M000202241

THE CAMBRIDGE COMPANION TO
AMERICAN CATHOLICISM

This *Companion* provides a comprehensive overview of American Catholicism's historical development and distinctive features. The essays – all specially commissioned for this volume – highlight the inner diversity of American Catholicism and trace the impact of American Catholics on all aspects of society, including education, social welfare, politics, and intellectual life. The volume also addresses topics of contemporary concern, such as gender and sexuality, arts and culture, social activism, and the experiences of Black, Latinx, Asian American, and cultural Catholics. Taken together, the essays in this *Companion* provide context for understanding American Catholicism as it is currently experienced and help to situate present-day developments and debates within their longer trajectory.

Margaret M. McGuinness is Professor of Religion at La Salle University. She is the author of *Called to Serve: A History of Nuns in America* (2013), which won the 2014 Catholic Press Association Book Award in History and received the 2016 Distinguished Book Award from the Conference on the History of Women Religious. She is also the author of *Neighbors and Missionaries: A History of the Sisters of Our Lady of Christian Doctrine* (2012).

Thomas F. Rzeznik is Associate Professor of History at Seton Hall University and coeditor of the quarterly journal, *American Catholic Studies*. He is author of *Church and Estate: Religion and Wealth in Industrial-Era Philadelphia* (2013).

(*continued after the index*)

THE CAMBRIDGE COMPANION TO

AMERICAN CATHOLICISM

Edited by

Margaret M. McGuinness
La Salle University

Thomas F. Rzeznik
Seton Hall University

CAMBRIDGE
UNIVERSITY PRESS

CAMBRIDGE
UNIVERSITY PRESS

University Printing House, Cambridge CB2 8BS, United Kingdom

One Liberty Plaza, 20th Floor, New York, NY 10006, USA

477 Williamstown Road, Port Melbourne, VIC 3207, Australia

314–321, 3rd Floor, Plot 3, Splendor Forum, Jasola District Centre,
New Delhi – 110025, India

79 Anson Road, #06–04/06, Singapore 079906

Cambridge University Press is part of the University of Cambridge.

It furthers the University's mission by disseminating knowledge in the pursuit of
education, learning, and research at the highest international levels of excellence.

www.cambridge.org
Information on this title: www.cambridge.org/9781108472654
DOI: 10.1017/9781108560900

© Cambridge University Press 2021

This publication is in copyright. Subject to statutory exception
and to the provisions of relevant collective licensing agreements,
no reproduction of any part may take place without the written
permission of Cambridge University Press.

First published 2021

Printed in the United Kingdom by TJ Books Limited, Padstow Cornwall

A catalogue record for this publication is available from the British Library.

Library of Congress Cataloging-in-Publication Data
NAMES: McGuinness, Margaret M., editor. | Rzeznik, Thomas F., editor.
TITLE: The Cambridge companion to American Catholicism / edited by Margaret
M. McGuinness, La Salle University, Philadelphia, Thomas F. Rzeznik, Seton Hall
University, New Jersey.
DESCRIPTION: Cambridge, United Kingdom ; New York, NY, USA : Cambridge University
Press, 2021. | Series: Cambridge companions to religion | Includes bibliographical
references and index.
IDENTIFIERS: LCCN 2020027579 (print) | LCCN 2020027580 (ebook) | ISBN 9781108472654
(hardback) | ISBN 9781108460088 (paperback) | ISBN 9781108560900 (epub)
SUBJECTS: LCSH: Catholic Church–United States–History.
CLASSIFICATION: LCC BX1406.3 .C35 2021 (print) | LCC BX1406.3 (ebook) |
DDC 282/.73–dc23
LC record available at https://lccn.loc.gov/2020027579
LC ebook record available at https://lccn.loc.gov/2020027580

ISBN 978-1-108-47265-4 Hardback
ISBN 978-1-108-46008-8 Paperback

Cambridge University Press has no responsibility for the persistence or accuracy of URLs
for external or third-party internet websites referred to in this publication and does not
guarantee that any content on such websites is, or will remain, accurate, or appropriate.

Contents

Contributors

Steven M. Avella is a graduate of the University of Notre Dame and a professor of history at Marquette University, Milwaukee, Wisconsin. He has written several books on the relationship of the church to American society. His work includes histories on the Archdioceses of Chicago and Milwaukee and the Diocese of Des Moines, Iowa; Catholicism in the American west; and journalism in California.

Tom Beaudoin is a professor in the Graduate School of Religion at Fordham University. He is the author of many publications about religion and theology in practice.

Mary Elizabeth Brown received a Ph.D. from Columbia University. She currently serves as an archivist at the Center for Migration Studies and as an archivist and adjunct professor at Marymount Manhattan College. Her most recent publication is a centennial history of Saint Joseph Patron of the Universal Church in Bushwick, Brooklyn.

Debra Campbell is Professor of Religious Studies Emerita at Colby College in Waterville, Maine. Her recent work, focused on Catholic life-writings, includes *Graceful Exits: Catholic Women and the Art of Departure* (2003) and a work in progress on the stories behind *The Nun's Story*.

Robert E. Carbonneau, CP, is an adjunct professor of history at the University of Scranton and a Passionist historian concentrating on American Catholic and Chinese history.

James T. Carroll is Professor of History at Iona College in New Rochelle, New York. He received his doctoral degree in American history from the University of Notre Dame. His research interests include Native American Catholicism, Gilded Age and Progressive Era history, and twentieth-century American Catholicism. He is currently researching the response of the Roman Catholic Church to the immigration restrictions of the 1920s.

Angelyn Dries, OSF, is Professor Emerita at Saint Louis University, St. Louis, Missouri, taught courses related to religion in America, mission history, and global Catholicism and continues to publish in these areas. She is the author of *The Missionary Movement in American Catholic History* (1998). She served on the editorial board of the Studies in World Christianity Series (Oxford University Press) and is contributing editor, *International Bulletin of Mission Research*. She is past president of the American Catholic Historical Association (2015).

Mary Beth Fraser Connolly is the author of *Women of Faith: The Chicago Sisters of Mercy and the Evolution of a Religious Community* (2014) and the coeditor of *Empowering the People of God: Catholic Action before and after Vatican II* (2013). She is currently a continuing lecturer in history at Purdue University Northwest in Indiana.

Maura Jane Farrelly is Associate Professor and Chair of American Studies at Brandeis University in Waltham, Massachusetts. She is the author of *Papist Patriots: The Making of an American Catholic Identity* and *Anti-Catholicism in America, 1620–1860* (2012).

Mary L. Gautier (Ph.D. Sociology, Louisiana State University) was a senior research associate at CARA, the Center for Applied Research in the Apostolate at Georgetown University for twenty-one years. Before coming to CARA in 1998, Gautier taught sociology at Louisiana State University and at Texas Christian University and served as a lay pastoral associate in Baton Rouge, Louisiana for six years. At CARA, she specialized in Catholic demographic trends in the United States, managed CARA databases, and conducted demographic projects and computer-aided mapping. She also edited *The CARA Report*, a quarterly research publication, and other CARA publications. She is the coauthor of twelve books on Catholicism in the United States, most recently *Migration for Mission: International Catholic Sisters in the United States* (2019).

Lauren Frances Guerra is Visiting Assistant Professor in the Department of Theological Studies at Loyola Marymount University. Her work on sacred sexualities and writing as a liberative practice appears in *Voices from the Ancestors: Xicanx and Latinx Spiritual Expressions and Healing Practices* (2019).

Katharine E. Harmon is Assistant Professor of Theology at Marian University in Indianapolis, Indiana, where she teaches undergraduate and graduate students, and college seminarians. A graduate of the University of Notre Dame's liturgical studies program, Harmon has contributed a dozen articles to the fields of both liturgical studies and American Catholicism and is the author of *There Were Also Many Women There: Lay Women in the Liturgical Movement in the United States, 1926–1959* (2013). She is the recipient of the 2017 Catholic Press Association First Place Award for the best scholarly article in a Catholic publication, and is a regular contributor and member of the editorial advisory council for the blog Pray Tell: Worship, Wit and Wisdom.

Brett C. Hoover is Associate Professor of Pastoral and Practical Theology at Loyola Marymount University in Los Angeles. He is the author of *The Shared Parish: Latinos, Anglos, and the Future of US Catholicism* (New York University Press, 2014) and the coeditor of *Hispanic Ministry in the Twenty-first Century: Urgent Matters* (2016).

Paula M. Kane is the John and Lucine O'Brien Marous Chair of Catholic Studies at the University of Pittsburgh. Her latest publication studied the relationship between the Jesuits and the emergence of psychoanalysis. Her latest book explored the case of an alleged stigmatic nun in New York in the 1920s and

1930s to investigate the history of mystical experiences among American Catholics and allied issues of ethnicity and sanctity.

Mark Massa, SJ, is Director of the Boisi Center for Religion and Public Life and Professor of Theology at Boston College. He is the author of eight books, most recently of *The Structure of Theological Revolution: How Debates over Birth Control Changed American Catholic Theology* (2018).

Lawrence J. McAndrews is Emeritus Professor of History at St. Norbert College. He is the author, most recently, of *The Presidents and the Poor: America Battles Poverty, 1964–2017* (2018).

James P. McCartin is Associate Professor of the History of American Christianity at Fordham University. He is the author of *Prayers of the Faithful: The Shifting Spiritual Life of American Catholics* (2010) and is presently at work on a history of US Catholics and sex in the nineteenth and twentieth centuries.

Margaret M. McGuinness is Professor of Religion and Theology at La Salle University. She is the author of *Called to Serve: A History of Nuns in America*, which won the 2014 Book Award in History (Catholic Press Association) and received the 2016 Distinguished Book Award from the Conference on the History of Women Religious. She is also the author of *Neighbors and Missionaries: A History of the Sisters of Our Lady of Christian Doctrine* (2015), and a former coeditor of the quarterly journal, *American Catholic Studies*.

Cecilia A. Moore teaches in the Department of Religious Studies at the University of Dayton and at Xavier University of Louisiana's Institute for Black Catholic Studies. She is a church historian who specializes in the history of Black Catholics in the United States.

James M. O'Toole is Clough Professor of History Emeritus and University Historian at Boston College. He is the author of *The Faithful: A History of Catholics in America* (2010).

William L. Portier is the Mary Ann Spearin Chair of Catholic Theology in the Religious Studies Department at the University of Dayton. He is the author of *Divided Friends: Portraits of the Roman Catholic Modernist Crisis in the United States* (2014) and *Every Catholic an Apostle: A Biography of Thomas A. Judge, CM, 1868–1933* (2017).

Thomas F. Rzeznik is Associate Professor of History at Seton Hall University and coeditor of the quarterly journal, *American Catholic Studies*. He is the author of *Church and Estate: Religion and Wealth in Industrial-Era Philadelphia* (2013).

Introduction

MARGARET M. MCGUINNESS AND
THOMAS F. RZEZNIK

The Catholic Church has been the largest single religious denomination in the United States since the mid-nineteenth century, consistently claiming between 20 and 25 percent of the nation's population over the past 170 years. Arriving in the Americas with the earliest Spanish and French missionaries, following pathways of settlement and expansion to all corners of the United States, and bolstered by successive waves of immigration, both in the past and today, Catholicism has been a constitutive element of American history from the very beginning. It has shaped the development of the nation in myriad ways, from formal political engagement and social activism to subtle cultural influence and anonymous works of charity. It is also one of the nation's most internally diverse religious denominations, drawing together members from all races and ethnicities, socioeconomic classes, ideological perspectives, and political persuasions. American Catholics espouse a wide range of beliefs, customs, and practices that reflects the church's cultural richness, but that has also given rise to numerous clashes and outright conflict. They continue to maintain a strong sense of collective unity, yet also exhibit much of the same polarization found within wider society. It is a church that today is at once growing and contracting, vibrant yet visibly scarred by scandal. For all these reasons, American Catholicism captivates and confounds, and it deserves scholarly attention.

This volume is designed to provide readers with a broad overview of American Catholicism in its diversity and complexity. It is intended to be accessible to those with little or no existing knowledge of the subject, yet also to serve as a resource for those who already possess some degree of familiarity with the topic. As a work of synthesis, the volume distills vast material into concise chapters that address different aspects of American Catholicism. In contributing to a unified whole, each chapter is also designed to stand on its own as an introduction to its particular topic or subject. The goal is to inform readers of broad trends and transformations rather than advance narrow scholarly arguments or a particular research agenda. Taken together, the volume provides context for understanding American Catholicism as it exists today, helping situate twenty-first century developments and debates within their longer trajectory.

Grappling with American Catholicism requires coming to terms with the inherent tension present in those two terms. Could one be both American and Catholic? As a religious minority within Protestant America, Catholics were viewed with suspicion, if not outright hostility. From the colonial era on through the twentieth century, waves of anti-Catholic sentiment relied on the conceit that Catholicism was essentially incompatible with American political values. It was viewed as a foreign faith whose core tenets and teachings were fundamentally at odds with American democracy, individual liberty, religious pluralism, and the separation of church and state. Such concerns spurred successive generations of Catholics to affirm their patriotism and defend the proposition that their faith was not an obstacle to full participation in American life.

One of the main trajectories of American Catholicism has been Catholics' movement from the margins to the mainstream. As they grew in number and in organizational strength, they claimed an increasingly powerful presence and voice in American affairs. By the mid-twentieth century, Catholics had attained a secure place within the social, political, and economic mainstream. Yet this movement into the American mainstream came at a cost. It eroded old markers of Catholic distinctiveness and erased some of the critical distance that Catholics had maintained towards American culture and its values. In many regards, they became virtually indistinguishable from their non-Catholic counterparts. While this trend signaled Catholic acceptance and respectability, it also had the effect of distancing American Catholics from their counterparts in other parts of the world, especially the global south and other developing regions. The pontificate of Pope Francis, in particular, has called attention to the fact that the concerns and priorities of church in the United States today do not always align with those stressed by the Vatican or held by Catholics in other parts of the world. To understand American Catholicism is to recognize a degree of exceptionalism that has long characterized the history of the church in the United States.

Guiding this analysis is a recognition that Catholics view the world through their own distinctive lens, which some have termed the "Catholic imagination."[1] This includes an emphasis on sacramentality, or the notion that physical reality is a reflection of the divine. Rooted in

---

[1]   See Andrew Greeley, *The Catholic Imagination* (Berkeley: University of California Press, 2001).

the doctrine of the incarnation, which teaches that Christ took human form and became one like us in all things but sin, sacramentality reflects a core Catholic belief that God is present in the created world and knowable to us in those myriad manifestations. It teaches that spiritual meaning can be found in diverse realms of human activity, including family and community life or in artistic and cultural production. As a result, the study of American Catholicism has long been attentive to the relationship between faith and culture. It recognizes that art, music, literature, architecture, fashion, and other forms of cultural expression are an integral part of Catholic life and provide a source of religious meaning. The Catholic imagination also recognizes how ordinary objects and everyday routines can acquire sacred significance. This helps account for the importance of devotional activity within Catholicism, with its emphasis on relics, rosaries, medals, holy cards, and other material objects, as well as the places and practices associated with them. For Catholics, the mundane and the miraculous are intimately intertwined. The experience of faith is connected not just to the church's formal rituals and official worship, but also to a range of popular practices and folk customs that operate in tandem with them.

Just as the Catholic population has grown and changed, so too has our historical understanding of its development. This volume reflects the tremendous transformations that have taken place within the field of American Catholic studies over the past thirty to forty years. The history of American Catholicism had traditionally been told through the lens of church history. This narrative framework tended to emphasize institutional development, internal church affairs, and the contributions of bishops, clergy, and others holding formal positions of authority within the church. Although these works provided a rich chronicling of Catholicism's growth as told through official church records – often with a triumphalist tone designed to glorify Catholic achievement, uphold Catholic truth, and extol Catholicism's contributions to the nation – they often contained little critical analysis.[2] But starting in the 1970s, a new generation of scholars inspired by the reforms of the Second Vatican Council and the shift towards social history within the historical profession began to approach Catholic

---

[2] The best works of the period – such as John Gilmary Shea, *History of the Catholic Church in the United States*, 4 vols. (Akron, OH: D.H. McBride, 1886–1892); Peter Guilday, *The Life and Times of John Carroll, Archbishop of Baltimore (1735–1815)* (New York: The Encyclopedia Press, 1922); and John Tracy Ellis, *The Life of James Cardinal Gibbons* (Milwaukee: Bruce, 1963) – demonstrate a great deal of scholarly sophistication, but gained little attention outside of Catholic academic circles.

history with an eye towards the experience of ordinary churchgoers and the diverse communities who comprised the "People of God." These works focused on the Catholic experience within the United States, drawing attention to the rich Catholic subculture that had marked and sustained Catholic distinctiveness and charting the gradual integration of Catholics into the American mainstream.[3]

In more recent decades, the study of American Catholicism has been influenced by scholarly interest in lived religious experience, with insights drawn from multidisciplinary perspectives. These works have explored the ways that Catholicism has been experienced and expressed in family and community life, in popular religious practice and folk customs, and through other forms of collective activity, including those that operate outside official institutional structures and spaces.[4] Scholars have also become much more attuned to the unique experiences of the many diverse groups found within American Catholicism, looking at how issues of gender, race, ethnicity, social class, geographic location, generational difference, and other sociological variables affect Catholics' relationship with the church and with one another. Their work reminds us that the Catholic Church has never been as unitary or monolithic as many have assumed, including Catholics themselves. They have also brought attention to the painful realities of racism and other forms of discrimination and inequality within American Catholicism, as well as how the church itself has been responsible for establishing institutional barriers to equality or complicit in perpetuating forms of systemic oppression.[5]

---

3   See, for example, James Hennesey, SJ, *American Catholics: A History of the Roman Catholic Community in the United States* (New York: Oxford University Press, 1981); Jay P. Dolan, *The American Catholic Experience: A History from Colonial Times to the Present* (Garden City, NY: Doubleday, 1985); and John Cogley and Rodger Van Allen, *Catholic America: Expanded and Updated Edition* (New York: Sheed and Ward, 1986).

4   This transformation began with Robert Anthony Orsi, *The Madonna of 115th Street: Faith and Community in Italian Harlem, 1880–1950* (New Haven, CT: Yale University Press, 1985). For other examples, see Thomas A. Tweed, *Our Lady of the Exile: Diasporic Religion at a Cuban Catholic Shrine in Miami* (New York: Oxford University Press, 1997); Kristy Nabhan-Warren, *The Virgin of El Barrio: Marian Apparitions, Catholic Evangelizing, and Mexican American Activism* (New York: New York University Press, 2005); James T. Fisher, *On the Irish Waterfront: The Crusader, the Movie, and the Soul of the Port of New York* (Ithaca, NY: Cornell University Press, 2009).

5   See, for example, John T. McGreevy, *Parish Boundaries: The Catholic Encounter with Race in the Twentieth-Century Urban North* (Chicago: University of Chicago Press, 1996); Steven W. Hackel, *Children of Coyote, Missionaries of Saint Francis: Indian–Spanish Relations in Colonial California* (Chapel Hill: University of North

The study of American Catholicism today reflects the disciplinary diversity of its practitioners. Once the domain of seminary professors and those housed in theology and history programs at Catholic institutions, the field of Catholic Studies now also includes those working in the broader field of religious studies and related disciplines, including an increasing number whose training has taken place at secular institutions. Their work has widened the scope of inquiry and helped move the field beyond some of its earlier parochialism. Catholic resources are now being mined to shed light on topics beyond the conventional confines of Catholic history, making a case for the relevance of Catholicism to larger trends and transformations in American history.[6] Another effort to expand the scope of American Catholicism has come from those who have sought to situate events within a global framework, highlighting patterns and connections that stretch beyond American borders. Their work calls attention to the fact that Catholic history is, by its very nature, transnational in scale and scope, with developments in the United States intimately connected to decisions made in Rome, the influence of international geopolitics, and the continuous movement of people and resources across countries and continents.[7]

Reflective of these wider scholarly trends, the nineteen essays contained in this volume comprise an effort to write histories of US Catholics attuned to the diversity found within the church and mindful of the continuous interplay between faith and culture. Some are more broadly historical in nature, while others are focused on a specific topic. While every effort has been made to provide comprehensive coverage, it is impossible to include everything in such surveys. These essays,

Carolina Press, 2005); Mary J. Henold, *Catholic and Feminist: The Surprising History of the American Catholic Feminist Movement* (Chapel Hill: University of North Carolina Press, 2008); Shannen Dee Williams, "Black Nuns and the Struggle to Desegregate America after World War I" (Ph.D. diss.: Rutgers University, 2013).

6 On this point, see R. Scott Appleby and Kathleen Sprows Cummings, eds., *Catholics in the American Century: Recasting Narratives of American History* (Ithaca, NY: Cornell University Press, 2012).

7 See, for instance, Peter R. D'Agostino, *Rome in America: Transnational Catholic Ideology from the Risorgimento to Fascism* (Chapel Hill: University of North Carolina Press, 2005); Gerald McKevitt, *Brokers of Culture: Italian Jesuits in the American West, 1848–1919* (Stanford, CA: Stanford University Press, 2007); John T. McGreevy, *American Jesuits and the World: How an Embattled Religious Order Made Modern Catholicism Global* (Princeton, NJ: Princeton University Press, 2016); and Kathleen Sprows Cummings, *A Saint of Our Own: How the Quest for a Holy Hero Helped Catholics Become American* (Chapel Hill: University of North Carolina Press, 2019).

however, offer foundational overviews of the most salient elements of the American Catholic experience. Also included in this volume are chapters on topics and themes not usually discussed in similar overviews of American Catholicism – such as gender and sexuality and Catholic art and culture.

The first section of the book provides a chronological overview of American Catholicism, with essays on colonial origins, the nineteenth century, and the twentieth century that allow readers to trace the general themes and issues that are part of the church's history. Catholics during the colonial and revolutionary eras were more integrated into the mostly Protestant environment of the United States than future generations. This would change as nineteenth-century Catholic immigrants arrived in the United States and developed a system of schools, hospitals, and social service institutions that would not only educate and care for American Catholics, but would insulate them from their non-Catholic neighbors and compatriots. Twentieth-century Catholicism would begin as a period of tremendous expansion within the church, but the end of the century would be marked by a decrease in the number of parishes, schools, and social service institutions as changes in the church and society led to new ways of living and practicing Catholicism.

After an introduction to the historical framework of Catholicism in the United States, the second section, entitled "Catholic Life and Culture," allows readers to understand the many facets of American Catholicism. The first essay is devoted to Catholic worship, which includes the Mass and formal prayer, but also a range of popular devotions. Although the way in which American Catholics worship, including at Mass, has changed over the decades, the focus on communal worship and prayer has remained a constant. The following chapter surveys Catholic intellectual life. Philosophers and theologians have traditionally played an important role in interpreting the teachings of the church to the Catholic faithful, but they have also responded to social, economic, and political issues in light of church teaching.

The parochial school system, which has been a significant part of American Catholic culture since the nineteenth century, is the subject of Chapter 6. US Catholics have been able to attend schools steeped in their faith from preschool through graduate school, and the system remains intact in the second decade of the twenty-first century despite demographic and societal changes in both the United States and the church. In addition to schools, Catholics developed a network of hospitals, orphanages, and social service agencies that have met the needs of many, Catholic and non-Catholic alike. Social welfare in the church includes both individual acts of charity and an emphasis on social justice that addresses a variety of systemic issues. In Chapter 7, readers will see the many ways in which the American Catholic Church responded to those in need. The church could not have developed its vast network of parochial schools and agencies devoted to reform and social justice without the work of women religious, who continue to serve the church in a variety of ways. Chapter 8 is devoted to a study of the ways in which sisters and nuns have shaped and served the church. Although declining numbers and an aging population, along with changes in education and health care, have changed the way in which women religious serve their church, they remain the face of Catholicism for many.

In addition to creating their own institutions devoted to "taking care of their own," Catholics actively participated in the larger culture. Chapter 9 describes the ways in which Catholics have engaged in the political process, noting that they went from being "outsiders" to political power brokers. The role Catholics have played in the arts is the subject of Chapter 10. Catholics helped shape, and at the same time, were shaped by television, movies, literature, and art. Their participation in these areas has expanded to social media in the late twentieth and twenty-first centuries. The very presence of Catholics in the United States and their participation and engagement in every aspect of American life and culture has resulted in anti-Catholicism, which is the subject of Chapter 11. The essay reminds readers that anti-Catholicism has its roots in puritanism and continues into the present.

The final chapters of this section discuss American Catholicism from the perspective of issues especially relevant to the twenty-first century. The subject of Chapter 12 is sexuality. In addition to discussing the ways in which issues related to gender and sexuality influenced how American Catholics were viewed by others, this essay explains the way in which this topic has been controversial in the US church. Evangelization has always been an important component of Catholicism. Chapter 13 focuses on the ways in which American Catholics experienced the many dimensions of mission – to, within, and from the United States – in order to help readers understand the global context in which the church in the United States functions.

The focus of the volume's third section is "The Many Faces of Catholicism." The first essay in this section is devoted to laywomen and feminism. Although Catholic laywomen have not necessarily followed the same path to liberation within their tradition as their Protestant and Jewish sisters, they have created spaces for themselves within the institutional church. The clergy sexual abuse crisis and the shortage of ordained clergy, combined with the growing number of women who possess the necessary educational credentials, has prompted many to call for women to exercise greater leadership roles in parishes and in dioceses. Chapter 15 is devoted to a survey of the history and presence of Black Catholics from the era of Spanish, French, and English colonization efforts until the twenty-first century. Included in this discussion are the topics of racism and racist practices within the church, and ways in which African Americans struggled to claim their rights and find their voice in an institution that remains predominantly white. Latinx Catholics are the subject of Chapter 16. Although there has been a Latinx presence in the church since the Spanish sought to colonize portions of what is now the United States, this group is currently emerging as an important part of the church's future. Areas covered in this chapter include the history of Latinx Catholics in the United States and themes in contemporary Latinx Catholicism. Chapter 17 focuses on Asian-American Catholics, specifically the Chinese, Japanese, Filipino, Vietnamese, and Korean presence in the church. The essay discusses the history of Chinese and Japanese Catholics in the US church in the nineteenth century, as well as Asian-American Catholics since the 1965 Immigration Act. The final chapter in this section is on the topic of the growing significance of so-called cultural Catholics within the church in the United States. As many American Catholics have moved away from traditional practices, the church has tried to keep them within the institution.

The final section is the concluding essay of the volume. This discussion of the church today also offers some reflections on how issues impacting today's American Catholic Church might influence the future. Examining trends that include population, practice, belief, and pastoral leadership, the essay offers some concluding thoughts on what might be next for American Catholicism. One issue that will certainly affect the future of the Catholic Church in the United States is the clergy sexual abuse crisis. As Mary L. Gautier correctly notes in the final chapter of this volume, "The clergy sexual abuse crisis is a cloud across the church in the United States at the beginning of the twenty-first century." What that means for the church in America remains to be seen.

When the *Boston Globe*'s Spotlight Team began its in-depth coverage of what has become known as the sexual abuse crisis in the Catholic Church on January 6, 2002, no one anticipated the tremendous impact this would have upon the church and its people. What started out as an investigative report of a systematic cover-up of priests engaged in the sexual abuse of minor children in the Archdiocese of Boston quickly evolved into a worldwide scandal involving thousands of priests and church leaders. The scandal has become a part of the recent history of every US diocese, and will impact the American church for decades to come. It is now clear that the topic of sexual abuse by Catholic priests – and in some cases, sisters – will clearly affect the future work of historians, sociologists, psychologists, and others working in the field of Catholic Studies, though it is far too early to understand the long-term impact of the crisis.

Scholarly work on the sexual abuse crisis is really just beginning, and as a result, readers of this volume will not find a chapter devoted to the topic. It is clear, however, that this subject will figure prominently in future work by historians of Catholicism in the United States, who are already discussing ways in which to incorporate this piece of history into the larger story. A panel at the 2016 American Catholic Historical Association's annual meeting, for instance, brought together historians and archivists to reflect upon the importance of including the sexual abuse crisis in works devoted to American Catholic history. The discussion ranged from best practices for archives holding materials related to the crisis faced by historians struggling to write on the topic.[8] It is worth noting at this juncture that this volume does not contain an essay specifically focused on the priesthood in the US Catholic Church because of the difficulties scholars have had researching this topic. The two topics are, of course, intimately entwined and a comprehensive history of one cannot be written without exploring the second. Researching and writing about these topics will be the work of future historians.

A full and accurate understanding of American Catholicism is essential for the history of Catholicism as well as the history of the United States. As these essays demonstrate, the place of Catholics in education, politics, arts and culture, and social reform must be included in any history dedicated to these topics. In addition, Black, Latinx, and Asian-American Catholics, as well as women religious and laywomen, now command a place in the larger histories of their church and their nation. It is our hope that this volume not only provides a foundation for those seeking to further their knowledge of the Catholic Church in the United States but also contributes to this effort to place American Catholicism within larger histories.

---

[8] See "Writing Catholic History After the Sex Abuse Crisis," *American Catholic Studies* 127 (Summer 2016), 1–27.

Part I

Historical Overview

1 American Catholicism's Early Foundations

MAURA JANE FARRELLY

Catholics were in the United States from the very beginning. Some were the descendants of people who had migrated to Maryland, Pennsylvania, and New York in the seventeenth and eighteenth centuries – primarily from England, but to a lesser extent from Ireland, Germany, and Portugal. Others were the descendants of people who had migrated to Florida and Louisiana from Spain, France, and Quebec during those same centuries.

When trying to understand the history and experiences of America's "first" Catholics, it is helpful to remember that the current boundaries of the continental United States were not defined all at once. When the Treaty of Paris that ended the Revolutionary War was signed in 1783, the new United States extended no farther west than the Mississippi River. Florida was still a Spanish colony. The Jefferson administration purchased the Louisiana Territory from France in 1803, expanding the country's boundaries to include most of what lies between the current states of Louisiana and Montana. A little more than a decade later, then, the Spanish government gave Florida to the United States after the Americans agreed to assume responsibility for some of Spain's debts. In the 1840s, Mexico was forced to sell the territory that stretches from Texas through Utah, Nevada, and California to the United States, following that country's defeat in the Mexican War. That same decade, what is now Oregon, Idaho, and Washington became a part of the continental United States, thanks to a treaty the Polk administration negotiated with Great Britain.

Native-born Catholics were living in all of these regions when the regions became "American." Indeed, the Catholic population in the United States more than doubled after Jefferson acquired the Louisiana territory, thanks to the 75,000 Catholic souls who were living in that part of New France.[1] Anyone who has ever traveled California's famous

---

[1]   J. F. Regis Canevin, "Loss and Gain in the Catholic Church in the United States, 1800–1916," *Catholic Historical Review* 4 (1917), 380.

Highway 101, which runs along the coast from Los Angeles to the Oregon border, has seen the evidence of Catholicism's early presence in California, long before it joined the United States. The highway traces the old *El Camino Real*, or "royal road," where Spanish priests established twenty-one mission outposts between 1769 and 1833 as part of their effort to convert the native Indians to Christianity. The missions are controversial today because the priests running them ignored – or sometimes even worked to destroy – many of the cultural traditions of the Chumash, Ohlone, Tongva, and Salinan peoples they evangelized. Nevertheless, the fact remains that the United States inherited thousands of native-born Catholics of European and Native ancestry when California became a state in 1850.

America's first Catholics were by no means a religious monolith; their sense of themselves as Catholics varied, depending upon the country or territory their ancestors had come from and the cultural traditions those ancestors had brought to North America with them. The religious identities of America's first Catholics were also shaped by the experiences they and their ancestors had, living for many generations in the vast territory that eventually became the United States. Before they became Americans, some of these first Catholics lived in European colonies where they were able to practice their faith freely, and the Catholic Church enjoyed the financial and legal support of the civil government. Others lived in colonies where they were legally marginalized and sometimes even persecuted because of their faith.

One thing all of America's first Catholics had in common was that they were different from the immigrants who came to the country later, in the nineteenth century. Those immigrants would ultimately be responsible for the powerful presence that Catholicism has on the religious landscape of the United States today. America's first Catholics were different from these later Catholics in terms of the way they understood their place in the Catholic Church; they were also different in terms of the way they understood their place in American society. Even in areas where Catholics were concentrated, there were not enough of them in colonial and early America to enable them to form the dynamic, but parochial enclaves that characterized the "immigrant" Catholic experience for most of the nineteenth and twentieth centuries. America's first Catholics were integrated, therefore, into the culture of their predominantly Protestant country in a way that the immigrants who followed them were not. This integration – when combined with the reality that many of America's first Catholics were far removed from the authority and infrastructure that defined the

Catholic Church in Europe – helped to make the first Catholics in the United States far more individualistic and religiously self-sufficient than their immigrant coreligionists from Europe who came later.

This chapter focuses on the legal, institutional, religious, and cultural experiences of Catholics living in what became the United States prior to the year 1820. That year marked the beginning of a massive and decades-long increase in Catholic immigration that ultimately changed the character of Catholicism in the United States.

SPANISH AND FRENCH MISSIONS IN FLORIDA AND LOUISIANA

The Catholic Church in America began in a southern context. Sixteen years before Sir Walter Raleigh attempted to found the first British colony in North America, thirty-seven years before the Virginia Company of London set up shop along the banks of the James River, and fifty years before the first English Calvinists anchored their ships on the tip of the arm of Massachusetts Bay, Spanish priests were serving soldiers on what eventually was known as Parris Island, South Carolina, and Jesuits were working to convert Algonquian Indians along what was then called the "Ajacán Peninsula," between the James and the York Rivers that empty into the Chesapeake Bay.

The Catholic presence in what became Virginia and South Carolina would not last for long. While the Escamacu Indians who converted on Parris Island seem to have remained Catholic into the early years of the seventeenth century, the Spanish were gone from the Port Royal Sound by 1587. Nevertheless, Catholicism continued to grow in other parts of the south – eventually dominating the religious landscape in Louisiana and parts of Florida, before it assumed an English accent in Maryland at the time of that British colony's founding in 1634.

Saint Augustine, Florida – the oldest continuously occupied city in the United States – provides an example of early Catholic missionary activity and its legacy. The community was founded in 1565 by a group of 1,500 soldiers, priests, and settlers who had been sent to the area by the Spanish government. King Phillip II of Spain was concerned about a fort that 300 Huguenots – i.e., French-speaking Calvinists – had built the year before in territory along the Saint Johns River that was claimed by Spain. Phillip hoped the new Spanish settlement, located just forty miles south of the Huguenots' Fort Caroline, would scare the French settlers enough that they would leave. Absent that, the king intended to have his soldiers remove the French from Florida by force.

In the early eighteenth century, while Saint Augustine was solidly Spanish, the city became home to a sizeable number of formerly enslaved Africans and African Americans who had fled to Florida from the British colonies of Georgia and South Carolina. In 1693, King Charles II of Spain had declared that any slaves who made it to Florida would be freed, provided they converted to Catholicism and agreed to be baptized. Although the 1819 treaty by which Spain ceded Florida to the United States stipulated that the free, Catholic descendants of these runaway slaves were to receive American citizenship following the colony's transfer, many Catholics of African descent fled to Cuba when the Florida Territory became part of the United States, understanding that their status in a country that condoned and depended upon hereditary, race-based slavery would always be tenuous.[2]

The Spaniards who settled Florida came from a solidly Catholic country where their king was a staunch supporter – ideologically and financially – of the Catholic Church's efforts to convert Native American Indians to Christianity. Indeed, the descendants of many of the earliest European settlers in Florida, known as *Floridanos*, often used the language of evangelization to justify their ancestors' conquest of the peninsula; European land-grabs were said to be an essential component of the pope's plan to bring the Native Indians to Christ.[3]

The church distinguished between "parishes" and "missions" in Florida. A parish served a settled population of Catholics, all or most of whom had been born into the faith (which at this point in time meant that they were almost exclusively Europeans). The job of a parish priest was to create the circumstances that allowed Catholics to sustain their religious identities – performing Masses, hearing confessions, officiating marriages, etc. Most of the clergy who served parishes in colonial Florida were secular priests, meaning they did not belong to a religious order such as the Dominicans, Franciscans, or Jesuits. Their salaries were paid for by the Spanish crown, and in some instances their appointments were approved by the crown, as well.

2 James M. Woods, *A History of the Catholic Church in the American South, 1513–1900* (Gainesville: University Press of Florida, 2011), 23–24; Frank Marotti, *The Cana Sanctuary: History, Diplomacy, and Black Catholic Marriage in Antebellum St. Augustine, Florida* (Tuscaloosa: University of Alabama Press, 2012), 1–7, 105.
3 Woods, *A History of the Catholic Church in the American South*, 1–31; Kevin Starr, *Continental Ambitions: Roman Catholics in North America* (San Francisco: Ignatius Press, 2016), 69.

In contrast, a mission had the conversion of Native American Indians as its focus. The missions in colonial Florida were run not by secular priests, but by priests who had taken vows of obedience to the superiors of particular orders. Early on, the mission clergy in Florida operated outside any episcopal framework, meaning their activities with native tribes were not subject to the review or supervision of bishops. Often, their evangelization efforts were complicated by the actions of nonclerical European explorers in the region. Men such as Juan Ponce de Léon, Lucas Vázquez de Ayllón, and Hernando de Sota plundered and burned native villages and captured and enslaved native men and women, despite a papal bull from 1537 that forbade the enslavement of the indigenous people of the western hemisphere and ordered all Catholics to treat Native Americans with dignity and respect. Pope Paul III's entreaty was one that Spain's *conquistadors* freely ignored. The indigenous people of Florida, therefore, were understandably suspicious of the motives of the Europeans in the region. As a consequence, the Jesuits and Dominicans who worked to bring native Floridians to Christ accomplished few long-lasting conversions.[4]

The conversion work of the Jesuits and Franciscan Recollects in New France was only slightly more successful, even though these priests did not have to contend with the undermining effects of rampant marauding by Europeans, the way their counterparts in Florida did. Like the Spanish, the French were primarily interested in the financial gains to be made from harnessing the natural resources of the New World. But also like the Spanish, the Catholic kings of France in the seventeenth and eighteenth centuries felt an obligation to support their church's efforts to bring the native people of North America to Christ.

For most of the seventeenth century, the economic and religious activities of French trappers, settlers, and priests were focused on territory in North America that is now the Canadian provinces of Nova Scotia, New Brunswick, Quebec, and Prince Edward Island. The colony that the French called "Acadia" when it was founded in 1605 became "Nova Scotia" in 1713, when the French were required to hand it over to the British government, following their defeat in Queen Anne's War (1702–1713). That war was one of several wars in the eighteenth century fought between the French and the British in North America. Following the conclusion of the largest of these wars, the French and Indian War (1754–1763), the French were required to

---

[4]   Starr, *Continental Ambitions*, 70–92; David J. Weber, *The Spanish Frontier in North America* (New Haven, CT: Yale University Press, 1992), 101.

give Quebec, which included present-day New Brunswick and Prince Edward Island, to the British as well.

These eighteenth-century colonial transfers had significant implications for the religious lives of the European people who had been living in New France since the seventeenth century. The Acadians were Catholic, meaning they subscribed to a faith that had been outlawed in England following the Glorious Revolution of 1689, during which England's Parliament rose up against King James II, who was a Catholic convert, and placed his Protestant daughter, Mary, and her Protestant husband, William, on the throne.

Would the French Catholic Acadians and the priests who served them be allowed to worship freely in the now-English colony of Nova Scotia following the colony's transfer in 1713? The initial answer from London was yes – provided the Acadians signed oaths, by which they agreed to remain neutral and not to assist the French, should England and France ever go to war with one another again. This conditional toleration characterized life in Nova Scotia for more than forty years, until the French and Indian War broke out and the British army officers tasked with winning that war became uncomfortable with the fact that a large, French-speaking, Catholic population was concentrated in a British colony. Between 1755 and 1764, nearly 12,000 Acadians were forcibly removed from their homes and dispersed throughout England's lower thirteen colonies, where they faced great animosity because of their religion. Many of these refugees eventually left England's colonies and headed south, making their way to a region along the Mississippi River that explorer Robert LaSalle had first claimed for the king of France in 1682. That region was called "Louisiana," in honor of France's King Louis XIV, and the Acadians who settled there became known as "Cajuns," a bastardization of the word "Acadian."

In the eighteenth century, the French government came to use the word "Louisiana" to describe all the of the territory it claimed in North America – from the northernmost parts of the present-day Canadian province of Quebec to the southernmost parts of the present-day American state of Louisiana. During the early decades of the eighteenth century, this entire territory was under the auspices of one bishop – the Bishop of Quebec, whose residence in Quebec City was nearly 3,000 miles away from the Mississippi delta. Because of the distance, Quebec's bishop divided Louisiana into territories and placed clerical representatives in charge of each region. The Jesuits were responsible for "Upper Louisiana" – the territory north of the Ohio River that is now Ohio, Indiana, Illinois, and Ontario. The Capuchins had "Lower

Louisiana," which is present-day Mississippi, Louisiana, Arkansas, Missouri, and parts of Tennessee and Kentucky.[5]

The Jesuits and the Capuchins were fierce competitors – rivals for souls – and the Society of Jesus was unwilling to allow the brown-hooded Capuchins to have complete control over Catholics living in Louisiana's largest city, New Orleans, no matter what the Bishop of Quebec said about territorial jurisdiction. In the late 1720s, a Jesuit missionary by the name of Nicholas Ignace de Beaubois purchased a house for his order in New Orleans. This decision proved to be very important to the city, as the Jesuits had a close relationship with the Ursulines, a group of European nuns who were devoted specifically to the education of women and girls and the care of the sick and elderly. Father Beaubois arranged for several Ursuline nuns from the French town of Rouen to found a convent near the house he had purchased. Nuns from that convent eventually founded the first orphanage, the first girls' school, and one of the first hospitals in Louisiana.[6]

Sixty-nine nuns lived and worked in the Ursuline convent in New Orleans between its founding in 1727 and the sale of Louisiana to the United States in 1803. Some of these nuns came from France, but as the years went on, many more of them were "Creoles," meaning they had been born in Louisiana. Several nuns also came from Cuba. The Creole population in Louisiana was a mixture of races – as were the nuns and girls who lived, worked, and learned in the Ursuline convent. Sometimes these racial differences generated friction, as the leaders of the Ursuline convent were not always willing to replicate the racial hierarchies that dominated the landscape in New Orleans outside the convent's walls.

The friction became particularly acute during the period between 1763 and 1800, when Lower Louisiana was briefly a possession of Spain. The Spanish government had an extensive collection of labels that were designed to categorize people according to their heritage and skin color, and the women who ran the Ursuline convent refused to enforce these distinctions – either among themselves or among the students who lived at their school. Although New Orleans's nuns never challenged the system of hereditary, race-based slavery that fueled the economy of their city, life within the walls of their convent was marked by an unusual degree of racial ecumenism for the time.[7]

5 Woods, *A History of the Catholic Church in the American South*, 88–89.
6 Woods, *A History of the Catholic Church in the American South*, 92.
7 Emily Clark, *Masterless Mistresses: The New Orleans Ursulines and the Development of a New World Society, 1727–1834* (Chapel Hill: University of North Carolina Press, 2007).

THE ENGLISH IN MARYLAND

Baltimore was the epicenter of the Catholic Church in the United States during the first few decades of the country's existence. The city was home to the first American diocese – created by the Holy See in 1789, six years after the Revolutionary War ended – and the country's first bishop, John Carroll, was from Maryland. The Carroll family was large, wealthy, prominent, and – by the mid-eighteenth century – thoroughly native-born. The family's history reveals much about the nature and status of Catholicism in the English colonies before the founding – and the faith's role in the development of the new American nation.

The Carroll family owned several tobacco plantations in Prince George's and Charles Counties. John Carroll's older brother, Daniel, was one of just five men who helped to design both the Articles of Confederation and the Constitution of the United States. His cousin, Charles – also from Maryland – was thought by many of his contemporaries to be the wealthiest man in America. Charles Carroll took a huge risk when he signed the Declaration of Independence, which, from the British perspective, was a declaration of treason. The only Catholic to sign that manifesto, he stood to lose a lot if the Patriots lost the war.

John Carroll joined the Society of Jesus (i.e., the Jesuits) in 1753, when he was eighteen years old. Twenty years later, the Jesuits were suppressed by Pope Clement XIV, but Carroll continued to work as a priest in Maryland, even traveling to Canada on behalf of the Continental Congress in an unsuccessful bid to convince the Quebecois to join the lower thirteen colonies in their struggle for independence. Maryland's Catholics supported the independence movement in numbers that were greater than those of their Protestant neighbors, in part because they believed the religious discrimination they endured in Maryland was a byproduct of the colony's connection to England.[8]

The colony where John Carroll was born in 1735 had been founded more than 100 years earlier by an English nobleman named Cecilius Calvert. Calvert was a convert to Catholicism, just like his father, George. George – the first Lord Baltimore – had been hoping to establish a haven for English-speaking Catholics in the New World; he died, however, before he could receive the charter to Maryland from King Charles I. His oldest son, therefore – the second Lord Baltimore – inherited the father's vision.

---

[8] Maura Jane Farrelly, *Papist Patriots: The Making of an American Catholic Identity* (New York: Oxford University Press, 2012), 17.

Maryland was an experiment. Catholicism had been restricted – and ultimately banned – in England, starting in 1606 when Queen Elizabeth I's successor, King James I, enacted legislation that required people to attend the Protestant Church of England and to swear an oath that denied the authority of the pope. England's Catholic population had been declining for decades by the time Cecilius Calvert received the charter to Maryland in 1632; estimates are that less than 2 percent of the population was Catholic by that decade. In Maryland, however, Catholics would constitute 10 percent of the population, with some counties, such as Charles and St. Mary's Counties, having as much as a third of their populations be Catholic.

English-speaking Protestants in Maryland, in other words, were going to have to deal with a Catholic population that was five-to-fifteen times larger than what they were used to in England. Not only that, but Cecilius Calvert fully intended for his coreligionists to be able to do things in Maryland that they were prohibited from doing in England – such as vote, hold office, and worship openly in free-standing Catholic chapels.[9]

The system that Calvert built in Maryland kept the peace and sustained the colony for more than fifty years. Its foundation was the first act of religious toleration passed in the English-speaking world, the "Act Concerning Religion," which Calvert pushed through Maryland's colonial assembly in 1649. The statute promised Maryland's residents – Catholics and Protestants alike – that the government would not meddle in anyone's private religious affairs. It also required the colony's residents to keep any religious bigotry they may have brought over with them from England to themselves. The act forbade the use of a long list of terms, some of them perfectly innocuous today, that were considered to be insults in the seventeenth century: "Puritan"; "Presbyterian"; "Popish Priest"; "Jesuited Priest"; "Lutheran"; "Calvinist"; "Anabaptist"; the list went on.[10]

Everything changed following the Glorious Revolution of 1689, however. Three years after William and Mary ousted Mary's Catholic father, James II, from the throne, Protestants in Maryland rebelled against the authority of their Catholic proprietor. William responded by revoking Maryland's charter, which was not restored to the Calvert

---

9   Farrelly, *Papist Patriots*, 27, 42–45, 116; Lois Green Carr and David William Jordan, *Maryland's Revolution of Government, 1689–1692* (Ithaca, NY: Cornell University Press, 1974), 33.

10   Farrelly, *Papist Patriots*, 98–99.

family until 1715, when all of Lord Baltimore's heirs had converted to the Church of England. The Protestant king's handpicked governor for Maryland established the Anglican Church in the colony in 1702, and over the course of the next few years, Maryland's Catholics were stripped of the franchise and their ability to own guns legally. A special tax was placed on Catholic servants who were brought into Maryland, and in the 1750s, in the midst of the French and Indian War, Catholics were required to pay a double tax on their land in order to finance Maryland's mandated contributions to the British war effort. Lawmakers justified the double tax by saying that Catholics could not contribute military service to the war, since they were prohibited from owning and using guns.[11]

All this religious discrimination meant that the experiences Catholics had in British colonial Maryland were different from the experiences their coreligionists had in Florida and Louisiana. In Maryland, it became decidedly difficult to be Catholic – and the difficulties were not just civil. They were also ecclesiastical. Free-standing Catholic chapels were outlawed in the colony; in fact, the Catholic Church in St. Mary's City, the colony's original capital, was torn down under the governor's orders in 1704.[12] This meant that priests had to say Mass in private rooms that laypeople set aside for that purpose in their own homes. Catholic clergy in Maryland could not rely upon the government to pay for their upkeep or expenses, as the priests in New France and Florida could. Maryland's Catholics were therefore served by the Jesuits, who shouldered the expenses of what they considered to be a "mission" to North America – something akin to the work their Spanish colleagues did with the natives in Florida – even though many of the Catholics they served had been born into the faith.

The Jesuits financed their work in British colonial America by running tobacco farms, which relied heavily on the labor of enslaved men and women. The Jesuits were an order of teachers – not laborers or soldiers. They had spent the bulk of their lives at the best universities in continental Europe, studying rhetoric, music, and language, rather than agriculture or animal husbandry. They had not been trained to farm, which meant they were dependent upon the labor and talents of the men and women they owned.

Many of these men and women became Catholics, as the Catholic Church was comfortable with bringing Christianity into the slave

---

[11]   Farrelly, *Papist Patriots*, 133–134, 193, 213.
[12]   Farrelly, *Papist Patriots*, 194.

quarters long before evangelical Protestants adopted the idea. Prior to the 1820s, most evangelicals in America resisted efforts to evangelize slaves because they feared what their slaves might to do with Christ's message of liberation and love. Protestants also worried they might be obliged, as Christians, to free anyone who had converted to Christianity.[13] Catholics did not share these fears, and the extent to which the Jesuits relied on slavery has recently come to light, thanks in part to the work of historians and alums at Georgetown University who have been trying to track down the descendants of men and women whom the Jesuits sold in 1838, after the Society of Jesus decided to abandon its tobacco farms and focus on the urban areas that Catholics were immigrating to from Europe.[14]

Maryland's Catholic population grew slowly, but steadily throughout the seventeenth and eighteenth centuries. The number of priests, however, remained consistently low throughout the entirety of Maryland's existence as an English colony. Indeed, in 1763, when a census commissioned by the Bishop of London found that there were more than 16,000 Catholics in Maryland and another 8,000 across the border in Pennsylvania, the total number of priests serving in British colonial America was just eighteen. There was one priest for every 940 Catholics, a less-than-ideal ratio for a faith that put so much emphasis on the guidance of its clergy, in an exceedingly rural environment that had few roads, no transportation infrastructure, and encompassed more than 8,000 square miles. Under such circumstances, it was not uncommon for Catholics in British colonial America to have to go for weeks or even months without receiving the sacraments, especially if they did not live in the Catholic strongholds of Charles and St. Mary's Counties, on the southern tip of the western shore of the Chesapeake.[15]

The paucity of priests, when combined with the legal discrimination Catholics faced, meant that in eighteenth-century Maryland, the decision to be and remain Catholic was a deliberate one. Catholic identity was not something one passively inherited from one's family or culture; it was, rather, something one consciously chose to retain in a

13   Thomas J. Murphy, *Jesuit Slaveholding in Maryland, 1717–1838* (New York: Routledge, 2001); Charles F. Irons, *The Origins of Proslavery Christianity: White and Black Evangelicals in Colonial and Antebellum Virginia* (Chapel Hill: University of North Carolina Press, 2008).

14   Rachel L. Swarns, "272 Slaves Were Sold to Save Georgetown. What Does It Owe Their Descendants?" *New York Times*, April 16, 2016.

15   Farrelly, *Papist Patriots*, 139; Tricia T. Pyne, "Ritual and Practice in the Maryland Catholic Community, 1634–1776," *U.S. Catholic Historian* 26 (Spring 2008), 24.

colony that had given people many earthly reasons to convert to a Protestant form of Christianity.

The dedication of the priests who served in Maryland was vital to the faith's survival there. Nevertheless, the real reason Catholicism endured in eighteenth-century Maryland – and went on to serve as the foundation for the Catholic Church in the United States – was that the laity refused to abandon their Catholic faith. At the same time, however, circumstances forced laypeople to redefine their faith in order to maintain it. When Catholic Masses were not available, for instance, laypeople insisted on attending Anglican services – a practice that the Catholic clergy in England had labeled "schimatick" (a pejorative term), but which the Jesuits in Maryland grudgingly came to accept.

Lay Catholics formed prayer groups – or what were known as "sodalities" – with or without the initial guidance of a priest, whereby they committed to one another to engage in prayer exercises that would sustain the community's collective religious identity during those weeks and months when the services of a priest were unavailable. Colonial Maryland's Catholics freely clashed with their priests over Holy Day fasting observances that did not mesh with the "real world" work requirements of colonial life, and they insisted upon marrying outside the Catholic faith – frequently in those counties where the Catholic population was small – because, as one priest finally came to accept, confining the laity just to Catholic marriage partners would "reduce many of the faithful to live in a state of celibacy."[16]

These experiences helped to create an identity among America's first Catholics that was fiercely independent, committed to the idea of individual rights, and different, therefore, from anything found in Catholic Europe or even within those Spanish and French colonies that eventually joined the United States. As John Carroll confessed to an English friend in the midst of the Revolution, "I have contracted the language of a republican."[17] He and the lay Catholics he served were comfortable with the rights-oriented political mandates of the independence movement – which was why Catholics in British colonial America supported the Patriots and believed it was time for Americans to assume a new national identity.

---

[16]   Farrelly, *Papist Patriots*, 162–174; John Carroll to Charles Plowden, February 12, 1803, in *The John Carroll Papers*, ed. Thomas O'Brien Hanley (Notre Dame, IN: University of Notre Dame Press, 1975), 2:408.

[17]   John Carroll to Charles Plowden, February 20, 1782, *John Carroll Papers*, 1:65.

REPUBLICAN CATHOLICISM

The strong current of republicanism that ran through the Catholic community at the time of the nation's founding touched more than just the national or political identity of America's first Catholics; it touched their religious identity, too. Indeed, the early decades of the church's development in the United States was marked by a certain degree of intrareligious conflict, and republican sentiments among the nation's first Catholics were what fueled much of this conflict.

Not long after the Treaty of Paris was signed in 1783, Maryland's clergy turned their attention to two important projects: (1) increasing the number of priests serving in the United States; and (2) building up an episcopal infrastructure for the Catholic Church, since the clergy working in British colonial America had been under the auspices of the Bishop of London, who resided in what was now a foreign country. Maryland's priests made these projects a priority because the developments were desperately needed – but also because Catholics who had supported the independence movement believed it would be a good thing if the Vatican paid more attention to the United States. The attention, they understood, would carry with it an implicit diplomatic recognition of America's status as an autonomous nation.[18]

Imposing an institutional framework onto a population that had been taking responsibility for its religious identity for generations was no easy task, however. America's first bishop was confronted with this reality early on; yet, John Carroll managed to devise a way of working with America's fiercely republican lay Catholics. That way was known as "lay trusteeism," and for a time, it played an important role in building up the church's infrastructure in the United States.

Trusteeism was not unusual in Christianity – though it was quite unusual in Catholicism. The system involved groups of laypeople who pooled their resources to purchase land, labor, and supplies so that new churches could be built. The laypeople typically incorporated, as a way of separating their personal finances from the finances of the churches. They then elected boards of lay trustees, and those boards made a host of decisions affecting life within the congregations – decisions ranging from whether and when a new roof would be placed on a chapel, to the selection of clergy and the payment of their salaries.

---

[18] Farrelly, *Anti-Catholicism in America, 1620–1820* (New York: Cambridge University Press, 2017).

Lay trusteeism was how Congregationalists, Baptists, and Presbyterians had built their churches across New England during the colonial period, and it was how Catholics in Philadelphia had built two churches in that city, as well – St. Joseph's in 1733 and St. Mary's in 1763. John Carroll accepted the lay trustee system as the best way to build up the Catholic Church's physical infrastructure in America, even though it gave lay Catholics a degree of authority over parishes that was unheard of in the old world. For many years, the system that Carroll accepted worked.

By 1815, when America's first Catholic bishop died, there were six dioceses in the territory that was the United States. Two Catholic seminaries had been established – St. Mary's in Baltimore and St. Thomas' in Bardstown, Kentucky – making it possible for men to stay in the country while they trained to be priests. There were two convents in the United States, one in Maryland and the other in Louisiana. A Catholic college, Georgetown, had been established in Washington, DC, and construction on nearly a dozen new Catholic churches – including the first Catholic cathedral in the United States – had also been started or completed.[19]

Lay trusteeism made it possible for the number of Catholic churches in the country to grow, but it also made it possible for disagreements that the laity had with one another to infect the governance of the church. Nearly all of the parishes in early America were afflicted with these disagreements – to John Carroll's chagrin. Philadelphia's Catholic community, however, may have been the one that was most acutely afflicted, and where the disagreements had the most obvious impact on the Catholic Church.

The disagreements that plagued Catholics in the City of Brotherly Love were a mixture of class and ethnic antagonisms, a reflection of the internal diversity and religious dynamics of the nation's first Catholics. Catholics of Irish ancestry resented the heavily accented English of German and French-speaking priests; Catholics of German and English ancestry resented the heavy drinking habits of Irish priests. Ethnic devotions to particular saints – Nicholas, Patrick, George, and Denis – became a source of competition between and among the various ethnic groups, and nontheological traditions such as congregational singing in the vernacular, which was important to Germans, and the funeral custom known as a "wake," which was important to the Irish,

---

19   Peter Guilday, *The Life and Times of John Carroll* (New York: Encyclopedia Press, 1922).

generated annoyance and sometimes even disgust among Catholics who were unfamiliar with these practices.[20]

The disagreements that Catholics of German and Irish ancestry had with one another resulted in the founding of a whole new parish in 1788; Holy Trinity was built on land that German-speaking Catholics purchased just two blocks away from St. Mary's Church. At a time when Bishop Carroll was facing a severe dearth of competent priests, his laity forced him to assign a new priest to work in a new church that was just a few hundred yards away from an existing church – and all because German- and Irish-American Catholics in Philadelphia could not get along.

Carroll did this with some reluctance. When the new trustees of Holy Trinity complained to him, however, that the German-speaking priest he had found for them was "not by any means agreeable to our wishes," that was when the bishop pulled rank on the trustees, warning them that "the authors of dissensions & sowers of discontent between Pastors & their flock have always been punished by the church with exemplary Severity."[21] Carroll may have accepted the American custom of lay trusteeism as the best way to build up the church's physical infrastructure, but that did not mean he was willing to give the laity unlimited power.

The tensions in Philadelphia were an example of the growing pains the Catholic Church in the United States went through, as an institution that has always seen authority and hierarchy as necessary guideposts in a fallen world attempted to establish itself on a landscape that was fiercely independent, among a people who had been taking individual responsibility for their religious identities for multiple generations. The Diocese of Philadelphia was unusually disputatious, but tussles between and among clergy and laypeople did crop up in a number of American dioceses during the early decades of the nineteenth century. Some bishops tried to work with the republican impulses they found among their laity; Charleston's Bishop John England, for example, rather famously drafted a constitution for his diocese in 1822, governing Catholics in the Carolinas and Georgia

---

[20] Helen A. Heinz, "'We Are All as One Fish in the Sea ...' Catholicism in Protestant Pennsylvania, 1730–1790" (Ph.D. diss.: Temple University, 2007), 108, 136, n. 14; Maura Jane Farrelly, "Conflict and Community in Early Pennsylvania's Catholic Church," *Pennsylvania Legacies* 15 (Fall 2015), 9.

[21] Quoted in Dale B. Light, *Rome and the New Republic: Conflict and Community in Philadelphia Catholicism between the Revolution and the Civil War* (Notre Dame, IN: University of Notre Dame Press, 1996), 4, 8.

through a bicameral "legislature" that had one house made up of
clergy, and another house made up of laypeople who had been selected
by and from among various parishes.[22]

Other bishops unabashedly resented the efforts of laypeople to
exert control over their parishes. When Catholics in Norfolk,
Virginia, locked their priest out of his church and tried to replace
him with a clergyman from New York in 1819, Archbishop
Ambrose Maréchal of Baltimore assured them under no uncertain
terms that their "pretended right" of choosing their own priest was
"perfectly unfounded." Even John Carroll, who had embraced lay
trusteeism as the best way to build up the church's infrastructure
in the United States – and had confessed in 1782 that he, too, had
"contracted the language of a republican" – found the independent
impulses of some of the trustees he worked with to be a tad
frustrating. Three years after he wrote to his friend about his own
republican sensibilities, Carroll warned New York's Catholics that
they were acting "nearly in the same manner as the Congregational
Presbyterians of your neighboring New England states" when they
insisted that they had certain "rights" within the community of the
church.[23]

In 1829, America's bishops convened in Baltimore for the first of
what ended up being ten "provincial councils," or meetings at which
the bishops determined how best to implement the mandates of the
Catholic Church within an American context. High on the bishops' list
of priorities during these meetings was the issue of lay trusteeism – or
what the bishops called a "scandalous insubordination toward lawful
pastors" and an "evil that tends to the ruin of Catholic discipline to
schism and heresy."[24]

It would be a "great good," the bishops decided at the First
Provincial Council of Baltimore, if "the system of church trustees [were]
entirely abolished." They took steps at that first meeting to ensure that
the property in any new parish created in the United States would

---

22   James M. O'Toole, *The Faithful: A History of Catholics in America* (Cambridge, MA:
      Belknap Press, 2008), 51.
23   Gerald P. Fogarty, *Commonwealth Catholicism: A History of the Catholic Church
      in Virginia* (Notre Dame, IN: University of Notre Dame Press, 2001), 33–55; John
      Carroll, "John Carroll's Letter on Lay Trusteeism in New York City," 1786, in
      American Catholic History: A Documentary Reader, ed. Mark Massa and
      Catherine Osborne (New York: New York University Press, 2008), 32.
24   Quoted in Light, *Rome and the New Republic*, 240.

legally belong to the bishop who oversaw the parish – regardless of whether laypeople had paid for the land or the construction of the church. The council also stipulated that all existing trustees were barred from having any say in the selection or dismissal of their priests.[25]

In the thirty years that followed, America's bishops worked hard to restrain the republican values of their laity and to dismantle the system of lay trusteeism. In older parishes where trusteeism already existed, trustees were pressured to transfer ownership of the parish's properties to the various bishops. Slowly, the bishops' campaign began to have success – and the reason for this success was that the population of Catholics in the United States started changing during these decades, becoming less native-born, more immigrant – and therefore less republican.

Specifically, the Catholic population in America became more *Irish* with each passing year. Irish immigrants tended to be more deferential than their fiercely republican, America-born counterparts to the authority of priests and bishops. The Irish laity deferred to their clergy because the Catholic Church in Ireland had been one of the few institutions that opposed the oppressive policies of the English government and tried to make the lives of Irish peasants better.

The thousands of Irish Catholic immigrants who began arriving in the United States in the 1830s and 1840s, fleeing poverty and starvation in their home country, radically altered the economic, political, religious, and cultural landscape in the United States. By 1850, immigrants from Ireland constituted nearly a quarter of all the inhabitants in Boston, New York, Philadelphia, and Baltimore – and the church that America's first Catholics had built in the United States would be forever changed.

FURTHER READING

Carey, Patrick W. *People, Priests, and Prelates: Ecclesiastical Democracy and the Tensions of Trusteeism.* Notre Dame, IN: University of Notre Dame Press, 1987.
Clark, Emily. *Masterless Mistresses: The New Orleans Ursulines and the Development of a New World Society, 1727–1834.* Chapel Hill: University of North Carolina Press, 2007.

[25]   Light, *Rome and the New Republic*, 241; Patrick W. Carey, *People, Priests, and Prelates: Ecclesiastical Democracy and the Tensions of Trusteeism* (Notre Dame, IN: University of Notre Dame Press, 1987), 264; Eric Vanden Eykel, "Scripture in the Pastoral Letters of the Provincial Councils of Baltimore," *American Catholic Studies* 121 (Fall 2010), 61–65.

Farrelly, Maura Jane. *Papist Patriots: The Making of an American Catholic Identity*. New York: Oxford University Press, 2012.

Pasquier, Michael. *Fathers on the Frontier: French Missionaries and the Roman Catholic Priesthood in the United States, 1789–1870*. New York: Oxford University Press, 2010.

Starr, Kevin. *Continental Ambitions: Roman Catholics in North America*. San Francisco: Ignatius Press, 2016.

2 The Immigrant Church, 1820–1908

STEVEN M. AVELLA

Between the first decades of the nineteenth century and the dawn of the twentieth, the numbers of US Catholics grew from 200,000 to more than 14 million. This growth was made possible by an increasing birth rate but also successive waves of immigration, predominantly from Europe. During this era, US Catholics developed a dense network of imposing and influential institutions: cathedrals (some of surpassing architectural elegance), parish churches, and various types of schools, orphanages, hospitals, convents, monasteries, and seminaries. Even in places where Catholics were a minority or whose Catholic populations grew slowly, Catholic enclaves often flourished.

This growth generated a host of administrative and organizational challenges. It also created a backlash among non-Catholic citizens and fueled anti-Catholic sentiment that sometimes became violent. In response, Catholics worked to protect their interests. Catholics built an institutional subculture designed to serve their spiritual and social needs, as well as to insulate them from ideas and values at odds with their faith. Amid this growth, Catholic leadership became more centralized and effective in directing church affairs and exercised a greater role in helping immigrants resist anti-Catholic xenophobia and maintain group solidarity.

This chapter focuses on several key themes: (1) early Catholic immigration and the church's response to the challenges it posed; (2) new waves of immigration in the late nineteenth century that established a more multiethnic Catholic presence; (3) debates among Catholics about their relationship to the nation and the pace of Americanization; (4) the impact of centralizing and Romanizing tendencies within the church and their impact on US Catholicism.

A GROWING CATHOLIC POPULATION

The best evidence of Catholic Church growth in numbers and presence in the United States is to be found in the creation of new dioceses. In

1808, the Congregation for the Propagation of the Faith – the Roman office that had authority over the young US church – elevated the Diocese of Baltimore, the first in the United States, to the status of an archbishopric and created four additional dioceses in Boston, New York, Philadelphia, and Bardstown, Kentucky. This began a continual process of dividing and subdividing portions of the United States into administrative units to deal with growth and guide further expansion. By 1908, the year the United States was no longer considered a missionary territory by Rome, there were ninety dioceses, two vicariates apostolic, and one prefecture apostolic serving 14.2 million Catholics.[1]

The first wave of nineteenth-century Catholic immigrants was primarily from northern and western Europe. Many of them, from Ireland or German-speaking areas, were fleeing economic insecurity, revolution, or oppressive government policies. These newcomers frequently settled in coastal cities like Boston, New York, Philadelphia, and Baltimore. They also landed in New Orleans, but most avoided the South, in part because of labor competition with enslaved African Americans. Catholics also expanded into areas designated the "Old Northwest" fronting the Great Lakes, settling in the Ohio River Valley, Indiana, Michigan, Illinois, and Wisconsin. Catholics were to be found on farms but the heaviest concentrations were in waterfront cities like Dubuque, Cleveland, Toledo, Cincinnati, Detroit, Milwaukee, and Chicago.

German-speaking Catholics were the first to arrive in great numbers, with many fleeing from revolutionary disorder and diminishing opportunities in Europe. While many settled along the East Coast, a considerable number moved into the American heartland, settling in cities and towns throughout the region between St. Louis, Cincinnati, and Milwaukee that came to be known as the "German Triangle." Their presence fueled the need for pastoral accommodations, which were often made at the insistence of the German community itself. In the 1790s, Bishop John Carroll permitted the foundation of a Catholic parish dedicated to German speakers: Holy Trinity Church in Philadelphia. It was the first parish in the nation to be established to serve a specific national group, initiating a trend towards ethnic separatism that would continue over the course of the nineteenth century. As their population grew, German Catholics staked out prime urban space for their churches and schools and recruited German-speaking priests

---

[1]   Figures taken from the *Official Catholic Directory* (New York: Kenedy, 1909).

and sisters to staff them. Important seed money for church construction was donated by European mission societies, such as the Society for the Propagation of the Faith, the Leopoldine Foundation, and the Ludwig Mission Society. The churches they established were often elaborately decorated in the style of their homelands in the German-speaking areas of Europe (Bavaria, Austria, and Switzerland). Most placed a heavy emphasis on church music and had substantial organs and choir lofts. A typical German parish also fostered a rich associational and devotional life with organizations (vereinen) formed on the basis of age and gender. These groups sponsored particular devotions and cultivated support for the church. German-speakers were determined to preserve their native language and culture – seeing it as an important vehicle for the preservation of their faith. The belief that "language preserves faith" was a long-held belief among German-American Catholics, which fueled their strong investment in parochial education. They saw Catholic schools as having an integral role to play in the transmission of faith, culture, and identity from one generation to the next.

Irish or English-speaking communities grew significantly in the wake of the 1845–1854 agricultural crises in Ireland known as the Great Hunger or the Great Famine. Although poorer than German-speaking immigrants at this time, they were hard workers and more capable of fitting into American society because they spoke English. They eventually overcame hostility in cities like Boston, and participated in city politics and secured public jobs, especially in teaching and law enforcement. They, too, built churches (generally more modestly decorated than the Germans), opened schools, and founded social welfare organizations to serve their constituencies. Over time, Irish Catholics came to dominate the US clergy in many places and were selected to fill the vast majority of episcopal appointments. Irish-Americans dominated the US hierarchy from the mid-nineteenth century until well into the twentieth. Adding to this were religious sisterhoods from Ireland – the Sisters of Mercy, the Sisters of Charity of the Blessed Virgin Mary, and the Sisters of the Presentation, among others – who were active in parochial education, health care, and various works of charity. Even as these communities became established in the United States, many continued to recruit members from Ireland to serve alongside their growing number of Irish-American vocations.

By 1850, the Catholic Church was the single largest religious denomination in the United States and Catholic institutions stretched from coast to coast. US expansion into the Louisiana Territory, the American Southwest, and the West Coast provided the nation with vast new territory, but also annexed regions of earlier colonial-era French and Spanish Catholic settlement, making their inhabitants part of the US church. Catholic missionaries plunged into the interior of the country, following settlers and reaching out to Native American tribes. One notable example was Father Pierre Jean de Smet (1801–1973), a Belgian Jesuit who traveled extensively in western North America, helping to establish the church's presence on the Great Plains and in the Pacific Northwest. He came to the United States in 1821 and moved to St. Louis in 1823, where he was ordained in 1827. He began his active ministry as the US government was forcibly removing Indians from their tribal lands east of the Mississippi. De Smet worked among the diverse tribes already present in the region, learning their languages and customs in order to evangelize them. His respect for native culture gained him the respect of many tribal leaders, and he became an important intermediary between them and US government officials. He established numerous missions in the region, from Nebraska to Montana.

Catholic expansion and numerical growth brought distinct challenges. In particular, the influx of foreigners often provoked negative and even violent reactions on the part of "native-born" Americans. Hatred or fear of foreigners (xenophobia) periodically convulsed American life, sometimes fomented by demagogic politicians and preachers. Anti-foreign invective often singled out certain social pathologies that were supposedly inbred in the despised immigrant cohort. They were derided as burdens on the public treasury, prone to indolence, drunkenness, crime, and disease. Catholicism was often seen as an added liability. Because of their loyalty to the pope, Catholics, it was believed, could not be trusted to be loyal Americans.

Public displeasure with Catholicism took many forms. One was the publication of lurid accounts of sexual misconduct by priests and nuns. One of the bestselling books of the early nineteenth century was Maria Monk's *Awful Disclosures of the Hotel Dieu Nunnery* (1831). This book was a form of pornography, with titillating stories of sexual relations between priests and nuns, followed by nauseating accounts of infanticide. This book was widely read and believed, and popular speakers vouched for its authenticity. Harsh anti-Catholic sermons from the Reverend Lyman Beecher in Boston led to the burning of an Ursuline convent in 1834 in Charlestown, Massachusetts. Suspicion of Catholics spawned intrusive "convent inspection" laws in some states. Several other popular tomes stoked fears of Catholic dominance in the United States. Samuel F. B. Morse's *A Foreign Conspiracy against the Liberties of the United States* (1832) took aim at European mission societies;

Lyman Beecher's *Plea for the West* (1834) warned of an immigrant take-over of America. These dark conspiracies and accusations of sexual profligacy on the part of Catholics appealed not only to the poorly educated, but also people of learning and prominence in American society.

In some places public schools exhibited hostility to the Catholic faith, eliciting complaints from Catholic parents who did not want their children being exposed to the King James Version of the Bible, singing Protestant church hymns, or having their children harangued by zealous Protestant teachers on the evils of "Romanism." When Bishop John Hughes of New York demanded that a percentage of the city's Public School Fund go to Catholic schools, he met strong opposition from those who objected to the use of public tax dollars to support the "Catholic religion." Hughes then insisted that Catholics build their own schools, pressing ahead with a program of parochial education that placed a considerable financial burden on the generally low-income Catholic population.[2] Bloody riots targeted Catholics in several locales, most notably Philadelphia in 1844 and Louisville in 1855.

Popular sentiment against Catholics reached into local, state, and national politics. These fears and other agitation led to the formation of nativist political parties and ultimately the Know-Nothing Party, which influenced electoral politics in the 1850s and even advanced a candidate for president, Millard Fillmore, in 1856. Anti-Catholicism persisted throughout the nineteenth and twentieth centuries and created a defensive mood among US Catholics. Persecution encouraged Catholics to build an extensive (and expensive) network of parallel institutions: schools, hospitals, and social welfare agencies to wall themselves off from aggressive Protestant proselytizing. In New York, Bishop John Hughes stationed Irish sharpshooters around the perimeters of churches in response to anti-Catholic hostility in 1844 and vowed to turn New York "into a second Moscow" if Catholics were attacked.[3]

Concern about growing Roman influence was not entirely unfounded. In the nineteenth century, the Roman papacy itself became a more prominent aspect of Catholicism and loyalty to the pope became an increasingly important mark of orthodoxy. Pope Pius IX (1846–1878) pressed this forcefully and convened Vatican Council I (1869–1871), which affirmed the direct jurisdiction of the Roman Pontiff in spiritual affairs and declared the pope infallible when he spoke on matters of faith

---

[2]   John Loughery, *Dagger John: Archbishop John Hughes and the Making of Modern America* (Ithaca, NY: Cornell University Press, 2018), 121–125.

[3]   Loughery, *Dagger John*, 160.

and morals. In response, US church leaders looked increasingly to the Vatican for direction. Another link to the Vatican came in 1859 with the establishment of the North American College in Rome, which provided American seminarians with an opportunity to pursue their priestly formation under Roman auspices. Over time, it cultivated a cohort of priests loyal to Roman direction, including many who came to occupy important positions in the US hierarchy.

On a national level, bishops worked together in group meetings called Provincial and Plenary Councils. Since there was no comprehensive code of canon law as yet (it would come in 1918) or much direct Roman governance of the US church for much of the nineteenth century, local churches had a hand in directing local affairs. The archbishops of Baltimore (the oldest US diocese) convened periodic gatherings of bishops to address mutual problems and concerns, such as lay trusteeism, sacramental practices, church discipline, marriage policies, clerical education, and the Catholic education of youth. The councils also played a role in the creation of new dioceses by conveying to Vatican officials the requests, petitions, and geographical realities of the church in the United States. Of singular importance were the Plenary Councils of 1852, 1866, and 1884, which brought together representatives of all the dioceses of the United States.

Called in the aftermath of the Civil War, the Plenary Council of 1866 focused primarily on clarifying theological teachings and addressing internal administrative affairs, but it also had to grapple with the legacy of sectionalism and slavery. Although the Catholic Church did not split along northern and southern lines like many of the nation's Protestant denominations, its members had been divided on the issue of slavery. Many Catholic religious orders had owned slaves, including the Jesuits, the Vincentians, the Ursulines, and the Daughters of Charity. Nineteenth-century Catholic theologians such as Bishop Francis Kenrick and Father Augustine Verot, defended the rights of slaveholders, asserting the moral "acceptability" of slavery as long as it was practiced in a humane fashion. Northern Catholics were more concerned about southern efforts to extend slavery into the territories where it threatened to crowd out wage labor than they were about the social and political equality of African Americans. Among the US bishops, Archbishop John B. Purcell of Cincinnati was one of the few who openly opposed slavery. During the war, northern dioceses tended to defend the Union cause, while southern dioceses supported the Confederacy. Racial prejudice remained entrenched and largely unacknowledged.

Although the convener of the council Kentucky-born Archbishop Martin J. Spalding of Baltimore promoted efforts to evangelize African Americans, the question of the treatment of the four million newly freed persons was never formally addressed by the bishops. Some religious communities of men and women accepted the challenge, but by and large neither northern nor southern Catholics viewed this task as a priority.

In 1884, the Third Plenary Council of Baltimore, convoked at the insistence of Roman authorities, produced a series of far-reaching decisions that would be of great importance in the US church. Among them, the bishops mandated that every parish should have a parochial school. Although it remained an elusive goal, the policy spurred considerable investment in the expansion of Catholic elementary education. The work of staffing these schools was largely undertaken by women religious, whose voluntary labor lessened the financial burden on parishes and dioceses and sustained the system of parochial education well into the middle decades of the twentieth century. The Third Plenary Council also authorized a popular catechism, known familiarly as the "Baltimore Catechism," which went through many editions and became a mainstay of catechetical formation for Catholic youth up through the time of the Second Vatican Council in the 1960s. Its familiar question and answer format outlined church teachings on matters of faith and morals in concise, authoritative language that students were frequently required to memorize and internalize.

By the closing decades of the nineteenth century, the Catholic Church was firmly established in the United States. In the nation's major cities, bishops announced Catholic presence and might by erecting cathedrals "of suitable magnificence" and grandeur that served as the focal point of diocesan life and sign of episcopal authority. St. Patrick's Cathedral in New York, built between 1853 and 1879, stands as the most representative of this majestic building tradition, with a Gothic design that celebrated the glories of the Catholic past in modern America. Standing alongside these cathedrals were the countless other parish churches – some of them equally impressive size and beauty – that made Catholicism visible in cities and towns across the country. They were joined by the growing number of schools and academies for both boys and girls, and colleges and universities that opened up pathways for higher education and social advancement. A range of health and social welfare institutions, including hospitals and orphanages, represented the church's stake in providing for community needs. All of this institutional growth reflected the increasing size, stability, and financial clout of Catholics throughout the United States.

THE IMMIGRANT PARISH AND
CATHOLIC SUBCULTURE

Parish life was the heart and soul of the US Catholic experience in the immigrant era. As new waves of immigration reshaped the face of the church in the United States during the second half of the nineteenth century, parish growth came to reflect the increasing diversity of the Catholic community. Like their Irish and German forebearers, newer Catholic immigrant groups settled together and formed ethnic neighborhoods that were anchored by churches, schools, and social welfare organizations. Often these churches were built within blocks of each other as dioceses responded to ethnic diversity by granting each group its own parish. In places like the "Back of the Yards" neighborhood in Chicago, there were eleven Catholic churches within an area of less than two square miles, serving Irish, Germans, Poles, Croatians, Lithuanians, Bohemians (Czechs), and Slovaks. The pattern was repeated not just in the nation's major cities and industrial towns, but even in rural communities. This proliferation of ethnic Catholic parishes reworked the geography of many cities and shaped Catholic social life. Most consisted of large church structures, schools, playgrounds, convents, and residences for priests. The parish, often located in the heart of an urban neighborhood, provided spiritual care, but it also was a social and cultural center for immigrant Catholics. People met their future spouses at church-run schools, choirs, and picnics. Church-supported social welfare programs provided money for Christian burial, mementos for the dead, and spiritual help in times of unemployment, illness, stress, and the inevitable joys and sadness of life. Church bells pealed the hours of the day, the thrice-daily Angelus prayer, and the doleful toll of the passing of friends and neighbors.[4]

Immigrant era Catholicism was marked by a strong emphasis on devotional activity that ran in tandem with the formal liturgical life of the Catholic Church found in the Mass and the sacraments. Popular piety included the honoring of patron saints: St. Patrick among the Irish, St. Boniface among the Germans, or St. Stanislaus among the Poles. Devotions also cut across ethnic lines, like prayers and novenas to the Sacred Heart of Jesus or to the Virgin Mary. Catholics also regularly honored the real presence of Christ in the consecrated host through a number of Eucharistic devotions, including adoration of the Blessed

---

[4] For a representative discussion, see Edward R. Kantowicz, "The Ethnic Church," in *Catholicism, Chicago Style*, ed. Ellen Skerrett, Edward R. Kantowicz, and Steven M. Avella (Chicago: Loyola University Press, 1993).

Sacrament and annual Corpus Christi celebrations. The latter often included solemn outdoor processions in which the priest carried the consecrated host, contained in an elaborate vessel known as a monstrance. These celebrations spilled out of the church and into the neighborhood and included representatives of parish organizations, groups of school children, and even musical bands or military honor guards. These and other events became important public markers and demonstrations of Catholic life. These devotional prayers and practices often helped immigrant Catholics feel close to God and to Mary and the saints.

Devotional activities of this type were frequently promoted during annual parish missions. In an era of Protestant revivalism, Catholics offered an alternative form of religious exercises in these week-long services. They were generally conducted by a member of a religious order such as the Redemptorists, the Jesuits, or the Paulists, but sometimes by local priests. These carefully scripted events were sometimes divided by gender (one week for men and one week for women) so that sermons and other activities could be tailored to address the needs and concerns of particular segments of the parish population. Mission preachers led participants to ponder deeply the direction of their lives and their fate after death: heaven, hell, or purgatory. Sacramental confession was available for the repentant. For those who had forgotten their religious training, missions refreshed key church teaching and reminded attendees of their religious obligations. Missions were extremely popular among US Catholics and often helped restore flagging parish membership and bolster Catholic institutional life.

As these immigrant communities grew and multiplied, ethnic diversity produced a new set of challenges for church leaders. Typical was the response to the huge influx of Italian immigrants mostly from southern Italy and Sicily. US bishops and local priests worried about Italians' lax observance of church law – especially Mass attendance and their general distaste for Catholic schools. Termed the "Italian Problem," Catholic leaders discussed how to inculcate good religious habits in Italians, such as financial support for the parish, attendance at Catholic schools, deference to the clerical and episcopal authority, and adherence to formal church teachings. Many Italians balked at "Irish" control of the American church and resented the accusation that they "suffered a spiritual destitution greater than that of all other immigrant groups."[5]

---

[5] "American Bishops and the Pastoral Care of Italians, 1884," in *Keeping Faith: European and Asian Catholic Immigrants*, ed. Jeffrey M. Burns, Ellen Skerrett, and Joseph M. White (Maryknoll, NY: Orbis Books, 2000), 163.

In addition, many Italian males were openly anticlerical because the church opposed Italian unification and also because clerical celibacy seemed to strike at traditional notions of masculinity. Over time, however, the groups learned to accommodate their differences. Italians supported their own ethnic parishes in order to carve out a space for themselves and their religious customs. Church leaders made efforts to support outreach ministries, often entrusting the work to missionary priests and sisters from Italy who could serve the immigrant community with greater cultural sensitivity.

The Catholic Church also struggled to respond to racial diversity as blacks began to migrate to northern cities in search of work and a refuge from southern racial violence. Quite often, they encountered similar discrimination among white Catholics. These attitudes caused bishops to form separate (segregated) parishes for African-American Catholics in many northern cities. Predominantly white parishes that permitted African Americans to worship sometimes relegated them to balconies or the rear of the church. Catholic seminaries, religious houses, convents, and other educational institutions turned away black candidates. Almost no diocese took in African-American candidates for the priesthood. When Father Augustus Tolton (1854–1897), the first African-American priest in the United States, felt the call to the priesthood, he was forced to go to Europe to pursue his studies since no seminary in the United States would admit him. Only a small number of religious communities, like the Society of St. Joseph (Josephites), the Oblate Sisters of Providence, and the Sisters of the Holy Family, took in African-American vocations.

Over the course of the late nineteenth century, parishes became a defining feature of Catholic life. They marked the Catholic presence in the United States, from its burgeoning cities to its rural regions. They met the spiritual and social needs of a largely immigrant flock, helping them preserve their culture while easing their adjustment to life in a new land. Parishes also created and reinforced a series of boundaries, not only between Catholics and the wider American culture but also among Catholics themselves, dividing them along ethnic and racial lines. They not only helped cultivate a sense of Catholic distinctiveness but also promoted a degree of defensiveness. They became the foundation of a Catholic subculture that would dominate the US Catholic community until well into the twentieth century.

INTERNAL DEBATES: AMERICANIZATION OR SEPARATISM

Ethnic parishes and the creation of a distinctive Catholic subculture were celebrated by many, but some church leaders in the United States fretted that excessive perpetuation of language, culture, and ethnic identity would slow the acceptance of Catholics into mainstream American life. Members of this "Americanist" wing of the church, as it came to be known, promoted assimilationist policies and tended to emphasize the fundamental compatibility of American values with Catholicism. Their critics, however, worried about the corrosive effects of "modern" thought and principles – such as the separation of church and state and religious pluralism – and sought to curtail their influences. These disagreements erupted in a series of public disputes and arguments – largely among bishops and priests – that shaped the church's response to a range of issues, both internal and external, during the closing decades of the nineteenth century.

During the 1870s and 1880s, a series of clashes emerged between the church's two largest immigrant groups, the Irish and Germans, over the direction of US Catholicism. One of its first soundings was a noisy public dispute over episcopal succession in Milwaukee. The aging archbishop, German-speaking John Martin Henni, was failing rapidly and wanted his friend, Bavarian Michael Heiss, Bishop of La Crosse, to be appointed his successor. Henni's petition met procedural difficulties as well as vigorous opposition from English-speaking priests who wanted an English speaker as bishop. Through the help of a German cardinal in Rome, and the intercession of the German-speaking Mother General of the School Sisters of Notre Dame, Heiss eventually received the appointment and was named archbishop in 1881. The dispute in Milwaukee paralleled battles over church leadership in other dioceses and reflected ongoing worry among German-American Catholics over "leakage" from the Catholic faith. Although they understood the inevitability of assimilation, they wanted it to happen more gradually. In 1886, a Milwaukee priest, Father Peter Abbelen, a chaplain to the School Sisters of Notre Dame – a large German congregation of sisters – brought attention to German Catholic concerns by issuing a public "memorial" addressed to the Congregation for the Propagation of the Faith in Rome. Its demands included that German parishes be considered equal to English-speaking parishes and that priests not suppress the German language or German customs and devotional practices.

The "Abbelen Memorial" caused a stir, especially among leading English-speaking bishops who opposed it, most notably Archbishop John Ireland of St. Paul, Cardinal James Gibbons of Baltimore, John J. Keane, rector of the Catholic University of America, and Denis O'Connell, rector of the North American College in Rome.[6]

Another flashpoint stemmed from Catholic support for labor unions. In the United States, concerns were raised over the Knights of Labor, a popular labor organization founded in 1869 and headed by a Catholic, Terence V. Powderly. The Knights had attracted a wide array of working people and launched and won several strikes. Nonetheless, it had the trappings of a "secret society" (an entity condemned by the Vatican) and in 1884, a Canadian bishop issued a condemnation of the organization. This alarmed US bishops who feared that a similar public statement would confuse and anger those Catholics who had joined the Knights. Some would just abandon the church if they were forced to choose. In 1887, Cardinal Gibbons drew up a strong defense of the organization. He underscored the fear that a condemnation might alienate scores of Catholic working class men and women who would have to choose between their church and their economic well-being. His arguments averted a papal condemnation and its potential fallout.

Tensions also erupted over the question of whether parochial schools continued to be necessary. For Germans, Poles, and others who considered schools an integral part of their parishes, the answer was clear. They argued that separate Catholic schooling was needed to provide children with sound religious instruction and to counteract the dangers of secular society. Catholic schools also cultivated future vocations to the priesthood and religious life. Some church leaders, like Archbishop Ireland, however, wondered if the schools were needed only in the short run. In his diocese, he supported the Faribault and Stillwater plans, experimental alternatives modeled on a program developed earlier in Poughkeepsie, New York. This plan integrated public and parochial schooling and carved out a special place for religious instruction after regular school hours. This arrangement had won tentative acceptance in Rome but aroused the suspicion of German-American bishops who mistrusted Ireland and the public schools.

---

[6] See "German Catholic Grievances in the Abbelen Memorial, 1886" and "Reply of Bishops John Ireland and John Keane to the Abbelen Memorial," in *Keeping Faith*, 60–74.

Complaints about Ireland and others flowed into the Vatican, which took a dim view of many of these developments. Roman authorities dispatched someone to give a close-up view of American affairs. In 1893, on the occasion of the Columbian Exposition in Chicago, the Vatican sent over a set of antique maps of the United States, and with them, an emissary, Archbishop Francesco Satolli. Once the fair was over, Satolli remained in the United States. American bishops had long resisted the idea of a Roman nuncio or delegate on American soil, fearing it would stir up anti-Catholic feelings in the country. Privately some expressed misgivings about having the peering eyes of Rome too close to their work. Nonetheless, Satolli would become the first Apostolic Delegate to the United States. Later, he and future delegates played a key role in selecting candidates for episcopal office, making sure only candidates acceptable to Rome would be appointed.

The Columbian Exposition also raised eyebrows among many Roman officials and some American bishops when Cardinal Gibbons and Bishop Keane participated in the World Parliament of Religions. This multifaith gathering assembled representatives from all the major world religions for discussion and common prayer. Gibbons and Keane never denied the Catholic Church's claim to be the "one true church" but their very presence on a stage with other religious leaders suggested a level of toleration of other traditions that was not acceptable according to formal Catholic teaching at that time.

Overarching these individual incidents were real differences about the extent to which the Catholic Church could be successfully adapted to America's political, social, and economic realities. Bishops like Ireland were supremely optimistic that Catholicism could flourish in America with its religious freedom, separation of church and state, and democratic principles. Bishop Keane and Cardinal Gibbons (perhaps America's most revered Catholic churchman) held to this view. Father Isaac Hecker, an American-born convert to Catholicism and founder of the Paulists, was an important intellectual force in this debate. In his writings and sermons, Hecker emphasized the creative work of the Holy Spirit in the lives of individuals and in the church. He believed that America's religious freedom produced a faith that was deeply personal and for Catholics, fortified by the sacraments. He sensed God's spirit worked strongly in the American experience and believed that divine providence would guide the United States to embrace Catholicism. He believed that Catholicism and American life were deeply compatible.

Others were highly skeptical, including Archbishop Michael Corrigan of New York, members of the Catholic University of America faculty, and the German-American bishops. More seriously, Roman authorities were suspicious of Hecker's ideas and those who shared them. Among the Roman critics was included Pope Leo XIII, who had called for the restoration of Thomistic philosophy and theology as an antidote to evolutionary modern thinking. Eventually, the pope and his advisors weighed in on the subject. In the encyclical *Longinqua Oceani* (1895) the pope took a dim view of American realities, such as the separation of church and state. His writing reflected a decades-long battle by the church against the forces of "modernity": science, individualism, rationalism, socialism, and materialism. In 1864, Pope Pius IX had issued a list of eighty false teachings of the modern age in his "Syllabus of Errors," including the notion that the "Roman Pontiff can, and ought to, reconcile himself, and come to terms with progress, liberalism, and modern civilization."[7] In such an atmosphere, any Catholic efforts to find common ground with modern times were suspect. When Father John Zahm, CSC, of the University of Notre Dame published *Evolution and Dogma* (1896), and suggested that Catholic thought was not hostile to evolutionary theory, the book provoked sharp reactions and was withdrawn, Zahm himself narrowly escaping public condemnation. Those who envisioned religious truths as timeless and unchanging had no patience for evolutionary ideas. For them, truth did not – and could not – change.[8]

When Americanizing US bishops seemed too eager to find common ground with secular society or champion democratic governance, alarm bells went off. The flashpoint was a translation into French of Walter Elliott's *Life of Father Hecker*, the founder of the Paulists, which included an introduction written by Abbé Felix Klein, a professor at the Institut Catholique in Paris. Klein affirmed Hecker's belief that the Holy Spirit could renew and transform the traditional structures of the Catholic Church. Change was possible. For a variety

---

[7] Joe Holland, *Modern Catholic Social Teaching: The Popes Confront the Industrial Age, 1740–1958* (Mahwah, NJ: Paulist Press, 2003), 94–98.

[8] On Zahm, see R. Scott Appleby, *Church and Age Unite: The Modernist Impulse in American Catholicism* (Notre Dame, IN: University of Notre Dame Press, 1992), 13–52. See also John P. Slattery, *Faith and Science at Notre Dame: John Zahm, Evolution, and the Catholic Church* (Notre Dame, IN: Notre Dame Press, 2019).

of reasons (none of them having to do with actual conditions in the United States), Klein's introduction struck a nerve in the French church and incited protest from French bishops who were at odds with the anticlerical French government. The legacy of Hecker and his interpreters was highly suspect when set against the reigning theological ideas of the day rooted in medieval thought and neo-scholasticism.

Pope Leo XIII and his advisers finally decided to confront what they considered a heresy they called "Americanism." Pro-Americanist prelates were removed from office: Father Denis O'Connell from the head of the North American College and Bishop John J. Keane as rector of the Catholic University of America. Archbishop Satolli, at first sympathetic to the Americanists, changed sides. In January 1899, in a letter addressed to Cardinal Gibbons, *Testem Benevolentiae*, the papal axe fell on the Americanists. While praising American enterprise and efforts to promote the church, the pope took aim at certain heterodox beliefs that he believed had sprung up in the US church: too rapid assimilation, religious subjectivism, and a certain form of ecclesiastical nationalism that considered the church in the United States as somehow different or distinct from the church universal.

The letter hit like a thunderbolt, pleasing conservative bishops like Corrigan who publicly thanked the pope for this clarification. It depressed and demoralized others like Gibbons and Ireland who denied that anyone held these heterodox positions, but who were apologists for some of the views Pope Leo condemned. Ultimately, the arguments about Catholic assimilation became moot when immigration to the United States slowed during World War I and was then formally restricted through quotas imposed by the US Congress in the Immigration Act of 1924.

Under Pope Pius X (1903–1914), papal power would be further centralized and Catholic identity would be even more firmly wedded to Roman direction and authority. Pius X tightened the screws on perceived theological dissent with *Lamentabili Sane Exitu* (July 1907) and *Pascendi Gregis* (September 1908), which leveled harsh charges against the heresy of "Modernism." These papal decrees created an atmosphere of anxiety around any scholarly research that seemed to deny, question, or modify accepted doctrinal teachings. Professional historians were ostracized if they even suggested that Catholic doctrine, liturgical practice, and governance were subject to change over the course of time. For many decades, the "perennial teaching" of neo-scholastic theological methods and manuals, pressed by Pope Leo XIII, prevailed as the official theology of the church. Catholic priests and laypeople were steeped in this particular theological framework.[9]

CONCLUSION

The story of nineteenth-century US Catholicism is that of the immigrant church, its struggles, and its triumphs. From the first streams of Irish and German immigration in the first half of the century through the growing swell of Southern and Eastern Europeans in its closing decades, these newcomers built churches and schools, formed local organizations, and expanded the church's institutional presence on American shores. During this time, Catholic numbers grew rapidly in almost every region of the United States. Bishops, priests, and women religious who served the church commanded respect and support. Yet this growth also provoked negative reactions in American society and incited bursts of intense anti-Catholic animosity, including violence. To defend themselves, church leaders insisted on creating separate institutions (especially schools) and encouraged Catholic solidarity when confronted by a sometimes hostile world. A rich Catholic subculture flourished, raising questions over the extent to which Catholics should adapt to American society. Though Catholics grew increasingly "at home" in the United States, a more militant and triumphant spirit developed among American bishops and clergy, and Roman authorities exerted greater influence over local US conditions. American Catholics, although deeply committed to their democratic and liberal principles, were also quite loyal to the pope and Roman guidelines were the touchstone of orthodoxy. The immigrant church became the most loyal daughter of the Roman Church.

FURTHER READING

Davis, Cyprian. *The History of Black Catholics in the United States.* New York: Crossroad Publishing, 1993.
Dolan, Jay P. *The Immigrant Church: New York's Irish and German Catholics.* Notre Dame, IN: University of Notre Dame Press, 1983.
Gjerde, John ed. by S. Deborah Kang. *Catholicism and the Shaping of Nineteenth Century America.* New York: Cambridge University Press, 2012.

---

9   For a full account of the Americanist controversy, see Thomas T. McAvoy, *The Great Crisis in American Catholic History, 1895–1900* (Chicago: H. Regnery, 1957).

Gleason, Philip. *The Conservative Reformers: German American Catholics and the Social Order.* Notre Dame, IN: University of Notre Dame Press, 1968.

McAvoy, Thomas T. *The Great Crisis in American Catholic History, 1895–1900.* Chicago: H. Regnery, 1957.

McGreevy, John T. *Catholicism and American Freedom: A History.* New York: W. W. Norton, 2003.

O'Brien, David J. *Isaac Hecker: An American Catholic.* New York: Paulist Press, 1992.

Orsi, Robert Anthony. *The Madonna of 115th Street: Faith and Community in Italian Harlem, 1880–1950.* New Haven: Yale University Press, 1985.

3 The Catholic Century

JAMES M. O'TOOLE

In June 1908, Pope Pius X published an apostolic constitution reorganizing the Roman curia. Apart from a few members of the clergy, virtually none of the roughly fourteen million Catholics in the United States in that year could have said, if asked, what an "apostolic constitution" was, nor could they have named the various departments in the remade curia or explain what any of them did. The church's central administrative structures had no bearing on their religious lives or their identity as Catholics: Sunday Mass was the same next week as it had been last week. But the obscure papal decree had symbolic significance, even if laypeople were blissfully unaware of it. The responsibilities of one of those departments – the Sacred Congregation de Propaganda Fide ("Propagation of the Faith"), whose origins lay in the supervision of missionaries to China and Japan in the sixteenth century – encompassed, the pope said, "those regions in which, the sacred hierarchy not being yet constituted, the missionary state still exists." By that standard, there were parts of the world that had once qualified as mission lands but now did not. Establishment of their own native churches had moved them into a different category. In 1850, for example, a system of dioceses and bishops had been reconstituted in Great Britain for the first time since the Reformation, allowing England and Scotland not to be considered missions anymore. In the New World, a century of growth also justified recognizing that the United States had ceased to be missionary territory; likewise Canada and Newfoundland (not yet a part of the Canadian confederation).[1] In less than a sentence in the middle of a document about something else, the status of the Catholic Church in America had been changed. No longer an uncertain outpost, it was a regular part of the church worldwide, as much as that in Italy or

[1] An English translation of the document appeared in the *Sacred Heart Review*, August 1, 1908.

France. Coming as it did at the opening of a new century, this technical papal order can be seen as marking the suitable beginning of a new era for the church in the United States.

Some commentators would later characterize the twentieth as the "American Century," but for Catholics, it was also to be a Catholic Century. At its start, if one word could have summarized their church's experience, that word was probably "progress." Since the appointment of the first bishop, just after the Revolution, the church had spread to every corner of the nation, divided now into ninety-three dioceses, containing more than 1,200 local parishes. About one in five Americans were Catholics, making them members of the largest single religious denomination in the country. The ranks of the clergy and (even more so) of religious sisters had multiplied rapidly, to 15,000 and 50,000, respectively, by 1908. Church institutions, most prominently the 6,000 schools at all levels, educating more than one million students, dotted the landscape.[2] Moreover, "progress" also seemed to predict the church's future: everything was already good, and it was getting better. Past achievement portended future success. Particularly given the nativist hostility some Catholics had experienced on first arrival, it was easy to take satisfaction from all this progress, collective and individual, and to suppose that it might go on indefinitely, uninterrupted.

But roughly two-thirds of the way through this Catholic Century, begun with such optimism, the picture would change. While the percentage of Catholics in the American population remained more or less the same and new parishes and dioceses were created as the population shifted around the country, the theme of "progress" was joined by another one: "contraction." The roster of priests and sisters both peaked in the 1960s, falling off thereafter as many left for secular lives and as fewer young people joined their ranks; those who remained were rapidly graying. The density of the church's infrastructure – convents, rectories, churches, schools, hospitals, social welfare institutions – once an outward sign of prosperity, now became problematic, with too much of it in some places, not enough in others, and all of it increasingly costly to maintain. Worst of all, just as the century ended, the exposure of widespread and persistent patterns of sexual abuse of minor children by members of the clergy riveted the nation's attention. In addition to the criminal and moral failings they exposed, these shocking revelations seriously undercut the church's moral authority and challenged

---

[2]   Unless otherwise noted, all statistical data in this essay are taken from the reports in the annual volumes of the *Official Catholic Directory* (New York: Kenedy and Sons).

Catholics' emotional ties to their church. The confidence with which
the century began was, by its end, giving way to uncertainty.

SOCIAL CHANGE

The composition of the Catholic population went through repeated
transitions over the course of the Catholic Century, but progress
seemed once again to be the consistent theme. For decades,
Catholicism in the United States had been predominantly a church of
immigrants and, therefore, a church of the working class. With time,
however, thanks in large part to the work of Catholic schools, from
kindergartens to universities, many Catholics were able to climb the
social and economic ladders and, with one generation giving way to the
next, to resist any tendency to slip back down. Immigrant grandparents
who had found work as day laborers and housekeepers lived to see their
sons and daughters, their grandsons and granddaughters, become
lawyers, doctors, teachers, and business executives. By mid-century,
Catholicism had become largely a church of the middle class, even the
upper-middle class. Movement into the professions was accompanied
by a move from crowded inner city neighborhoods into leafier suburbs,
and the institutions of the church followed the people. At the end of the
Second World War, there were just shy of 300 parishes on Long Island,
for example, 214 of them in the boroughs of Brooklyn and Queens. In
1960, there were still that many in the city, but the count of parishes on
the rest of the island had grown from 81 to 114 in only fifteen years.
Levittown, New York, had not even existed in 1900, but by the early
1960s, it had a parish staffed by five priests with a school that enrolled
600 pupils taught by fifteen Sisters of Saint Joseph. Such growth was not
unusual. Outside Los Angeles, the one parish in Anaheim, California, in
1945 grew to three by 1960, while in Van Nuys, one parish had become
four over the same period. Three of those four had schools, with more
than 2,300 students and thirty-one sisters of various orders.

Following a major overhaul of the nation's immigration laws in 1965,
the social picture became more complex, as newcomers from Latin
America, Asia, and Africa took the places on the ships and planes of
passage once occupied by their fellow Catholics from Europe. This meant
that even as the second and third generations of earlier immigrants were
prospering, Catholicism was also becoming a church of the working class
again. The largest numbers of new Catholic Americans were identified
collectively as "Hispanic," a term that blurred distinct nationalities, each
with its own particular religious traditions and practices, united only by

Spanish as a mother tongue. The impact was geographical as much as it was racial and ethnic. Church membership fell off in the former Catholic heartland of northeastern and midwestern cities, but it grew just as rapidly in the West and Southwest, where many of the newcomers settled. Between 1970 and the end of the century, the number of parishes in Houston, Texas, for instance, went from fifty-three to seventy-eight while, over the same decades, the forty-two parishes in Toledo, Ohio, shrank to thirty. Introduction of the vernacular into the liturgy of the Mass, replacing the Latin of centuries, initiated by the Second Vatican Council of the 1960s, enhanced the church's role in preserving the language of immigrants, and thus it assisted their acculturation to new surroundings. At one of those new Houston parishes, Mass was celebrated every Sunday in English, Spanish, and Vietnamese, and polyglot churches became common everywhere. These newly arrived Catholics helped the church maintain its membership at between 20 and 24 percent of the American population as a whole, while the internal culture of the church evolved, with new devotional emphases replacing older ones. Dramatic processions in honor of Our Lady of Guadalupe became more common than monthly meetings of the parish rosary society. The Irish writer James Joyce had once described Catholicism as a matter of "here comes everybody." By the end of the twentieth century "everybody" was significantly more inclusive.

PUBLIC LIFE

When Catholic immigrants first began arriving in large numbers in the nineteenth century, they often faced nativist hostility, sometimes in the form of political and legal discrimination. Their religious allegiance to the pope – a foreign prince, after all – was thought by some Americans to render them unreliable citizens by definition. Just before the Civil War, an anti-immigrant, anti-Catholic "Know Nothing" movement briefly captured the legislatures of several states, authorizing "convent inspections" and other measures designed to expose the sinister activities that, its adherents were sure, infected church institutions. By the opening of the twentieth century, however, the force of numbers led to increasing Catholic influence in the public square. Voting strength allowed them to win political office, first in cities that were dominated, for better or worse, by machines. As the new century began, there were already Catholic mayors in the obvious places, such as New York and Chicago. But even in Kansas City and Omaha, for instance, Catholics were coming to control city governments. For decades, Boston politics

turned on the fortunes of James Michael Curley, as conspicuously
devout (his son became a Jesuit) as he was conspicuously corrupt. In
San Francisco, a more reform-minded Catholic political tradition
emerged in the 1930s, promoting labor peace and the economic development of the city. Nearly everywhere, Catholic voting strength was
powerfully apparent.[3]

Political success on the local level soon expanded upward to state
and federal governments, if not without setbacks. Al Smith, the
Catholic governor of New York, became the first member of his
church to receive a major party's nomination for president in 1928,
but he went down to crushing defeat in a campaign marked by the
reappearance of overt anti-Catholic fear mongering. In 1960, Senator
John Kennedy of Massachusetts finally broke through the barrier that
had excluded Catholics from the White House, and by then Catholics
were regularly taking their seats in political office across the board.
They were increasingly represented in Congress, and in some state
legislatures, the percentages of Catholics were even larger. More telling in the last third of the century was changing party allegiances.
Between 1965 and 1995, the number of Catholics in Congress grew
steadily from 108 to 148 (out of a total of 535), but their party identification shifted dramatically. Catholic Democrats in the House shrank
from eighty-one to seventy-one, while the count of their Republican
colleagues rose from thirteen to fifty-six; in the Senate, the number of
Catholic Democrats held steady throughout the period at twelve,
while Catholic Republicans increased from two to twenty-one.
Catholics had once been an essential pillar of the New Deal
Democratic coalition, but the Republican Party had begun courting
white ethnic voters in the 1960s. After the Supreme Court's ruling in
the case of Roe v. Wade in 1973, Catholic opposition to abortion
inclined many to a more conservative politics and, starting in the
1980s, Catholics became the prototypical swing voters. Ronald
Reagan, a Republican, won the Catholic vote twice (1980 and 1984)
and so did Bill Clinton, a Democrat (1992 and 1996). Moreover, the
support that most Catholic Democratic candidates gave to abortion
rights brought them criticism from within their own church. When
John Kerry, the first Catholic presidential candidate since Kennedy,

---

3   The literature on early twentieth century urban politics is extensive. For an
    interesting contrast to machine politics, see William Issel, *Church and State in the
    City: Catholics and Politics in Twentieth-Century San Francisco* (Philadelphia:
    Temple University Press, 2013).

led the Democratic ticket in 2004, several bishops denounced his stand, even arguing that he should be denied communion; Kerry lost the close election.[4]

Catholics' impact on public life was not limited to electoral politics. Their role in the labor movement in the first half of the century was crucial to its many successes. The substantial number of Catholics in the industrial labor force inevitably brought many of them to leadership positions. George Meany, a plumber and the son of Irish immigrants to the Bronx, New York, rose to the presidency of the American Federation of Labor (AFL), while Philip Murray, a miner from Pittsburgh and a near-daily communicant, headed the Congress of Industrial Organizations (CIO). (The AFL and CIO merged in 1955 under Meany.) At the local level, Catholic working men and women found active support from their church, attending "labor schools" that were organized in neighborhood parishes. There, members of the clergy led them through the study of church teachings that supported workers' rights to organize and to bargain for fair wages and better working conditions. These efforts were even memorialized on film. *On the Waterfront* (1953) featured the actor Karl Malden (himself Serbian Orthodox) portraying a thinly disguised Jesuit "labor priest," John Corridan, fighting corruption in the dockworkers union. No less committed to campaigns for economic and social justice were members of the Catholic Worker movement, founded in the depths of the Great Depression by Dorothy Day, a journalist and convert to the church from socialism, and Peter Maurin, a self-declared philosopher originally from France. Catholic Workers dedicated themselves to serving the poorest of the urban poor by living among them as equals, providing such basic necessities as food, shelter, and clothing. Actual membership in the movement was small, but its influence was great, through the publication of a monthly newspaper, *The Catholic Worker*, which proudly sold for a penny a copy so that anyone could afford it.[5]

Concern for issues of social justice also led some Catholics into the movement for African-American civil rights in the 1950s and 1960s. The number of African Americans who were Catholics was always small – less than 10 percent – and when many Catholic leaders spoke

---

4 Brookings Institution, "Vital Statistics on Congress," May 21, 2018, www.brookings .edu/multi-chapter-report/vital-statistics-on-congress.

5 James T. Fisher, *On the Irish Waterfront: The Crusader, the Movie, and the Soul of the Port of New York* (Ithaca, NY: Cornell University Press, 2009); William Miller, *Dorothy Day: A Biography* (New York: Harper and Row, 1982).

of "racial" distinctions, they were trying to denote the difference between Poles and Italians. However, led by a few crusading priests, the Jesuit John LaFarge most prominent among them, local churches organized Catholic Interracial Councils to bring black and white Catholics together to encourage mutual understanding and to work for change in their own neighborhoods. As the moral clarity of black demands for voting and other civil rights gathered force, support grew among priests, sisters, and laypeople. Newspaper photographs of lines of nuns marching in support of other marchers in Selma, Alabama, and elsewhere reinforced the growing realization that the Christian message demanded fundamental fairness. With time, dissenting voices were heard too. White Catholics in urban areas often resisted the integration of their neighborhoods, and opposition to school desegregation proved particularly strong in some places.[6]

The Catholic influence on American public life extended to popular culture as well. With the movie business growing into a significant vehicle for mass entertainment, Catholics were regularly depicted on the screen, and Catholic actors publicly identified as such. America may have had a tradition of nativist suspicion, but no nation in which Father Chuck O'Malley, the singing priest (played by Bing Crosby) of Going My Way (1944) and Bells of St. Mary's (1945), was a popular cultural hero could be described as unremittingly anti-Catholic. Loretta Young, who had a long career in film and television, made no secret of her faith, and she devoted herself actively to Catholic charitable causes. So did Danny Thomas, a singer and comedian who turned his personal support for a children's hospital in Memphis, Tennessee, into a national crusade. Sometimes, even priests might become media stars. In the 1930s, Father Charles Coughlin, from a parish outside Detroit, won nationwide fame with his Sunday afternoon radio broadcasts on the social and political issues of the day. It was said that one could walk down the street of any Catholic neighborhood and hear Coughlin's voice in the very air: every radio in every house was tuned in. He veered increasingly into cranky and anti-Semitic rants and was eventually forced to stop, but he had paved the way for others. Fulton Sheen, a priest from Illinois who taught at the Catholic University of America, had some early experience on the radio, but with the arrival of television, he proved

---

6   David W. Southern, *John LaFarge and the Limits of Catholic Interracialism, 1911–1963* (Baton Rouge: Louisiana State University Press, 1996); John T. McGreevy, *Parish Boundaries: The Catholic Encounter with Race in the Twentieth-Century Urban North* (Chicago: University of Chicago Press, 1996).

himself master of the medium. He was made an auxiliary bishop of New York in 1951, and he appeared on the small screen in his full episcopal regalia, sweeping his cape and fingering his pectoral cross while speaking in deep Shakespearean tones. Despite the religious trappings, his messages were for the most part agreeably inspirational and nondenominational, summarized by his program's title: *Life Is Worth Living*. In the 1980s, as cable television expanded, a nun from Alabama went Sheen one better. Mother Angelica (born Rita Rizzo), after founding her own religious community and monastery, established the Eternal Word Television Network (EWTN), which eventually added radio and internet programming and made hers a household name. Her extended, often ad-libbed monologues were especially popular with Catholics of more traditional religious tastes, and her programs continued to be rebroadcast long after a stroke restricted her direct involvement; they are still aired today.[7]

RELIGIOUS LIFE

Since their first arrival in large numbers in the nineteenth century, Catholics in America had been a church-going people. Regular attendance was the hallmark of their religion, a tradition that solidified throughout the first two-thirds of the Catholic Century. As the population grew, the opening of new parishes meant that Catholics had increasingly easy access to the official services of their faith. Reliable statistics on church attendance are notoriously hard to come by – Gallup Poll surveys shortly after World War II placed it at just under 50 percent for all American denominations, taken together – but every observer agreed that Catholics' consistent practice reached and remained at historically high levels. The schedule of Masses in local churches every Sunday morning seemed to prove a fundamental rule of economics: supply rose in response to high demand. A priest-sociologist, studying a parish in New Orleans in the 1950s, took note of half a dozen Sunday Masses there every week, hourly from 6 to 10 o'clock with another at 11:30; attendance varied from 350 at the earliest to 900 at the last. Roughly 85 percent

---

[7] Alan Brinkley, *Voices of Protest: Huey Long, Father Coughlin, and the Great Depression* (New York: Vintage, 1983); Fulton J. Sheen, *Life Is Worth Living* (New York: McGraw-Hill, 1953); Christopher Owen Lynch, *Selling Catholicism: Bishop Sheen and the Power of Television* (Lexington: University of Kentucky Press, 1998); Paul Vitello, "Mother Mary Angelica, Popular TV Host, Dies at 92," *New York Times*, March 29, 2016.

of those on the parish rolls were in their pews regularly, the scholar concluded, making faithful Mass attendance "one of the identifiable characteristics of Catholic behavior." Rising numbers of vocations to the priesthood made it possible to sustain this level of access to the central ceremony of the church. The clergy-laity ratio in New Orleans in that decade was 1:2,600 (improved from 1:3,200 when the century began); in Philadelphia, it was 1:1,000.[8]

The religious life of American Catholics was not, however, confined to the minimal requirement of weekly Mass. They participated in the other sacraments and rites of their church in record numbers. Infants were baptized in the local parish as soon after birth as possible, often the same day, cementing their church membership. A few years after that, parents turned the occasion of a child's first reception of Communion – in 1910, Pope Pius X lowered the age for this to seven from the traditional twelve – into a major family event, with boys dressed (probably for the first time) in a formal suit of clothes and girls arrayed as little brides. Priests encouraged the frequent confession of sins in the sacrament of penance, and despite the fear of shame that might accompany it (even though confession was anonymous), Catholics lined up in their churches, usually on Saturday afternoons and evenings, to comply. One priest in one parish in New York City at the beginning of the century counted 175 penitents at a single sitting, a number he considered normal; a week or two later, when he noted in his diary that he heard "only 88," he worried that the pace was "slack." Two priests in the 1950s in Salt Lake City (hardly a Catholic stronghold) had similar experiences, together tallying nearly 9,500 confessions in a single year, an average of about 180 per week.[9]

Devotional practice also spilled out into the public streets. In the summer of 1926, more than half a million Catholics from around the country gathered outside Chicago for a Eucharistic Congress, five days of prayers, sermons, and devotions designed to highlight the distinctive Catholic theology of the real presence of God in the Eucharist. Not even a driving rainstorm on the festival's final day dampened their

---

[8]   Joseph Fichter, *Dynamics of a City Church* (Chicago: University of Chicago Press, 1951).

[9]   Margaret M. McGuinness, "Let Us Go to the Altar: American Catholics and the Eucharist, 1926–1976"; and James M. O'Toole, "In the Court of Conscience: American Catholics and Confession, 1900–1975," both in *Habits of Devotion: Catholic Religious Practice in Twentieth-Century America*, ed. James M. O'Toole (Ithaca, NY: Cornell University Press, 2004).

enthusiasm. Smaller versions of this were held in later years in cities around the country, often packing the local baseball stadium, and parades of Catholic organizations became commonplace. In 1947 and again in 1948, Catholics in Boston swelled day-long marches, the first by the Holy Name Society (the principal parish organization for men), the second by the Catholic Youth Organization (for adolescents); these remain today the largest parades in the history of New England. Planners of the Chicago event had insisted that their devotions were not intended as "a flaunting of vast numbers before non-Catholics," but whatever else they were, these spectacles were that, too.[10]

Such high levels of participation in the traditional rites of their church had perhaps left American Catholics unprepared for the changes that came with the Second Vatican Council (1962–1965). For many of them, the church's supposed unchanging character had been no small part of its appeal. Nevertheless, they exhibited enthusiasm for those changes almost from the beginning. The council's adoption of the "People of God" as the governing metaphor for the church – replacing the earlier "Mystical Body of Christ," an image that was hard for many to grasp – appealed to fundamentally democratic American sensibilities. The visible changes were impossible to miss. Formerly, the Mass had been focused on the actions of the priest, praying in Latin (with his back turned to them) on behalf of the people in the pews, who might or might not be paying any attention. This was replaced with a "new Mass," implemented in stages between 1964 and 1969. A new altar had been set up in the sanctuary of every church, and the priest now stood behind it, facing the people. The text of the service had been translated into the vernacular, and Mass-goers were expected to respond to the priest's invitations to prayer and to recite some of the key texts of the liturgy aloud with him. Perhaps even more alarming to some, they were expected to sing, a task previously delegated to a choir and only on those rare occasions (a "High Mass") when there was any music at all. There were some pockets of resistance to all this. A Catholic Traditionalist Movement objected to what it saw as a "Protestantizing" of the church, hoping instead for a restoration of the older forms, but its numbers and influence were small. For the most part, wide acceptance of the new liturgical practices was the norm, despite the speed and extent of the change. The experience of going to Mass was radically different in

---

[10] Edward R. Kantowicz, *Corporation Sole: Cardinal Mundelein and Chicago Catholicism* (Notre Dame, IN: University of Notre Dame Press, 1983); for the Eucharistic Congress, see ch. 11.

1970 from what it had been in 1960, but American Catholics made the shift readily.[11]

Other developments in the aftermath of the council elicited a more mixed reaction, and together they heralded deeper changes in the ways Catholics related to their church. The numbers of priests and sisters reached their historic high points (58,000 and 180,000 respectively) by the end of the 1960s, with a "vocation crisis" setting in thereafter. Enhanced educational and professional opportunities, especially for women, combined with Vatican II's emphasis on the important role of laypeople in the church, prompted fewer young adults to seek ordination or embrace lives as vowed religious. New lay ministries (in religious education, for instance) became available to help fill the gaps, but the traditional sources of church authority were drying up. At the same time, confidence in church leadership was seriously undercut by controversy over contraception. A Vatican commission, including laypeople, had been appointed to study the question of whether the church's traditional teaching on the subject could be modified. Its deliberations were confidential, but the open secret spread quickly that the group was going to recommend a change, permitting "artificial" as well as "natural" means of birth control. (The government had approved the contraceptive pill for use in the United States in 1960.) In July 1968, however, Pope Paul VI sided with a minority view and reaffirmed the sinfulness of the pill and other contraceptive measures. Negative reaction from laypeople, joined by some priests, was widespread, and the pope's encyclical almost immediately became a dead letter. Within a few years, Catholics' attitudes and practices regarding contraception were indistinguishable from those of their non-Catholic neighbors; they simply disregarded the church's official teaching. Meanwhile, routine recourse to confession suddenly declined, a larger trend not exclusively tied to contraception. Parishes that had once scheduled three or four hours for confessions every week cut them back first to an hour, then to half an hour, then to "any time by request." Once again, supply responded to demand.[12]

A more general shift was underway in how Catholics related to the church and understood their membership in it. They were encouraged,

---

[11]   Mark S. Massa, *The American Catholic Revolution: How the Sixties Changed the Church Forever* (New York: Oxford University Press, 2010).

[12]   Leslie Woodcock Tentler, *Catholics and Contraception: An American History* (Ithaca, NY: Cornell University Press, 2004); Robert McClory, *Turning Point: The Inside Story of the Papal Birth Control Commission* (New York: Crossroad Publishing, 1997).

through preaching and religious publications, to take more personal responsibility for their own spiritual lives. The church was obviously there to assist them in this, but merely going through the motions of religion was no longer enough. Watching a priest say Mass while lay-people sat or knelt quietly – a few trying to follow along in a missal, some silently reciting the rosary or other private prayers, many simply daydreaming – was discouraged; full, active participation in the liturgy was the new ideal. More broadly, following church law just because it was the law was not sufficient. "The Church has begun to acknow-ledge," a layman from Iowa wrote to a national magazine, "that as adults, with all that the term implies, we can make moral decisions." Such an attitude had wide implications. If certain beliefs or practices no longer meant something to them, Catholics felt newly empowered to ignore them, without endangering their identification with the church. "I and countless other ... thinking Catholics," a man from New Hampshire added, were no longer willing to accept church authority just because it was the constituted authority. Instead, they could focus on those dimensions of the church that meant something to them personally, leaving others behind. "Thinking" and "adult" Catholics were free to make those choices. The loosening of former strictures led some critics to speak disparagingly of "cafeteria Catholics" who, without jeopardizing their faith, picked the teachings they liked and left alone those they did not.[13]

Whether a good or a bad thing, by the 1970s, Catholicism in America had without a doubt become a more voluntary church, just as American Protestantism had always been. Members participated to an extent that they themselves determined. One indicator of this was that the high levels of regular Mass attendance began to decline. A poll in 1958 had found that 74 percent of American Catholics reported having gone to church the previous week. In 1970, just five years after the council's conclusion, that number was down to 60 percent – still significantly higher than the 40 percent of Protestants who said they had attended a religious service, but down nonetheless. The decline continued, to about 50 percent in the middle 1980s and finally settling in just above 30 percent by the century's end. Other changes in religious practice were evident too, and some of them might be more welcome. Even as rates of confession plummeted, for instance, rates of reception of the Eucharist skyrocketed. Where once only a minority of those at

---

[13]   Quotations are in O'Toole, "In the Court of Conscience," 173.

any given Mass came forward for the sacrament at the appropriate time –
fear of unworthiness was common – now virtually everyone in attendance did so, and most probably would have thought it strange not to.[14]
A proliferation of new lay organizations, with self-selected membership,
also gave Catholics the chance to tailor their religious practice along
lines that appealed to them. A small but widespread Catholic charismatic movement began in the 1960s, for example, self-consciously
trying to replicate the experience of the ancient church as recorded in
the scriptures. Small groups of lay people, often without any supervision
or involvement by the clergy, gathered for spontaneous prayer in
unknown tongues, a practice previously confined in America to
Pentecostal Protestant sects. Not every such movement attracted every
Catholic, but laypeople had confidence now that they could pursue such
particular interests if they wanted to, all the while remaining under a
broad Catholic umbrella.

CRISIS

If Catholics had at first been surprised by the enormous changes that
came from the Vatican Council, they were similarly surprised by the
crisis that engulfed their church as the Catholic Century came to an
end – though perhaps they should not have been. Starting in the middle
1980s, scattered news reports began to expose cases of the sexual abuse
of young children and adolescents by members of the clergy. A priest in
Louisiana, two in Rhode Island, others in New Jersey, Texas,
Washington State, and elsewhere: all were charged criminally, and they
either pled guilty or were convicted. At first, these cases attracted
mostly local attention, though some had a higher profile. Bruce Ritter,
a member of the Franciscan order, had achieved national recognition (in
the form of financial support and honorary degrees) for his work in
directing a home for runaway teenagers in New York City; he resigned
in 1990 amid revelations that he had abused some of the boys in his
care. Wherever such a case arose, it could seem like an aberration, a
particular problem with a particular priest; once that one case had been
resolved, the problem had apparently been successfully addressed. "We
don't want to give the impression that it's a rampant problem," said an

---

[14]   George Gallup, Jr. and Jim Castelli, *The American Catholic People: Their Beliefs,
       Practices, and Values* (New York: Doubleday, 1987), 26–28; Bryan T. Froehle and
       Mary L. Gautier, *Catholicism, U.S.A.: A Portrait of the Catholic Church in the
       United States* (Maryknoll, NY: Orbis, 2000), 22–24.

official of the national bishops' conference in 1985, allowing that "even one case is too many."[15]

Starting in January 2002, all Americans, regardless of their religious affiliation, became aware of just how rampant the problem in fact was. Boston was the epicenter of the crisis. Investigations by reporters from the *Globe*, the city's principal newspaper, laid out in detail the patterns both of abuse and of the ways in which church officials had dealt with it. Most of the abuse had been directed at boys. Abusers often targeted those who came from difficult family circumstances – low-income households, divorced parents, previous experiences of minor delinquency – and most parents initially appreciated the attention that priests lavished on their kids, convinced that it would have a good effect. When a complaint was registered against a priest, the bishop's office would examine the allegations, with two common outcomes. First, a sum of money would be paid to the family in exchange for their agreement not to press a legal case or to disclose the matter publicly in any other way. Families were usually willing to accept such offers, eager to avoid the embarrassment that might otherwise come to them, even though they, the victims, had nothing to be embarrassed about. Next, the abusing priest would usually be transferred quietly to another parish assignment, often without notice to his new pastor that there had ever been a problem, and always without notice to the people of the new parish. Sometimes, a priest might also be sent for a brief period to a psychological treatment facility, but most of the time he was then returned to work, having been declared "cured." Once in place, the offender usually resumed his habits of abuse in his new setting.[16]

The cases carefully documented in the newspaper's accounts were gruesome in their detail, extending back over decades, with dozens of abusers (some of them dead by then) and hundreds of victims. That the revelations were coming only a few months after the terrorist attacks of September 11, 2001, heightened their emotional impact, and they soon prompted similar investigations across the country. It was immediately apparent that this was neither just a Boston problem nor a problem of a few individual "bad apples." Rather, there were deeper systemic failings that needed to be addressed, harder questions that needed answers. What was it in the recruitment and seminary training of the clergy that

---

15   "Sex Charges against Priest Embroil Louisiana Parish," *New York Times*, June 20, 1985, A24.

16   The *Boston Globe*'s daily reports were subsequently compiled in book form in *Betrayal: The Crisis in the Catholic Church* (Boston: Little Brown, 2002).

had failed to identify potential abusers and to keep them from the priesthood in the first place? To what extent were homosexuality and clerical celibacy contributing causes of abuse? What was it in church administrative structures that had led bishops and other officials to be more concerned with protecting the public image of the church than protecting its youngest and most vulnerable members? Some bishops became special targets for condemnation, particularly when the documents of their handling of abuse cases came to light in criminal proceedings. The cardinal archbishop of Boston, Bernard Law, was forced to resign in disgrace less than a year after the story there had first come to light. Two bishops in Florida also resigned when it was revealed that they themselves had engaged in abuse, while another bishop in Massachusetts was indicted but subsequently disappeared before any prosecution could take place. For all the seeming health and success of the church in the United States, there was apparently a rot at its core.

In response, the anger of American Catholics was universal, and it found expression in the formation of an organization calling itself Voice of the Faithful. Nearly half a century of having been told that they, the People of God, *were* the church convinced laypeople that they could indeed organize in order (as their slogan put it) to "Keep the Faith, Change the Church." From a small group of parents meeting in a church basement in suburban Boston to share their concerns, they grew into a national organization that, within a matter of months, convened 4,000 people for a day of discussion, protest, and planning. For their part, the nation's bishops gathered in June 2002 to address the crisis. After listening to frank condemnations of their actions by laypeople and victims, they drafted a "charter" for the protection of children, laying out uniform procedures to be followed in the future when charges of abuse were made. They also commissioned a detailed academic study, compiling comprehensive data on the phenomenon of abuse in general and its impact on the church. The formerly secret financial settlements that had been paid to the families of victims were added up, amounting at the time to hundreds of millions of dollars. The totals would grow in subsequent years into the billions, as many dioceses came to new agreements with victims. Several dioceses were forced to file for bankruptcy.[17]

---

[17]   National Review Board for the Protection of Children and Young People, *A Report on the Crisis in the Catholic Church in the United States* (Washington, DC: United States Conference of Catholic Bishops, 2004); John Jay College of Criminal Justice, *The Nature and Scope of Sexual Abuse of Minors by Catholic Priests and Deacons in the United States, 1950–2002* (Washington, DC: United States Conference of Catholic Bishops, 2004).

As far as it went, the bishops' charter seemed to work. Dioceses everywhere implemented the program for investigating charges when they arose, immediately removing from active ministry, pending full investigation, any priest who had been "credibly accused." The definition of that crucial phrase was subject to some variation from place to place, but the incidence of new cases of abuse declined dramatically after 2002. Even so, the details of older cases, dating as far back as the 1950s, continued to be reported, keeping the issue alive in the public consciousness. A report from the attorney general of Pennsylvania in 2018 documented the by-then familiar patterns of abuse and cover-up as they had played out in six of the state's dioceses; its impact was enhanced by a 500-page "appendix of offenders" that included accounts, name by name, of more than three hundred priests with credible accusations against them. Other states and even the federal justice department undertook similar investigations, some of which are still ongoing at this writing. Attention began to focus less on priest-perpetrators and more on the actions and inactions of bishops, for their handling of these previous cases and for their own abusive behavior. Most shocking of these (also exposed in 2018) was the example of Theodore McCarrick, the retired archbishop of Washington, DC. Rumors of his abuse of both minors and adult seminarians under his authority had circulated quietly in church circles for years, and yet they had not served as any impediment to his advancement. He was stripped of his rank as a cardinal and sent to the seclusion of a monastery; several months later, he was dismissed from the priesthood altogether.[18]

The crisis over sexual abuse, coming at the end of the Catholic Century, was unlike any other challenge that the church in America had previously faced, and its effects, both near- and long-term, were real. In the immediate aftermath of the disclosures, a surprising number of American Catholics did not simply leave the church for another one or for none. Some surely did, but on the whole, the attitude was one of "keeping the faith" (as Voice of the Faithful had put it) despite the moral failings and mismanagement of church leaders. In a few places, financial support for local parishes actually went up during the crisis, a sign that, while parishioners might dislike and distrust their bishop, they supported their own local pastor, whom they knew personally and saw

---

[18] For a detailed analysis of the strengths and weaknesses of the Pennsylvania report, see Peter Steinfels, "Vehemently Misleading," *Commonweal* (January 25, 2019): 13–26. The McCarrick case is summarized in "Former Cardinal Expelled As Pope Confronts Abuse," *New York Times*, February 17, 2019.

every week. The national impact of Voice of the Faithful lessened over time, but the organization endured and, together with other groups (such as Bishop Accountability, which published documents relating to abuse cases on the internet), kept the issue before the public at large.

More generally, however, the palpable sense of a church in crisis, initiated by the abuse scandal, lingered in the wake of less dramatic but no less powerful challenges. Though the church was steadily becoming more diverse racially and ethnically, the integration of local Catholic communities was harder to accomplish. There might be more parishes with mixed populations, but distinct liturgies for speakers of English, Spanish, Vietnamese, and other languages meant that (just as Martin Luther King, Jr., had once said in a different context) ten o'clock on Sunday morning was perhaps the most segregated hour in Catholic America. Divisions between self-described liberal and conservative Catholics, particularly during the papacies of John Paul II and Benedict XVI, also had a polarizing effect, each side asserting that its position – on theological as well as social and political issues – was the more authentically Catholic view. Finally, a steady decline in church membership and attendance among young adults, with many of them joining the "nones" (those who replied "none" when asked what religion they belonged to), seemed to suggest that a demographic bottom had yet to be touched.

CONCLUSION

The canvas of American Catholics at the end of their century thus presented a complex picture of light and darkness. It had been an era of remarkable successes, characterized by the flowering of a rich religious culture that attracted and held the loyalty of millions. Over successive generations, men and women – clergy, vowed religious, laity – had continually committed themselves and their resources to advancing the welfare of their own community and that of the nation as a whole. Catholics had built and sustained the largest private systems of education, health care, and social service in history and these institutions were open not merely to Catholics but to anyone. They had repeatedly demonstrated their loyalty to both church and country. At the same time, as the century ended, they had been forced to acknowledge a dark underside to all their success. The same culture that produced the visible signs of faithful achievement had also produced a closed, secretive world in which defending the interests of fellow members of a priestly club was a higher priority than defending children. The church's moral authority, once simply taken for granted, had first been undermined and then squandered. Whether and how that authority could be restored remained open questions. The church could no longer count on the automatic support of those who identified themselves as its members. They would be a part of the church on their own terms, considering themselves no less Catholic for that. The future was unknown, as all futures are, but their history offered American Catholics examples both of what to emulate and what to avoid as they moved into it.

FURTHER READING

Appleby, R. Scott and Kathleen Sprows Cummings, eds. *Catholics in the American Century: Recasting Narratives of U.S. History*. Ithaca, NY: Cornell University Press, 2012.

Massa, Mark S. *The American Catholic Revolution: How the Sixties Changed the Church Forever*. New York: Oxford University Press, 2010.

McCartin, James P. *Prayers of the Faithful: The Shifting Spiritual Life of American Catholics*. Cambridge, MA: Harvard University Press, 2010.

McGreevy, John T. *Catholicism and American Freedom: A History*. New York: Norton, 2003.

O'Toole, James M. *The Faithful: A History of Catholics in America*. Cambridge, MA: Belknap Press, 2008.

Steinfels, Peter. *A People Adrift: The Crisis of the Roman Catholic Church in America*. New York: Simon and Schuster, 2003.

Part II

Catholic Life and Culture

4 Catholic Worship

KATHARINE E. HARMON

Describing American Catholic worship demands grappling with the broad expanse of peoples and places that have experienced the Catholic faith between the moment of the first Mass, celebrated by globe-trotting Spanish explorers in 1494, and Mass in the twenty-first century, when the first American-born pope, Francis, assumed leadership of the global church. Yet, American Catholic worship asks that we look at far more than formal ritual experiences such as the Mass, the Divine Office, or the sacraments. For much of American Catholic history, a rich panoply of devotions to Mary, Jesus, the saints, and the Blessed Sacrament played a major, if not central, role in supporting and sustaining Catholic identity on the American continent – a role that would not be challenged until liturgical renewal advocates began to question the relationship of popular piety and formal liturgical prayer in the second quarter of the twentieth century.

This chapter introduces four major trends significant for understanding Catholic worship and experiences of popular piety. Beginning in the sixteenth and seventeenth centuries, the demands of effectively evangelizing in mission territories called for a certain amount of creativity and flexibility with regard to how worship was practiced and interpreted, even while the church as a whole was instituting significant moves toward uniformity following the Council of Trent. Second, the rise of devotionalism in the eighteenth and nineteenth centuries intersected with the increased organizational power of the growing Catholic population in the expanding United States. Whether or not Catholics had regular sacramental access, Catholics adopted a wide variety of devotional exercises to meet their spiritual needs. Third, liturgical renewal paired with ecclesial directives in the twentieth century to refocus the faithful's spiritual attention on participation in the Eucharist and, following the Second Vatican Council, on the Mass. Finally, social and cultural shifts among American Catholics in the post-Conciliar period have revealed a church in deep need of effective and creative evangelization, but also have resulted in significant tensions among the faithful regarding how the Mass is celebrated. While Catholics of past generations could express spiritual preferences with their choice in devotions, Catholics in the present express their spiritual identity through their preferred aesthetic (music, architecture style), specific elements of the Mass which they find important (good preaching, welcoming atmosphere), or by choosing a Mass which is "progressive," "traditional," or even "pre-Conciliar" in its style.

MISSION AND EVANGELIZATION

Worship in the "new world" was fluid and multiform, both due to the flexibility which was still at play in the Roman Rite prior to the liturgical reforms following the Council of Trent (1545–1563), but also because of the creativity demanded by the needs of mission territories. The mendicant missionaries who accompanied European explorers to the "new world" introduced Catholic worship to the American continent, and, for them, the principal practice in which they were interested was not the regular celebration of the Eucharist, but baptism. Some of the earliest Spanish friars reported astonishing success in numbers of baptisms (which, in 1531, could number between 300 and 500 infants per week),[1] though the processes of indoctrination, the treatment of new converts, and the subsequent maintenance of the Catholic faith were undeniably dubious. Despite the need to view the entirety of the mission system with a critical eye, recognizing the flexibility and creativity with which Franciscan and, later, Jesuit missionaries approached evangelization reveals surprising strategies of inculturation. "Inculturation," as liturgical scholar Mark Francis explains, describes a "dialogue between faith and culture that transforms and enriches *both* the culture in which the faith is proclaimed and the universal church."[2] To this end, these early missionaries revised ritual language and created new resources with which to communicate the Catholic faith. For example, Franciscan friars created new rituals uniquely suited for their converts, such as the 1540 *Manual de Adultos* (Manual for Adults), which included instructions borrowing from indigenous cultural forms and vocabulary in order to prepare and baptize new adherents to the faith. Later, the Franciscan

---

[1]   Jaime Lara, "'Precious Green Jade Water': A Sixteenth-Century Adult Catechumenate in the New World," *Worship* 71, no. 5 (1997): 415–428.
[2]   Mark R. Francis, *Shape a Circle Ever Wider: Liturgical Inculturation in the United States* (Collegeville, MN: Liturgical Press, 2000), 59–60.

ethnographer Bernardino de Sahagún (1500–1590) and his collaborators assembled a collection of hymns for communal singing and dancing in a 1583 volume titled *Psalmnodia Christiana* (Christian Psalms). The hymnal included songs evoking indigenous culture and society, such as a baptismal hymn which described the "green jade water of baptism" (signifying that baptism was precious) and likening Christian initiation to a "divine sweat bath" (an indigenous penitential practice).[3] Aside from newly composed sources for worship, some characteristics of medieval piety – such as an emphasis upon visual imagery, the use of processions, or allegorical readings of the liturgy – intersected well with indigenous sensibilities. Friars took advantage of festive celebrations of the year (like a patron saint's day or Christmas) and particularly dramatic moments (such as Palm Sunday or Good Friday) to make use of processions, dances, feasts, and reenactments of events in Christ's life.

In the seventeenth century, French Jesuits arriving in New France in the northeastern part of the continent encouraged conversion through rigorous catechesis in the native peoples' own languages, working with native *dogiques*, or catechists, to instruct local communities. After conversion, new Catholics regularly experienced the zealous preaching of the Jesuit missionaries, hearing about the terrors of hell and being encouraged to abandon "pagan" practices for Christian religious observances and a Christianized, European culture. Despite such worldviews, the Jesuits also attempted to approach evangelization with inculturation in mind, translating Christian concepts in ways that evidenced an awareness of indigenous cultures. For example, French Jesuits interacting with the Huron in the Great Lakes region avoided explaining the doctrine of transubstantiation because they wished to circumvent the Huron people's interpretation of Eucharistic reception as an accepted form of cannibalism. Instead, Jean de Brébeuf (1593–1649), who had translated the catechism and numerous Christian prayers into Huron, translated *"eucharist"* as *"atonesta,"* a Huron word that conveyed a sense of a symbolic act, performed with an attitude of thanksgiving, rather than emphasizing the "real presence" of Christ's body.[4]

The earliest missions of America displayed significant creativity in their experiences of Catholic worship in part because late medieval liturgical and ritual books had not yet been codified. The compilation

3   Lara, "'Precious Green Jade Water,'" 427.
4   Cornelius J. Jaenen, *Friend and Foe: Aspects of French-Amerindian Cultural Contact in the Sixteenth and Seventeenth Centuries* (New York: Columbia University Press, 1976), 145.

of official liturgical books would not take place until after the Council of Trent. Once published, however, the new *Missal* of Pius V (1570, the book used for celebrating Mass) and the *Roman Ritual* (1614, a book of rituals for sacraments) served to typify a new era in Catholicism, demanding an unprecedented amount of uniformity in practice and demonstrating the authority of the pope in all matters liturgical. Settling questions of practice and authority was particularly important for nations grappling with Protestant reformers and related political upheaval on the European continent. Yet, the effects of "Tridentine" Catholicism also were felt in the Americas through the banning of vernacular manuals which had been in use among the missions, and through papal support of the Society of Jesus, whose aforementioned missionary efforts were instrumental in the New World.

A Tridentine approach to liturgy and sacrament also affected how Catholics interacted with the Eucharist. Eucharistic piety (but not sacramental reception) had long been highly encouraged and popular among Catholics. By the time of the Reformation, the faithful had developed a robust and sometimes boisterous system of Eucharistic devotions, including pilgrimages, Eucharistic processions, adoration, and the popular Corpus Christi (Body of Christ) Feast. Yet, Eucharistic participation and belief in the real presence did not extend to sacramental reception. Thus, while the sacraments and the Mass themselves became more structured, the worship patterns of American Catholics continued to diversify over the course of the eighteenth, nineteenth, and twentieth centuries, with an increasing variety of devotional practices emerging to fill the *space* of the Mass (if it were available) or to be practiced *in place* of the Mass (if it were not).

DEVOTIONALISM

In the "priestless church" of the early United States, Catholics who sought to maintain their faith when priestly visits were few needed to pursue alternative avenues to practice piety. Among Catholics of the former British colonies, home-centered worship and reading, either with a nuclear family or a gathering of neighbors, became one strategy used to practice "spiritual communion" with the church. And, thanks to technological advancements that made print material more readily available on the mass market, a variety of prayer books and devotional handbooks aided the faithful in their pursuit of home-based religious experiences and prepared them for the next opportunities of confession and Mass.

For example, the prolific pamphleteer, John Gother (d. 1704), composed his *Prayers for Sundays & Festivals, Adapted to the Use of Private Families and Congregations* as a means for the faithful to keep in tune with the church through the liturgical seasons. This text included Gospel passages, a short paragraph commenting on the text, and a list of short prayers that could be read by "the head of the family" or another person who could read "freely and distinctly."[5] Likewise, Richard Challoner (1691–1781), one of the most significant devotional authors for English-speaking Catholics in the eighteenth century, authored the frequently reprinted *Garden of the Soul*, which included a variety of prayers, commentaries, and ritual instructions. From this text, for example, the "Morning Exercises" described how to cultivate an appropriate attitude for prayer and included texts of devotional prayers and traditional components from the Mass, including the Lord's Prayer, Creed, and Confiteor (penitential prayer).[6] While few testimonies exist from laypersons who used these resources, as historian James O'Toole describes, the "wide distribution of devotional manuals [...] testifies to their use."[7]

Implicit in the production of manuals such as these is their ready intelligibility to English-speaking American Catholics. As the American church became organized into dioceses, John Carroll (1736–1815), its first bishop, repeatedly advocated for the use of the vernacular as a critical evangelization tool, arguing that, "in this country either for want of books or inability to read, the great part of our congregations must be utterly ignorant of the meaning and sense of the publick offices of the Church."[8] While Carroll stressed that vernacular usage would be important for the edification of the faithful, later bishops discarded this concern by the Third Provincial Council's meeting of 1837. Worries that the US church might be "out of step" with Rome caused attempts for greater alignment of American practice with that of Rome, including a rejection of vernacular language and hymnody.[9] Calls for the vernacular would not

---

5   Quoted in James O'Toole, *The Faithful: A History of Catholics in America* (Cambridge, MA: Harvard University Press, 2008), 29.

6   Richard Challoner, *Garden of the Soul: A Manual of Spiritual Exercises and Instructions for Christians Who, Living in the World, Aspire to Devotion* (London: n.p., 1775), 19–28.

7   O'Toole, *The Faithful*, 33.

8   Cited in John Tracy Ellis, "Archbishop Carroll and the Liturgy in the Vernacular," *Worship* 26, no. 12 (1952): 548, n. 3.

9   Nathan D. Mitchell, *Cult and Controversy: The Worship of the Eucharist Outside Mass* (Collegeville, MN: Liturgical Press, 1982), 326.

reemerge with any frequency in American contexts until the 1940s, in concert with liturgical renewal efforts.

Another important evangelization method in the absence of regular sacramental access centered on the parish mission. Parish missions emerged, in part, as a response to Protestant revivalism in the midst of the Second Great Awakening. Intense preaching about hellfire and damnation, calls for repentance, and the opportunity for the sacraments of confession and the Eucharist presented the Catholic faith as an embodied and experiential event that intimately relied upon the ministers of the institutional church.[10] Parish missions also served to link together isolated Catholics, to cultivate and maintain Catholic identity in an environment which, at times, was hostile to Catholicism, and to encourage the participation of Catholics in their faith despite irregular access to the sacraments.

As the Catholic population increased over the course of the nineteenth century, immigrant Catholics, often in cities, encouraged priests and women religious from their home countries to serve parochial needs, creating a network of national parishes (based on cultural identity) mapped on top of burgeoning territorial parishes (based on location) throughout the growing United States. National parishes brought their own particular edge to worship practices, such as the popularity of hymn-singing among Bavarian German congregations, or Marian processions among Italians. And, with increased organizational power and resources, parishes could offer a robust variety of regular devotional practices in a public context, including numerous Masses each day. By the turn of the twentieth century, regardless of location in the United States, Sunday schedules at urban parishes almost universally began with two or three "low Masses" (a spoken Mass, said in a "low" voice, which followed a more simplified form, allowed plenty of room for devotion and private prayer, and could be "said" quite quickly), followed by one "high Mass" (a chanted Mass which usually included an organist and choir to sing responses, additional ministers, and often a vernacular-language sermon). Some parishes designated a specific Mass as the "children's Mass," which children were encouraged to attend. Others attended to the needs of

---

10   Joseph Dougherty, *From Altar-Throne to Table: The Campaign for Frequent Holy Communion in the Catholic Church* (Lanham, MD: Scarecrow Press, 2010), 26–27; Jay P. Dolan, *Catholic Revivalism: The American Experience, 1830–1900* (Notre Dame, IN: University of Notre Dame Press, 1978), 11–18.

their multiple ethnic groups, offering vernacular Gospels and sermons in various languages on a rotating basis.

It is important to note that for most Catholics, devotional practices paired with "low Mass" provided their normative experience of the Mass. "Low Masses" readily allowed a space for the development of personal prayer life fueled by devotional material, and the frequency with which "low Masses" were made available suggests that they were in high demand by the faithful. Interestingly, despite the greater significance assigned to the "high Mass," with its more elaborate ceremonial and accompanying music and preaching, some pastors noted that churches were "half empty when the chief service of the Sunday [took] place," or that "high Masses" were even completely dropped during the summer due to poor attendance.[11]

Aside from increased access to Mass, whatever form it may have been, American Catholics likewise received strong encouragement to partake regularly in the sacrament of confession. When access to sacramental ministers had been slim, devotional manuals, like those mentioned above, included exercises to prepare for confession, such as an examination of conscience, which offered the faithful a systematic list of sins to consider and to determine whether these would need to be included in one's next confession. But, following the meeting of the plenary councils in Baltimore in 1852 and 1866, American bishops legislated that confessionals needed to be "in a public and conspicuous place," resulting in the installation of confessional boxes along the perimeter of the church's nave (the central area with pews). While statistics regarding confessional attendance are rare, some do exist, and the numbers are impressive: an individual priest could hear more than 750 individual confessions in a given month, while a larger operation, like a cathedral, might have as many as 1800.[12] Just as with determining preferences for Mass, the frequency and quantity of scheduled confessional times suggest high demand for the sacrament. This flowed in part from the admonition that in order to make a communion, one would need to confess beforehand. Confessions in preparation for Sunday worship took place on Saturday afternoons and evenings, often beginning around 4:00 pm and lasting until 9:00 pm, with a break for

---

[11] "The Apostolate," *Orate Fratres* 11, no. 9 (1937): 416; Hans Anscar Reinhold, "Merely Suggesting," *Orate Fratres* 15, no. 9 (1941): 391.

[12] See James O'Toole, "In the Court of Conscience: American Catholics and Confession, 1900–1975," in *Habits of Devotion: Catholic Religious Practice in Twentieth-Century America*, ed. James O'Toole (Ithaca, NY: Cornell University Press, 2004), 132–135.

dinner. Thursday evenings also proved popular, due to "First Friday" devotions to the Sacred Heart, which promised that if one were to make a communion on the first Friday of the month for nine consecutive months, one was assured of not dying without receiving the sacraments (and thus being better prepared to die without the consequences of grave sin). This tight connection of confession in preparation for communion remained even after Pope Pius X's decree, *On Frequent Communion* (1905), allowed sacramental reception without confession (when no grave sin had been committed), and would not break down until the 1970s, when confession (and many other devotional practices) virtually disappeared from the lives of the faithful.

Within the immigrant church, increased organizational power and social ascendency among American Catholics also enabled the development of sodalities and associations at the local and national levels, as well as the development of media which promoted Catholic identity within an increasingly literate audience. Catholics could join any number of associations, many of which centered upon devotions to Mary (e.g., Sodality of the Blessed Virgin Mary, Sodality of Our Lady), the Eucharist (e.g., Sodality of the Blessed Sacrament), the rosary (e.g., Holy Rosary Society), or any number of the saints. Greater access to mass market materials significantly increased the availability of, and American Catholics' familiarity with, devotional content – including prayer books, prayer cards, statues, paintings, medals, and print media. Particularly after the 1840s, lay Catholics saw an increase in the number of types of popular devotions. Prayer books included not only several versions of the rosary and benediction with the Blessed Sacrament, but a great variety of Marian devotions (e.g., the seven dolors [sorrows], the Immaculate Conception, and the Sacred Heart of Mary); an increased variety of devotions to the Blessed Sacrament (e.g., Forty Hours' Devotion and visits to the Blessed Sacrament); and meditations on Jesus' Passion and suffering (e.g., devotions to the Sacred Heart of Jesus, the Way of the Cross, the seven last words, the five wounds, and the Precious Blood).[13] Popular magazines emerged that praised the merits of such devotions, including *Ave Maria* (1865–1970, sponsored by the Holy Cross Fathers of Notre Dame), *Sentinel of the Blessed Sacrament* (1897–1982, sponsored by the People's Eucharistic League), and, above all, the *Messenger of the Sacred Heart* (1866–present, sponsored by the Jesuits).

---

[13] Ann Taves, *The Household of Faith: Roman Catholic Devotions in Mid-Nineteenth-Century America* (Notre Dame, IN: University of Notre Dame Press, 1986), 21–45.

Likewise, the attachment of indulgences to devotional practices significantly served to increase their popularity. An "indulgence" (from a Latin root meaning "kind, tender, fond") referred to the church's *indulgent* attitude toward sinners. In response to an individual saying particular prayers, conducting works of charity, or visiting sacred locales, the church could grant an "indulgence," freeing the individual from some of the temporal punishment due on account of sins committed during one's lifetime – in other words, an indulgence could erase time in purgatory. Garnering indulgences was a powerful motivator for the faithful, and the seeking of indulgences was encouraged by papal pronouncements. In particular, Pope Pius IX (1846–1878) accelerated the number of devotions tied to indulgences, a collected list of which was compiled in *The Raccolta*, an "official handbook of indulgenced prayers."[14] Catholic publishers in the US market turned to this volume in the development of English resources, which included indulgenced devotions, such as *The Golden Manual* and *St. Vincent's Manual*, both of which went through numerous editions.[15]

Among the wide variety of devotional options, the Blessed Mother received special attention and only increased in popularity over the course of the nineteenth century. Many Catholic immigrants came to the United States with a particular iteration of Marian devotion, reminding them of their country of origin – as the Basilica of the National Shrine of the Immaculate Conception in Washington, DC so materially realizes in its dozens of shrines, such as that of the Mother of Sorrows (former Czechoslovakia); Our Lady of Brezje (Slovenia); or Our Lady of Altötting (Bavaria, Germany). Aside from this, Pope Pius IX affirmed Mary's Immaculate Conception on December 8, 1854, adding a new holy day to the liturgical calendar. Then, the apparition of Mary at Lourdes in France in 1858 further captured the Catholic imagination, prompting the establishment of homegrown Marian shrines throughout the country – from the National Shrine Grotto of Our Lady of Lourdes, constructed in the 1870s in Emmitsburg, Maryland, to the Grotto at the University of Notre Dame, begun in 1896. Shrines such as these became the object of pilgrimages coordinated by Catholic schools, clubs, and parishes well into the twentieth century.

---

[14] Taves, *The Household of Faith*, 27.
[15] *The Golden Manual: Being a Guide to Catholic Devotion, Public and Private* (New York: D & J Sadlier, 1851); and St. Vincent's *Manual: Containing a Selection of Prayers and Devotional Exercises*, 2nd revised and enlarged ed. (Baltimore: Murphy, 1848).

But perhaps the most powerful impetus for Marian devotion came from Pope Leo XIII (1878–1903), who not only encouraged the recitation of the rosary and the development of rosary societies but also explicitly encouraged Catholics to bring their rosaries to Mass – prompting a powerful spiritual practice among the faithful which would continue until the Second Vatican Council. Between 1883 and 1898, Leo XIII composed twelve encyclicals and five apostolic letters encouraging devotion to the rosary, including the recitation of the rosary within the month of October; the granting of indulgences for reciting the rosary in various circumstances; and assurances to the faithful that the rosary provided an easy, yet fruitful spiritual practice.

Aside from Marian devotion, American Catholics were encouraged to foster devotions to the Blessed Sacrament. Visits to and prayer before the Blessed Sacrament, Eucharistic processions, exposition, and Benediction were all included in the faithful's repertoire of Eucharistic devotions and were often paired with attendance at Mass itself. One of the most popular Eucharistically inspired devotions was the ritual of Benediction of the Blessed Sacrament. Benediction (Latin for "blessing") often served as a formal close to another devotional event. It was led by a priest who blessed the assembly with the Eucharist contained in an elaborate vessel known as a monstrance, and often included traditional hymnody such as the *Pange Lingua* (*Sing, my Tongue*). In instances from the mid-nineteenth century through the middle of the twentieth, Benedictions appeared in conjunction with vespers, feast days, and celebrations such as Candlemas or confirmations, novenas (a set of prayers prayed on nine consecutive days), parish missions, and the Mass itself.

Such prayer practices were not only private and individualized but also served as public displays of faith and identity for Catholics. The death of Pope Pius IX in February 1878 provided such an occasion. A Solemn Requiem Mass at St. Vincent de Paul Church in Oshkosh, Wisconsin, presented an opportunity for "all the Catholics to turn out" for a "grand street procession of societies and Catholics" in the midst of a cold Wisconsin February. Oshkosh churches were "draped in mourning, displayed black flags, and tolled their bells from noon until 1 o'clock," and, on Sunday, a grand procession, replete with music bands and furled banners, crisscrossed the city, stopping at various churches for devotional ceremonies and the delivery of short sermons, and concluding the pilgrimage with a Benediction of the Blessed Sacrament.[16]

---

16   *The Oshkosh Northwestern*, February 15, 1878, p. 4.

Public displays of devotion to the Eucharist took place on an even larger scale with Eucharistic Congresses, the Twenty-Eighth of which took place in Chicago, Illinois on June 20–24, 1926. According to the *Chicago Tribune*, one million visitors arrived in the city during the Congress, filling Soldier Field to participate in "spectacle after spectacle," including an outdoor Mass attended by 145,000 persons, while "other thousands" stood outside. Aside from the drama of worship services at this Eucharistic Congress, a variety of talks focused on Eucharistic themes from Family Communion to Priestly Vocations, and some 30,000 schoolchildren were gathered into a single chorus to chant the *Mass of Angels*, which resulted in the release of a record, made available for 75 cents a copy.[17]

LITURGICAL RENEWAL

Interest in the Eucharist began to refocus as some members of the Catholic faithful became increasingly attentive to liturgical renewal in the second quarter of the twentieth century. Advocates of the "liturgical movement" challenged widespread reliance on extra-liturgical devotions as the primary source of Catholic spirituality, and instead began encouraging not only Eucharistic reception (which had increased significantly with Pope Pius X's encouragement) but active and intelligent participation within the Mass itself. Such participation took place in a variety of ways. First, participation required access to the texts of the Mass, often by means of vernacular translations, which allowed the faithful to read the readings of the day and the prayers of the presider. The use of these hand missals (books with the texts of the Mass designed for congregational use) asked the faithful to shift their attention from general devotion focused on, say, Christ's passion, to specific moments in salvation history, as emphasized by the rotating calendar of feasts and seasons in use by the church, often described as the "Church Year," or "liturgical calendar." Participation might also take place vocally, with the entire congregation joining in oral responses, instead of the altar servers alone responding to the priest presider as had been traditionally practiced. This format was referred to as the "dialogue

---

[17] "Chicago Staged the 28th Eucharistic Congress," photo byline, *Chicago Tribune*, January 2, 1927, p. 99; *XXVIII International Eucharistic Congress June 28–24 Chicago Ill* (Chicago: XXVIII International Eucharistic Congress, Inc., 1926), 13; "Welcome! Chicago Guests," advertisement for the Brunswick Shop, *Chicago Tribune*, June 21, 1926, p. 14.

Mass," referencing the call and response of the presider and congregation. Participation was also encouraged through singing, and the restoration of congregational song and the promotion of chant served to support this. Finally, participation might take place through sacramental Eucharistic reception, not only during the Mass, but within the communion rite of the Mass – that is, Catholics were invited to participate in the ritual taking place, receiving communion immediately following the presiding priest.

These practical iterations of active, intelligent participation in the Mass closely aligned with the Catholic intellectual revival and coordinated with increased interest in lay participation in the life of the church. These social and cultural movements also coincided with the retrieval of a theological image: the Mystical Body of Christ, an archetype used by the Apostle Paul to describe the church, emphasizing that all members of the faithful coordinated together to act as Christ's body in the world. The conflux of intellectual renewal, social regeneration, and theological retrieval inspired twentieth-century Catholics to promote liturgical renewal. Notable among them, Virgil Michel, OSB (1890–1938) claimed, "The more wholeheartedly and intelligently the member of the mystical body enters into this corporate worship of the Church, the more should the divine life and the spirit there imbibed affect his daily conduct" and allow the "liturgical spirit to radiate forth from the altar of Christ into every aspect of the daily life of the Christian."[18] This renewal movement found support in Catholic organizations, publications, educators, laywomen and men, pastors, and the popes themselves.

Yet, an increased interest in the Mass as the center of devotion had profound consequences on the perception and use of devotions. Among some groups of American Catholics, devotions and devotionalism began to be associated with a rejection of communal worship in the Mystical Body of Christ, and as emphasizing an isolated individualism. Even though Pope Pius XII (1939–1958) explicitly had affirmed the practice of "personal" piety (i.e., private devotions) among the faithful in his encyclical on the liturgy, *Mediator Dei* (*On the Sacred Liturgy*, 1947), and the Second Vatican Council's document on the liturgy, *Sacrosanctum Concilium* (*Constitution on the Sacred Liturgy*, 1963), likewise described devotions as "highly commended," a concurrent emphasis upon participating intelligently in the Mass itself had the

---

[18]   Virgil Michel, "The Scope of the Liturgical Movement," *Orate Fratres* 10, no. 11–12 (1936): 485.

practical result of pushing devotions to the margins of Catholic spiritual life.

This move from devotion-based spirituality to a Mass-centered spirituality caused, in the words of historian Philip Gleason, a "clashing of tectonic plates of culture" which produced "nothing less than a spiritual earthquake in the American Church."[19] By the mid-1960s, devotional cultures rapidly began disappearing, to the point that even Catholic journalists described American Catholics as experiencing a "piety void."[20] Yet, as historian Joseph Chinnici has observed, to see the gain of active, intelligent participation in the Mass as the cause of the loss of devotions oversimplifies the situation.[21] Changing social patterns, such as the dissipation of ethnic-based parishes and neighborhoods and the population dispersion of Catholics to the suburbs, meant that by the time the Second Vatican Council opened in 1962, the social structures which supported an extra-liturgical devotional life were no longer in place. Likewise, the post-Conciliar Mass afforded opportunities for participation, including congregational singing and the use of vernacular language, which had been characteristics of numerous popular devotions. Finally, the charismatic movement among Roman Catholics, which emphasized spiritual conversion, filled some of the same emotional space which devotions had occupied.

WORSHIP AFTER THE SECOND VATICAN COUNCIL

The implementation of the norms expressed in *Sacrosanctum Concilium* on the First Sunday of Advent in 1964, began in the midst of a complex series of social and cultural changes taking place in the 1960s.[22] Vatican II asked the church to become more pastoral in its evangelization – throwing its doors open to the modern world – and called for a new ritual, which invited the faithful to experience the Mass as the source and font of their spiritual life. At an address given at the National Liturgical Week meeting in Houston, Texas in 1966, theologian James J. Megivern described how, with the new liturgical norms,

---

[19] Philip Gleason, *Contending with Modernity: Catholic Higher Education in the Twentieth Century* (New York: Oxford University Press, 1995), 305.

[20] Dan Herr, "Stop Pushing," *The Critic* 24, no. 2 (October–November 1965): 4, 6.

[21] See Joseph P. Chinnici, "The Catholic Community at Prayer, 1926–1976," in *Habits of Devotion: Catholic Religious Practice in Twentieth-Century America*, ed. James M. O'Toole (Ithaca, NY: Cornell University Press, 2004), 9–87.

[22] Joseph P. Chinnici, "Reception of Vatican II in the United States," *Theological Studies* 64, no. 3 (2003): 472–473.

"Sanctuaries have been rearranged, altars turned around, English sacramentaries and lectionaries rushed together, vernacular hymns scouted up, congregations instructed in new postures at various parts of the mass, rites for concelebration and communion under both kinds learned for the proper occasions." He concluded that "All this has been rightly greeted with grateful hearts by those who have in recent years been concerned to make the church's worship come to life."[23] Nonetheless, historians, such as Colleen McDannell, have found that implementation of the liturgical instructions tended to be "uneven, disjointed, and disorganized."[24] At the parish level, acceptance of liturgical reform had much to do with how much preparation had been received beforehand, and how much exposure had been afforded by the efforts of liturgical renewal enthusiasts. In places where the liturgical movement had been most active, particularly the Midwest, implementation of reformed practices tended to occur more rapidly.

Despite such challenges, surveys issued within five years of the post-Conciliar reforms suggest that reception of liturgical renewal among Americans was decidedly positive – both among pastors and parishioners. According to data presented by sociologist Andrew Greeley in 1977, between 85 and 87 percent of Catholics in the United States preferred the "new Mass" to the Mass as celebrated in the previous *Roman Missal*.[25]

While celebration of the Mass had a significantly positive reception, encouraging the faithful to accept any other reformed liturgical experience *aside* from that of the Mass proved difficult. The restoration of the Liturgy of the Hours as a regular practice within parishes was, largely, a failed experiment and, even in the wake of renewed interest in Scripture among Roman Catholics, attempts at Bible services, likewise, failed to gain traction in parish life.[26] Such text-heavy services tended to demand far more of the faithful than did traditional devotions. They required a certain amount of competency to conduct (navigating a breviary, for

---

[23]   James J. Megivern, "American Catholic Worship Tomorrow," *Worship* 40, no. 8 (1966): 483.

[24]   Colleen McDannell, *The Spirit of Vatican II: A History of Catholic Reform in America* (New York: Basic Books, 2011), 119.

[25]   Andrew M. Greeley, *The American Catholic: A Social Portrait* (New York: Basic Books, 1977), 127–151.

[26]   William Storey, "The Liturgy of the Hours: Cathedral versus Monastery," *Worship* 50, no. 1 (1976): 50–70; Paul Ford, "Whatever Became of Bible Services?" *Pray Tell: Worship, Wit, & Wisdom*, September 30, 2012, www.praytellblog.com/index.php/2012/09/30/whatever-became-of-bible-services/

example), continually varied in focus and theme (according to the liturgical year), and demanded a certain amount of intellectual effort (interpreting texts and their meaning). In the end, the desire of liturgical renewal advocates of the twentieth century was partly met: the Eucharist became the summit and font from which the church's activity flowed and to which its activity was directed. But, for most parishes, the Eucharist became the only remaining commonly practiced worship experience among the American Catholic faithful.

In the decades following the Second Vatican Council, Roman Catholics in the United States have continued to experience marked sociological and demographic changes that have shaped parochial worship experiences. By 2010, 57 percent of Roman Catholics in the United States had no living memory of Vatican II. The number of parishes has both skyrocketed (to 19,559 in 1990), and plummeted to levels below that of 1965 (17,337 in 2015). While parishes have been closed by the dozens in dioceses in the Northeast and Midwest, parishes have been opened in the West and South to accommodate a shifting American population. And, among the youngest groups of Catholics (those born in 1961 and later), more than four in ten identify as Hispanic or Latino/a.[27] In the twenty-first century, pastoral challenges which confronted the first Catholics on American soil remain relevant: how does one attend to questions of inculturation and effective evangelization as the Catholic population becomes more ethnically diverse, particularly among Spanish-speaking Catholics, and how does one negotiate a scarcity of ordained ministers, which has demanded parish consolidations and closures, and resulted in less frequent access to the sacraments?

Aside from these issues, Roman Catholics have experienced a series of changes in the twenty-first century which have been welcomed by Catholics seeking a more "traditional" worship style and a revival of devotional practices, particularly surrounding the Eucharist. Of particular note are Pope John Paul II's (1978–2005) encouragement for the retrieval of Eucharistic adoration, Pope Benedict XVI's (2005–2013) granting of permission to celebrate the "Extraordinary Form" of the Roman Rite, and the Vatican's implementation of the Third English edition of the Roman Missal in 2011, which altered the prayer texts at Mass to make them adhere more strictly to the original Latin.

Interestingly, preferences for "traditional" aesthetics and practices tend to be embraced most frequently by younger Catholics who lack

---

[27] See Charles E. Zech et al., *Catholic Parishes of the Twenty-first Century* (New York: Oxford University Press, 2017), 7–19.

memories of pre-Conciliar worship, and who often seek flexibility and individual choice in their practices of piety. As liturgical scholar Kimberly Hope Belcher describes, young women and men college students who practice Eucharistic adoration do not only expect to gather for "collective, quasi-liturgical worship before the Eucharist exposed in a monstrance," but will often engage in a variety of practices, "ranging from active, contemporary praise and worship music to silent prayer and journaling [. . .] to private unscripted prayer."[28] Such trends in worship among young Catholics are reflected in the spiritual practices promoted within the various Catholic youth conferences and programs, such as rosaries and adoration, as well as more traditional aesthetic choices (e.g., the use of the "mantilla" or "chapel veil" among young women). Such movements toward traditional aesthetics and rituals, the allowance of the Extraordinary Form of the Roman Rite, as well as the rejection of the more fluid translation techniques employed in the production of the previous English editions of the Roman Missal (1974 and 1985), have been welcomed by some Catholics as a needed "reform of the reform," and lamented by others as problematic dividing forces within the Roman Catholic Church that neglect pastoral, theological, and evangelical realities.

CONCLUSION

Catholic worship in the twenty-first century reflects the countervailing movements of the post-Vatican II era. More "progressive" reforms have demanded increased flexibility regarding local cultures, encouraged active liturgical participation, and called for a central focus on the communal celebration of the Mass. Meanwhile, more "traditionalist" reforms have tempered creative approaches to liturgical rites by choosing traditional aesthetics for music and architecture, seeking the retrieval of a variety of Catholic devotions, and even questioning the structure of the reformed rites promulgated by Pope Paul VI (1963–1978). With hope, the worship of the future American church will draw together these two extremes. As liturgical theologian Nathan D. Mitchell has observed, worship in the third millennium will likely "look, feel and sound very different from anything we can imagine today."[29] By looking at their past,

---

28   Kimberly Hope Belcher, "Eucharistic Adoration and Ecumenical Dialogue: Ritual Practice and Authority among Catholic College Students," *Questions Liturgiques* 99 (2018): 4.

29   Nathan D. Mitchell, "The Renewal that Awaits Us," *Worship* 70, no. 2 (1996): 165.

Catholic worshippers in the present United States of America may be inspired to resist temptations toward polarization, and instead, draw upon legacies of inculturation and evangelization, and rely on collaboration among laypeople, religious, and clergy to advance a robust spiritual life of public and private prayers, in a church ever in need of reform.

FURTHER READING

Chinnici, Joseph P., "Reception of Vatican II in the United States," *Theological Studies* 64, no. 3 (2003): 461–494.

Dougherty, Joseph, *From Altar-Throne to Table: The Campaign for Frequent Holy Communion in the Catholic Church.* Lanham, MD: Scarecrow Press, 2010.

Francis, Mark R., *Shape a Circle Ever Wider: Liturgical Inculturation in the United States.* Collegeville, MN: Liturgical Press, 2000.

Harmon, Katharine E., "Learning Your Catholic Language: Attitudes and Approaches to Latin and Vernacular in the United States' Liturgical Movement," *Worship* 87, no. 4 (2013): 309–337.

McGuinness, Margaret M., "Let Us Go to the Altar: American Catholics and the Eucharist, 1926–1975," in *Habits of Devotion: Catholic Religious Practice in Twentieth-Century America,* ed. James O'Toole. Ithaca, NY: Cornell University Press, 2004, 187–235.

Mitchell, Nathan D., *Cult and Controversy: The Worship of the Eucharist Outside Mass.* Collegeville, MN: Liturgical Press, 1982.

Taves, Ann, *The Household of Faith: Roman Catholic Devotions in Mid-Nineteenth-Century America.* Notre Dame, IN: University of Notre Dame Press, 1986.

Turner, Paul, *Whose Mass Is It? Why People Care So Much about Catholic Liturgy.* Collegeville, MN: Liturgical Press, 2015.

5   Catholic Intellectual Life

WILLIAM L. PORTIER

Few New York theatergoers who pass Father Francis Duffy's statue in Times Square know that the beloved chaplain to New York's "Fighting 69th" regiment was also a leading turn of the century Catholic intellectual. In 1905, Duffy (1871–1932) and colleagues sought to join "the ancient faith and modern thought" in their new journal, *The New York Review*, arguably the boldest American expression of Catholic intellectual life of its own or any time.[1] He and *The Review*'s other founders hoped to encourage a homegrown Catholic intellectual culture among the nation's growing body of upwardly mobile Catholics.

For Duffy and his colleagues, *culture* was a central concern of Catholic intellectual life. The question of how biblical faith – and the historical ensemble of liturgy, devotion, doctrine, and church structure to which it gives rise – relates to the local cultures in which it takes root is the beating heart of Catholic intellectual life. In this dynamic of assimilation and separation, Catholics tend to stress continuity, coming down on the side of an integral relationship between faith and reason and religion and culture. Such a perspective has enabled Catholics to make significant contributions to public debate in American society on numerous issues.

Could there be an American Catholic culture? Were Catholic principles compatible with American values? Initially, it was not clear whether such a synthesis was even possible. On one side, the history of English anti-Catholicism expressed in penal laws barring Catholics from full participation in public life made some Catholics dubious about their American prospects. On the other, the welcome promise of the founding documents' appeal to the

[1]   Michael J. DeVito, *The New York Review (1905–1908)* (New York: United States Catholic Historical Society, 1977).

Creator as the source of citizens' rights and freedoms made other Catholics hopeful.

This chapter surveys the history of American Catholic intellectual life through three periods: (1) from the Early Republic to 1870, (2) during the Americanism-Modernism controversies of the late nineteenth century and the Catholic Renaissance of the early twentieth, and (3) and post–World War II developments. It reveals a dynamic of assimilation and separation as Catholics reflected on their ongoing negotiation between positive engagement with American culture and more cautious forms of involvement in public life.

CATHOLICS NEGOTIATING AMERICA: EARLY REPUBLIC TO 1870

Few in number and culturally marginalized, Catholics prior to 1850 based their intellectual life on European models. Despite exceptions such as lay publisher and controversialist Mathew Carey (1760–1839), most Catholic intellectual production came from a small group of bishops and clergy, including Maryland-born John Carroll (1736–1815), John England (1786–1842) and Francis Kenrick (1797–1863), both born in Ireland, and Kentucky-born Martin Spalding (1810–1872). Kenrick and Spalding studied theology in Rome where their intellectual formation was heavily shaped by Scholasticism, a Latin-language system of commentary on medieval authors, especially St. Thomas Aquinas. This training included a heavy emphasis on natural law. Natural law approaches combine classical philosophy's sense of an ordered cosmos with the biblical doctrine of creation to emphasize that intellectual and moral life, including politics, should be conducted rationally, or in keeping with God's order. Two issues preoccupied these prelates and other Catholic intellectuals of this era: the relationship between church and state, and the "church question."

In the wake of the American Revolution, fellow citizens pressed "papists" to defend their American loyalty. Suspecting papal teaching authority extended to politics, they questioned Catholic claims that limited it to religious matters. Both Carroll, whose family originated in Ireland, and John England, a pastor there before coming to Charleston, South Carolina, found the US Constitution's First Amendment a great benefit to Catholics. "Freedom and independence," Carroll wrote, "acquired by the united efforts, and cemented with the mingled blood of protestant and catholic fellow-citizens, should be equally enjoyed by all."[2] England's Constitution for the Diocese of Charleston, issued in 1826, displayed his own embrace of modern politics by providing for lay participation in diocesan governance. Carroll and England lived in times of weak popes, and confidently described papal powers as purely spiritual. In an address before Congress that same year, England told legislators, "We know of no tribunal in our church which can interfere in our proceedings as citizens."[3]

As the nineteenth century advanced, the pope emerged more and more as the face of Catholicism, problematizing Carroll's and England's claims about the limits of papal power. In 1864, Pope Pius IX, beleaguered by nationalist European governments, issued an inflammatory document known as the "Syllabus of Errors," which listed eighty errors of the modern age. Among its propositions, it condemned religious freedom and the separation of church and state and denied any need for papal reconciliation with "liberalism, progress, and modern civilization." Archbishop Martin Spalding of Baltimore responded immediately. His pastoral letter took an exceptionalist approach, describing European liberalism as anarchical and distinct from American understandings of liberty. It would be "manifestly unfair and unjust," he concluded, to apply papal strictures against "European radicals and infidels" to "the state of things established in our noble Constitution, in regard to the liberty of conscience, of worship, and of the press."[4]

The Syllabus and Spalding's response came during the American Civil War when the slavery question divided American Christians. As Francis Kenrick's *Theologia Moralis* [*Moral Theology*] illustrates, Catholics approached slavery as a "natural" institution. They were obliged to treat enslaved people "justly." After a long citation from Pope Gregory XVI's 1839 condemnation of the slave trade, Kenrick asks: "Now how should we feel about domestic slavery which flourishes in many areas of the West and of the East? Should the descendants of those who had been abducted from Africa still be subject to this yoke?" Though he laments the laws that uphold the system of chattel slavery, he stated that "one should not attempt anything that contravenes the

2   Cited in James Hennesey, SJ, *American Catholics: A History of the Roman Catholic Community in the United States* (New York: Oxford University Press, 1981), 68.

3   England's "Address before Congress," January 8, 1826, in *Creative Fidelity: American Catholic Intellectual Traditions*, ed. R. Scott Appleby, Patricia Byrne, and William L. Portier (Maryknoll, NY: Orbis Books, 2004), 143.

4   *Pastoral Letter of the Most Reverend Martin J. Spalding, D.D.*, 2nd ed. (Baltimore: Kelly & Piet, 1865), 9–10, as cited in *Creative Fidelity*, 140.

laws" or that "might promote emancipation or the bearing [of slavery] more lightly."[5]

Kenrick's position on enslaved people reveals the chronic weakness of natural law thinking: its inability to mount the prophetic social critiques demanded by its own premises. Kenrick failed to act on his own critique of the obviously unjust practices of chattel slavery in the United States. Most tragically, natural law's presumption in favor of inherited social and political orders blinded Kenrick, even as he exhorted masters to treat slaves "justly," to the raw moral heinousness of owning fellow human beings.

By the 1840s, proliferating Christian denominations prompted renewed Protestant interest in historical Christianity and encouraged vigorous debate over what came to be known as the "church question." Which denomination represented the true church of history? Emphasis on liturgical and doctrinal history moved some Protestants, especially among Episcopalians and German Reformed, in what seemed to Catholics as a Romeward direction. Amid these Protestant debates, Catholic apologists relished their chance to address standard objections to Catholic ecclesiology, especially in regard to the papacy. In 1845, Kenrick, described as "the most accomplished American theologian of the era," published *The Primacy of the Apostolic See Vindicated*, which England's liberal Catholic *Rambler* called "the best vindication of the Holy See, in all its relations, we know of in our language."[6]

With its emphasis on papal authority, the First Vatican Council (1869–1870) challenged American Catholic thinkers with their own "church question." Until 1908 the Vatican considered the United States a "mission" territory, not bound by universal canon law. Without government interference and little oversight from a weak Vatican, American bishops governed themselves in a series of thirty-four provincial and plenary councils. They developed, in the words of historian James Hennesey, "the strongest nineteenth-century conciliar tradition in the Western Church."[7] They rivaled European defenders of the papacy in their personal devotion to the pope, but relative isolation

---

5   Francis Patrick Kenrick, *De Servitute, from Theologia Moralis*, vol. 1, translated by Maureen Tilley (Philadelphia: Eugene Commiskey, 1841), 255–258, as cited in *Creative Fidelity*, 168–169.

6   E. Brooks Holifield, *Theology in America, Christian Thought from the Age of the Puritans to the Civil War* (New Haven, CT: Yale University Press, 2003), 416; "Short Notices," *The Rambler* 5 (1857): 292.

7   James Hennesey, SJ, "The Baltimore Council of 1866: An American Syllabus," *Records of the American Catholic Historical Society of Philadelphia* 76 (1965): 165.

protected them from the extremes of Roman centralization. The Council forced them to face this trend, challenging their theology of episcopal autonomy and collegiality.

The American contingent of forty-nine episcopal representatives arrived in Rome for the Vatican Council before the issue of papal infallibility officially appeared on the agenda. As the question loomed, the lack of any agreed upon understanding of "papal infallibility" became clear. In the final vote on July 18, 1870, only ten American bishops voted for the definition. One of only two who voted against it was an American. The rest absented themselves. An entry in one observer's council notebook captured the American dilemma: "How can the Bishops define on infallibility, unless they be by Divine right, judges of what is of faith? And, if so, how can the Pope be declared to be alone unerring?"[8] Based on their tradition of episcopal autonomy and collegiality, the Americans sought clarity on how the college of bishops was related to infallible papal teaching, a question later addressed by the Second Vatican Council's Constitution on the Church.

Unlike most leading nineteenth-century Catholic spokespersons, who were trained in a Latin-based European tradition and who remained outsiders to the American cultural and intellectual mainstream, the voices of Orestes Brownson (1803–1876) and Isaac Hecker (1819–1888) signaled a shift away from inner church questions toward a more positive engagement with American culture. Turning from purely doctrinal debates of the post-Reformation era, they appealed, with inspiration from European romantics and New England Transcendentalists, to the interior needs of religious seekers. Passing through various Protestant denominations, Brownson lived the church question's restlessness. In 1835, he emerged as a founding member of Boston's Transcendentalist Club. Three years later, he founded the *Boston Quarterly Review*. In 1844, the year both he and Hecker entered the Catholic Church, it became *Brownson's Quarterly Review*, "one of the stellar intellectual journals of the period." A provocative controversialist, "no American contemporary matched him as a philosophical theologian."[9]

Hecker accompanied Brownson through New England Transcendentalism. As a Catholic, he and a group of companions founded the

<hr/>

8   Isaac Hecker, "Notes in Italy, 1869–'70," Appendix I in William L. Portier, *Isaac Hecker and the First Vatican Council* (Lewiston, NY: Edwin Mellen Press, 1985), 185–186.

9   Holifield, *Theology in America*, 418, 482–483. On the Brownson–Hecker relationship, see David J. O'Brien, *Isaac Hecker: An American Catholic* (Mahwah, NJ: Paulist Press, 1992), chapter 14.

Paulist Fathers in 1858. When Brownson suspended his *Review* in 1864, Hecker founded the *Catholic World*, modeling it on New England's *Atlantic Monthly*. Lacking Brownson's rigor and philosophical depth, the younger Hecker combined mystic genius with a strong pastoral bent. He addressed his creative mix of New England Calvinism's providentialism and Romantic Catholicism to Emersonian "earnest seekers." His *Questions of the Soul* (1855) epitomized this new apologetic approach.

Beginning in the 1850s, Brownson and Hecker articulated the twin themes that would inspire those in the next generation known as Catholic "Americanists": (1) the fit between America and Catholicism; and (2) the Catholic role in realizing America's providential world-historical mission to create "a new order of civilization." Brownson's 1856 essay "Mission of America" appeared in the wake of stunning victories by the anti-Catholic Know Nothing party in the elections of 1854, and gave full-blown expression to these Americanist themes. Brownson's response to nativism urged Catholics to enter fully into American life. He argued that the founders built American political order on "natural justice and reason as explained by Catholic doctors."[10] Brownson's *American Republic* (1865) gave systematic expression to this Americanist vision. Brownson's and Hecker's messianic belief in a Catholic America's providential role in world history passed in the 1890s to a new generation of "Americanists."

AMERICANISM, MODERNISM, AND THE CATHOLIC RENNAISSANCE

Usually dated from 1884 to Pope Leo XIII's censure of religious "Americanism" in his encyclical *Testem Benevolentiae* (1899), the Americanism episode marks a key chapter in Catholic immigrants' long history of negotiating a place in America. Could Catholics fully accept American political values? Or should they keep a safe distance from national culture? Were religious liberty and the separation of church and state primarily benign or inherently hostile for Catholics?

At the nineteenth century's end, such tensions erupted in a series of controversies over practical issues such as work, school, and even beer. Should Catholics participate in labor unions? Despite benefits such as

---

[10] Orestes A. Brownson, "Mission of America," in *The Works of Orestes A. Brownson,* ed. Henry F. Brownson, 20 vols. (Detroit, MI: Thorndike Nourse, 1882–1887), 11: 566–567, 572, 576.

insurance and credit, unions were sometimes anti-Catholic. Should Catholics have their own schools, or go to public schools, which seemed de facto Protestant schools? Irish Catholics, who tended to dominate the immigrant church, asked why German Catholics didn't just learn English instead of preserving German-language newspapers and organizations. Why should Catholics, with their Irish pubs and German beer gardens, support the temperance movement promoted by evangelical Protestants?

Leaders who advocated more rapid Catholic assimilation were called "Americanists." Less trustful of US political institutions, their opponents urged a certain separatism. John Ireland (1838–1918), Archbishop of St. Paul, Minnesota, led the Americanists. With episcopal allies Denis J. O'Connell (1849–1927) and John J. Keane (1839–1918), Ireland shared a common providential vision of history in which a Catholic America occupied a messianic role in leading church and world into a new age of voluntary religious culture. Americanists promoted their program of church reform both nationally and on the world stage. Vatican opposition, as expressed in *Testem Benevolentiae*, took the wind from Ireland's sails.

Although many of the Americanists' practical proposals proved largely unsuccessful, they nevertheless secured for Brownson's and Hecker's Americanist vision of history a lasting place in Catholic thought. This vision, with its impulse for creative, critical engagement with American culture, survived the censure of Americanism and took on various twentieth-century forms, including (1) the founding of the Catholic University of America, (2) a modernist intellectual flowering, (3) a new appreciation for history and historical development, (4) an embrace of the Social Sciences, and (5) the establishment of the National Catholic War Council.

Founded as a graduate school, the Catholic University of America (CUA) opened in 1889, the first Anglophone Catholic university since the Reformation. Closely aligned with the Americanist vision, it soon "became the chief center from which the research-oriented ideal that marks the modern university diffused itself outward into the world of Catholic higher education."[11] A distinguished international faculty developed strong programs in semitics, biblical studies, patristics, classics, and church history. Its School of the Social Sciences, founded in 1895 by Belgian Thomas Bouquillon (1840–1902), eventually included

---

[11]   Philip Gleason, *Contending with Modernity: Catholic Higher Education in the Twentieth Century* (New York: Oxford University Press, 1995), 7.

psychology, sociology, and anthropology. As Catholic public intellectuals, its faculty had a wide-reaching impact on American society in the first half of the twentieth century.

CUA's founding was only one expression of a widespread and extraordinary burst of intellectual activity inspired by Americanism that emerged between 1889 and 1908. At the University of Notre Dame, Father John Zahm (1851–1921) took to heart Bishop Ireland's exhortation for the church to "regain the scepter of science."[12] Zahm's popular teaching and publications challenged the materialism of contemporary evolutionists such as Cornell University's president, Andrew Dixon White. Zahm published his theological defense of theistic evolution, *Evolution and Dogma* (1896), in the same year as White's *A History of the Warfare of Science with Theology in Christendom.* Translated into French and Italian, Zahm's book became an international bestseller. But due to his association with Americanist Denis O'Connell, the Vatican forced him to withdraw his book from publication in 1898; he published a later work, *Woman in Science,* under the pseudonym H. J. Mozans in 1913.[13]

Americanist rhetoric likewise inspired a new generation of priest professors, including the faculty at St. Joseph's Seminary in Yonkers, New York, who launched *The New York Review* in 1905. Seeking alternatives to reigning forms of Scholasticism, they found in the writings of John Henry Newman (1801–1890) a model for a modern Catholic culture of the intellect in the English language. In the *Review*'s pages, both European and American authors advanced historical-critical study of the Bible and church history, as well as engagement with subjective approaches to religious thought characteristic of modern philosophy. A few years earlier, John Talbot Smith in *Our Seminaries: An Essay in Clerical Training* (1897) and John B. Hogan in *Clerical Studies* (1899) urged reform of seminary curricula.

The same year as the *Review* was launched, an editorial team assembled by John Wynne, SJ, (1859–1948) began work on the *Catholic Encyclopedia.* Its 350,000 articles by 1,500 contributors, 145 of whom were women, offered a comprehensive foundation for the English-language "culture of the intellect" of which Newman,

---

[12]   Ireland, "The Mission of Catholics in America," in *Church and Modern Society,* 1:92.

[13]   On Zahm, see Mariano Artigas, Thomas F. Glick, and Rafael A. Martinez, *Negotiating Darwin: The Vatican Confronts Evolution, 1877–1902* (Baltimore: Johns Hopkins University Press, 2006), chapter 7.

Spalding, and Duffy dreamed. The *Dublin Review* praised the *Encyclopedia*, complete in fifteen volumes by 1915, as "the greatest triumph of Christian science in the English tongue."[14]

Yet these new intellectual currents were not immune to scrutiny. On September 8, 1907, Pope Pius X signed *Pascendi Domenici Gregis*, an encyclical condemning "Modernism" as "the synthesis of all heresies" and abruptly ending almost two decades of unprecedented Catholic creativity in biblical studies and theology. For Pius such scholarship led only to subjective truth "of no use to the man who wants to know above all things whether outside himself there is a God into whose hands he is one day to fall."[15] He found Aquinas more than up to this task of knowing God and in *Pascendi* he endorsed Scholasticism in the strongest terms. But despite Vatican efforts to stamp out this Americanist inspired intellectual awakening, it had fueled fires that *Pascendi* could not extinguish. Shifting cultural winds sent them off in new directions. As the twentieth century began, two new paths for Catholic intellectual life opened up: history and social science.

In 1884 lay groups in Philadelphia and New York started historical societies. The contemporary journals *American Catholic Studies* and *U.S. Catholic Historian* originated with their publications. A member of the New York group, John Gilmary Shea (1826–1892) introduced American Catholics to scientific history with his four-volume *History of the Catholic Church in the United States* (1886–1892). As an independent scholar, supporting his family with editorial work, Shea prepared the way for university historians who followed. Peter Guilday rightly named him "father of American Catholic history." Thomas J. Shahan (1837–1932) joined CUA's faculty in 1891. Three prior years of postdoctoral studies in history at Berlin and the Institut Catholique, prepared him to begin the programs in church history, especially patristics, for which the university became known. In 1895, he began the *Catholic University Bulletin* and made major contributions to the *Catholic Encyclopedia*.

Trained in history at Louvain, Peter Guilday (1887–1947) came to CUA in 1914 and founded the field of American Catholic history as a university discipline. In 1915, he helped launch the *Catholic Historical*

---

[14]   As cited in Margaret M. Reher, *Catholic Intellectual Life in America: A Historical Study of Persons and Movements* (New York: Macmillan, 1989), 103, 166n79. See also *The Catholic Encyclopedia and Its Makers* (Washington, DC: Encyclopedia Press, 1915).

[15]   *Pascendi*, para. 39.

Review and, with Shahan and others, the American Catholic Historical Association in 1919, as an affiliated society of the larger American Historical Association.[16] Such scholars institutionalized critical history among American Catholics. Guilday's student, John Tracy Ellis (1905–1992), taught at CUA from 1938 to 1964, served as long-time editor of the *Catholic Historical Review*, and solidified American Catholic history as a professional field. As in Europe, church history provided a sanctuary for serious Catholic intellectual work in a post-*Pascendi* environment that repressed intellectual innovation in biblical studies and theology. In addition, American Catholic history helped Catholic immigrants defend themselves against periodic nativist outbursts and find a place in American life.

After *Pascendi*, Americanist impulses also found a home in CUA's School of the Social Sciences, where scholars approached America in "a complex pattern of engagement and resistance."[17] Their work reveals how Catholic intellectual life was attuned to, yet still distinct from, mainstream contemporary scholarship. Trained in Neo-Scholastic philosophy, their sense of the continuity between faith and reason predisposed them to appreciate contemporary science but distinguished them from many secular peers in the social sciences. More confident than embattled, they enlisted empirical research in the service of social justice. They approached their work with a forward-looking spirit that shaped their teaching and research. Their empirical commitments separated them from many fellow Catholic academics whose work was rooted in philosophical and theological methodologies.

Most distinguished of these pioneer social thinkers was John A. Ryan (1869–1945), a priest of the Archdiocese of St. Paul, Minnesota, who was sent in 1902 to study moral theology at CUA, where Thomas Bouquillon and William Kerby mentored him. In 1906, he published *A Living Wage*, which presented a natural law argument, based on Leo XIII's *Rerum Novarum*, for workers' rights in justice to a minimum wage sufficient to support their families. Ryan's work greatly influenced the work of the National Catholic War Council (NCWC), founded by the US bishops in response to World War I. John A. Ryan's

---

[16] David O'Brien, "Peter Guilday: The Catholic Intellectual in the Post-Modernist Church," in *Studies in Catholic History in Honor of John Tracy Ellis*, ed. Nelson H. Minnich, Robert B. Eno, and Robert Trisco (Wilmington, DE: Michael Glazier, 1985), 260–306.

[17] Elizabeth McKeown, "From Pascendi to Primitive Man: The Apologetics and Anthropology of John Montgomery Cooper," *U.S. Catholic Historian* 13 (Winter 1995): 21.

name became synonymous with the work of the Council and its successor organizations. In 1919, the NCWC appointed him Director of its Social Action Department, a position he held until 1944. That same year, Ryan drafted a postwar Program of Social Reconstruction, which the bishops adopted the following year. Focusing on reform in labor and social services, Ryan based the program, despite its Progressive ring, in a Thomistic vision of goods and ends. He used his position to intervene in national debates about social policy and even served on the board of the American Civil Liberties Union. During the 1930s, New Deal legislation enacted many reforms he advocated and his work helped bring Catholics into the New Deal coalition.

In contrast to such progressive public engagement, other intellectual forces gave rise to a Catholic Renaissance in the early twentieth century that looked to an idealized past. Physician James J. Walsh's *The Thirteenth: Greatest of the Centuries*, published in the same year as *Pascendi*, anticipated a new mood of selective antimodernism. After the Great War, Americanism took a surprising medieval turn. Catholics defended their devotion to America with a "medieval roots of democracy theory," trying to make historical connections between American institutions and Catholic natural law. Lacking any urgency for America's conversion, this internally focused, Neo-Scholastic variant on Americanism was "the earliest clear-cut version of the Catholic Renaissance in the United States."[18]

The Catholic Renaissance that emerged in the 1920s took off after Al Smith's defeat in the 1928 presidential election and lasted until the end of World War II. During this time, Neo-Scholasticism functioned "ideologically" to unify Catholics across their immigrant subcultures.[19] Centers of Thomistic thought sprang up in the 1920s. Étienne Gilson (1884–1978) taught at Harvard and then founded the Pontifical Institute of Medieval Studies at Toronto, which, along with Laval University in Québec, trained a generation who established Thomism in American Catholic universities. By the 1940s Thomistic philosophy had become professionalized at Catholic universities such as Saint Louis and Notre Dame, where Jacques Maritain (1882–1973) exercised strong influence. CUA professors founded the American Catholic Philosophical Association in

---

[18]   Gleason, *Contending with Modernity*, 125–130.
[19]   Philip Gleason, "American Catholics and the Mythic Middle Ages," in *Keeping the Faith: American Catholicism Past and Present* (Notre Dame, IN: University of Notre Dame Press, 1987), 26, 169, 176.

1926 and the *New Scholasticism* (now *The American Catholic Philosophical Quarterly*) in 1927. The year 1926 also saw the founding of two other important scholarly publications: *Thought* at Fordham University and *Orate Fratres* (now *Worship*), begun by Louvain Thomist and liturgical reformer, Virgil Michel, OSB (1890–1938) at St. John's Abbey in Collegeville, Minnesota.

If a Thomistic sense of reality's emphasis on intelligible order gave progressive-era Catholic intellectuals such as the CUA social scientists confidence in their engagement with empirical methods, denizens of the Catholic Renaissance found reality's intelligible order threatened by Depression-era social chaos and modern scientific materialism. They wanted to return to the kind of Catholic culture Christopher Dawson (1889–1970) wrote about in the 1920s and 1930s, and for which an idealized Medieval civilization served as a model. Selective readings of influential English writers John Henry Newman and G. K. Chesterton (1878–1936) offered additional literary inspiration. Newman's *Apologia Pro Vita Sua* and *Idea of a University* critiqued liberalism and urged the unity and integration of learning. Chesterton's *Heretics* (1905) and *Orthodoxy* (1908), his novels, and epic poems inspired resistance to modern civilization.

The medievalism and rejection of modern materialism in earlier French Catholic literary revival writers, such as Charles Péguy and J.-K. Huysmans, also attracted Catholic Renaissance readers. From the 1930s through the 1950s, such authors, inspired by Newman on the unity of learning, populated integrated humanities curricula at Catholic colleges and universities, where students typically took at least twelve sequenced hours of Thomistic philosophy. Eventually, college-educated women religious passed on to their elementary and high school students this Catholic Renaissance ethos.

Countervailing currents also emerged, especially among the laity. In 1924 in New York City, Michael Williams (1877–1950) launched *Commonweal*. Four years later he hired as managing editor a former Notre Dame professor, George N. Shuster (1894–1977). Both Shuster and Williams shared the Catholic Renaissance's resistance to prevailing cultural disintegration.[20] Along with their radical poverty and pacifism, Dorothy Day's (1897–1980) Catholic Workers shared a Catholic Renaissance conviction that the times required a supernaturally

---

[20] On Williams and Shuster, see William M. Halsey, *The Survival of American Innocence: Catholicism in an Era of Disillusionment, 1920–1940* (Notre Dame, IN: University of Notre Dame Press, 1980), chapters 2 and 5.

energized Mystical Body of Christ.[21] Other Depression-era Catholic reformers, such as Catherine de Hueck (1896–1985), sociologist Paul Hanly Furfey, and Howard University biology professor and civil rights activist Thomas Wyatt Turner (1877–1978), inhabited the same world. A former student at CUA, Turner protested to the bishops gathered at the university in 1919 its present exclusion of African Americans.

From the end of the 1920s up to the 1950s, the Catholic Renaissance spirit predominated in Catholic intellectual life. It encouraged a certain sense of selective withdrawal from dominant intellectual trends and helped to shape a relatively unified immigrant Catholic subculture in the volatile and uncertain years between the world wars.

POSTWAR DEVELOPMENTS

The second half of the twentieth century witnessed the emergence of new theological trends and perspectives that challenged the dominant place of Thomistic philosophy in Catholic intellectual life. Theology, taught primarily in seminaries, had, by the 1940s, begun to professionalize. In 1941, the Jesuits began publication of *Theological Studies*. The Catholic Theological Society of America (CTSA), with a membership comprised mostly of seminary professors, began in 1946. The Catholic Biblical Association, founded a decade earlier, focused primarily on biblical translations until 1943, when Pope Pius XII's *Divino Afflante Spiritu* opened the field to historical-critical approaches. Association members started the *Catholic Biblical Quarterly* in 1939, with Mother Kathryn Sullivan, RSCJ (1905–2006), a founding editorial board member.

Responding to requests for theology programs for laity, John Montgomery Cooper at CUA, who founded the school's Department of Religious Education in 1929, developed religion as an alternative to seminary theology. Enlisting his home discipline of anthropology to promote Christian life, Cooper's five-volume textbook series connected doctrine to liturgical and devotional practice. Sounding much like Cooper, a young John Courtney Murray, SJ, (1904–1967) also proposed an alternative to "scientific" Thomism. But he called it "Theology." In 1943 Sister Madeleva Wolff, CSC, (1887–1964), a published poet and Berkeley Ph.D. in English, established St. Mary's Graduate School of Sacred Theology, the only US school offering women doctorates in

---

[21] Gleason, *Contending with Modernity*, 154–155.

theology. The program lasted until 1966. In 1953 Sister Rose Eileen Masterman, CSC, from Dunbarton College in Washington, DC, proposed a professional organization for college instructors. Begun in 1954, its cumbersome name, the Society of Catholic College Teachers of Sacred Doctrine, allowed the new organization to include proponents of both Theology and Religion. In 1967, it became the College Theology Society. Its journal *Horizons* began publishing in 1974.[22]

After World War II, John Courtney Murray emerged as a significant Catholic public intellectual. In the spirit of the Americanists of the 1890s, Murray revisited and updated Catholic thought on church–state relations. Amid unprecedented economic prosperity and Catholic movement into the American mainstream, Murray's work on church and state provided intellectual justification for Catholic participation in the postwar consensus. Forbidden in the 1950s to publish on church and state, Murray turned to a natural-law-based "public philosophy." Responding to longstanding suspicions of Catholic patriotism and Vatican misgivings about America, he argued that religious liberty promoted the good of public peace. In 1960, encouraged by Sheed and Ward editor Philip Scharper (1920–1985), Murray collected his public philosophy essays in *We Hold These Truths: Reflections on the American Proposition*. In November, John F. Kennedy narrowly defeated Richard Nixon to become America's first Catholic President. On December 12, publisher Henry Luce put Murray on the cover of *Time* magazine.

If Murray gave theoretical justification for a full Catholic embrace of American institutions, John Tracy Ellis's historical retrieval of the Americanists of the 1890s offered 1950s Catholics strong precedents and historical models for what Murray proposed. Ellis began publishing on Americanism in the mid-1940s, directing dissertations on every aspect of the controversies. His massive 1952 biography of Cardinal James Gibbons gave immigrant Catholics a benign, patriotic face. With the publication of "American Catholics and the Intellectual Life" (1955), Ellis set off an ongoing debate on Catholic intellectual life. He blamed Catholic intellectual "inadequacy" on a "self-imposed ghetto-mentality which prevents them from mingling as they should with their non-Catholic colleagues."[23] As Ellis pulled Catholics away

---

[22] Sandra Yocum, *Joining the Revolution in Theology: The College Theology Society, 1954–2014* (New York: Sheed &Ward, 2014).

[23] John Tracy Ellis, "American Catholics and the Intellectual Life," *Thought* 30 (Spring 1955): 387–388. On the intellectual life debate, see *Creative Fidelity*, Part 1.

from their own self-complacent culture toward the dominant culture, critics accused him of imposing alien standards on them.

Murray and Ellis, however, were not the only Catholic public intellectuals of the 1950s. In 1955, William F. Buckley, Jr. (1925–2008) founded the *National Review*. Joining classical liberalism's emphasis on fiscal responsibility and objection to needless governmental intrusions on personal freedom to a fervid anticommunism and a growing cultural conservatism, Buckley shaped American political conservatism in the latter twentieth century. His brother-in-law and colleague, L. Brent Bozell, wrote Buckley's vision into Barry Goldwater's 1964 *Conscience of a Conservative*.

By the early 1960s, the Thomistic synthesis began to crack. Thomistic revival historical scholarship showed that Aquinas, far from the strict Aristotelian of modern manuals, differed significantly from his modern interpreters. The many Thomisms of Toronto, Louvain, Rome, and various American schools showed that Thomism had been historicized.[24] Though these schools had much in common, they differed over many issues, not least the interpretation of Aquinas on the key doctrine of analogy, with its confidence in human ability to see the Creator's reflection in creation. Analogy was central to a Thomistic understanding of what Pope Pius X thought to be at stake in the modernist crisis, our ability to know God. A clear sign of Thomism's intellectual vitality, this diversity ironically meant that Thomism could no longer symbolically unify Catholic thought.

Despite signs of new intellectual currents drifting over from Europe, Pope John XXIII still surprised most American Catholics when, in 1959, he announced a new council. From 1962 to 1965, the Second Vatican Council drew from twentieth-century biblical, patristic, and liturgical movements to renew the church's self-understanding and reposition it with respect to modern democratic politics, especially through the Declaration on Religious Liberty, of which Murray was one of the principal architects. Vatican II's US implementation coincided with the demographic dissolution of the European immigrant Catholic subculture in the mid-1960s. Assimilated European-American Catholics no longer differed significantly from other Americans in such measures as salary and levels of education.

---

[24]   Helen James John, SND, *The Thomist Spectrum* (New York: Fordham University Press, 1966).

Educated, upwardly mobile Catholics, amid increasing cultural upheaval, found themselves in a position to learn and take seriously the church's traditional teaching on the primacy of conscience in moral life. The Vietnam War chastened Americanist fervor among many Catholics and drew them to the conscientious positions of Dorothy Day, brothers Daniel (1921–2016) and Philip (1923–2002) Berrigan, and the Catholic peace movement. The sexual revolution challenged Catholic sexual teaching. *Humanae Vitae*, Pope Paul VI's 1968 encyclical forbidding "artificial" birth control, ignited widespread theological "dissent." The postwar consensus had blown up, leaving Catholics divided and adrift. American pluralism once normed by consensus was now normed by diversity, a trend increasingly present in Catholic thought as well.

In the wake of the reforms of the Second Vatican Council and the social and demographic changes of the 1960s, Catholics searched for identity and integrity amid the institutional remains of an intellectual culture once based on the unity and integration of learning. On this fractured landscape, what might replace fading Thomisms and the hegemony of philosophy? The American Catholic Philosophical Association's president noted in 1967 that Scholasticism's collapse brought on "a massive failure of confidence." He suggested replacing *Catholic* with *Christian* as more "relevant." In 1970, the American Catholic Sociological Society became the Association for the Sociology of Religion. The American Catholic Psychological Association, abandoning its "divisive, sectarian, ghetto mentality," became Psychologists Interested in Religious Issues.[25]

Amid these changes, many felt that Catholic higher education needed renewal. At Land O'Lakes, Wisconsin, in 1967, the president of the University of Notre Dame, Father Theodore Hesburgh, CSC, and a group of Catholic university presidents laid out a hopeful vision of "the nature and role of the contemporary Catholic university." They claimed for the Catholic university "a true autonomy and academic freedom." Still committed to the Catholic Renaissance ideal of the unity and integration of learning and the interdisciplinary dialogue it requires, they saw a renewed Vatican II theology assuming the integrative role once played by philosophy. In the face of disciplinary specialization and diversification of Catholic universities, however, their vision proved elusive. Catholic universities never became

---

[25]   On the Catholic professional societies, see Gleason, *Contending with Modernity*, 319–320.

the "critical reflective intelligence of the church" envisioned by the Land O'Lakes statement.[26]

By 1968, Walter Burghardt, editor of *Theological Studies* and president of the Catholic Theological Society of America (CTSA), chided theologians for their "relative isolation from where the American action is" and doubted that the CTSA could continue to justify its "relatively unproductive existence."[27] Theology survived as a legitimate humanities discipline in Catholic universities, but, as David Tracy argued, its primary "public" was neither church nor society, but the academy.[28] Like scholars in every university discipline at this time, theologians with specialized training felt more loyalty and responsibility to their professional guilds than to any ideal of the unity and integration of learning.

Amid ensuing agonizing over institutional and disciplinary identities, voices excluded from the postwar consensus began to emerge. A founding member of the National Black Catholic Clergy Caucus in 1968, Louvain-trained medieval historian Cyprian Davis, OSB, (1930–2015) pioneered the field of Black Catholic Studies. *The History of Black Catholics in the United States* (1990) bore fruit in the Institute for Black Catholic Studies at Xavier University, New Orleans, the Black Catholic Theological Symposium, and distinguished scholars such as M. Shawn Copeland and Father Bryan Massingale. With *The Church and the Second Sex* (1968), Mary Daly, (1928–2010), caught the crest of second-wave feminism. Rosemary Radford Ruether, Elisabeth Schüssler-Fiorenza, Sister Elizabeth Johnson, CSJ, and others walked in her footsteps. In more recent decades, the Academy of Catholic Hispanic Theologians in the United States (ACHTUS) and their *Journal of Hispanic/Latino Theology*, founded in 1993, focuses on the critical appropriation of Hispanic experience, especially that of immigrants from the Caribbean and Latin America. These scholars continue to participate in larger groups, challenging European Americans to appropriate critically their own ambivalent histories.

With their pastoral letters *The Challenge of Peace* (1983) and *Economic Justice for All* (1986), American bishops intervened in

26   "Land O'Lakes Statement," in *American Catholic Higher Education: Essential Documents, 1967–1990*, ed. Alice Gallin, OSU (Notre Dame, IN: University of Notre Dame Press, 1992), 7–12.
27   Walter J. Burghardt, SJ, "Toward an American Theology," *American Ecclesiastical Review* 159 (September 1968): 181–187, 185, 187.
28   David Tracy, *The Analogical Imagination: Christian Theology and the Culture of Pluralism* (New York: Crossroad Publishing, 1981), chapter 1.

important public debates of the era hoping for a united Catholic voice. In hindsight, these letters look more like the last hurrah of the Vatican II generation of bishops, shaped by the postwar consensus. The fate of a hoped-for women's pastoral, abandoned under Vatican pressure, and an alternative neo-conservative economics pastoral, signaled the divided state of the American church.

The flashpoint for present divisions over gender and cultural issues is the legacy of Pope John Paul II (1978–2005). After the vital but chaotic post-Vatican II decade, he redrew blurred boundaries, responding to confusion and fragmentation by highlighting the central role Jesus Christ plays in each of the council's contested major documents. And although his 1998 encyclical *Fides et Ratio* emphasized the compatibility of faith and reason and his writings on inculturation seemed to support perspectival diversification in Catholic thought, he sought to enforce theological discipline in other areas, particularly on issues pertaining to the reproductive family.[29] He staked his papacy on the defense of *Humanae Vitae* and opposition to women's ordination. His teachings in the area of marriage, sexual morality, abortion, and end-of-life care tended to restrict personal discretion in matters of conscience. In the United States, these ideas found favor with neo-conservative political and economic commentators, such as *First Things* founder Richard John Neuhaus (1936–2009), many of whom came to see the very meaning of "Catholic," and indeed the fate of civilization, to hang on holding the line on birth control, abortion, women's ordination, and gay marriage.

In the opening decades of the twenty-first century, the Catholic intellectual landscape reflects a fractured political culture. The conversations taking place in the rival spheres of *Commonweal* and *First Things*, *Theological Studies* and *Nova et Vetera*'s US edition, the CTSA and the Academy of Catholic Theology, feel more like alternative universes than participants in an ongoing argument of a tradition. In 2005, a journalist asked theologian Charles Curran, "Where have the dominant theologians gone?" His response applies to every discipline on the Catholic intellectual landscape: "Now and in the future, we need many different Catholic theologies emerging in different cultures and contexts and diverse areas of specialization. No one person or small

---

[29] James Chappel, *Catholic Modern: The Challenge of Totalitarianism and the Remaking of the Church* (Cambridge, MA: Harvard University Press, 2018), chapter 2 on "Paternal Catholic Modernism."

group of theologians of one station in life, or one sex, or one color, will ever again dominate Catholic theology."[30]

Catholic intellectual life today feels unsettled and uncertain. A vision of Catholicism as a culture looks as distant and idealistic as Newman's unity and integration of learning. Yet, can we imagine Catholic intellectual life without a culture? Many want a separate culture, a new Catholic Renaissance. Others argue that changed times require a Catholic intellectual culture without triumphalist antimodernism and the embarrassing blind spots of earlier eras. Despite these challenges, Catholics in the United States, as heirs to a long and rich intellectual heritage, have considerable resources to draw upon, as they cast off into the deep of an uncertain future.

FURTHER READING

Appleby, R. Scott, Patricia Byrne, and William L. Portier, eds. *Creative Fidelity: American Catholic Intellectual Traditions*. Maryknoll, NY: Orbis Books, 2004.

Carey, Patrick W. *American Catholic Religious Thought: The Shaping of a Theological and Social Tradition*. Milwaukee, WI: Marquette University Press, 2004.

Holifield, E. Brooks. *Theology in America: Christian Thought from the Age of the Puritans to the Civil War*. New Haven, CT: Yale University Press, 2003.

Gleason, Philip. *Contending with Modernity: Catholic Higher Education in the Twentieth Century*. New York: Oxford University Press, 1995.

McGreevy, John T. *Catholicism and American Freedom: A History*. New York: W. W. Norton, 2003.

Reher, Margaret M. *Catholic Intellectual Life in America: A Historical Study of Persons and Movements*. New York: Macmillan, 1989.

Sparr, Arnold. *To Promote, Defend, and Redeem: The Catholic Literary Revival and the Cultural Transformation of American Catholicism*. Westport, CT: Greenwood Press, 1990.

---

[30]   *National Catholic Reporter*, February 4, 2005.

6 Catholic Education

JAMES T. CARROLL

The growth and development of Catholic schools in the United States represented an ambitious, ideologically motivated, and faith-based effort on the part of both church leaders and the Catholic faithful to educate youth and young adults and provide an alternative to public schools, which were considered hostile to the tenets of Catholicism. The opening of the Ursuline Academy in New Orleans in 1727 laid a foundation for the most extensive privately funded system of schools in history. The Catholic school system – both parish schools and private institutions founded by religious orders – grew at a slow rate in the early years of the republic, but quickly accelerated with the arrival of Catholic immigrants at the midpoint of the nineteenth century, primarily from Ireland and Germany. This growth continued unabated until the mid-1960s, when the baby boom generation fueled demands for seats in classrooms across the nation. In 1965, the apex of Catholic school enrollments, 4.5 million children attended parish elementary schools. Over the years, the Catholic Church built an incredible network of educational institutions in every corner of the nation.

The breadth and scope of Catholic education in the United States were vast and wide-ranging, encompassing schools associated with parishes, secondary schools sponsored by religious orders, protectorates for vulnerable youth, colleges and universities for men and women, nursing schools, law schools, graduate and professional schools, minor and major seminaries, and catechetical schools, to name a few. The Catholic school system that developed in the United States was the most significant private philanthropic endeavor in history. The strenuous efforts of the hierarchy, local pastors, faithful parishioners, and countless religious teachers, particularly Catholic sisters, provided a means for young Catholics to become well educated and firmly situated in the middle class.

This chapter traces the history of Catholic education in the United States from one small academy to a complex educational bureaucracy. It was a process that unfolded in three distinct phases: establishment and early growth (1790–1900), expansion and centralization (1900–1945), and postwar surge and challenges to sustainability (1945–present).

ESTABLISHMENT AND EARLY GROWTH, 1790–1900

The hundred years between the founding of Georgetown University (1789) and the implementation of the bold mandates of the Third Plenary Council of Baltimore (1884) witnessed the emergence of a Catholic educational enterprise that began with the establishment of elite private academies and a smattering of colleges for both men and women. Gifted and charismatic leaders spearheaded these developments and directed the expansion of Catholic education in the United States. Some examples include John Carroll, the first bishop in the United States, who wanted his schools to produce "intelligent and cultured Christian gentlemen"; Archbishop John Hughes of New York who considered Catholic education as a vital quiver in his efforts to combat anti-Catholicism; and Elizabeth Ann Seton who offered quality academic preparation to young women, both rich and poor. During the first half of the nineteenth century, a disparate group of visionary leaders worked independently and with virtually no coordination to open Catholic educational institutions. By 1850, there were over 200 elementary schools, approximately 125 secondary schools for young men and academies for young women, and nearly two dozen colleges. The elementary schools provided a standard common school curriculum; the secondary schools for boys granted a broad-based college preparatory program; and the girls' academies provided a practical curriculum. The colleges were all single-sex with traditional theological and philosophical course of study for men, and a humanities-based and professional preparation program for women. A majority of these institutions were small, and many served both Catholics and non-Catholics without prejudice. Many were short-lived, while others continue their mission in the twenty-first century.

The earliest endeavors of Catholic education in North America – the Ursuline Academy in New Orleans (1727) and Georgetown Preparatory School in Washington, DC (1789) – reflected the composition of the Catholic population in North America in the opening years of the nineteenth century. The student population came from wealthy and prominent families who wanted a classical and traditional education for their children. The sizeable presence of non-Catholics in the student population testified to the excellent education provided at these institutions.

The mid-nineteenth century was a significant transition point in the history of Catholic education in the United States. The sudden arrival of nearly two million famine immigrants from Ireland, many fiercely devoted to their Catholic faith, fanned virulent forms of anti-Catholicism, highlighted the necessity of creating a systematic plan for Catholic schools, and challenged church leaders to mobilize priests and the faithful. The majority of the Irish immigrants opted to live in urban areas (Boston, New York, Philadelphia, Chicago), which explains the explosive growth of Catholic schools in these cities after 1850.

John Hughes, Archbishop of New York, was an early supporter of a centralized and comprehensive system of Catholic education. In the 1840s, he focused his well-honed oratorical skills in numerous public debates to refute attacks on the church. He strongly opposed state support for common schools, the use of the King James Bible, and the recitation of a Protestant version of the Lord's Prayer. Hughes considered these efforts to be a direct attack on the church and saw them as apparent attempts to proselytize the growing Catholic school-age population in New York City public schools. The so-called "Bible Wars," which raged in New York City throughout the 1840s, were a significant impetus for the opening of Catholic schools, especially after Irish immigrants began to arrive in large numbers. This conflict awakened opponents of Catholic education to the increasing political influence of Irish Catholics in New York City and forced them to temper their antagonistic policies. In 1850, Hughes issued a circular letter to the priests of the archdiocese asserting "that the time has almost come when it will be necessary to build the school-house first, and the Church afterward." This decree started the steady progression of expanding and centralizing a Catholic school system in the United States and serves as one of the justifications for considering him the "father" of the parochial school system.[1]

The school campaign launched by Archbishop Hughes spread to other parts of the country, predictably following throngs of immigrants leaving cities in the northeast for points further west. The idea of a Catholic school system posed a daunting set of challenges: convincing bishops of the importance of Catholic schools, identifying methods of financing the various institutions, publishing textbooks, and, most

---

[1] John Hassard, *Life of the Most Reverend John Hughes: First Archbishop of New York* (New York: D. Appleton, 1866), 338; and John Loughery, *Dagger John: Archbishop John Hughes and the Making of Irish America* (Ithaca, NY: Cornell University Press, 2018), 111–138.

importantly, securing the services of well-trained religious teachers, primarily Catholic sisters, to staff institutions. Initially, many US bishops recruited teaching sisters from Europe; in time, however, diocesan communities were founded for this purpose. For example, in the 1840s, Archbishop Hughes secured the assistance of the Ladies of the Sacred Heart (France), Sisters of Mercy (Ireland), and the School Sisters of Notre Dame (Germany), and in 1846 he welcomed a new diocesan community, the Sisters of Charity of New York, a branch of Mother Seton's original community, to conduct schools. Most Catholic dioceses followed a similar pattern to staff a growing and increasingly complex array of educational institutions.

When the US bishops met in 1884 at the Third Plenary Council, they addressed the issue of Catholic education boldly and directly. The bishops realized that attitudes regarding education in the United States were changing; many reformers advocated for mandatory school attendance laws, supported a standardized curriculum, and called for financial support from state and local governments. The rumblings for a comprehensive plan for Catholic schools, starting with Archbishop Hughes in the 1840s and continuing with various council decrees in 1852 and 1866, garnered significant support from both the clergy and laity and was the dominant agenda item in 1884. The edicts issued in 1884 included: mandating that all parish pastors build a school, instituting policies and procedures for assessing teacher quality, requiring careful planning for the establishment of a Catholic university, drafting a new catechism (*The Baltimore Catechism*), and opening normal schools for the professional preparation of Catholic school teachers.

While council decrees in 1884 focused on a multitude of educational concerns, covering issues as disparate as defining the course of study for seminaries to suggesting standardized textbooks be used in Catholic schools, the primary debate, and the immediate challenge was opening schools in every parish in the country. Specifically, the council "mandated" that every parish open a school within two years. This decree was part of a broader discussion that took place over at least forty years among powerful bishops, yet this abrupt directive on the school question caught many priests by surprise and raised numerous concerns. A parish school required adequate and ongoing financial support, dedicated and competent teachers, and the positive support of parishioners. On the last point, the council "commanded" Catholic parents to enroll their children in parish schools unless they received a dispensation from the bishop.

The strong emphasis on parochial schools that emerged from the council was enthusiastically received by many Catholics across the nation. The laity joined forces with members of the clergy to plan and finance the opening of parochial schools. Both clergy and laypeople recognized the importance of schools as sites of cultural reproduction of Catholic values, particularly religious education and sacramental preparation. The bedrock of "cultural Catholicism" in the United States was cemented by these schools.

The school question exposed deep ideological and theological divisions among the Catholic bishops in the United States. The breach had many points of contention; but, in regards to education, the issues centered on differing views regarding the assimilation of Catholics into the broader fabric of American life and culture. Michael Augustine Corrigan, Archbishop of New York, and Bernard McQuaid, Bishop of Rochester, led the more conservative faction who favored separate schools for Catholic children and firm alliance with Roman authorities. This group supported a more limited accommodation of American values and ideas while maintaining a unique Catholic (and ethnic) culture. John Ireland, Archbishop of Saint Paul, and John Lancaster Spalding, Bishop of Peoria, represented the "Americanist" contingent who favored greater assimilation of Catholics into American culture. While supporters of this position were not opposed to Catholic schools, they believed that compromise and cooperation with state officials in the area of education was wise and appropriate. For example, Archbishop Ireland adopted the "Poughkeepsie (NY) Plan," an arrangement where local school boards funded Catholic schools, employed religious sisters as civil servants, and maintained facilities in exchange for agreeing not to teach religious subjects during regular school hours, for his schools in Faribault and Stillwater, Minnesota. This program was unpopular with conservative Catholics who argued that it diminished the religious nature of the schools and eventually disappeared by 1900 due to legal and political challenges.

The Third Plenary Council also appointed several bishops to develop a plan for a Catholic university in the United States. The opening of an institution of advanced study for intellectually motivated clerics to pursue philosophy, theology, canon law, and the natural sciences was much needed in the United States. To this point, opportunities for graduate and advanced studies for Catholic priests in the United States were available only in Europe. There was some debate on the location: Ireland favored Washington, DC; Corrigan nominated Seton Hall in New Jersey. One ambitious idea proposed three Catholic universities in the United States, one in the East, one in the Mississippi Valley, and one in the West. Ultimately, the Catholic University of

America opened in 1887 in Washington, DC, providing a Catholic institution for advanced study and research in the United States.

The broader growth of Catholic colleges and universities in the United States was fitful and unfocused throughout most of the nineteenth century. The exact number of institutions is difficult to determine with any degree of accuracy since many were very short-lived and frequently served a specific population, such as members of a particular religious community or individuals studying one specific discipline. In the nineteenth century, nearly 200 Catholic institutions received charters to grant degrees; only one-quarter survived to the twentieth century.[2] Among those that flourished were Mount Saint Mary College (1830), Fordham University (1841), the University of Notre Dame (1842), Saint Thomas of Villanova College (1842), and Loyola University Chicago (1870), all of which remain vibrant.

A number of Catholic colleges began as seminaries to prepare candidates for priestly ordination. For instance, Mount Saint Mary started as a minor seminary to educate teenage boys, but finances and demands for increased enrollments required extending admission to candidates seeking a classical college education. By the midpoint of the nineteenth century, major dioceses and religious orders offered an array of structures to train candidates for the priesthood, ranging from small cathedral colleges conducted by the local bishop to larger free-standing seminaries serving large dioceses. The Society of Saint Sulpice (Sulpicians) and the Congregation of the Mission (Vincentians), founded to staff and administer diocesan seminaries, were recruited by several bishops to assist in the training and formation of future priests in the United States.[3]

The Third Plenary Council did not specifically address Catholic secondary schools apart from some discussion on minor seminaries; however, nearly 700 Catholic secondary schools, coming in the form of colleges, academies, and prep schools, offered a variety of programs, ranging from commercial subjects to classical college-preparatory courses of study. These schools were overwhelmingly single-sex institutions founded by religious orders. Since it was uncommon for working-class youth to pursue secondary education in this period, most

---

[2]   Matthew Garrett, "The Identity of American Catholic Higher Education: A Historical Overview," *Catholic Education: A Journal of Inquiry and Practice* 10:2 (2006): 229–233.

[3]   See Joseph White, "Perspectives on the Nineteenth-Century Diocesan Seminary in the United States," *U.S. Catholic Historian* 19:1 (Winter 2001): 21–35.

Catholic secondary schools in the nineteenth century served a small and wealthy clientele.

The parochial school mandate coincided with a rapid increase in the Roman Catholic population in the United States. Between 1860 and 1890 the Catholic population tripled, compared with a doubling of the general population during the same period. Local bishops faced a myriad of challenges: establishing new parishes, opening schools, attracting priestly vocations, recruiting religious teachers, and, in many cases, pondering approaches to funding these endeavors while serving an overwhelmingly poor and immigrant population. In typical Catholic tradition, pastoral demands exceeded the financial resources of the faithful.

The challenges and setbacks that confronted Catholic schools at the end of the nineteenth century did not overshadow the steady increase in the number of schools, especially in the Northeast and Midwest. In 1900, more than 3,800 schools were funded by local parishes and staffed by numerous congregations of religious women. The total number of students enrolled approached 900,000.[4] However, as the *Catholic Review* accurately noted in 1881, Catholic schools were "little more than a congeries of fortuitous atoms," lacking both administrative structures and organizational strategies.[5] These shortcomings would become more pronounced in the opening decades of the twentieth century as the number of schools grew at a rapid rate to accommodate the needs of a growing Catholic population.

EXPANSION AND CENTRALIZATION, 1900–1945

By 1900, every diocese in the United States, with the single exception of Brownsville, Texas, operated at least one school. Chicago was the largest (a distinction it would retain throughout the twentieth century), followed closely by New York. The pressures facing bishops, pastors, and the laity, as they sought to maintain their commitment to Catholic education, were both extensive and complex. Between 1900 and 1940, the number of parochial schools doubled and the student population nearly tripled, which demanded better strategies to monitor this growth and more efficient structures to attend to the day-to-day affairs of the

---

4   Unless otherwise noted, statistical data throughout this chapter has been drawn from the annual volumes of the *Official Catholic Directory* (New York: Kenedy and Sons).
5   Cited in F. Michael Perko, SJ, ed., *Enlightening the Next Generation: Catholics and Their Schools, 1830–1980* (New York: Garland, 1988), 172.

schools. In short, a more centralized and bureaucratic approach for administering Catholic schools was required.

By 1920, the larger archdioceses – Chicago, New York, and Philadelphia, for example – appointed school superintendents, primarily priests, to represent the bishop in educational matters. These men were responsible for planning and coordinating the expansion of schools, establishing policies and procedures, developing curriculum and instructional materials, liaising with state officials, overseeing finances, and negotiating with religious orders on matters of staffing. The superintendents were frequently assisted by "community supervisors," akin to assistant superintendents, who represented individual religious communities and monitored the schools they operated. At the local level, the pastor and principal were responsible for administering the parish school. This bureaucratic model eventually extended to all parts of the country.

The growing number of Catholic schools in the United States created staffing challenges. While some priests and brothers taught, the overwhelming majority of teachers were Catholic sisters. In 1900, approximately 100 communities of women were teaching in schools; by 1940 that number had doubled. The tradition of recruiting religious communities from Europe was no longer sufficient to meet the demand for teachers. In the minds of many members of the hierarchy, the best approach was to establish teaching communities of women religious within a particular diocese. In many places, these diocesan communities provided a majority of the teachers. One example will suffice: in the Diocese of Brooklyn, the Sisters of Saint Dominic (Amityville) and the Sisters of Saint Joseph (Brentwood) served in 80 percent of the parish schools. In addition to the large communities of religious women, several served particular populations: the Missionary Helpers of the Sacred Heart attended to children who were not enrolled in parochial schools; the Sisters of the Blessed Sacrament ministered to African Americans and Native Americans, and a sizeable number of communities served specific ethnic groups in national parishes.

The Great Depression and World War II hampered the growth of parochial schools due to pressing financial constraints on Catholic parishes and a lack of tradesmen and materials during the war. Between 1920 and 1930, the number of schools grew by nearly 20 percent, from approximately 4,800 to 5,800 (though student population increased by 41 percent, accounting for a rapid increase in class size). The next 20 years (1930–1950) witnessed a continued growth in Catholic schools, albeit at a slower pace, approximating a 4 percent increase each decade.

While the parish elementary school was the main focus of church officials in the first years of the twentieth century, changing attitudes about formal education, growing affluence among some Catholics, and increasing attention to professional preparation in American society required serious reconsideration of the place of Catholic secondary schools. The Catholic preparatory schools for boys and academies for women founded in the nineteenth century were largely elitist institutions delivering a classical education to the sons and daughters of wealthy Americans, both Catholic and Protestant. The changing economy and culture in the United States in the early twentieth century required more egalitarian and broad-based curriculums in Catholic secondary schools. The church and various religious orders responded to these changes by opening comprehensive high schools, technical schools, and commercial and secretarial schools. The comprehensive high schools offered a range of options, including a traditional academic program for those students hoping to enroll in colleges or universities, business courses for those seeking employment in white-collar occupations after high school, and technical education for students pursuing blue-collar positions. Two examples will suffice: Roman Catholic High School for Boys opened in Philadelphia in 1890 offering a tuition-free comprehensive program of studies, and Grace Institute commenced operations in 1897 in New York City providing two years of secretarial training for young women.

As noted earlier, the opening (and closing) of Catholic colleges was erratic and commonly reflected particular needs of a diocese or religious order. The institutions remained firmly single-sex with those for men providing a liberal arts core supplemented with professional preparation and those for women focusing on traditional feminine occupations, particularly teaching and nursing. One significant change in the 1920s was a sustained focus on assessing and improving the academic reputations of Catholic colleges and universities. With a couple of notable exceptions, most did not have rigorous admissions standards, did not employ properly credentialed faculty members, and did not amass large endowments. Insightful college presidents suggested creating a coherent strategy relating to the opening of new institutions, revising curriculum, expanding programmatic offerings, and encouraging competent individuals (mainly Catholic sisters) to earn doctoral degrees at world-class institutions. Ironically, the quest for academic excellence and reform was led by a cadre of sister-presidents in the 1920s and 1930s. A small number of institutions embraced changes and gradually raised their academic profiles (the College of Saint Catherine in St. Paul,

Minnesota, a women's institution run by the Sisters of Saint Joseph, was the first Catholic institution to have a chapter of Phi Beta Kappa), but many Catholic colleges struggled to improve their reputations.

The growing size and prominence of parochial schools instilled fear and anxiety among those committed to maintaining traditional ("Protestant") American values. During the 1920s – the decade fixated on "100% Americanism" – state legislatures, local school boards, and nativist fraternal organizations, including the Ku Klux Klan, united and mobilized to thwart the continued expansion of these schools. The failed Towner-Sterling bill (1922) proposed establishing a federal department of education to provide school funding and to develop a national curriculum to be used across the nation. That same year, the state of Oregon passed legislation requiring parents to send their children to local public schools. Since the law would have effectively eliminated parochial school education in Oregon, the Society of Sisters of the Holy Names of Jesus and Mary, with the support of the US bishops and the National Catholic Welfare Conference, sought an injunction against it in federal court. In *Pierce v. Society of Sisters* (1925), a unanimous Supreme Court ruled the law unconstitutional, arguing that the legislation violated parents' liberty to educate their children as they saw fit. This ruling affirmed the constitutionality of parochial schools and other sectarian institutions. However, this case also upheld that states have the authority to regulate and monitor schools, including private ones.

The positive ruling in the Oregon school case emboldened the church hierarchy and laity to expand the nationwide system of parochial schools. In the mid-1940s, there were approximately 7,500 parochial schools with enrollments reaching 2.5 million students. During the 1950s, the number of schools approached 10,000 with more than 4 million enrolled. The spike after World War II was the result of continued growth in urban areas, along with the baby boom and the movement of many Catholic families into suburban areas.[6]

POSTWAR SURGE, 1945–1965

In the years following World War II, Catholic schools faced two significant challenges: a growing number of school-age children and increasing movement to the suburbs. The number of children seeking admission to Catholic schools grew exponentially between 1950 and 1960; the

---

[6]   "Catholic School Statistics," *The Official Catholic Directory*, 1940–1960.

number nearly doubled that decade. At the same time, Catholics started to relocate to suburban communities that rose up across the nation in the postwar years. Earlier schools were mostly urban, but the increasing number of students, combined with opening new parishes in the burgeoning suburbs, proved to be a two-edged sword for Catholic schools: student populations in urban areas grew simultaneously with the opening of new schools in more bucolic settings. This development pressured infrastructure, complicated finances, and, most importantly, increased demand for competent teachers.

Fortunately, both the baby boom and the suburbanization of the Catholic population coincided with a significant increase in vocations to orders and congregations dedicated to teaching in parochial schools. Most religious communities (both women and men) in the 1950s were admitting double and even triple numbers of novices compared with prewar classes. As a result, in September 1966, 104,000 Catholic sisters were teaching in schools, assisted by nearly 18,000 priests and brothers who primarily taught in secondary schools.[7] Despite the substantial increase in vocations, most religious communities were in the untenable position of accepting only three new missions each year during the 1950s. The larger communities received an average of fifteen requests annually and were pressured to add teaching sisters to their existing missions to accommodate growing student populations. The numeric growth of Catholic schools overwhelmed the capacity of teaching orders to staff all of the classrooms. In the Diocese of Brooklyn, for example, the Sisters of Saint Dominic (Amityville) and the Sisters of Saint Joseph (Brentwood) – the major communities of teachers in the diocese – received nearly 250 novices in 1955, yet in that same year, the number of new classrooms exceeded 400 hundred. In 1960, 40 percent of teachers in Catholic schools in the Diocese of Brooklyn were laypeople.

At the same time, the postwar era ushered in a broader vision of secondary education that the Catholic community enthusiastically embraced. Prior to 1950, approximately 2,300 Catholic secondary schools were serving nearly 600,000 students in the United States. The schools founded after World War II tended to be larger than their predecessors in order to accommodate a growing population of high school students, to be co-institutional (boys on one side; girls on the other), to meet the needs of a specific geographic region, and to be

---

[7]   Tom O'Donoghue, *Come Follow Me and Forsake Temptation: Catholic Schooling and the Recruitment and Retention of Teachers for Religious Teaching Orders, 1922–1965* (New York: Peter Lang, 2004), 42.

located in the suburbs. The postwar schools tended to follow a college preparatory curriculum and attracted a diverse student body. Sweeping campuses and playing fields replaced the vertical structures of prewar Catholic high schools in the inner city.

The prominent role of Catholic colleges and universities in the United States was also evident at the midpoint of the twentieth century. In 1950, approximately 225 institutions of higher learning were operated by religious orders and dioceses. These included major research institutions, such as the University of Notre Dame, Georgetown, and the Catholic University of America, which provided a wide range of academic programs, including undergraduate, professional, and doctoral degrees. However, most were single-sex institutions offering traditional programs in the humanities and undergraduate professional preparation. The generous education benefits associated with the Servicemen's Readjustment Act of 1944 (the G. I. Bill) and additional funding from state and federal sources in the postwar period allowed Catholic colleges to expand and enabled large numbers of students to pursue a college degree. In fact, for the first time, American Catholics from the working classes envisioned and embraced the notion that the baccalaureate, and, in some cases, graduate degrees, were the surest path to a middle-class life.

A unique aspect of Catholic higher education was the small colleges operated by religious orders to train their members. The vast majority were opened by religious sisters to prepare women for the various ministries of a particular community, especially teaching, nursing, and social work. Since these places were small, served a specific population, and were often short-lived, they are often overlooked. It is important to note, however, that institutions like Marywood College in Pennsylvania, Siena Heights College in Michigan, and Brentwood College in New York joined nearly 150 similar institutions that trained several generations of Catholic sisters. By the mid-1960s, many of these sister-training institutions became colleges and universities providing unprecedented educational opportunities for women.

The years following World War II were halcyon days for Catholic schools in the United States. The number of students and schools increased each year; in 1960, nearly 10,000 parish schools educated a student population that exceeded four million students. Approximately one million students attended over 2,000 Catholic secondary schools. The critical role that Catholic education has played in the spiritual and academic preparation of its students is beyond dispute. The Catholic school system prepared generations of students to advance across a broad spectrum of occupations and professions, ranging from civil service to law and medicine. These schools accommodated students of varying intellectual abilities and provided academic programs tailored to individual needs. Rural schools countered the urban elementary schools, prestigious college preparatory schools balanced trade and technical high schools, and sister-training colleges augmented large research universities. In 1965, the Catholic Church in the United States offered the most comprehensive, privately funded school system in the world. The commitment and perseverance of bishops, pastors, the faithful, and, most notably, Catholic sisters, built the Catholic school system.

CHALLENGES OF SUSTAINABILITY, 1965–PRESENT

The 1970s were a decade of massive changes for Roman Catholicism throughout the world. The meetings of the Second Vatican Council (1962–1965) produced documents and decrees that transformed the church. Some of these changes included updating the liturgy to encourage more participation by the laity; mandating religious orders and congregations to reexamine their founding charism and mission; and considering ways that the church could respond to demands in the modern world. These changes were dramatic and did not meet with complete approval by Catholics, yet they certainly marked a shift.

The Council coincided with massive social changes occurring in the United States in the 1960s and 1970s. The opposition to the Vietnam War, the promotion of the civil rights of African Americans, the women's movement, and revelations of political corruption, produced tumult and alienation across the nation. Challenging traditional American norms and values was an essential characteristic of these years and touched every corner of the country, including education. During this era, Catholics reassessed the nature and mission of their educational commitments. Some turned away from Catholic schools in favor of public education; others sought renewal and revitalization amid demographic challenges.

One significant shift was the noticeable difference in the make-up of the teaching staff in Catholic schools. The number of religious teaching in schools dropped from 104,000 in 1966 to 85,000 in 1970, a decline of nearly 20 percent. Many factors account for this decrease including a steep decline in vocations to religious communities, a significant spike in numbers leaving religious life, and a considerable shift towards new (nontraditional) ministries, especially among Catholic sisters. The popular face of parochial schools – Catholic sisters in distinctive garb – faded quickly in the 1970s. This shift required Catholic schools to employ increasing numbers of lay teachers who commanded higher salaries and better benefits than members of religious communities. This change coincided with a significant setback for Catholic schools in the United States Supreme Court. In *Lemon v. Kurtzman* (1971), the court ruled that state aid to sectarian parochial schools violated the religion clauses of the First Amendment and was thus unconstitutional, but allowed for indirect aid like busing and textbooks.

Meanwhile, the suburbanization of American Catholicism continued unabated in the 1960s and 1970s and significantly altered its demographic character. The urban Catholic neighborhood marked by recognizable institutions – church, school, convent, rectory, and frequently gymnasiums and parish halls – receded rapidly during these years. The mass exodus of Catholics to the suburban environs – a visible result of their increasing affluence and educational attainment – occurred alongside a steep decline in the number of priests and religious. As early as the late 1950s, a principal of a Catholic elementary school in Brooklyn commented that the cement had not cured on the latest addition to her school when waves of students transferred to a parish school in suburban Long Island. Both schools, ironically, were served by the same religious community.

The postwar growth of Catholic schools in the suburbs was impressive, yet never matched the scope of those in urban settings. The high-quality public schools that opened in these areas compared favorably with Catholic schools and a growing number of Catholic parents opted to send their children to those schools. Moreover, an increase in the number of lay teachers needed to staff the schools presented financial challenges and forced most parishes to start charging tuition. This idea was foreign to many Catholics who were accustomed to free education supported by the local parish community.

Those remaining in the urban neighborhoods were often poor and unable to support existing institutions financially. The economic pressures eventually forced church officials to make tough decisions, including closing and consolidating schools. In 1980, 2.2 million students attended 7,800 parish schools and nearly 500,000 enrolled in Catholic secondary schools. The decline of Catholic schools between 1970 and 1980 eerily mirrored the incline of the 1950s and 1960s. It was a complete reversal of fortunes: 20 percent both ways.

The ongoing decline in enrollments, particularly in parish elementary schools, led many dioceses and religious orders to consider new organizational structures. In places where consolidation of schools appeared to be the appropriate solution, regional schools (sometimes called "Catholic academies") replaced parish schools. Also, new types of structures emerged that promoted an entirely new philosophy of Catholic education better positioned for the realities of the twenty-first century. This included initiatives like the Cristo Rey network, which solicits financial support from the business community and philanthropic foundations to replace funding historically provided by members of the local parish. Also, the number of single-sex secondary schools declined significantly after 1980; some closed and many more became coeducational.

The National Catholic Education Association reported in 2016 that approximately 5,000 elementary schools and 1,200 secondary schools enrolled over two million students. While closures and consolidations have stabilized in the twenty-first century, a steady and consistent decline continues in all parts of the United States. More startling, however, is the fact that nearly 98 percent of administrators and teachers in Catholic schools are laypeople. Despite challenges and set-backs, the Catholic school system remains the largest privately funded educational endeavor in the United States.

A definite bright spot for Catholic education since the 1970s is the continuing growth and increasing quality of Catholic colleges and universities in the United States. While total numbers have declined, the number of students has increased steadily. Approximately 221 institutions are serving 720,000 students in the twenty-first century. Among these institutions are prestigious and world-class research universities: University of Notre Dame, Georgetown University, Boston College, and Villanova University; places committed to a humanities-based curriculum: College of the Holy Cross, University of Dayton, Loyola College of Maryland, Santa Clara University; and a large number of midsize teaching institutions serving first-generation college students. These institutions attract a very diverse student population; many are non-Catholic, recent immigrants, and from racial and ethnic groups underrepresented in American higher education.

The ongoing contributions of Catholic institutions of higher learning continue to shape intellectual life in the United States. Catholic colleges and universities offer a wide array of academic programs, ranging from community colleges to doctoral-granting institutions. Georgetown University and the University of Notre Dame are ranked among the best institutions in the nation. Most of these colleges and universities adopted the directives of the *Land O' Lakes Statement*, drafted in 1967 by a diverse group of college and university leaders under the leadership of Father Theodore Hesburgh, CSC, president of the University of Notre Dame, which affirmed the academic and legal freedom of Catholic higher education from interference from the church hierarchy. In practical terms, this resulted in severing formal relations between colleges and universities and their founding orders and congregations, as well as establishing lay boards to govern institutional operations. With notable exceptions – including the Franciscan University of Steubenville (Ohio), Thomas Aquinas College (California), and Ave Maria University (Florida), which espouse fidelity to church teachings as their primary mission – most Catholic institutions of higher learning are private, albeit with unique missions within the Catholic tradition.

Since the implementation of the reforms of the Second Vatican Council – now, over fifty years ago – the Catholic Church in the United States has undergone a sweeping and, at times, a traumatic transformation of its core beliefs and values and its place in American society. In many respects, these changes were most apparent in the diminishing size and stature of Catholic education across the nation because schools were the public face of the church. Yet regardless of religion or politics, most Americans would point to education as the most significant contribution of Catholicism to the nation.

CONCLUSION

The multiple contributions of the Catholic Church to formal education in the United States deserve careful consideration and proper recognition. In the early period, educational institutions founded by the church commonly preceded endeavors by public entities. The comprehensive scope of Catholic education – elementary schools, secondary schools, technical schools, practical educational institutions, junior colleges, sister-training colleges, baccalaureate institutions, and universities – is rivaled only by state-sponsored systems. Although the intellectual, social, and financial contributions of Catholic education in the United States are impossible to determine with any measure of accuracy, there is no dispute that the Catholic Church and numerous religious orders established the most significant private system of education in history.

The importance of Catholic schools in the United States is best measured on three levels: first, the meteoric rise of the socioeconomic status of American Catholics; second, the preservation of the Catholic faith tradition; and finally, the persistence of the church and the faithful to provide schools serving a wide range of students. Clearly, these schools provided opportunities for generations of young Catholics to take positions in all strata of American society. Catholics are well-represented in the professions, business community, and local and national politics. The bedrock of these achievements is Catholic schools. In addition, those who attend Catholic schools, particularly those who attend both a parochial elementary school and a Catholic high school, are more likely to identify as Catholic. Finally, both church officials and leaders of religious orders continue actively to support new forms of Catholic education to meet the needs of the poor and recent immigrants.

The Catholic schools of the twenty-first century in some respects have reverted to their historical origins, private academies and preparatory schools for wealthy students. The tuition-free parish schools and heavily subsidized secondary schools have disappeared forever. Happily, a sizeable number of inner city students, mostly African American and Latino, are being served by Catholic schools with very different organizational and financial structures. In many cities, Catholic schools receive funds from private individuals and corporate supporters. In most secondary schools, tuition-assistance programs provide aid to reduce the burden of high tuitions. In the final analysis, however, there are never enough seats or adequate funds to meet the pressing needs of these schools.

In conclusion, the opening of the Ursuline Academy in New Orleans in 1727 ignited a mythical connection between the Catholic Church and its schools in the imagination of most Americans. The memories of generations of students adorned in solid pants and plaid dresses marching into thousands of local schools still resonate with many Catholics who attended these schools, and others who lived close to those institutions. In many cases, this may be their most enduring encounter with the church. The consistent goal of Catholic education was to meet the spiritual and intellectual needs of successive generations of children, ranging from school-age immigrants in the nineteenth century who spoke little English to undergraduates at top Catholic universities in the twenty-first century. The Catholic school system – which peaked at over 10,000 parish schools, 2,300 secondary schools, and 250 colleges and universities – was the product of a grand vision that captivated the imagination of the entire community: bishops, pastors, religious teachers, lay parishioners, and millions of students. It was a uniquely American phenomenon, funded by private contributions, staffed by faithful teachers, and supported by the laity. In addition to fulfilling its primary mission of providing a solid religious education, these institutions readied generations of Catholics to attend college and pursue professional training and to join the middle class. The years following World War II were a highpoint for Catholics due, in large part, to the outstanding success of Catholic schools, which prepared them to take full advantage of economic opportunities and to join the mass migration to the suburbs.

FURTHER READING

Brinig, Margaret and Nicole Garnett. *Lost Classroom, Lost Community: Catholic Schools' Importance in Urban America.* Chicago: University of Chicago Press, 2014.

Dolan, Jay P. *The American Catholic Experience: A History from Colonial Times to the Present.* Garden City, NY: Doubleday, 1985.

Gleason, Philip. *Contending with Modernity: Catholic Higher Education in the United States.* New York: Oxford University Press, 1995.

Hunt, Thomas, et al. *Urban Catholic Education: The Best of Times, The Worst of Times.* New York: Peter Lang, 2013.

Oates, Mary J., CSJ. "The Development of Catholic Colleges for Women, 1895–1960." *U.S. Catholic Historian* 7:4 (Fall 1988): 413–428.

Perko, F. Michael, SJ, ed. *Enlightening the Next Generation: Catholics and Their Schools, 1830–1980.* New York: Garland Publishing, 1988.

Walch, Timothy. *Parish School: American Catholic Parochial Education From Colonial Times to the Present.* New York: Crossroad Publishing, 1996.

White, Joseph. *The Diocesan Seminary in the United States: A History from the 1780s to the Present.* Notre Dame, IN: University of Notre Dame Press, 1990.

7 Social Welfare and Social Reform

MARY ELIZABETH BROWN

The Catholic Church in the United States includes among its institutions a vast social welfare network that has been important for countless individuals, including the Catholics who support it, the Catholics who benefit from it, and the non-Catholics who have been recipients of its services. This essay provides a narrative of that development, identifying the key characters and turning points from the eighteenth century to the present day. It explores the intersection of "American" and "Catholic": what the church learned from the American culture around it, and what the church contributed to it through its teachings about charity and its example of putting those teachings into action.

In contrast with today's notion of philanthropy, Catholics historically used the word *charity* to describe the key motivations for their work. By the end of the nineteenth century, however, assisting individuals through charity was deemed insufficient when not accompanied by efforts to address the sources of their problems through *social action*. This shift conveyed the idea that those in need are partners in resolving problems, and that individual problems are rooted in social conditions. By the end of the twentieth century, social action was seen as an activity with the goal of achieving *social justice*, which conveys a sense of giving individuals in society their due, so that those in need get what they need to live as human beings.

The transition in Catholic thought and action from individuals performing acts of charity that benefited other individuals to a search for social justice that benefited the whole community was shaped by multiple factors: changing human needs, changes in church resources for meeting those needs, evolving interaction with other groups in US society, and the developing thought of Catholic theologians, scholars, and pastors. These factors point to a rich tradition of social welfare work and social activism that has had a major impact on the United States in various realms, including health care, immigration, and labor. In the process, the Catholic tradition of social welfare and social reform has changed the lives of countless individuals, added to the services communities could offer their members, and contributed to the American conversation about what constitutes the best care for those in need.

FROM INCEPTION TO 1845

The Protestant Reformation, which began shortly after Columbus's voyages, stimulated interest in questions of salvation, and, of particular interest to the development of charity, whether souls were saved by "faith" or by "works." In France, Vincent de Paul (1581–1660) emphasized obedience to the biblical command of care of the poor as the standard for judging Christian life, a view that inspired the work of his religious congregation and others. The Daughters of Charity that de Paul founded together with Louise de Marillac (1591–1660) relied on the support of benefactors, together with their own voluntary poverty, to sustain their charitable activities. Other communities of women religious adopted a similar model of a life shared with the poor. The model carried over to the Americas, where religious communities took the lead in establishing schools, hospitals, and other social welfare institutions.

Among the pioneering figures in establishing a tradition of Catholic charity in the United States is Elizabeth Ann Bayley Seton (1774–1821). Indeed, it was charity that drew Seton to Catholicism: she converted partly in response to the kindness shown to her by her husband's Catholic business partner's family when her husband fell ill and died. In 1809, upon the invitation of Bishop John Carroll, she relocated from her native New York to Emmitsburg, Maryland, where she founded a community of women religious. Influenced by Vincent de Paul and his Daughters of Charity, she adopted their rule for her own community, which she called the Sisters of Charity of Saint Joseph.

Alongside their pioneering work in parochial schooling, the influence of the Vincentian model allowed Seton's Sisters of Charity to undertake varied services the church needed in its early years, including the institutional care of children. Their institutions, the first of which opened in Philadelphia in 1814, were usually called "orphanages" and took in children who might have lost both parents or only one parent (leaving the other unable to be both breadwinner and caretaker), or who had two living but uninvolved parents. In their work, they emphasized supporting the family, not just the child, with the goal of reuniting children with their families whenever possible.

Health care was another important manifestation of charity and played a role in shaping the image of Catholicism. In 1734, Ursuline nuns in New Orleans opened the first Catholic hospital in what is now the United States. Among the nation's oldest Catholic institutions founded specifically for the care of the sick was the Baltimore Infirmary, opened by Elizabeth Ann Seton's community in Emmitsburg. Women religious also expanded their efforts in emergencies. The 1832 cholera epidemic brought many sisters temporarily into nursing, and gave them a permanent reputation for heroism in the face of deadly disease.

By the 1830s, two lines of development in American Catholic charity had become clear. The first was that charity began, if not at home then close to it, with Catholic communities organizing for the care of their own. However, in the process of caring for their own, Catholics were also contributing to the institutional life of the secular communities around them, and creating an image of Catholicism in the American mind.

FAMINE MIGRATION THROUGH WORLD WAR I

A second period in American Catholic charity opened in the 1840s with the Irish potato famine and lasted until 1920, when Catholics institutionalized their response to World War I. While one might argue the Progressive Era that began in the 1890s introduced new philosophies supporting charitable action and new institutions to carry it out, this eighty-year period is held together by the emphasis on action at the local level. As the Vatican established more and more dioceses to structure Catholic life in the United States, each one developed its own charitable institutions. Some of these, such as the maritime ministry, were found only in certain areas. Others were quite common: most dioceses made provision for the care for the sick. However, not until World War I were national institutions created to address cross-diocesan problems.

Although the years are not synchronous, the trajectory of charity might be summed up in the life of Blandina Segale (1850–1941). Born Rosa Maria Segale in Ciccagna, Genoa, she came to the United States as a child with her family and settled in Cincinnati, where she joined the Sisters of Charity. From 1872 to 1894 she served on the frontier; her adventures there were published in 1931 as *At the End of the Santa Fe Trail*. Recalled to Cincinnati in 1897, she and her birth sister, also a member of the Sisters of Charity, were charged with the care of Italian immigrants. They organized the Santa Maria Institute, modeled after settlement houses, and in a step unusual for the time, affiliated it with the local nondenominational community chest to contribute to its economic security. Sister Blandina's career reflects the main thrust of this period. When she entered the Sisters of Charity, the emphasis was still on charitable work. But as the number of Catholic immigrants increased, charity workers became increasingly attentive to the impoverishing effects of industrialism and developed new institutions to meet changing needs.

For the next century, the most important charity remained the care of children. While many communities of women religious continued to open orphanages, an innovation in child care took place in the work of Father John Christopher Drumgoole (1816–1888). The only son of a widowed mother, he served as a sexton at Saint Mary's church on Manhattan's Lower East Side, where he opened the church to the neighborhood's homeless children. When he became a priest, he responded to the work of Charles Loring Brace and other Protestant reformers who advocated sending children to rural areas for adoption, a system ripe for labor exploitation. Drumgoole advanced another alternative: placing children in a Catholic institution that offered them the benefits of a rural environment. He purchased a tract on Staten Island's south shore, invited the School Sisters of Saint Francis to staff it, and developed it into the Mission of the Immaculate Virgin of Mount Loretto. The property still hosts children's residences, since 2016 as part of the Catholic Charities of Staten Island.

By the end of the nineteenth century, new understandings of child development prompted Catholics and others to reexamine institutional child care. Father Edward J. Flanagan (1886–1948) created an institution that incorporated a number of notable reforms. His "Boys Town" outside of Omaha, Nebraska, housed small groups of boys in "cottages," under the supervision of adults who promoted various aspect of their development. Boys Town structured community life so the boys were citizens rather than inmates, voting for a Boy Mayor and exercising responsibilities rather than being assigned tasks.

During the nineteenth and early twentieth centuries, Catholic health care also followed the pattern of expanding service within an increasingly urban, industrial, immigrant, and diocesan-oriented framework. During the nineteenth and early twentieth centuries, Catholic health care evolved from emergency service in epidemics to a full-time ministry. In New York City, the Sisters of Charity founded Saint Vincent's Hospital in 1849, just at the time a cholera epidemic hit the city. Later in the century, Mother Frances Xavier Cabrini (1850–1917) founded hospitals in New York, Chicago, and Seattle to meet the needs of Italian immigrants.

The career of Marianne Cope (1838–1918) shows how a religious community that focused on a particular mission could, over time, expand its understanding of its calling to adapt to a more secular understanding of a profession. Born Maria Anna Barbara Koob in the Grand Duchy of Hesse to parents who emigrated to the United States the following year, she entered the Sisters of Saint Francis of Syracuse in 1862. By 1870, she was elected to the community's governing council and helped steer the community toward hospital work. As Superior of Saint Joseph's Hospital in Syracuse, she implemented the new theories of antisepsis, which taught that a clean environment could prevent germs from reaching patients and causing disease. She participated in the movement to improve medical training by welcoming medical school graduates to serve as interns, and required that patients be informed who was treating them and why so that patients retained some agency in their care. By 1883, in response to a request from the native Hawaiian government, she left her position as Superior General of her community to assist Father Damien DeVeuster by running a hospital for Hansen's Disease (leprosy) patients.

The nineteenth century also saw Catholics recognize several new groups as persons in need of charitable attention and develop institutions to respond to their needs. Among them, considerable attention was devoted to women, partly because nineteenth-century ideology argued females needed protection, and partly because women truly were vulnerable to sexual and economic exploitation. The Sisters of Mercy, founded in Ireland in 1831, established shelters for girls and young women, offering them education and training for domestic service. The Sisters of the Good Shepherd, founded in France in 1835, extended domestic-service training to women whose sex lives deviated from the ideal. In 1869, Sister Mary Irene Fitzgibbon (1823–1896) of the Sisters of Charity established the New York Foundling Asylum, which provided both care for infants and support for mothers. Recognizing the dire economic conditions that led many to give up their children, the sisters employed mothers to nurse the infants under their care. This arrangement provided women with a means of financial support and allowed them to preserve maternal bonds.

The other group that received much charitable attention in the nineteenth century was immigrants. While almost all American Catholic charities borrowed from European models, the care of immigrants required real interaction between European and American institutions. The pioneer was Peter Paul Cahensly (1838–1923), who in 1866 organized the Saint Raphael Society for the Protection of German Catholic Emigrants, with an office at the port of Hamburg. In 1889, the Saint Raphael Society (named for the patron saint of travelers), in cooperation with the German Central Verein in the United States and the Archdiocese of New York, opened Leo House, named for Pope Leo XIII, to provide inexpensive meals and hotel facilities for those detained in New York by untimely transportation connections or other circumstances. Charlotte Grace O'Brien, daughter of Irish patriot William Smith O'Brien, focused on the care of Irish immigrant women traveling alone, and led the Archdiocese of New York to create the Mission of the Holy Rosary on property in Lower Manhattan where Elizabeth Ann Bayley Seton had once lived. Another significant figure in the field was Bishop Giovanni Battista Scalabrini (1839–1905), who organized a congregation of male religious to minister to migrants in transit and in their new homes. He helped organize three communities of women religious and created an Italian Saint Raphael Society to further advance this work.

The late nineteenth century also saw the first sustained efforts at charity across racial lines. Catholic missionaries had long been involved in evangelizing Native American tribes. In 1873, the US bishops appointed Charles B. Ewing, formerly a Civil War general, to work toward a greater Catholic presence in the Indian missions. The next year, the bishops created the Bureau of Catholic Indian Missions, with Ewing as Commissioner. In addition to raising funds to support missionary activity, the bureau also pressed the government to assign Catholic clergy to work on the reservations. Although the federal government looked to religious denominations to Christianize native peoples and introduce them to white American ways, the results were not always what government officials expected: the Catholic Church often recruited clergy and sisters from non-English-speaking parts of Europe to serve in this field.

Katharine Drexel (1858–1955) pushed the boundaries of Catholic charity in her day by working across racial lines to include both Native and African Americans in her ministry. The second of three girls (two sisters and a half-sister) born to a wealthy, cultivated, and devout Philadelphia family, Katharine was exposed in her youth to hands-on charity by her stepmother. She became aware of African Americans' special needs through her brother-in-law, Edward de Veaux Morrell, a Republican Congressman who supported the rights of newly freed blacks, and of the special needs of Native Americans by seeing first-hand the conditions on reservations in the Far West. When she and her sisters came into their inheritance in 1885, Katharine began using the money to assist Catholic missionary outreach. She later founded a new religious order, the Sisters of the Blessed Sacrament, to work among the black and Indian communities.

Amid these efforts, Catholics began to reassess the causes and nature of poverty, from seeing it as a result of misfortune to viewing it as rooted in underlying social conditions in need of reform. Labor activists often took the lead in rethinking the nature of economic inequality. Those in power, though, tended to treat all questioning of capitalism as radical. A case in point came in the 1886 New York City mayoral campaign of Henry George, who advocated a tax on the unearned increase in land value as a way to address the problem of investors who focused on personal financial return instead of the community good. When Father Edward McGlynn (1837–1900) campaigned in favor of George, he was excommunicated not just because he disobeyed an episcopal order to desist but because of the reform he was advocating, which Archbishop Michael Augustine Corrigan considered too radical.

Another controversy concerned the Knights of Labor, an organization founded in 1869 that attracted significant working-class Catholic support in the 1880s partly because its leader, Terence V. Powderly (1849–1924), was Catholic. Like many organizations, the Knights required members to keep its plans secret, which made the organization seem more dangerous than it was and also led the clergy to worry penitents would keep their vow of secrecy rather than making adequate confessions. The Vatican's Congregation for the Propagation of the Faith, which at the time oversaw American Catholic affairs, undertook to resolve the pastoral issue. Cardinal James Gibbons (1834–1921), Archbishop of Baltimore, sent a "memorial" to Rome arguing that Americans were forging a new path that deserved forbearance; he painted a contrast between a Europe in which working classes were deserting the church and an America in which well-educated Catholics brought church teaching into political and economic society through membership in and even leadership of organizations such as the Knights of Labor.

Amid the rise of Progressive Era reform, Catholics took inspiration and impetus from the writings of Pope Leo XIII, whose 1891 encyclical *Rerum Novarum* served as a foundational document in modern Catholic social teaching. In it, Pope Leo XIII applied church teaching to industrial society. One emphasis was on the "dignity" (derived from the Latin word for "worth") of human beings, which was innate, not derived from their usefulness to the economic system. It followed that people participated in the economy *as people*, and that labor was not just something capitalists used to produce goods, but individuals with rights and responsibilities. The emphasis on individual dignity also led Leo to introduce a second principle, subsidiarity, whereby responsibility fell to the lowest level of social organization that could accomplish the task. As individual workers were overmatched vis-à-vis employers, they should be able to organize among themselves. However, given the imbalance between workers and employers that the economy created, Leo argued, it was incumbent on the state to intervene to insure the type of economic security that respected workers' dignity.

One person whose life's work was influenced by *Rerum Novarum* was John A. Ryan (1869–1945), who first read the encyclical while studying for the priesthood. It continued to guide his thought during his graduate studies at the Catholic University of America, where his dissertation became the foundation for his 1906 book, *A Living Wage*, which applied Catholic moral teachings on labor and economic life to concrete realities. Although many aspects of his work reinforced the "separate spheres" concept of gender of his time and place, he used those principles to advocate for equal pay for both sexes. Otherwise, employers would gravitate toward women, who typically earned less. Ryan wanted employers to gravitate toward men, who would marry and use their wages to support wives who tended husbands, households, and as many children as naturally occurred. Ryan later contributed to the developing Catholic critique of birth control, and of a society that commodified children by arguing parents should have no more than they could "afford."

By the eve of the First World War, two developments in American Catholic history were reinforcing each other. In diocese after diocese, generations of Catholics had organized welfare institutions that provided systematic care to those in need, mostly women, children, and the sick and injured, but also, depending upon local populations, immigrants and racial minorities. Meanwhile, Ryan's arguments for an economy that recognized human dignity spread through American Catholicism as clergy trained at the Catholic University took their places in parishes, in diocesan administration, and in other institutions of higher education. The two sources of authority, church teaching and lived experience, supported the trends of the early twentieth century: ever-greater systemization of charity, and, as part of the systemization, investigations into the causes of poverty and experimentation with means to prevent it.

FROM WORLD WAR I TO VATICAN II

The period from the end of World War I through the reforms of the Second Vatican Council saw the steady reorganization of American Catholic charity. Inspired individuals could still make generous contributions, as performer Danny Thomas did in 1962 when, in fulfillment of a vow, he established Saint Jude's Hospital, which continues to conduct research into childhood cancer and to use that knowledge to treat patients free of charge. By and large, however, the emphasis shifted from individual and localized action to corporate effort directed under centralized, hierarchical auspices. This new shift had some advantages; the hierarchy, for example, could cultivate leadership and command the resources needed to support charitable institutions. The Catholic Church was in a position to *think* about charity as well as to conduct it, and to bring the church's social teaching to bear on the social issues of the day.

The nation's entry into World War I in 1917 led to an expansion of Catholic charitable organizations. The Knights of Columbus, a men's social organization founded in 1887, established centers offering recreational activities to military personnel. In 1917, the American Catholic hierarchy established the National Catholic War Council to organize national fundraising, aid soldiers and servicemen, meet domestic needs that arose from the war, and communicate with Catholics about the war effort. The next year, the hierarchy established a program to train women in social work.

The war proved the usefulness of a national approach to national issues. An episcopal steering committee asked Father John Ryan to draft what became the 1919 *Bishops' Program of Social Reconstruction*. In the document, Ryan laid out a series of "practical proposals" based on the church's traditional teachings on social and industrial conditions. The program identified desirable outcomes such as a minimum wage, "social [old-age] insurance," and standards of occupational health and safety that precluded child labor. It adopted the principle of subsidiarity in advocating means for achieving these goals. This meant that society should rely on the smallest social unit that could solve the problem so that a charitable individual might meet a local need, a labor union could negotiate for a particular trade or business, and federal law might be required to address national issues. The *Bishops' Program* also signaled a Catholic effort to transform society by advocating for programs that would serve as a social safety net.

The hierarchy's national efforts in World War I found an echo in individual bishops' efforts, as they began establishing centralized

Catholic Charities bureaus on the diocesan level. This move toward greater centralization allowed for greater episcopal control, but it also positioned church leaders to ensure compliance with state and local standards and to impose their own. It allowed for greater planning, as the bishop could survey the diocese, identify needs, and then find a way to meet them rather than waiting for a religious order to respond. Catholic Charities also transformed models of funding. They limited individual organizations' fundraising and instituted diocesan-wide collections, the proceeds of which were distributed to charities according to diocesan leadership's perception of the need.

Yet alongside this trend toward centralization, localized action still persisted. During the 1930s, Catholic social teaching found an active advocate in Dorothy Day (1897–1980), the cofounder of the Catholic Worker movement, which established "houses" in multiple locations, from rural farms to urban settlement-type homes. She and other Catholic workers embraced a "radical" approach to poverty: "radical" in that it borrowed from Marxist thought and emphasis on how the concept of private property enriched some at the expense of others, "radical" in that it called upon the church's medieval history in challenging modern capitalism, and "radical" in its ability to see the interconnections between issues of war and peace and issues of wealth and poverty. Similarly, Day advocated a "radical" approach to peace in forswearing violence. Day, though, did not usually call hers a "radical" program. She emphasized love. For all her calls for specific reforms, what she really called for was love of neighbor. And for all her participation in protests, she was sure that love – not the violence of war or even violent protest – was the only way to reach that goal.

Catholic Workers, though, were a distinct minority. Much more popular, albeit briefly, was Charles Coughlin (1891–1979), who gave voice to Catholic views on politics and the economy during the Great Depression. Founding pastor of the Shrine of the Little Flower in Royal Oak, Michigan, Coughlin pioneered Catholic radio, broadcasting locally in 1926 and going national in 1930. Coughlin also expanded media outlets, publishing *Social Justice* magazine and organizing a politically influential National Union for Social Justice. Coughlin initially supported President Franklin Roosevelt's New Deal, but soon saw FDR's monetary policies as the same sort of currency manipulation Midwesterners had opposed during the Populism of the 1890s, which eventually led him down a well-trod path to virulent anti-Semitism. Although a combination of episcopal and governmental action shut down Coughlin's media outlets, his message politicized the Catholic populace and stirred up the call for government action.

During the New Deal era, Catholics became powerful champions of the rights of labor, as exemplified by the work of a generation of "labor priests." Monsignor Francis J. Haas (1889–1953) worked for the National Labor Relations Board as a mediator. In a later generation, Father John Corridan, SJ, a native New Yorker serving at the Jesuits' Xavier Institute of Industrial Relations in Manhattan became involved in longshoremen's labor issues; his activities were later fictionalized in the 1954 movie *On the Waterfront*. Although these Catholic labor activists were in agreement on fundamental principles, they held mixed opinions on other issues, like whether unions should organize workers by skills or by industry. Father John P. Monaghan, SJ, for instance, helped to organize the Association of Catholic Trade Unionists, which emphasized unions organized by skill. In contrast, Father Robert E. Lucey (1891–1977), the future Archbishop of San Antonio, started his reputation as a reformer advocating for the Congress of Industrial Organizations (CIO), which advocated one union for all those working in a particular industry.

While much thinking about labor justice developed in industrial settings, agriculture also received attention. Peter Maurin's emphasis on Catholic Worker farms is an early example. Later, Monsignor Luigi Ligutti (1895–1983), an Italian immigrant to rural Iowa, became part of the National Catholic Rural Life Conference in 1924, and ended his career as Vatican liaison to the United Nations Food and Agricultural Organization.

As it was for the New Deal itself, race was a niche issue for 1930s Catholic social teaching, of interest mostly to Catholics who were or who had contact with African Americans. The most famous of the latter was Father John LaFarge, SJ (1880–1963), founder of the Catholic Interracial Council of New York and advocate for racial justice. LaFarge's very being symbolized the problems of overcoming racism. Descended from Benjamin Franklin and Oliver Hazard Perry, a son of wealth and of a famous artist, LaFarge had a hard time avoiding a patronizing attitude toward other people. Also, LaFarge's strategy was reform from the top–down, disseminating church teaching via his own writings, his role as an editor of the Jesuits' *America* magazine, and his participation in drafting an encyclical on racism for Pope Pius XI, rather than supporting African-American Catholics' vision for themselves and their efforts to attain it.

Refugee care was another niche issue. In the 1930s, the National Catholic Welfare Conference's Bureau of Immigration carried out the wishes of the US hierarchy and assisted the German Saint Raphael Society in aiding non-Aryan Catholics affected by the Nuremberg Law in Germany and other nations under Nazi occupation. NCWC officials found their work hampered by a lack of legislation specifically for refugees and by limits on all migration that had been imposed in the 1920s. However, they did not call for change in US immigration law, fearful that the public would be concerned about adding to the Depression's unemployment problem.

On the broader topic of immigration, however, Catholics were especially active in the fight to repeal discriminatory laws and quota-based restrictions. The example of Italian Americans is instructive. As World War II came to a close in Italy, the American-born son of an Italian immigrant language professor, Juvenal Marchisio, took a leave from his position as a judge in Brooklyn's Family Court to head American Relief for Italy, an agency that gathered the results of local food and clothing drives, transported the goods to Italy, and worked with government and the private sector to distribute them. The experience taught Marchisio that immigration was a factor in long-term economic recovery. When in 1952, under the leadership of the Irish-American Catholic Senator from Nevada Pat McCarren, Congress failed to lift immigration restrictions that affected Italy, Marchisio became president of a new organization, the American Committee on Italian Migration (ACIM), dedicated first to obtaining special legislation to meet emergencies such as floods that required the relocation of populations in Italy, and then to a complete end to the laws that treated Italian immigrants as less desirable than others. ACIM also pioneered collaborative efforts, working with secular organizations and with organizations based in other faiths to advocate for the passage of immigration reform.

As World War II turned into the Cold War, American Catholic charitable institutions became a part of US efforts abroad. Catholic War Services was founded in 1943 to alleviate suffering in World War II. In 1955, it renamed itself Catholic Relief Services, emphasizing its move into technical and economic development designed to sustain human security, and it used federal funds to carry out its programs. But participation in the Cold War could at times endanger Catholic credibility, as seen in the career of Doctor Thomas A. Dooley III (1927–1961), who became a celebrity among American Catholics for his work in Vietnam among refugees from the communist North and then in a clinic in Laos. Recruited by the CIA, Dooley used his position to gather intelligence and built on the authority of his reputation to falsify the extent of communist atrocities in Vietnam.

The election of the Catholic John F. Kennedy (1917–1963) to the presidency in 1960 was an important marker in American Catholic charity and social teaching. Although Kennedy himself was not particularly outspoken on social reform, he supported those who brought their religious values to bear on public life. Most notably, Kennedy appointed Sargent Shriver (1915–2011) to head the Peace Corps in part because he knew his brother-in-law to be loyal and efficient, but also because Shriver brought to the job a commitment to service that owed something to his approach to his faith. As he looked forward to running for reelection in 1964, Kennedy began to think of advocating antipoverty programs, drawing inspiration from Dwight MacDonald's *New Yorker* review of former Catholic Worker Michael Harrington's *The Other America*, which called attention to the persistent poverty present in the midst of America's postwar economic expansion.

Under the Johnson administration, Shriver brought Catholic thought to bear on the War on Poverty through his work as head of the agency directing it, the Office of Economic Opportunity. Although some of the agency's projects would prove controversial – particularly urban renewal efforts that greatly affected those living in "blighted" inner city neighborhoods, Catholics among them – considerable funding flowed toward causes that Catholics had long championed. Student assistance in the form of Pell grants and work-study programs aided Catholic colleges and universities, while funding from Medicare and Medicaid enabled Catholic healthcare institutions to sustain the care they provided to the sick and the elderly.

Support for the war in Vietnam, however, proved a greater test of Catholic convictions. There were some Catholics, such as Cardinal Francis Spellman, who accepted Johnson's actions as a necessary part of the policy of containing communism. Beginning in 1965, however, aspects of the conflict troubled even those who accepted the idea that war was sometimes necessary. The issue came to the attention of the general public when a Catholic pacifist, Roger Allen LaPorte (1943–1965), borrowed a form of protest already in use among Vietnamese Buddhists and set himself on fire in front of the United Nations headquarters in New York in November of that year. The protest movement soon escalated from street demonstrations to civil disobedience. Philip Berrigan (1923–2002) and his brother Daniel (1921–2016) provided both the philosophical underpinnings that guided this development and much of the actual protest. Along with author Thomas Merton (1915–1968) and a number of people of many different faiths, they helped to form Clergy and Laity Concerned About Vietnam

(CALCAV) in 1965. Their most famous action came in 1968, when the Berrigans and several other activists entered the Selective Service office in Catonsville, Maryland, stole 378 draft records, and set them aflame in the office's parking lot. Daniel Berrigan extended the reach of the action by using it as material for a play, *The Catonsville Nine*.

By the third quarter of the twentieth century, Catholics had made significant contributions to the way American society cared for its needy. Catholic teaching on labor was part of the support that within seventy-five years turned the miserably impoverishing industrial jobs of the early twentieth century into "good" jobs that Americans were afraid to lose. Catholic advocacy helped focus immigration law on human rights and family unity. The benefits of these changes also flowed toward Catholic institutions. Medicaid, Medicare, educational legislation, and funds from the War on Poverty allowed Catholic hospitals, nursing homes, educational institutions, and even parishes to do more for those in their care. The rise of an educated laity also offered the promise that Catholic thought would extend beyond the institutional church to the human community.

VATICAN II AND THE FIFTY YEARS AFTER

The reforms of the Second Vatican Council led American Catholics to re-evaluate their institutions and responses to social needs. On the national level, the US bishops implemented a restructuring plan in 1969, splitting the NCWC into the National Conference of Catholic Bishops, which focused on internal ecclesiastical concerns, and the United States Catholic Conference, which presented Catholic social teaching to society and addressed national social concerns. In 1973, the hierarchy's reaction to the Supreme Court decision *Roe v. Wade* launched a new development in which the bishops more frequently issued statements about Catholic social teaching on current events. Their willingness to speak out on policy matters and lay out moral responses to controversial issues can be read as a sign of how the US church had reached a stage of development at which the bishops no longer feared the charge that Catholics were disloyal when they disagreed with a national consensus.

A key figure shaping the bishops' response to social issues during the post–Vatican II period was Cardinal Joseph Bernardin (1928–1996). Born to Italian immigrants who had settled in South Carolina, Bernardin was ordained for the Diocese of Charleston in 1952. In 1968, he became the first General Secretary of the National Conference of Catholic

Bishops, and the innovator behind the hierarchy's Campaign for Human Development, a national antipoverty initiative. Bernardin's experience with that effort later shaped his most important work, *A Consistent Ethic of Life* (1984), which introduced the metaphor of right-to-life issues as a "seamless garment" (John 19:23). Bernardin argued that all issues that threatened life needed to be viewed and evaluated holistically. The work is sometimes considered an effort to reconcile two approaches, one arguing for the primacy of individual decisions about specific lives, especially in cases of abortion, and the other arguing for the importance of bringing ethics to bear on the scourges of poverty and war. Bernardin also raised concerns about intellectual frontiers Catholics had yet to explore, such as medical advances that called into question when life really began or ended. His "seamless" garment approach meant that nothing was too far from the bishops' mandate to preach and teach and that Catholics who focused on pro-life and Catholics who focused on anti-war issues were still bound together by common values.

The attention the bishops gave to *Roe v. Wade* helped to popularize Bernadin's book by raising questions about other issues that called the value of life into question, such as the suicide of the terminally ill and those suffering from chronic pain, or the use of the death penalty. In 1993, Sister Helen Prejean, CSJ (1939–) published *Dead Men Walking*, her personal experience with the administration of the death penalty, and after that, the hierarchy increasingly emphasized moral limits on executions.

During the 1980s, as the Reagan administration ratcheted up Cold War military spending and promoted a policy of nuclear deterrence, Catholics began to question the legitimacy of those actions. At the grassroots level, Philip and Daniel Berrigan organized Plowshares, a movement of anti-war and anti-militarization activists whose members carry out acts of civil disobedience inspired by the protest movements of the 1960s. In 1980, the Berrigans and six other Plowshares members were arrested and imprisoned for trespassing on a General Electric plant in King of Prussia, Pennsylvania, where they destroyed documents and damaged nuclear missiles in the making. Individuals within the American hierarchy offered their own forms of civil disobedience. Archbishop Raymund Hunthausen of Seattle (1921–2018) paid only half the federal income tax he owed, claiming the other half supported only unethical expenses such as nuclear weapons. The hierarchy also acted as a whole, issuing the 1983 statement on *The Challenge of Peace*, which drew upon a long tradition of Catholic just war theory to lay out moral arguments against nuclear deterrence and the arms race and to affirm peacemaking as "a requirement of our faith."

Catholics also became increasingly attentive during this period to issues of poverty and inequality, leading to debates over the nature and morality of the capitalist economy that exposed divisions within the church. When Pope John XXIII issued his 1961 encyclical *Mater et Magistra*, on how the church, as "mother and teacher," championed its "children," the needy, William F. Buckley (1925–2008) – Catholic and publisher of the *The National Review*, a journal that identified and championed conservative positions on the issues of the day – borrowed a phrase from his colleague Garry Wills that summed up his approach. His *"Mater Sì, Magistra No"* argued not that Pope John was wrong, but that Catholics were justified in ignoring him. During the 1960s and 1970s, as the War on Poverty found expression in law, other Catholics such as Michael Novak (1933–2017) moved from supporters of Presidents Kennedy and Johnson to their critics. Arguments over the economy could be muted when that economy provided for most people, but when it became clear the economy favored some over others, Catholics again reacted both as individuals and as a group. Geno Baroni (1930–1984) went from inner city pastor to an Assistant Secretary of Housing and Urban Development during President Jimmy Carter's administration, before the 1983 revised code of canon law forbade clergy to hold political offices that involved exercising civil power. In the Diocese of Brooklyn, as Bishop Francis J. Mugavero closed parishes and demolished church buildings, he turned the land over to reasonably priced housing units. The US bishops spoke out collectively on economic issues in their 1986 pastoral letter, *Economic Justice for All*, which emphasized that all members of society have "a special obligation to the poor and the vulnerable" and the need to "make economic decisions more accountable to the common good."

In more recent decades, two issues demonstrate Catholics' continued efforts to respond to the social needs of their day through both action and advocacy: health care and immigration. During the 1980s, when acquired immune deficiency syndrome (AIDS) was a disease that was little understood, Catholic institutions provided critical care to those who had nowhere else to turn. Saint Vincent's Hospital in New York City, for instance, established one of the nation's first hospice programs for persons with AIDS, extending a tradition of care established by the Sisters of Charity, who established the hospital with a commitment to serve all those in need, regardless of race, creed, ability to pay, or now, in the case of AIDS, regardless of sexual orientation.

Later, in the midst of the health care reform debates of the early twenty-first century, Catholic sisters expanded their focus to this new issue, drawing upon their years of experience staffing and managing hospitals and other health care facilities, to advocate for health care as a fundamental human right. While the American hierarchy refused to support the Affordable Care Act of 2010 because of its impact on funding for abortion and birth control, Sister Carol Keehan, a Daughter of Charity and then-president of the Catholic Health Association of the United States, argued that the law did not itself fund abortion or birth control directly and that Catholics should not withhold support for something with such potential for good. Her efforts helped ensure the bill's passage.

Catholic action and advocacy were equally visible on the issue of immigration. In 1965, the federal government increased the total number of immigrant visas and made them available on a more equal basis to the inhabitants of countries around the world. Ironically, the first consequence was a spike in unauthorized entry from Mexico, as the new law did not take into account the longstanding economic ties between the two countries. The individual migrants, who came without visas and were not entitled to many government social services, needed the traditional charitable services of the Catholic Church. The debate over whether to uphold the law or to recognize economic realities drew the Catholic Church into a newer field of commenting on the ethics of the law. The immigration situation became more acute in the 1980s as impoverished, terrorized people fled authoritarian governments in Central America. In the twenty-first century, masses of refugees fled both Central America and the Middle East. With each turn of events, the American hierarchy became more vocal. In 1999, the American hierarchy issued the statement *From Newcomers to Citizens: All Come Bearing Gifts*, reminding both Catholics and the American government of their moral obligations toward those in need.

CONCLUSION

This chapter has identified some of the forces that shaped American Catholicism's response to those in need and guided its contributions to social welfare. First, there was the nature of the need, whether the church was serving nineteenth-century orphans or twenty-first century senior citizens seeking help with Social Security paperwork. Second, there was a change over time in who responded to the need. While the hierarchy always had some role in establishing local charities, its leadership became more visible over time, as the public face of charity changed from sisters nursing the sick poor in an epidemic to members of the hierarchy issuing statements on moral issues. Third, there was an expansion in what was done to meet the need, as the church added advocacy on behalf of the needy to its tradition of hands-on care. It is a legacy that continues through the present day, as the church and its members continue to address social needs and promote the common good.

FURTHER READING

Abell, Aaron, ed. *American Catholic Thought on Social Questions.* New York: Macmillan, 1968.

Battisti, Danielle. *Whom We Shall Welcome: Italian Americans and Immigration Reform.* New York: Fordham University Press, 2018.

Brown, Dorothy M., and Elizabeth McKeown. *The Poor Belong to Us: Catholic Charities and American Welfare.* Cambridge, MA: Harvard University Press, 2000.

Gleason, Philip. *The Conservative Reformers: German-American Catholics and the Social Order.* South Bend, IN: University of Notre Dame Press, 1968.

Kauffman, Christopher J. *Ministry and Meaning: A Religious History of Catholic Health Care in the United States.* New York: Crossroad Publishing, 1995.

McShane, Joseph Michael. *"Sufficiently Radical": Catholicism, Progressivism, and the Bishops' Program of 1919.* Washington, DC: Catholic University of America, 1986.

O'Brien, David J., and Thomas A. Shannon, eds. *Catholic Social Thought: The Documentary Heritage.* Maryknoll, NY: Orbis Books, 1992.

Wall, Barbra Mann. *American Catholic Hospitals: A Century of Changing Markets and Missions.* New Brunswick, NJ: Rutgers University Press, 2016.

8 Women Religious

MARY BETH FRASER CONNOLLY

In 1966, Catholic philosopher Michael Novak published a story on the "New Nuns" in the popular American magazine, *The Saturday Evening Post*, that portrayed a new image of Catholic sisterhood. The new fresh face of American sisters, or Catholic women religious, sported a modified habit that altered the veil to expose a sister's hair (her bangs) and a shortened skirt that may have revealed that nuns did have legs, but also allowed for freer movement.[1] Sisters appeared to be on the move by the mid-1960s, leaving behind traditional ministries such as parish schools. This first modification of religious life was followed by another, as many congregations shed their religious habits for secular dress by the 1970s.

Novak's new nuns were partially the result of the changes in religious life taking place since the Second Vatican Council altered the familiar landscape for American Catholics, religious and lay alike. Although the transformation appeared radical, the change from religious habit to secular dress and the move from a handful of traditional ministries to ever-multiplying new nontraditional ministries evolved after decades of reflection, study, and community response to the needs of a changing world. That many observers felt the changes as sudden, and even radical, speaks to the specific cultural and religious place that nuns and sisters occupied in the preceding 300 years in North America.

To understand the longer history of Catholic women religious – which includes both nuns (those who take solemn vows that do not need renewal every year and often live in a cloistered community) and sisters (members of active congregations who take simple vows that are renewed yearly) – we must examine their ministries as well as the lives they led as faithful women of their church and communities. While immigration brought new and different religious foundations from those

---

[1] Michael Novak, "The New Nuns," *The Saturday Evening Post*, July 30, 1966.

that had been established in the eighteenth and early nineteenth centuries, the mid-to-late nineteenth century saw significant expansion of Catholic institutions with women religious playing an important role in the triumphant American Catholic Church that emerged by the mid-twentieth century. With the opening of the Second Vatican Council in the 1960s, the church entered a new age, and since then, women religious moved into it in ways that both adhered to tradition and expanded our understanding of their roles in the world.

EARLY FOUNDATIONS AND GROWTH IN ANTEBELLUM AMERICA

The first congregation of women religious to establish itself in what is now the United States was the Ursuline nuns of the Congregation of Paris in New Orleans, Louisiana, in 1727. After the United States was established, the Ursulines were joined by the Belgian Discalced Carmelites in Port Tobacco, Maryland, in 1790, a contemplative religious congregation. Many of these first congregations in the United States came from European communities escaping war and revolution. The French Poor Clares arrived in America in 1793, hoping to find a new home in Baltimore. Failing to establish a foothold there, they moved to New Orleans, then Cuba, and returned to Baltimore by 1797. The French Poor Clares opened a school but struggled with a language barrier and their austere religious life did not appeal to students. Their work was supported by a group of "Pious Ladies" who bridged the language barrier for the nuns. Three of these pious women – Maria Sharpe, Alice Lalor, and Frances McDermott – established a religious community in Georgetown, and became known as the Visitation nuns. They also assumed responsibility for the school.[2]

As Catholicism spread in America, whether by natural increase, conversion, or immigration, the church needed more religious to staff schools, establish and administer hospitals, and care for orphans. Consequently, the clergy and laypeople both imported and fostered the development of congregations of women religious. The first home-grown congregation came from an unlikely source, an Episcopalian widowed mother of five, Elizabeth Ann Seton, whose religious journey brought her to Catholicism in 1805 and to establish the Sisters of Charity, based on the French Daughters of Charity's constitution, in

---

[2]   George C. Stewart, Jr., *Marvels of Charity: History of American Sisters and Nuns* (Huntington, IN: Our Sunday Visitor, 1994), 48–55.

1809. Seton made her living teaching, after her husband's death, and this continued once she established her American congregation in Emmitsburg, Maryland. From this foundation, Seton's Sisters of Charity spread throughout the United States and eastern Canada.[3]

While Mother Seton's Sisters of Charity expanded and European congregations migrated to shepherd white immigrant Catholics, little attention was paid to black Catholics. Racist views of enslaved and free blacks barred admittance of women of color from religious congregations. The establishment of the Oblate Sisters of Providence in 1828 began the first black congregation in the United States. Among their ministries in Baltimore, the Sisters of Providence created the St. Francis School for Colored Girls, which provided an education received by white girls and issued an "implicit challenge to antebellum white society's efforts to circumscribe black life."[4]

Meanwhile, European women religious who arrived in this same period encountered obstacles of arduous travel, underfunding or absence of financial support from local clergy, and fear of Protestant anti-Catholic attacks, which led many sisters to wear secular dress when traveling to avoid calling attention to themselves. The first Sisters of St. Joseph of Carondelet (who ventured to Cahokia, Illinois, in 1836) and the Sisters of Mercy (escorted by Mother Frances Warde from Pittsburgh to their new foundation in Chicago in 1846) hid their religious identity by not wearing habits.

Travel to new foundations was seldom straightforward, hardly luxurious, and potentially dangerous. Sisters used whatever modes of travel were available to them, including trains, horse carts, and wagons. Mary Monholland, for example, left her native New York City to enter the Sisters of Mercy in Chicago in 1846, and, according to her biographer, nearly drowned in Lake Michigan. The future Mary Francis de Sales traveled by rail to the Great Lakes, only to have her steamship tragically sink with Milwaukee in sight. Monholland was rescued from the deadly Lake Michigan waters, despite calling to her rescuers to "Save my companions – leave me to my fate."[5]

---

3   Catherine O'Donnell, *Elizabeth Seton: American Saint* (Ithaca, NY: Cornell University Press, 2018).

4   Diane Batts Morrow, *Persons of Color and Religious at the Same Time: The Oblate Sisters of Providence, 1828–1860* (Chapel Hill: University of North Carolina Press, 2002), 218–219.

5   Isidore O'Connor, RSM, *The Life of Mary Monholland: One of the Pioneer Sisters of the Order of Mercy in the West* (Chicago: J. S. Hyland & Company, 1894), 22–23.

Religious congregations in North America offered an opportunity for some women to embrace their religious vocation (or calling), especially considering the limited options in the late-eighteenth and early-nineteenth centuries. Women who entered religious congregations were understood as something different and elevated from everyday lay-women. Accounts of these first congregations of nuns in North America refer to the religious zeal of women who sought a vocation, and who persisted in realizing their holy calling despite circumstances of class, race, parental approval, or dowry. The United States in the nineteenth century was a mission field and Catholic women found an opportunity to engage in a religious life that afforded them an education and lifelong work in the service of others.

TIME OF GROWTH: THE 1860S TO 1940S

In the early nineteenth century, sisters accompanied and supported the growing immigrant Catholic population. They established thousands of parish schools, owned and operated hundreds of academies and high schools for wealthier Catholic and Protestant girls, founded over forty colleges and universities for women, and administered and staffed more than 100 hospitals and orphanages. Increasing numbers of sisters facilitated this institutional growth. In the early 1800s, there were fewer than 500 sisters and nuns. By 1860, there were slightly more than 5,000. By the end of the nineteenth century, there were some 46,000 women religious.[6]

Catholics in the United States had, by the mid-nineteenth century, become the nation's largest single denomination. To provide for the material and spiritual well-being of this expanding population, church leaders sought congregations of sisters to teach, care for orphans, provide health care, and conduct works of mercy for those in need. Bishops recruited some congregations to emigrate to the United States to serve immigrant populations, and soon the landscape was dotted with European imports like the Sisters of Mercy, Ursulines, Sisters of St. Joseph, Franciscans, and Felicians. Homegrown congregations like the Sisters of Charity ministered in various locations from Maryland, New York, Kentucky, Ohio, and points West. What united all these communities was a dedication to serving the growing Catholic population and,

6   Stewart, *Marvels of Charity*, 564.

at the same time, offering thousands of Catholic young women another choice beyond marriage and motherhood.

Education and health care often come to mind as the dominant contribution of women religious in the United States. Catholic immigrants were largely under or uneducated, and clergy and women religious alike sought to address this need. Many, like the Sisters of Charity, started free schools for families who could not afford private schooling, operating them alongside academies for the daughters of elite Catholic and Protestant families. The Kentucky Sisters of Loretto at the Foot of the Cross in Bardstown and the Sisters of Charity of Nazareth established boarding schools for girls, as did the Sisters of St. Joseph of Carondolet in St. Louis. Despite their Catholic identity, convent schools also appealed to Protestant families because they offered girls a refined education within the protective walls of a convent. By the 1880s and 1890s, a larger percentage of Catholic elite took advantage of the convent school, which provided young women with a sound education in languages, history, literature, some mathematics, and sciences, as well as refined skills such as sewing, embroidery, comportment, and music.[7]

Both convent and parish schools offered Catholic girls an example of a different avenue than marriage and family, and enabled congregations to recruit members. Marriage and motherhood were equally respected among Protestants and Catholics, but this was a lauded third option. Not all families, however, wanted their daughters to become a vowed religious. It meant the loss of a family member, and in some cases a blow to the family economy. Parents feared losing a close connection with their daughters once women entered religious life. Despite these concerns, many parents saw their daughters' entrance into a religious congregation as an elevation in status. Young women found education and work in valued and meaningful ways through a lifelong commitment to answering God's call.

While religious life attracted some, it repulsed others. Protestant America's unfamiliarity with Catholic religious life sometimes resulted in open hostility and condemnation. Fear of Protestant attacks was not unfounded in the 1830s and 1840s, and the persistence of "escaped nun" literature added to Protestant animosity. Rebecca Reed's *Six Months in a Convent* (1835) detailed the abuse of young Protestant girls in convent

[7]   Carol K. Coburn and Martha J. Smith, *Spirited Lives: How Nuns Shaped Catholic Culture and American Life, 1836–1920* (Chapel Hill: University of North Carolina Press), chapter 6.

schools coerced to convert to Roman Catholicism, and *The Awful Disclosures of Maria Monk* (1836) depicted sisters at the hands of nefarious priests, unwanted pregnancies, and murdered babies buried on convent grounds. Rumors of Reed's experience emerged before she published her tale of abuse at the hands of the Ursulines in Charlestown, Massachusetts, and instigated an attack on their convent in 1834. A largely working-class crowd fueled with anti-Catholic rhetoric from Presbyterian minister, Lyman Beecher, rioted and destroyed the convent. Similar rioting and attacks occurred in Baltimore in 1839 and in Philadelphia in 1844.[8] As the number of religious congregations, including convent academies, grew in antebellum America, so did concerns over an encroachment of Catholicism into what was believed to be a Protestant nation.

INSTITUTION BUILDERS

Exposure to sisters and their ministries was the fundamental factor that changed the minds of those hostile to Catholicism and women religious. The Civil War helped convert Protestant America to a different way of thinking and made possible the growth of nursing as an acceptable role for women. While Clara Barton and Dorothea Dix professionalized nursing for women, sisters who had decades of nursing experience joined the ranks of sisters temporarily assigned to serve on the battlefields. The French Daughters of Charity had an established health care ministry, but others adopted or expanded services to include the administration of hospitals and nursing care. Most religious congregations had a component to their community that included "visiting the sick," but this did not necessarily entail nursing or hospital work.

When the Civil War began, there was a need for skilled nursing staff in military hospitals, and roughly 20 percent of all nurses were Catholic sisters. The Daughters of Charity in Emmitsburg, Maryland, sent women to the front to care for northern and southern soldiers alike. The Sisters of Mercy sent nurses from New York, Pittsburgh, Cincinnati, Chicago, Baltimore, Vicksburg, and Little Rock. Sisters, regardless of region and personal views, gained the respect of both sides of the conflict for their neutrality and many, like the Daughters of Charity stationed in Confederate Mobile, Alabama, managed to travel relatively unfettered across territories into

---

[8]   Nancy Lusignan Schultz, *Fire & Roses: The Burning of the Charlestown Convent, 1834* (New York: The Free Press, 2000).

Northern-controlled New Orleans, primarily because of their commitment to providing nursing care to all troops. Religious formation directed sisters to care for the body, but not actively convert the soul.[9]

Hospitals owned and operated by sisters expanded in the nineteenth century. Prior to the Civil War, nine congregations of women religious operated twenty-two hospitals. The number of institutions nearly doubled during the 1860s, while the congregations engaged in hospital ministry rose to nineteen. By the 1890s, Catholic health care expanded to nearly ninety hospitals, which opened their doors to non-Catholic patients. As a result of their growing reputation in health care, calls for women religious to offer this ministry in the west continued. The Sisters of St. Joseph of Carondelet went to Kansas City, Missouri, in 1866, responding to a cholera epidemic there, and later served in Prescott and Tucson, Arizona, and Georgetown, Colorado, where railroad workers and miners were in need of medical care. Health care reached more non-Catholics than education as hospitals expanded generally in the United States in the nineteenth century. By 1900, 10 percent of the nation's hospitals were Catholic.[10]

Where need arose, sisters also operated homes for children, single women, and the elderly; they conducted specific missions to Native Americans and African Americans; and undertook the care of the mentally and terminally ill. Some communities, like Katharine Drexel's Sisters of the Blessed Sacrament, were established for specific ministries; Drexel's sisters conducted missionary work among African Americans and Native Americans. Others adapted their ministries to include a wider range of charitable efforts in the United States, and in some cases expanded to foreign missions, like the Sisters of Charity of New York, who established a mission in the Bahamas in 1889.[11]

The growing immigrant and second-generation Catholic populations, however, required more sister-led parish schools to compete with free public education. In 1884, US bishops at the Third Plenary Council of Baltimore promoted the development of parochial education and required that all parishes establish a school. Good Catholic families sent their children to the parish school and supported it financially. The Catholic school stood in opposition to the free public

---

[9] Mary Denis Maher, *To Bind Up the Wounds: Catholic Sister Nurses in the U.S. Civil War* (Baton Rouge: Louisiana State University Press, 1989).

[10] Ursula Stepsis, CSA and Dolores Liptak, RSM, eds., *Pioneer Healers: The History of Women Religious in American Health Care* (New York: Crossroad Publishing, 1989), 30, 287.

[11] Stewart, *Marvels of Charity*, 320–367.

schools which progressive reformers eyed as a means of "Americanizing" immigrants by 1900.[12]

Efforts to Americanize immigrants – or make foreign-born residents more palatable to native-born Americans – became formalized in the 1900s in public schools, as well as in social settlement houses and other material welfare programs. Nativist critiques of Catholic immigrants never fully subsided; it ebbed and flowed but became more aggressive once again by the end of the nineteenth century. Ten million immigrants entered the United States between 1860 and 1890, and eighteen million more arrived from 1890 to 1920. The increase in immigrants from outside northern Europe rejuvenated the call to close American borders to new immigrants from southern and eastern Europe, who were largely Jews, Orthodox Christians, and Roman Catholics. Established American Catholic clergy, dominated by Irish Americans, looked to the growing number of their foreign Catholic brothers and sisters, and sought to Americanize them and prevent them from leaving their church.[13]

Parish schools and neighborhood houses operated by Catholic sisters were ideal means of reaching immigrants at risk of succumbing to Protestant missionaries and progressive reformers. To compete with social settlements like Jane Addams' Hull House, sisters created their own welfare centers. Sisters Blandina and Justina Segale (biological sisters) established the Santa Maria Institute in Cincinnati in 1897, and the Sisters of Our Lady of Christian Doctrine founded Madonna House in 1910 on the Lower East Side of New York City. The collective goal of these works of mercy, of course, was to provide support and aid to those in need, but they also created the modern Catholic social welfare system. Sisters' vows of poverty and religious charisms made them the ideal labor force to conduct these ministries.[14]

INTO A MODERN AGE

Catholic sisters conducted dynamic and needed ministries throughout the nineteenth century and their efforts contributed to a more mature

---

[12]   Jay P. Dolan, *The American Catholic Experience: A History from Colonial Times to the Present* (Garden City, NY: Doubleday, 1985), 273.

[13]   Gary Gerstle, *American Crucible: Race and Nation in the Twentieth Century* (Princeton, NJ: Princeton University Press, 2017), 83, 136, 170.

[14]   Suellen Hoy, *Good Hearts: Catholic Sisters in Chicago's Past* (Urbana: University of Illinois Press, 2006); Margaret M. McGuinness, *Neighbors and Missionaries: A History of the Sisters of Our Lady of Christian Doctrine* (New York: Fordham University Press, 2012), 6–8.

Catholic population in the first decades of the twentieth century. Despite their successes, sisters faced a conservative movement to regulate their religious life infusing it with more monastic-style structures. This came at a time when local bishops sought centralized authority, attempting to control all Catholic services within their dioceses by creating Catholic Charities offices and Catholic boards of education. Sisters had little control over these changes and this often led to conflicts with bishops. When relations were positive between bishop and communities, clerical authority benefited sisters. If sisters challenged or outright disobeyed clerical authority, there were consequences, such a bishop denying the expansion of a ministry, assuming control of property owned by a congregation, or in times of extreme conflict, stripping a congregation of its mission and expelling it from the diocese.

Globally, the church desired to formalize the status of women religious' within the ecclesiastical structure. Women within active religious congregations – those who took simple vows – caused concern, as their status was ambiguous. Many active congregations established since the eighteenth and nineteenth centuries did not follow rules of enclosure or cloister and did not practice a regimented monastic life. They had relative freedom to conduct their ministries in the streets, going to hospital wards and battlefields, entering classrooms, working with orphans, and conducting works of mercy desperately needed in the United States. In the short run, their ambiguous status aided the construction of the church's infrastructure and helped evangelize thousands of Catholic immigrants and their children. It also meant that sisters had some freedom of movement to expand congregations to different regions of the country.

Some church authorities, though, chaffed at the idea of female religious autonomy and expressed concern about the lack of uniformity and adherence to religious rule. In 1900, the papal bull, *Conditae a Christo*, officially gave active religious congregations canonical status and recognition, but it also compelled them to follow more strict rules of enclosure and live a more structured and rigid religious life. *Conditae* led to the revision of the Code of canon law in 1917, taking effect the following year. This meant that religious congregations in the United States had to comply with the mandates of Canon Law to the point where many had to revise their system of governance. Some who were already diocesan congregations were tied more directly to their local bishop. Others operated with a generalate system, where religious houses in different dioceses regulated their religious rule to meet the requirements of the revision. The Sisters of Mercy, who by their foundation in Ireland were a papal community, conducted each foundation independently of the original motherhouse in Dublin. Those in the United States did the same. Once a new foundation was established in a different area and could stand independent of its motherhouse, it took on the characteristics of a diocesan community, owing obedience to the local bishop. Technically, however, these foundations remained papal communities. In the case of the Mercys, pressure mounted as early as 1905 to merge the disparate foundations into a generalate system. The sisters deflected this demand by relying on the original intent of their foundress, Catherine McAuley, not to unify. By 1918, the revision of the Code of Canon Law started a new conversation for unification, which caused problems and ignited opposition from various church authorities, such as Chicago's Cardinal George Mundelein, who wanted to maintain control over the religious communities working within the archdiocese. Mundelein actively worked against the unification of the Mercy foundations. He opposed the attempts of the Sisters of Mercy in his diocese to engage in a generalate system, even going so far as forbidding a vote within the communities. The Chicago Mercys, understanding that papal authority wished union, collaborated with other Mercy foundations, like the Milwaukee community (outside of Mundelein's territory), and voted to join the Sisters of Mercy of the Union in 1929.[15]

If religious congregations did not have the full support of their bishops, they simply had to adapt. In Cincinnati, Sisters Blandina and Justina Segale had steadily grown their welfare mission to Italians since 1897, extending their work to three welfare centers by the early 1920s. By 1923, Italian support for the San Antonio Welfare Center had grown to the point that some wanted to establish an Italian parish; Archbishop Henry K. Moeller and lay representatives went ahead with that plan, despite the Segales' objection, and began using the building that the sisters had funded as a welfare center without compensation. By early 1924, Moeller directed the sisters to continue their work in a neighboring building that they would have to convert into a welfare center, starting that mission from scratch. The Segales were left with little choice. They remained in the neighborhood, conducting a welfare center around the newly established San Antonio parish.[16]

[15]   Stewart, *Marvels of Charity*, 376; Mary Beth Fraser Connolly, *Women of Faith: The Chicago Sisters of Mercy and the Evolution of a Religious Community* (New York: Fordham University Press, 2014), 67–73.
[16]   Journal 10, August 13, 1923; October 31, 1923; November 6, 1923; January 15, 1924, Santa Maria Institute Collection, Sisters of Charity Archives, Mount St. Joseph, Ohio.

Beginning in 1918, religious life was associated with more structure and more emphasis on conformity to rule, but this era also saw an increase in vocations. The twentieth century began with more than 46,000 professed sisters, and by 1920 that number nearly doubled. Part of the increase, again, was due to the importation of religious congregations from Europe; some women continued to immigrate to the United States to join an American community; others came from the ranks of American Catholic women. The numbers continued to rise each decade, reaching nearly 200,000 by 1960.[17] These numbers are striking, but what is more compelling is the way sisters and nuns came to dominate the Catholic, and by extension, the American landscape. By the mid-twentieth century, American congregations were even sending sisters to foreign missions in Asia, Latin America, and Africa.

While clergy clamored for more sisters and pressured superiors to put young, barely professed sisters into classrooms or other ministries, the movement toward professionalization resulted in pushback from congregational leaders who wanted sisters to earn their undergraduate, and in some cases graduate degrees, before superiors placed them in ministries. Women who entered religious life typically became postulants for six months; this was followed by one to two years in the novitiate and culminated with the profession of simple vows. Sisters then entered the juniorate phase, continuing their formation for another three to five years until their final profession. Although novices and juniors earned college degrees in the twentieth century, many took a decade to complete their undergraduate education because they could not be spared from the classroom or hospital ward. By the early 1940s, thinking began to shift towards making sure women religious completed their college degrees before beginning full-time ministry.

As education for girls and young women evolved, more women enrolled in higher education. Roughly 20 percent of all college-age women attend some institution of higher learning by 1870, and that percentage rose to 32 percent by the next decade. Increasingly, these were Catholic women. The hierarchy, however, viewed early secular women's colleges as a potential danger to the faith of Catholic women, and sisters' colleges offered a solution by the early twentieth century. Some congregations expanded their existing academies to create colleges, like the Mercys' Southside Chicago Saint Xavier Academy, which added Saint Xavier College in 1915. Others, like the Sisters of Notre

---

17 Stewart, *Marvels of Charity*, 374, 564–565.

Dame de Namur, established wholly new institutions, like Trinity College in 1900 in Washington, DC.[18]

Catholic women's colleges offered a comparable education to secular institutions in part to attract students, but also to prepare young women to thrive in the late nineteenth and twentieth centuries. They offered a thoroughly Catholic education to produce future mothers or religious and prepared graduates for positions in the working world. These institutions, however, served another purpose: they provided novices and newly professed sisters access to education in preparation for teaching and nursing ministries. Many communities also sent sisters to various non-Catholic institutions for advanced degrees in order to fill faculty and administrative positions in their own colleges, hospitals, and other institutions.

NEW NUNS IN THE WORLD: THE 1940S TO THE TWENTY-FIRST CENTURY

That "new" nun who graced the pages of the *Saturday Evening Post* in 1966 was one of many who impacted the cultural view of women religious in the second half of the twentieth century. Films dramatized nuns, offering Ingrid Berman's Sister Mary Benedict in *The Bells of St. Mary's* (1945), Audrey Hepburn's struggles as Sister Luke in *The Nun's Story* (1959), and even the lighthearted Rosalind Russell's Mother Superior in *The Trouble with Angels* (1966) and *Where Angels Go Trouble Follows!* (1968). Television followed with Sister Bertrille, played by Sally Field in *The Flying Nun* (1967–1970). The pull of the world, changes of Vatican II, and the sociopolitical upheavals of American culture impacted sisters and nuns in the 1960s. Even Mary Tyler Moore felt the tug of the modern world (and Elvis Presley) in the 1969 *A Change of Habit*. While Hollywood had its own insight into Vatican II and women religious, the reality of sisters' experiences was more complex.[19]

---

[18]   Kathleen Sprows Cummings, *New Women of the Old Faith: Gender and American Catholicism in the Progressive Era* (Chapel Hill: University of North Carolina Press, 2009), 59, 61, and 91; Kathleen A. Mahoney, "American Catholic Colleges for Women: Historical Origins," in *Catholic Women's Colleges in America*, ed. Tracy Schier and Cynthia Russett (Baltimore: Johns Hopkins University Press, 2002), 26–27.

[19]   Rebecca Sullivan, "Gidget Goes to the Convent: Taking the Veil as a Girl's Adventure in *The Flying Nun*," *Canadian Review of American Studies* 31(2) (2001): 16.

Women religious did not wake up one morning and decide to leave their traditional ministries, their habits, and in some cases, religious life. Changes of the 1960s had their roots in the preceding decades, as well as the process of renewal called for by Vatican II, which transformed traditional understandings of vocation. What emerged as religious life for women in the post-renewal period was, in many instances, a renewed embrace of the founding charisms of their religious congregations.

The significance of the demands placed upon congregations for personnel and expertise in the mid-twentieth century cannot be minimized; by the 1950s, the desire to prepare young sisters for ministries resulted in the Sister Formation Conference. A survey of communities and education conducted by Sister Bertrande Meyers of the Daughters of Charity in 1941 found that sisters overall lacked full preparation for work in schools, hospitals, and social services, and recommended that religious leaders wait to send sisters into ministry until they completed their degrees. Sister Madeleva Wolff, of the Sisters of the Holy Cross, spoke at the National Catholic Education Association convention in 1949 and echoed Meyers's call for a complete education, which must include theology.[20]

Help came in the form of Pope Pius XII's address to the Sacred Congregation of Religious meeting in Rome in 1950, and the First International Congress of Teaching Sisters in 1951. Pius stressed the importance of meeting the modern world and the professionalization of educators (the conversation already going on in the American context). While the pope's words took time to reach the American religious audience, attendees at the 1952 National Catholic Education Association (NCEA) in Kansas City, Missouri, discussed the pope's addresses. The NCEA conference gave space for Immaculate Heart of Mary Sister Mary Emil Penet to address Meyers's and Wolff's ideas as well; sisters needed more than a six-month novitiate and two years of juniorate training to be ready to enter the classroom. After two more years of surveys and studies, the Sister Formation Conference was established.[21]

Along with Vatican II's call for the renewal of religious life, the Sister Formation Conference laid the groundwork for change. So too

---

[20] Carol K. Coburn, "Ahead of Its Time ... Or, Right on Time? The Role of the Sister Formation Conference for American Women Religious," *American Catholic Studies* 126(3) (2015): 28.

[21] Karen M. Kennelly, CSJ, *The Religious Formation Conference, 1954–2004* (Silver Spring, MD: Religious Formation Conference, 2009).

did the establishment of the Conference of Major Superiors of Women Religious (the precursor of the Leadership Conference of Women Religious) in November 1956. Under the guidance of superiors, the Sisters Formation Conference studied sisters' ministries and examined the role sisters played in society. It was this work that opened many communities to renewal.

Women who entered religious life in the 1950s and 1960s were not isolated from American culture and politics. They were informed by the civil rights and nascent feminist movements. These political and cultural shifts merged with the global church's call for a reinvigorated women religious population in the 1960 treatise, *The Nun in the World*, by Belgian Cardinal Leon Joseph Suenens, who challenged sisters to engage in the world beyond their convents. Although they had been doing that work for centuries, some sisters embraced Suenens's call to do more and in a dynamic way, going beyond their traditional ministries. The rigid structures of religious life implemented since 1918 had hemmed them in, and although canonical status may have elevated sisters above the laity, many were dissatisfied with the distance between themselves and the people in parishes, schools, hospitals, and the streets. Sisters wanted to break through the religious rules that prevented them from authentic interactions with the laity.[22]

Works like Suenens's volume fed the desire for change, as did the rumblings of second-wave feminism. Betty Friedan's *The Feminine Mystique* was one of the catalysts for the women's liberation movement and it impacted sisters within congregations. With the experiences of the 1950s and early 1960s to support them, many communities when given the directive to revise and renew their religious governments, community life, and ministries took on the hard work of doing just that. The changes they adopted came through months and years of discernment concerning communities' charisms or founding spirit, the study of their foundresses' intent and original purposes, and an assessment of what members understood God wanted.

As church teachings emanating from the Second Vatican Council emphasized human dignity and spoke of the solidarity of persons in the modern world, Catholic sisters, whose missions had always been to respond to the needs of their age, whether in contemplative prayer or by educating impoverished immigrant children, embraced this message with enthusiasm. Many sisters questioned their continued presence

---

[22]   Fraser Connolly, *Women of Faith*, 129–161; Anne Buckley, "After Cardinal Suenens: New Role for Nuns? 'Yes!' 'No!' 'Well ...'" *The Catholic Advocate* (May 14, 1964).

among middle class and suburban populations. Some discerned new ministries, which took advantage of established locations, if not traditional populations. They chose to remain in urban parishes, even though those areas were increasingly neither Catholic nor populated by European-Americans. Others questioned the need to remain in parish schools and sought new avenues to provide education to those in need. Some sisters left hospitals to open public health centers in rural and urban areas. Still others responded to the call for missionary work in other parts of the world.

All these changes did not happen immediately in 1965. First, congregations had to address religious governance and structure to fit the modern world, as directed in the 1965 Council document, *Perfectae Caritatis*, which provided the official church approval, or blessing, to reimagine religious life, to consider what holy obedience, poverty, and chastity meant to themselves and their communities, and to understand what membership in a religious community truly meant. A misconception of this process is that *Perfectae Caritatis* was published in 1965, and by 1966 nuns left their habits, traditional ministries, and even religious life. The reality was that to engage properly in renewal meant time, study, surveys, experimentation, and ultimately the revision of religious constitutions. The renewal process began in the mid-1960s, with chapter meetings, drafts of revised constitutions, and the start of experimentation, which included small groups living in a former parish convent, house, or an apartment, grouped not by their ministry but by geographic necessity. It also included the modified habit and, in some cases, secular dress.

By the end of the 1960s, some congregations had determined that mother superiors should not place sisters in their ministries, but rather allow individuals the opportunity to discern their own path. Some chose to remain in Catholic schools and hospitals long affiliated with their communities. Others embraced new ministries, like the Traveling Workshops in Inter-Group Relations, which consisted of groups of five sisters who traveled throughout the country to conduct workshops on race, poverty, and injustice. The possibility of a new or different kind of ministry drew Presentation Sister Therese Rooney to the Loretto Educational Advancement Program, a literacy center in the Woodlawn and Lawndale neighborhoods of Chicago.[23] By the 1970s and 1980s,

---

[23] Sister Therese Rooney, PBVM, "I Know a Man ... and a Woman, a Young Boy ... and a Young Girl," in *New Work for New Nuns*, ed. Sister Mary Peter Traxler, SSND (St. Louis: B. Herder, 1968), 129–141.

some sisters entered pastoral ministry in hospitals and parishes. They pursued psychology degrees and became therapists, and others took positions outside their congregations' and Catholic institutions, entering government social services, welfare, and, even secular businesses. This was not an immediate change for religious congregations; it required a shift in mindset for both leadership and the community members at large.[24]

The 1960s was also the moment when religious vocations began to decline noticeably. Religious vocations had always ebbed and flowed throughout the American church's history, but women leaving their communities by the 1970s were not replaced by new vocations. In 1965, there were 209,000 women in religious life. George Stewart's study of sisters and nuns found that over the next twenty-five years, that number declined to 102,000. The number of women in formation in 1965 was about 11,000 and by 1990 it had dropped to about 2,200. Some communities fared worse than others, but across congregations, the loss in membership was about 50 percent.[25]

Why did sisters leave? They left for various and personal reasons. Many realized they did not have a true vocation, while others believed they could serve God and their neighbors outside a religious congregation. Some left because they found romantic love with another person. Whatever the reason, religious life no longer was their vocation, but leaving did not mark these women as failures or lost to the community. Many congregations found ways to maintain relationships with the women who left. By the 1980s, some communities welcomed former sisters, laywomen, and men into connections with their religious life as associates, including the Sisters of Charity, Sisters of Mercy, and Visitation Sisters.

The renewal process lasted for over a decade. By the time revised constitutions were approved in the 1980s, sisters had moved into a new phase of religious life. Now a smaller population, sisters' ministries concentrated more on social justice. Congregations with decreased and aging populations no longer administered their hospitals or colleges, but created new partnerships with lay boards sponsoring these institutions. Declining vocations and an aging population forced leadership to take a hard look at population projections and resources and determine their next steps into the twenty-first century. Since 2000, religious sisters have declined from nearly 80,000 to about 44,000 in 2018. One response

---

[24]   Fraser Connolly, *Women of Faith*, chapters 5 and 6.
[25]   Stewart, *Marvels of Charity*, 462–463.

to these population shifts has been for congregations with similar charisms or a shared foundress to combine. Along with consolidations, communities have divested themselves of larger motherhouses or converted them into assisted living and nursing care institutions, opening convents to other religious, retired priests, and the laity.[26]

What lies ahead for women religious? Amid reports of declining vocations, a new coterie of women dedicated to social justice and political activism replaced the 1960s "new nun" in popular culture. Some protested the School of Americas, championed immigration rights, worked to end the death penalty, and promoted environmental sustainability. In 2012, a group of sisters and their lay associates made headlines when they organized Nuns on the Bus, traveling the country in a large passenger bus to bring attention to issues of poverty, immigration, and health care to the voting public. On a congregational level, communities used their collective financial power to change company practices from within as shareholders, as in the case of Smith and Wesson to combat gun violence. In this case, they introduced resolutions on gun safety at shareholder meetings.[27] Not without controversy, such activism raised concerns in the Vatican, which ordered an investigation of US women religious in 2008. The resulting 2014 report praised American sisters for their service to the church but expressed criticism of spiritual practices and ministry that were not in concert with church doctrine, especially on homosexuality, birth control and abortion, and women's ordination.[28]

Alongside this new generation of activist sisters, some younger women have been drawn to contemplative religious congregations with traditional practices. These traditional communities – like the Cistercians of the Strict Observance (Trappistine nuns) or the Poor Clares – offer them the opportunity to live a life dedicated to prayer for the world. Yet even these communities often demonstrate a remarkably modern sensibility, meeting the twenty-first century with sophisticated public relations to draw attention to their ministry, social charism, and spirituality. Individual sisters conduct their ministry

[26] "Frequently Requested Church Statistics," *Center for Applied Research in the Apostolate* https://cara.georgetown.edu/frequently-requested-church-statistics/; and Erick Berrelleza, SJ, Mary L. Gautier, and Mark M. Gray, "Population Trends among Religious Institutes of Women," *CARA Special Report*, Fall 2014, 3–4.

[27] Carol K. Coburn, "The Selma Effect: Catholic Nuns and Social Justice 50 Years On," *The Global Sisters Report*, March 9, 2015.

[28] Dan Stockman and Dawn Araujo-Hawkins, "Women Religious and Others React to Apostolic Visitation Report Release," *Global Sisters Report*, December 12, 2014.

through Twitter and other social media platforms, while contemplative congregations open their communities virtually to followers to share religious messages and attract vocations.

In the end, women religious continue to adapt and evolve in the early twenty-first century. While religious life prior to 1965 has changed and likely will not return in that form, as some congregations reach completion, sisters still offer a model for the laity to engage in their world on a spiritual and human level. Since the eighteenth century, women religious have built the American Catholic Church, adapted their lives and missions to fit the needs of their time, and continue into the twenty-first century to follow their religious charism where they discern God has called them.

FURTHER READING

Butler, Anne M. *Across God's Frontiers: Catholic Sisters in the American West, 1850–1920.* Chapel Hill: University of North Carolina Press, 2012.

Coburn, Carol K., and Martha J. Smith. *Spirited Lives: How Nuns Shaped Catholic Culture and American Life, 1836–1920.* Chapel Hill: University of North Carolina Press, 1999.

Cummings, Kathleen Sprows. *New Women of the Old Faith: Gender and American Catholicism in the Progressive Era.* Chapel Hill: University of North Carolina Press, 2009.

Fraser Connolly, Mary Beth. *Women of Faith: The Chicago Sisters of Mercy and the Evolution of a Religious Community.* New York: Fordham University Press, 2014.

Koehlinger, Amy L. *The New Nuns: Racial Justice and Religious Reform in the 1960s.* Cambridge, MA: Harvard University Press, 2007.

McGuinness, Margaret M. *Neighbors and Missionaries: A History of the Sisters of Our Lady of Christian Doctrine.* New York: Fordham University Press, 2012.

9 Catholics and Politics

LAWRENCE J. MCANDREWS

The political history of American Catholics reflects the larger struggle of Catholic outsiders to overcome an often hostile Protestant society. Theirs was ultimately a battle for full citizenship in the American republic, from cultural acceptance to economic achievement to political prominence. And when they finally achieved it, theirs was a victory not only for Catholics, but for those countless other Americans who helped them get there.

This chapter will first examine the colonial era of the sixteenth through eighteenth centuries, when Spanish and French Catholics warily vied for control of the continent with English Protestants. It will then investigate the national era during the nineteenth century, when Catholics uneasily strove to become Americans, and during the early and middle twentieth century, when Catholics arrived in the American mainstream. Finally, it will assess the modern era of the late twentieth and early twenty-first centuries, when many American Catholics – locally, nationally, and internationally – have increasingly identified themselves more with their politics than with their religion.

COLONIAL POLITICS: FROM INSIDE TO OUTSIDE

The story of American Catholic outsiders began on the inside, from the privileged perches of the Spanish crown and the church that it sanctioned. In 1492, before Queen Isabella and King Ferdinand of Spain sent the Italian navigator Christopher Columbus on the first of his four voyages to the Caribbean, he attended Mass. Though no priests or nuns accompanied him on his initial expedition, he considered himself on a mission to save souls. Those Spaniards who followed him would bring clergy and, by their force of faith and their faith in force, they would convert numerous Native Americans to the religion of Rome.

This journey of cross and sword reached what is today the United States in 1565, when Captain-General Pedro Menendez de Aviles and his troops slaughtered French Protestant settlers and founded their own colony of St. Augustine in northeastern Florida, with Menendez as its governor. The Spanish introduced the mission system, under which priests not only offered religious instruction to Native Americans, but taught cooking, sewing, weaving, and farming, and acted as representatives of the Spanish government. The missions spread in the seventeenth and eighteenth centuries to Louisiana, Texas, New Mexico, Arizona, and California. But Spanish missionaries and soldiers exacted a steep price, with the priests enslaving and flogging the Natives, and the military hunting runaways and lassoing women.

As with Spanish colonization, the French settlement of North America mixed church with state, compassion with contempt, and success with failure. French colonization in what is today the United States began in Maine in 1604. Jesuits also evangelized in New York, Michigan, Indiana, Wisconsin, and Illinois, while Franciscans explored Michigan and Minnesota. The French settlement of the Louisiana territory by Quebec seminary priests originated in 1699 in Biloxi, Mississippi. Political hegemony by the mother country, already challenged by distance, would confront the even greater obstacle of division – between the Huron and Iroquois nations the French were trying to convert, and between the clergy and the traders they were trying to control.

In 1763, France and Spain lost the Seven Years' War to England, confining the French colonists to the north, the Spaniards to the south and west. By that time, the story of American Catholics had already turned inside out. In the thirteen English colonies, beginning with Virginia in 1607, Catholics were not choosing the leaders and enforcing the laws. Only Maryland, started by George Calvert in 1634, had Catholic foundations, reinforced by a Toleration Act in 1649. Of the other twelve colonies, eight had official religions, either Puritan or Anglican. Puritan Massachusetts expelled a citizen in 1631 for endorsing papal decrees, while Anglican Virginia deprived Catholics of the vote in 1642. In New Jersey, South Carolina, and Georgia, all were free to worship – "except papists."[1]

Following England's Glorious Revolution of 1688, which supplanted its Catholic king with a pair of Protestant monarchs, Maryland followed suit, making Anglicanism the colony's official religion and Catholics second-class citizens. Colonial schoolchildren read the *New England*

---

[1]   Manlio Graziano, *In Rome We Trust: The Rise of Catholics in American Political Life* (Stanford, CA: Stanford University Press, 2017), 30.

Primer, which called the Catholic Church "that arrant Whore of Rome." When England went to war with Spain in Europe and North America in 1739, a Protestant minister in the colonies, Parson Moody, "joined the troops as chaplain, and carried an axe at the shoulder, with which to hew down Catholic images in the churches."[2]

Rhode Island was the lone colony to award Catholics full legal equality – at least, on paper. Puritan Roger Williams, who established the colony in 1636, portrayed the Catholic Church as a "popish leviathan"; there was not a single Catholic in the colony in 1680; and there would be no Catholic church in Rhode Island until 1837. New York had two Catholic governors, Anthony Brockholls (1681–1682) and Thomas Dongan (1682–1688), but their Anglican successors banished Catholic priests and teachers. One Catholic teacher was not so lucky. He was hanged on the charge of being a "Popish priest."[3]

No wonder there were so few Catholics in the colonies. Of the 2.5 million colonists on the eve of independence, only about 25,000, or 1 percent, were Catholic, with nearly all of them living in Maryland, New York, and Pennsylvania. Those who were willing and able to worship risked the kind of ridicule that future president John Adams, a Unitarian, leveled when he attended a Catholic vespers service in Philadelphia in 1774. "This Afternoon's Entertainment was to me most awfull [sic] and affecting: the poor wretches fingering their beads, chanting Latin, not a word of which they understood," he wrote. "I wonder how Luther ever broke the spell."[4]

EARLY NATIONAL POLITICS: FROM OUTSIDE TO INSIDE

Although a minority among the colonists, Catholics fought alongside Protestants in the War for Independence from 1775 to 1783. Catholics and non-Catholics discovered a common enemy in British colonial rule. And when France and Spain joined the fight, they gained Catholic allies. During the war, a number of Catholics gained distinction for their contributions to the cause of independence. A Pennsylvania Catholic,

---

[2] Thomas J. Carty, *A Catholic in the White House? Religion, Politics, and John F. Kennedy's Presidential Campaign* (New York: Palgrave MacMillan, 2004), 14; Sister Mary Augustina Ray, *American Opinion of Roman Catholicism in the Eighteenth Century* (New York: Octagon Books, 1974), 221.

[3] Carty, *A Catholic in the White House?*, 13; Graziano, *In Rome We Trust*, 29–30.

[4] James Hennesey, *American Catholics: A History of the Roman Catholic Community in the United States* (New York: Oxford University Press, 1981), 62.

Captain John Barry, earned the moniker "Father of the American Navy." A Maryland Catholic, Charles Carroll, signed the Declaration of Independence. A French Catholic, the Marquis de Lafayette, heroically came to the aid of the American forces. At war's end, General George Washington would salute Catholics for playing their "patriot part."[5]

While some American Catholic patriots made significant political inroads, Catholics as a whole still faced barriers to equality. Two Catholics were among the fifty-five men who gathered to write the Constitution in Philadelphia in 1787. Thomas Fitzsimons was a merchant and banker in Philadelphia, and Daniel Carroll, Charles' cousin and John's brother, was a plantation owner in Maryland. Article VI of the document which they signed forbade a religious test for national office. And the First Amendment to which they agreed proscribed Congress from instituting an official religion or interfering with the free exercise of religion. But these provisions did not apply to the states, many of which persisted in keeping Catholics out of public office. Massachusetts, New Hampshire, New Jersey, North Carolina, South Carolina, and Georgia still required that their citizens practice Protestantism.

Many Catholics struggled to overcome these obstacles. Despite Protestant obstruction, the American Revolution had ensured, in historian Jay Dolan's words, that "heaven was democratized, and salvation now became a possibility for all God's children, not just the Calvinist elect." In 1789, in the spirit of the nation's newly ratified Constitution and newly elected president, Baltimore's Catholic clergy elected John Carroll as the first American bishop.[6]

Carroll set out to prove that, in the wake of a troubled past and in the face of an uncertain future, the members of his church were just as American as their Protestant counterparts. He modeled the nation's first Catholic cathedral, in Baltimore, after the capitol building in Washington, DC. He instructed the priests of his diocese to oversee "not Irish, nor English, nor French congregations and churches, but Catholic-American congregations and churches." And out of respect for the First Amendment, Carroll pledged to stay out of partisan politics because "when ministers of Religion leave the duties of their profession to take a busy part in political affairs, they fall into contempt."[7]

---

[5]   James T. Fisher, *Catholics in America* (New York: Oxford University Press, 2000), 30.
[6]   Jay P. Dolan, *In Search of an American Catholicism: A History of Religion and Culture in Tension* (New York: Oxford University Press, 2002), 29.
[7]   Timothy Byrnes, *Catholic Bishops in American Politics* (Princeton, NJ: Princeton University Press, 1991), 13.

But Carroll couldn't stay out of religious politics, for while heaven may have become a democracy, his church had not. Consistent with the post-independence movement away from official religions, many states had passed laws recognizing lay church members as the owners of church property – laws that violated the Catholic tradition of clerical land ownership. Though Carroll had reluctantly accepted this political reality, he had drawn the line at these same church members, known as trustees, choosing the pastors of their parishes. That was *his* job, and he would have to go to court to preclude any further erosion of his episcopal authority.

If it was difficult to be a Catholic man in the early republic, it was even more challenging to be a Catholic woman. Between 1789 and 1829, the United States gave birth to eight communities of women religious, led by Elizabeth Bayley Seton, a convert to Catholicism who founded the Sisters of Charity in Emmitsburg, Maryland, and would become the first native-born American saint. It would be another century before all women of any religion could vote in the United States, but the schools, hospitals, and asylums that these nuns operated were vital to the growth of the nation.

The noble efforts of Carroll, Seton, and other Catholics to coexist peacefully with the nation's Protestant majority could not deter the wave of nativism rekindled by the large-scale immigration of Irish, German, and Mexican Catholics into the United States beginning in the 1830s. Of the eleven million Americans in 1826, only about 250,000 were Catholic. Within three decades, there were over three million Catholics in the country. Many of them spoke a foreign language, and most of them were poor.

For some Americans, Catholics posed an existential threat. "The Catholic Church holds now in darkness and bondage nearly half the civilized world," Congregationalist minister Lyman Beecher preached in Charlestown, Massachusetts, in 1834. Beecher warned that the pope was about to seize the Mississippi Valley. Then an Ursuline nun, Elizabeth Harrison, left a Charlestown convent while suffering from depression. When she voluntarily returned, false rumors of her imprisonment spread. A mob set upon the convent, demanding Harrison's release. The invaders drunkenly donned nuns' habits, danced provocatively, and burned the convent before torching the homes of Irish Catholics.[8]

---

[8]   Hennesey, *American Catholics*, 119.

A decade later in Philadelphia, violence erupted in response to false rumors that a Catholic school board member, Hugh Clark, had interfered with the reading of the King James Bible in one of the schools. A protest meeting organized by the local nativist American Republican party sparked gun violence and the burning of two Catholic churches. A few weeks later, nativists attacked a church that doubled as an arsenal for Irish Catholics. When the militia arrived, the Irish Catholics tripped their horses with ropes and fired upon them from cannons. Thirteen people died, and many were wounded.

The level of suspicion in the country was so high that a band of nativists stole a 2,000-year-old inscribed stone that Pope Pius IX had sent in 1854 as a gift to the American people for their monument to George Washington. The thieves in the nation's capital were members of the American Party, which sought to prevent foreign-born Americans from voting or holding office. It had originated as a secret society, the Order of the Star Spangled Banner, whose members claimed to "know nothing" of its activities, before growing into a full-fledged political party. The "Know-Nothings" would elect eight governors and more than 100 members of Congress, and, in 1856, would nominate former Whig chief executive Millard Fillmore for president. Fillmore, who would carry only Maryland in the race won by Democrat James Buchanan, was not present to accept his nomination. He was in Rome, visiting the pope.

This resurgence of nativism kept American Catholics on the defensive. "We owe no religious allegiance to any State in this Union, nor to its central government," Bishop John England of Charleston, South Carolina, wrote in the American bishops' Pastoral Letter of 1837. But he added, "Nor do we acknowledge any civil or political supremacy or power over us in any foreign potentate, though that potentate might be the chief pastor [pope] of our church."[9]

When the United States went to war with predominantly Catholic Mexico in 1846, the American bishops stayed silent, lest they be accused of treason. When the United States won the war and annexed over one-third of Mexican territory in 1848, thousands of Mexican Catholics became an American underclass, subject to discriminatory legislation like California's 1855 "Greaser Act," which defined vagrants in racial terms.

Catholic leaders were also largely silent on the country's most pressing political issue, African-American slavery. In 1839 Pope Gregory XVI

<hr>

[9]   Byrnes, *Catholic Bishops in American Politics*, 14.

denounced the international slave trade, but he stopped short of condemning slavery itself. Many Catholic clergy and laypersons owned enslaved persons, and no prominent Catholic advocated immediate abolition before the Civil War. To Archbishop John Hughes of New York, Africans were "as dark in their spirit as in their complexion." To Chief Justice Roger Taney, who authored the majority opinion in the Supreme Court's 1857 *Dred Scott v. Sandford* decision upholding slavery, blacks were "beings of an inferior order." Some Catholics argued that it was easier to Christianize slaves than free persons, while others dreaded the disorder that widespread emancipation would bring. Most Catholics, like Taney, were Democrats, attracted by the party's sympathy toward immigrants and the working class if not its attachment to slavery. Most abolitionists were Whigs or Republicans, and many of them were anti-Catholic.[10]

Still, a few Catholics did take up the fight against slavery. In 1797, Charles Carroll proposed a bill in the Maryland state senate that would have gradually abolished slavery. After the effort failed, Carroll began freeing the slaves on his vast estate, as many as thirty at a time. Other Catholics claimed to agree with Carroll, but their actions belied their words. A Kentucky priest named John Thayer encouraged gradual abolition and chastised his congregants for selling slaves to buy land. But Thayer himself was a slaveholder, and a brutal one. In February 1801, Father Stephen Badin, the Catholic Vicar General of the West, wrote Bishop Carroll that Thayer's slave "Henny has run (a)way from her master for the third time. M[r] T [hayer] by stripping the poor woman half naked to (w)hip her has brought upon himself the indignation of all good men but more especially of the sex [women] and of the negroes."[11] Badin suspended Thayer's priestly duties after several female parishioners complained that he had inappropriately touched them. When Thayer died in 1845, he paid his own penance for his mistreatment of women. His inheritance would rebuild the Charlestown convent that went up in smoke in 1834.

The civil war that exploded in April 1861 divided the church as well as the country. A few more courageous voices finally emerged in the American Catholic community to renounce the peculiar institution

[10]   John T. McGreevy, *Catholicism and American Freedom: A History* (New York: Norton, 2003), 51.

[11]   C. Walker Gollar, "The Controversial and Contradictory Anti-Slavery of Father John Thayer," *Records of the American Catholic Historical Society of Philadelphia* 109: 3–4 (Fall–Winter 1998), 139.

that had shackled about four million Americans, 100,000 of whom were Catholic. In June 1861, prominent editor Orestes Brownson delivered an antislavery commencement address at St. John's College in New York (later Fordham University). In August 1862, Archbishop John Purcell of Cincinnati became the first member of the American hierarchy to censure slavery as "an unchristian evil, opposed to the freedom of mankind, and to the growth and glory of a Republican country."[12]

But Archbishop Hughes "anonymously" attacked Brownson, asserting that Catholic Union soldiers were not sacrificing "blood and treasure" to "satisfy a clique of abolitionists in the North." Bishop Martin Spalding of Louisville wrote in his diary that Republican President Abraham Lincoln's January 1863 Emancipation Proclamation had given license to "three to four millions of half-civilized Africans to murder their Masters and Mistresses!" Six months later, Irish Catholics were murdering African Americans on the streets of New York, as part of a violent protest against the draft.[13]

From the Civil War's carnage there emerged a nation, and Catholics played a bigger part in it. During the war, President Lincoln selected Archbishop Hughes as a special envoy to Rome to appeal for papal support of the Union effort. After the war, Republican President Ulysses Grant replaced federal agents on reservations with Protestant and Catholic missionaries in an ill-fated attempt to substitute a "Peace Policy" for the nation's tragic Indian Wars. The Knights of Labor, led by Irish-Catholic machinist Terence Powderly, became the country's largest union, enrolling many unskilled immigrants and helping to erode the church's traditional suspicion of organized labor as too secular and too secretive. Pope Leo XIII's 1891 encyclical *Rerum Novarum* (Of New Things) defended the right of workers to join unions while decrying the extremes of socialism and unfettered capitalism. During the coal strike in Pennsylvania in 1902, a Wilkes Barre priest, John Curran, went to the White House to plead with Republican President Theodore Roosevelt to settle the dispute.

The late nineteenth century brought a second wave of immigration, mainly from Canada and East Asia as well as eastern and southern Europe (including large numbers of Polish and Italian Catholics). It also featured growing Catholic power in electoral politics, especially at the local level. Boston and Chicago elected their first Catholic mayors before the end of the nineteenth century. In New York, Catholics

---

12 McGreevy, *Catholicism and American Freedom*, 80.
13 McGreevy, *Catholicism and American Freedom*, 80.

operated the corrupt Tammany Hall machine that picked most of the mayors. By 1905, Rhode Island had become the first state with a Catholic majority. The next year, Irish-Catholic Democrat Patrick McCarthy became the first foreign-born mayor of Providence, where nearly seven in ten residents were first or second-generation immigrants. To win his election and fortify his political base, McCarthy turned to the native-born and the newly arrived men and women of his church, with its well-established network of fundraising, public speaking, and social activism, as parish records supplied the names of potential voters. Similar patterns appeared across the country, as Catholic parishes and organizations became powerful tools of political mobilization.

Despite this progress, Catholics remained largely outside the mainstream of American politics. In 1867, when the Republican Congress voted to defund the American legation in Rome, Democratic President Andrew Johnson had no choice but to sever diplomatic relations with the Holy See, and the United States would not send an ambassador to the Vatican for another 117 years. In 1875, President Grant espoused a constitutional amendment to prohibit public funding of religious schools. The next year Maine Republican Representative James Blaine proposed a similar measure which passed the House, failed in the Senate, but would become the template for several successful state "Blaine Amendments." In 1884, when Blaine ran for president against Grover Cleveland, one of Blaine's supporters, a Presbyterian minister named Samuel Burchard, depicted Cleveland's Democrats as the party of "Rum, Romanism, and Rebellion," a slur against the Irish Catholics and former Confederates who comprised much of its membership. The attack appeared to backfire, as Irish Catholics surged to the polls to help Cleveland capture the crucial state of New York and win the election.

These renewed assaults on American Catholics provoked conflicting responses. At the Third Plenary Council in Baltimore in 1884, the bishops authorized schools for all their parishes, which were increasingly dividing along ethnic lines. But so-called Americanists in the church disagreed. One of them, New York priest Edward McGlynn, contended that parish funds would be better spent promoting social causes, such as 1886 mayoral candidate Henry George's proposed "single tax" on land. George lost the election to the Tammany Hall candidate Abram Hewitt, Archbishop Michael Corrigan (allied with the Tammany machine) suspended McGlynn for his partisan political activities, and the Vatican's Sacred Congregation for the Propagation of the Faith (*Propaganda Fide*) excommunicated him in 1887. To the surprise of many, Pope Leo XIII refused Corrigan's request to criticize George, and he reinstated McGlynn.

If an American ambassador would not go to Rome, a Vatican diplomat would have to come to the United States. In 1892, 400 years after Columbus first set sail for the Americas, Archbishop Francesco Satolli departed Rome for Washington, where he would become the first permanent papal representative to the United States. The pope would return the favor by employing Archbishop John Ireland of St. Paul, Minnesota, as a mediator between the United States and Spain during the Cuban-Spanish-American War of 1898. But after the United States easily won what Secretary of State John Hay called a "splendid little war," the peace treaty barely passed the Senate amid pleas to "Christianize" (convert to Protestantism) the largely Catholic population of the Philippines, which the United States had acquired along with Guam and Puerto Rico.

LATER NATIONAL POLITICS: FROM BOTTOM TO TOP

The nation's entrance into World War I in April 1917 against Germany, Austria-Hungary, and the Ottoman Turks presented a new opportunity for Catholics to certify their American credentials. One in five American combatants was a Catholic. Representatives from sixty-eight dioceses and twenty-eight national organizations convened at Catholic University in Washington, DC, in August 1917 "to devise a plan of organization throughout the United States to promote the spiritual and material welfare of the United States troops at home and abroad and to study, coordinate, unify, and put into operation all Catholic activities incidental to the war." In November this organization became the National Catholic War Council.[14]

After the war ended with an Allied triumph in November 1918, Democratic President Woodrow Wilson traveled to Paris to negotiate the peace. Along the way, he stopped in Rome, where in January 1919, Wilson, the son of a Presbyterian minister, became the first American president to meet with a pope, Benedict XV. Later that year the National Catholic War Council became the National Catholic Welfare Council. In 1922, the Vatican approved the council, soon renamed the National Catholic Welfare Conference (NCWC).

---

[14]   Lawrence J. McAndrews, *What They Wished For: American Catholics and American Presidents, 1960–2004* (Athens: University of Georgia Press, 2014), 3.

The bishops moved quickly to help shape public policy. In 1919, the NCWC adopted the Bishops' Program of Social Reconstruction, the hierarchy's answer to the Protestant Social Gospel movement. Authored by Monsignor John A. Ryan – a moral theologian from St. Paul, Minnesota – the document advocated a minimum wage, vocational training, and unemployment insurance while opposing child labor. In the 1930s, Democratic President Franklin Roosevelt would assign the priest to several boards and commissions and implement many of his ideas. The National Catholic Welfare Conference accomplished a major success in 1925 when the Supreme Court in *Pierce v. Society of Sisters* unanimously overturned an Oregon law mandating that children could attend only public schools.

The wait finally ended for proponents of Prohibition and women's suffrage. These movements, launched in the mid-nineteenth century, climaxed with the ratification of the Eighteenth and Nineteenth Amendments in 1919 and 1920. Although there were prominent Catholics on both sides of both issues, advocates too often invoked nativist stereotypes of drunken Irishmen or servile papists to advance their agendas. Women's rights champion Elizabeth Cady Stanton had employed both, lamenting that "drunkards" and "ignorant foreigners" were able to vote though native-born women were not. "It is not possible for a foreigner and a Catholic to take in the grandeur of the American idea of individual rights," Stanton said, "as more sacred than any civil or ecclesiastical organizations."[15]

A new nativist tide washed up on American shores in the 1920s, as Republican Presidents Warren Harding and Calvin Coolidge signed restrictive immigration statutes in 1921 and 1924, and the delegates to the Democratic convention in 1924 failed by one vote to disavow the rejuvenated Ku Klux Klan, which had helped elect governors and state legislators everywhere but the Northeast. Four years later, Democratic Governor Al Smith, a product of New York's Irish-American Tammany machine, became the first Catholic to win a major party presidential nomination. He could not conquer bigotry, however, especially in the heavily Baptist South. In "An Open Letter to the Honorable Alfred E. Smith," a Protestant attorney named Charles Marshall asked the candidate how he would govern if a papal encyclical violated the

---

[15] Elizabeth Cady Stanton, "Seneca Falls Keynote Address," July 19, 1848, www .greatamericandocuments.com/speeches/stanton-seneca-falls/; McGreevy, *Catholicism and American Freedom*, 95.

national interest. "Will somebody please tell me," Smith purportedly replied, "what in hell an 'enkyclical' is?"[16]

Despite Smith's defeat – which spared him the challenge of grappling with the Great Depression – Catholics would exhibit extensive influence during the 1930s and 1940s. President Roosevelt appointed several Catholics to his cabinet and the courts, and Catholics were a major component of the political coalition that reelected him an unprecedented three times, tightening the grip of the Democratic Party on the Catholic electorate at all levels of government.

In local politics, Catholics continued to exercise considerable political might. When not cleaning the streets, reducing crime, enhancing his power, and enriching his pocketbook, Jersey City's Catholic Democratic boss Frank "I am the Law" Hague (1917–1947) was allying with his dear friend, Monsignor John Sheppard, the pastor of St. Michael's Church, to promote Catholic education by limiting the construction of public schools. San Francisco Archbishops Edward Hanna and John Mitty viewed Roosevelt's labor legislation as the fulfillment of *Quadragesimo Anno* (In the Fortieth Year), Pope Pius XI's 1931 encyclical reaffirming the principles of *Rerum Novarum*. After Hanna steered a middle course between what the archdiocesan newspaper called "laissez-faire extremists" and "communist fanatics" in successfully mediating the Pacific Coast maritime strike of 1934, Mitty would defend the city's unions against the anti-New Deal backlash of the 1940s and 1950s.[17]

Other Catholic voices pushed politics to the left and to the right. Peter Maurin and Dorothy Day ushered in the Catholic Worker movement, which grew from a penny-a-copy newspaper published on May Day 1933 to a network of rural and urban halfway houses that rejected capitalism and affirmed pacifism. Charles Coughlin, a Canadian-born priest, had his own parish outside of Detroit; his own political organization, the National Union of Social Justice; his own newspaper, *Social Justice*; and, most importantly, his own radio show, which counted as many as ten million listeners. By the time the United States intervened in the Second World War in 1941, Coughlin's rhetoric had become extreme, his critiques of international finance having

---

[16]   Martin E. Marty, *A Short History of American Catholicism* (Allen, TX: Thomas More Press, 1995), 46.

[17]   Leonard F. Vernon, *The Life and Times of Jersey City Mayor Frank Hague: "I Am the Law"* (Mount Pleasant, SC: The History Press, 2011), 9–19; William Issel, "A Stern Struggle: Catholic Activism and San Francisco Labor, 1934–1958," in *American Labor and the Cold War*, ed. Robert W. Cherry, William Issel, and Kiernan Walsh Taylor (New Brunswick, NJ: Rutgers University Press, 2004), 156.

crossed over into anti-Semitism. So Roosevelt pulled the plug on Coughlin's program and put an end to Coughlin's demagoguery.

The Allied victory over Fascist Italy, Nazi Germany, and Imperial Japan was also a Catholic victory. Up to a third of the American forces in World War II was Catholic. During the war, Roosevelt dispatched New York Archbishop Francis Spellman on a diplomatic mission to Europe, Africa, and the Middle East, and he appointed Myron Taylor as a special envoy to the Vatican. Taylor, the Protestant former board chairman of United States Steel, did not receive the rank of ambassador, but he was the first American representative in Rome since 1867.

American Catholic education made important political advances in the postwar era. The G. I. Bill, signed by Roosevelt in 1944, rewarded returning veterans with free higher education and low-cost mortgages, providing a boon to Catholic colleges and universities, which many students could not otherwise afford to attend, and an opportunity for their graduates to move to thriving suburbs. In the same year, the American Catholic bishops for the first time sought federal aid for their elementary and secondary schools as well. Three years later, in *Everson v. Board of Education*, the Supreme Court furnished the bishops with a compelling argument for their new stance – that public funds for nonpublic schools were constitutional if they went to the students, not to the schools.

The nation's postwar prosperity ushered in a golden age for American Catholics, as Catholics would climb the socioeconomic ladder faster than Protestants. In 1946, Archbishop Spellman became a cardinal. He leveraged his friendship with Pope Pius XII and New York's role as a media and financial center to turn the archdiocesan headquarters into "the Powerhouse," where he brokered deals with the city's business and political leaders, restored the church's finances, and presided over a church and school construction boom. Herman Badillo, who would become the Bronx borough president and the country's first Puerto Rican member of Congress, recalled being summoned early in his career to the archdiocesan office, where one of the cardinal's subordinates told him that "we think you're a young man who's going to go far, and we're always looking for Catholics we can push along." Badillo replied that he appreciated the favor, but he wasn't a Catholic. Spellman was as popular as he was powerful – in 1957, the celebration of the twenty-fifth anniversary of his consecration as a bishop filled Yankee Stadium.[18]

---

[18]   Henry Sheinkopf, "The Archdiocese of New York: Transition from Urban Powerhouse to Suburban Institution, 1950–2000; A Case Study" (Ph.D. diss.: New York University, 2015), 67.

The outbreak of the Cold War demonstrated, however, that Catholics still had a way to go in American politics. In February 1950, Catholic Republican Senator Joseph McCarthy of Wisconsin alleged, without naming any, that there were over 200 communists in Democratic President Harry Truman's State Department. Coming shortly after the Soviet takeover of Eastern Europe and the communist conquest of China, and shortly before the Korean War and the execution of Julius and Ethel Rosenberg for passing atomic secrets to the Soviets, McCarthy's unsubstantiated charges resonated with many Americans. Catholics, acting in part out of religious solidarity, supported McCarthy in greater percentages than the general population. Catholic Democratic Senator John Kennedy of Massachusetts never repudiated McCarthy, even after televised Senate hearings in 1954 discredited McCarthy's accusations of communist infiltration of the US army. He shared with McCarthy and many American Catholics of both parties a fear and loathing of communism, with its atheistic ideology and religious persecution.

In 1960, Kennedy shattered the historical Protestant monopoly on the White House, but only after he promised that, if any conflict should arise between his religious beliefs and the national interest, he would follow the latter. "No Catholic prelate," he assured the Greater Houston Ministerial Association in September 1960, would "tell the president how to act." Kennedy received over three-quarters of the ballots of his fellow Catholics to squeak by Republican Vice President Richard Nixon in the twentieth century's closest popular vote. Assistance from the well-oiled machine of Chicago's Catholic Democratic boss Richard Daley, Nixon believed, had helped Kennedy steal the critical state of Illinois. In his first year in office, President Kennedy kept his promise. In a highly publicized showdown with the bishops of his church, Kennedy refused their pleas for federal aid for construction and teachers' salaries in nonpublic schools, then watched as a fellow Catholic Democrat, James Delaney of New York, helped forestall a compromise bill from obtaining a vote in the House of Representatives.[19]

As his presidency progressed, however, Kennedy revealed more and more of his faith. In the wake of the Cuban Missile Crisis, with *Saturday Review* editor Norman Cousins acting as an intermediary, Kennedy, Soviet Premier Nikita Khrushchev, and Pope John XXIII

---

[19]   Lawrence J. McAndrews, "Promoting the Poor: Catholic Leaders and the Economic Opportunity Act of 1964," *Catholic Historical Review* 104 (Spring 2018), 299.

discussed a ban on nuclear testing. Formal talks between the United States, the Soviet Union, and Great Britain commenced in January 1963. In his April 1963 encyclical *Pacem in Terris* (Peace on Earth), Pope John called for nuclear arms reduction. A week later at Boston College, Kennedy said of the encyclical, "As a Catholic, I am proud of it. As an American, I have learned from it." In September, the Senate voted to ratify the Nuclear Test Ban Treaty.[20]

MODERN POLITICS: THE CATHOLIC TWO-PARTY SYSTEM

Kennedy's assassination in November 1963 left a good deal of unfinished business for his country and his church. On such issues as civil rights, immigration, education, and abortion, American politics finally gave voice to voiceless minorities and women, while unraveling the age-old alliance between Catholics and Democrats.

Catholics had long been on both sides of the nation's burgeoning civil rights movement. In 1934 in New York, Jesuit priest John LaFarge unveiled the first of several Catholic Interracial Councils; twenty-five years later, the councils would form the National Catholic Conference for Interracial Justice (NCCIJ). Cesar Chavez and Dolores Huerta fought for the rights of Mexican-American farmworkers. Archbishop Joseph Ritter desegregated St. Louis's Catholic schools in 1947 (seven years before the Supreme Court ordered the integration of the nation's public schools), and Archbishop Patrick O'Boyle offered the invocation at the March on Washington (where Martin Luther King, Jr. delivered his "I Have a Dream" speech) in 1963. But Archbishop Thomas Toolen of Mobile prohibited his priests and nuns from protesting Alabama's segregation laws, and Archbishop John Cody of New Orleans (and later Chicago) expressed suspicions about King's communist sympathies. Chicago's Mayor Daley, who attended daily Mass and whose daughter was a nun, was so tepid in his support for civil rights that Catholic activists tried to move an African-American family into his neighborhood.

Yet when the moment arrived in 1964 for a civil rights law that would finally slay Jim Crow, Catholics proved indispensable to ensuring its passage. A decade after the inception of the Civil Rights Act under Democratic President Lyndon Johnson, Monsignor George Higgins,

---

[20] McAndrews, *What They Wished For*, 20.

director of the NCWC's Social Action Department, would recall that the NCWC had "lobbied more consistently and more effectively in favor of the landmark 1964 civil rights bill than it has ever lobbied before or since on any single issue."[21]

The bishops also helped enact the Economic Opportunity Act of 1964, which created the Office of Economic Opportunity (OEO), the centerpiece of Johnson's War on Poverty. Johnson appointed a founding member of the National Catholic Conference for Interracial Justice (NCCIJ), Peace Corps director Sargent Shriver, to head the OEO, and Shriver enlisted Catholics across the country in his agency's fight. A priest, John Maurice, assisted Tejano migrant workers in Milwaukee. A black priest, August Thompson, oversaw the South Delta Community Action Program in Louisiana. A nun and nurse midwife, Mary Stella Simpson, ministered to the needy at the free Tufts-Delta Hospital in Mississippi. When Democratic President Jimmy Carter continued the antipoverty campaign in 1977, Assistant Secretary of Housing and Urban Development Geno Baroni became the highest-ranking Catholic priest ever in the federal government.

The bishops supported the Immigration and Nationality Act, which removed the quotas that had substantially limited immigration for over forty years. The law, signed by President Johnson in 1965, prioritized families over skills, doubled the number of immigrants accepted into the country, and shifted the origins of most newcomers from Canada and Europe to Asia and heavily Catholic Latin America. In the next half-century, the church in the United States would undergo a dramatic political transformation, as its expanding Latino membership helped raise the profile and heighten the urgency of its increasingly generous immigration agenda.

The bishops' record on education showed mixed results. Negotiations among the NCWC's Monsignor Francis Hurley, the National Education Association's Robert Wyatt, and Commissioner of Education Francis Keppel, initiated during the Kennedy administration, produced the "aid to the child" compromise in the Elementary and Secondary Education Act (ESEA), the first large-scale federal school assistance, signed by Johnson in 1965. Consistent with the *Everson* ruling, federal dollars would flow primarily to impoverished school districts, not to the public schools for construction and teachers' salaries, but to public and nonpublic school students through

---

[21]   McAndrews, *What They Wished For*, 67.

public agencies. Johnson's Higher Education Act of 1965 extended scholarships and loans to students in nonpublic as well as public colleges and universities.

The end of the bishops' two-decade wait for federal funding of their schools was welcome, but it was hardly the answer to their prayers. Much of the ESEA money was not reaching Catholic students due to state Blaine Amendments. With instructional costs increasing and the Catholic "baby boom" ending, Catholic schools began to close at an alarming rate starting as early as the 1970s. The bishops would soon switch their focus to other forms of parochial school aid, such as tuition tax credits and vouchers for their largely Latino, Asian-American, African-American, and non-Catholic pupils. These efforts, backed by Republican presidents Richard Nixon, Gerald Ford, Ronald Reagan, George H. W. Bush, George W. Bush, and Donald Trump, enjoyed some local and state success but were less fruitful at the national level.

The resistance to such legislation by Democratic presidents Jimmy Carter, Bill Clinton, and Barack Obama (along with the first Catholic vice president, Joseph Biden) evinced the end of Democratic dominance over American Catholics. This development owed not only to the dramatic rise of many descendants of Catholic immigrants from the working class to the middle and upper classes, and to the growing identification of the Democratic Party with racial minorities and abortion rights, but to the aggressive Republican courtship of working-class white ethnic Catholics, first as members of Nixon's "Silent Majority," and later as "Reagan Democrats." The bishops found themselves on the opposite side of many of these Catholics when, in 1971, they abandoned their support for the six-year-old American combat role in Vietnam, leavening their traditional anticommunism and following the lead of the more radical Catholic Left, spearheaded by priests Philip and Daniel Berrigan, who landed in prison for defacing and destroying draft records.

But the bishops heartened their more conservative congregants when, five days before the agreement to withdraw American troops from Vietnam, the Supreme Court announced its landmark 1973 *Roe v. Wade* decision protecting abortion rights in all fifty states. The prelates would spend much of the next four decades seeking the reversal of *Roe*, first through a constitutional amendment and then through an antiabortion majority on the Supreme Court. Despite the election of four pro-life Republican presidents from Reagan to Trump, the presence of six Catholics (including the first Hispanic justice, Sonia Sotomayor) on the Supreme Court from 2009 to 2016, and the fact that one in five Americans was a Catholic, they would achieve neither.

The bishops further alienated Catholic progressives, including many women, when they undercut their ostensible neutrality on the proposed Equal Rights Amendment to the Constitution by conveying fears that it would promote abortion. These concerns helped the coalition, led by Catholic activist Phyllis Schlafly, to defeat the amendment in 1982. But the bishops unsettled Catholic conservatives on other fronts. Their 1983 pastoral letter "The Challenge of Peace" criticized the Reagan administration's nuclear arms buildup. Along with Pope John Paul II's efforts in his native Poland, it helped pressure Reagan to decelerate the arms race and hasten the end of the Cold War, which would arrive in 1991 under George H. W. Bush.

In the late twentieth and early twenty-first centuries, the bishops would continue to press for smaller defense budgets and a larger welfare state. They hailed President Reagan's restoration of diplomatic relations with the Vatican in 1984. They questioned the first war with Iraq under the first President Bush in 1991, opposed the second war with Iraq under the second President Bush in 2003, and supported the second President Bush's war in Afghanistan in the aftermath of the attacks on the United States by Islamic terrorists on September 11, 2001. The prelates were instrumental in the formulation and execution of George W. Bush's faith-based initiative, as federal funding of Catholic charities swelled. They applauded Reagan's amnesty for undocumented immigrants in 1986. They endorsed unsuccessful comprehensive immigration reform efforts during the George W. Bush and Barack Obama presidencies, at a time when one-third of American Catholics were Latinos, and many (authorized and unauthorized) immigrants, like those who had come to the United States in previous centuries, were Catholics.

But did the faithful listen to their bishops? According to a 2009 Zogby poll, fewer than one in four American Catholics favored the earned legalization of undocumented immigrants that the hierarchy was prescribing. A 2010 Pew survey found that two-thirds of church-going Catholics never remembered hearing about immigration from their parish priests. As Chicago's Cardinal Joseph Bernardin, the architect of "The Challenge of Peace," said of his fellow prelates in 1992, "Often we are not in the same ballpark as our people."[22]

In 2002, further evidence revealed that the bishops were not in the same universe as their people. A sexual abuse scandal spread from

22   Lawrence J. McAndrews, *Refuge in the Lord: Catholics, Presidents, and the Politics of Immigration, 1981–2013* (Washington, DC: Catholic University of America Press, 2015), 202–203.

Cardinal Bernard Law's Boston archdiocese to involve 11,000 priests in 95 percent of the country's dioceses. Despite the prelates' adoption of a zero-tolerance approach to such misconduct, weekly Mass attendance fell from 52 percent of Catholics in 2002 to 35 percent in 2003, and donations dropped by half between 2002 and 2004. When the Supreme Court in *Obergefell v. Hodges* in 2015 validated same-sex marriage in all fifty states, it was even easier than usual for many Catholics to disregard the hierarchy's rejection of the verdict.

Ever since the Democratic Party lost its hold on American Catholics in the 1970s and 1980s, scholars have searched in vain to unlock the mystery of the "Catholic vote." In local, state, and national elections, some Catholics have cast their ballots, at least in part, on the basis of their religious beliefs. But others have not let their faith determine their votes. Although Latino Catholics have usually voted for Democrats, and non-Hispanic white Catholics have tended to pick Republicans, Catholics have become important "swing" voters wooed by both parties. And in presidential elections from 1972 to 2016, Catholics have chosen winners. Only in 2000, when Democrat Al Gore won the popular vote but lost the electoral vote to George W. Bush in the Supreme Court, was a plurality or majority of Catholics on the losing side.

In 2004, for the first time, more Catholics voted against one of their own, Massachusetts Democratic Senator John Kerry (the third-ever Catholic major-party presidential nominee), than voted for him. Kerry had aligned himself with the church hierarchy on matters of war and peace and social justice, but his pro-choice views on abortion ignited a campaign by a few bishops to forbid him from receiving the Eucharist. The effort ultimately failed, but it attracted so much media attention that Chicago's Cardinal Francis George mused that he was considering "denying communion to reporters."[23]

Anti-Catholic prejudice has not completely disappeared from the United States. But when it comes to politics, American Catholics, so different for so long, are now in many ways just like everybody else.

FURTHER READING

Heclo, Hugh, and Wilfred McClay. *Religion Returns to the Public Square: Faith and Policy in America.* Baltimore: Johns Hopkins University Press, 2003.
Heyer, Kristin, Mark Rozell, and Michael Genovese, eds. *Catholics and Politics: The Dynamic Tension between Faith and Power.* Washington, DC: Georgetown University Press, 2008.

[23]   McAndrews, *What They Wished For*, 369.

Hudson, Deal. *Onward Christian Soldiers: The Growing Political Power of Catholics and Evangelicals in the United States*. New York: Simon and Schuster, 2008.

Issel, William. *Church and State in the City: Catholics and Politics in Twentieth-Century San Francisco*. Philadelphia: Temple University Press, 2012.

McAndrews, Lawrence J. *The Era of Education: The Presidents and the Schools, 1965–2001*. Urbana: University of Illinois Press, 2006.

McGreevy, John T. *Parish Boundaries: The Catholic Encounter with Race in the Twentieth-Century Urban North*. Chicago: University of Chicago Press, 1996.

Millies, Steven P. *Good Intentions: A History of Catholic Voters' Road from Roe to Trump*. Collegeville, MN: Liturgical Press, 2018.

Sterne, Evelyn. *Ballots and Bibles: Ethnic Politics and the Catholic Church in Providence*. Ithaca, NY: Cornell University Press, 2004.

10 Arts and Culture

DEBRA CAMPBELL

> When people have told me that because I am a Catholic, I cannot be an
> artist, I have had to reply, ruefully, that because I am a Catholic,
> I cannot afford to be less than an artist.
>
> Flannery O'Connor[1]

American Catholics were well represented among those transfixed by the
BBC miniseries *Brideshead Revisited* when it first aired on PBS in the
winter of 1982. There are many reasons why they found it so captivating –
aside from the costumes, and the exceptional beauty of its two male
protagonists. One is certainly the treatment of Catholic difference running through it, as it does through Evelyn Waugh's novel, which it
follows very closely. When the Anglican agnostic Charles Ryder
(Jeremy Irons) observes that Catholics seem "just like everyone else,"
the Catholic aristocrat Sebastian Flyte (Anthony Andrews) appears
deeply shocked: "My dear Charles, that's exactly what they're not ...
Everything they think's important is different from other people."

No matter that the scene is set in an English country house in the
1920s. It resonated with American Catholics in the early 1980s, who
were no strangers to discussions of the topic by parish clergy and the
contrasting treatment it received at the hands of Catholic authors,
artists, and filmmakers. This chapter examines the difference that
Catholic faith has made in the lives and work of American writers and
artists since the nineteenth century. The adjective "Catholic" is applied
broadly to individuals whose Catholic background or experiences have
informed their artistic vision, whether or not they continue to receive
the sacraments or call themselves Catholics. Art and literature produced by these individuals, rooted in Catholic ritual and community

---

[1] Flannery O'Connor, "The Church and the Fiction Writer," in *Mystery and Manners*,
   ed. Sally and Robert Fitzgerald (New York: Farrar, Straus & Giroux, 1969), 146.

life, has made its mark upon American values and popular culture, especially during the pivotal twentieth century.

ARTS AND CULTURE BEFORE 1920

American Catholics were latecomers to the world of art and literature. This is not surprising. Catholics were a marginal – often suspect – minority in the original thirteen colonies. Their communal culture was insular, centered on the Mass and private devotions. Their music and religious art came from Catholic Europe. In the wake of the Revolution, they kept a low profile and sought to show that they were loyal Americans. They tended to downplay how their religion differed from that of the Protestant majority. This situation and strategy changed with escalating waves of Catholic immigration from the 1820s to the 1920s, first primarily from Ireland and Germany and later from Italy and Eastern Europe. The dramatic growth, increasing ethnic heterogeneity, and sudden visibility of the Catholic community during these years produced a backlash that took the form of nativist attitudes and organizations, and occasionally erupted into violence.

Immigrant roots and fear of reprisals by Protestant Americans encouraged a "ghetto Catholicism," structured around ethnic parishes and schools, which sought to preserve the language and mores of the home country. Most nineteenth-century American Catholics lived in insular ethnic enclaves and received their (often limited) education in parochial schools. They were aliens in Protestant-dominated American culture. The immigrants' struggle to emerge from poverty, combined with the hierarchy's iron grip on Catholic education and culture, produced a Catholic community that emphasized piety, obedience, and material success. Mary McCarthy's description of her parochial school in Minneapolis near the end of the immigrant era provides us with a glimpse of the pressure placed upon immigrants and their children to take advantage of every opportunity for "bettering themselves." McCarthy and her classmates were trained to see their school and the world beyond as a meritocracy where one must compete to get ahead. She was more than half serious when she recalled that "Equality was a species of unfairness which the good Sisters of St. Joseph would not have tolerated."[2]

---

[2]   Mary McCarthy, "To the Reader," in *Memories of a Catholic Girlhood* (1957; reprint San Diego: Harvest Book/Harcourt, 1985), 19.

At times the equality enshrined in the American constitution clashed with the emphasis on Catholic religious and moral superiority taught in the parish. The ghetto mentality promoted by nineteenth-century bishops and clergy insulated devout Catholics from aspects of American society that might test their faith. For example, many in leadership positions within the American Catholic Church, like their Protestant counterparts, had strong misgivings about the practice of reading (or writing) novels because they believed it could lead to senti-mentality, triviality, anti-intellectualism, and worldliness. Still, it was hard to deny the novel's potential: it could be used to explain the faith to outsiders, correct misunderstandings of Catholicism, and even pave the way for the conversion of those who would never think of entering a Catholic church.

In his pioneering American Catholic novel, *Father Rowland* (1829), Charles Constantine Pise, a priest who served as chaplain to the US Senate, describes how three wealthy Virginia women raised Episcopalian are converted by a Jesuit. He shows how well suited Catholic teachings and rituals are to the lives of virtuous, genteel women, and treats the paterfamilias, General Woburn, a Deist Revolutionary War veteran, gently, despite his lack of interest in the newfound faith of his wife and daughters.[3] Pise's novel soothed the hierarchy's concerns and proved that there was an audience for Catholic fiction. By the final decades of the nineteenth century, the American Catholic community had produced a substantial number of writers, including a disproportionate number of women. The collection *Immortales of Catholic Columbian Literature* (1897), compiled by the Ursuline Sisters of New York, contains the work of sixty-three female Catholic authors who wrote stories, poetry, essays, and short historical studies. These authors – including Eleanor Donnelly, Agnes Repplier, Katherine Conway, and Anna Sadlier – were well known among their coreligionists, but not in non-Catholic circles.

The contents – and even the very existence – of *Immortales* help readers today understand why the hierarchy soon overcame its initial skepticism about the novel and other forms of imaginative literature and eventually gave its blessing to a whole array of Catholic publica-tions. Magazines such as *Ave Maria*, *Catholic World*, and *Messenger of the Sacred Heart* published the works of the *Immortales* and their male counterparts and propagated a specific vision of Catholic art, including

---

[3]   Charles Constantine Pise, *Father Rowland* (Baltimore: F. Lucas, Jr., [1841]).

fiction, that was warmly embraced by nineteenth-century Catholic women and many members of the clergy. These journals only accepted works that were *truly* Catholic, i.e., uplifting, moral pieces that never touched the ugly, demeaning side of life and were written from a Catholic point of view. Catholic clerics and scholars justified these criteria for Catholic art by references to the writings of Thomas Aquinas (ca. 1225–1274), a philosopher-theologian whose work constituted the foundation of Catholic thought from the late nineteenth through the mid-twentieth century. The skill with which nineteenth-century American bishops organized every aspect of their growing church, including literary productivity, is impressive, but it had a negative side. Writers and artists do not welcome management (and censorship) by institutions; American Catholics with literary or artistic ambitions have found various ways to distance themselves from the institutional church.

The period between the 1880s and the 1920s witnessed the flight of American writers and artists to Europe, where they found working conditions more congenial than back home. Among the Catholic exiles was Louise Imogen Guiney (1861–1920), daughter of an Irish General who arrived in Boston in 1839. After her father's death in 1877, she worked as a postmistress and later a librarian. She wrote poetry and essays, which she shared with a circle of Boston aesthetes, but she never felt at home in America. In 1901, she moved to England, and was welcomed by a heterogeneous group of writers and artists, many of them Catholics and converts to the faith, including Lionel Johnson and Alice Meynell. She settled in Oxford, which she considered the best place in England to experience remnants of pre-Reformation Catholic life. In her poetry, especially the "XII Oxford Sonnets" (1895) and the collection *Happy Ending* (1909), and as editor of the ambitious volume, *Recusant Poets*, published posthumously (1938), she explored the meaning of the older forms of Catholic spirituality and community that she discovered when transplanted to a place with deeper Catholic roots than her native Boston.

The artist John LaFarge (1835–1910) felt equally at home in diverse locations across the globe: in his Washington Square studio in New York; in his Newport, Rhode Island, home among the monied Protestant elite; and in England, France, Japan, and the South Pacific, where he studied and perfected his craft. He was known for his landscapes, his works in stained glass, and his murals, notably, *The Ascension of Christ* (1886–1888), commissioned by the Episcopal Church of the Ascension in New York. He was considered a leading light of the American Renaissance movement, which sought to show through art that late nineteenth-century America represented the culmination of what was best in European culture. Prosperous parents and aristocratic French roots made it easier for LaFarge to be openly Catholic and still accepted by artists and writers like Henry James who were deeply skeptical of Catholics.

Like LaFarge, Kate O'Flaherty Chopin (1850–1904) found that her French background nurtured a creativity and openness to artistic experimentation rarely found in American Catholic circles in the nineteenth century. Descended from an old Louisiana Creole family on her mother's side, Kate was educated at the Convent of the Sacred Heart in St. Louis, Missouri, where they followed a French curriculum far more ambitious than that of most American female academies. Students were taught science, history, literature, and current events and trained to discuss these topics intelligently, drawing their own conclusions. In her early teens, when suffering from trauma (possibly a sexual assault by a Union soldier), Kate was taken under the wing of one of the younger nuns, Madam Mary O'Meara, RSCJ, who urged her to write about what she knew, praised the result, and remained her valued friend and mentor into adulthood.

Kate married Oscar Chopin in 1870, moved to Louisiana, and had six children in quick succession. In the mid-1880s, widowed and saddled with her husband's debts, she became a full-time author. Her stories about Catholics in New Orleans and rural small town Louisiana were published in newspapers and magazines and in the collection *Bayou Folk* (1893), which established her national reputation. Chopin is best known for her controversial novel *The Awakening* (1899) explores her evolving views on marriage, sexuality, and a woman's need to be free to discover her identity and destiny. It shocked contemporary reviewers but probably not her former teachers at the Convent of the Sacred Heart. It was later recovered by feminists of the 1970s and is taught in literature courses across the globe.

CATHOLIC REVIVAL AMERICAN STYLE, 1920–1960

The lives of LaFarge and Chopin illustrate the influence of European and English models upon pioneering American Catholic writers and artists. Nineteenth and early twentieth-century Catholics in France, England, and Germany responded to modern society's challenges to traditional Catholicism by exploring how Catholic beliefs and rituals provide resources to grapple with change and trauma. G. K. Chesterton,

Hilaire Belloc, François Mauriac, Karl Adam, and others, writing in a variety of genres from history and polemic to poetry and fiction, self-consciously promoted a Catholic Revival. They maintained that Catholicism need not be irrelevant in a changing world dominated by modern ideologies and technologies, but might instead be the answer (or antidote) many were seeking.

In 1920, George Shuster (1894–1977) who had recently returned from military service in France to join the English Department at Notre Dame, issued a call for a Catholic Revival in America. He saw how the European Revival had helped Catholics respond to the experience and aftermath of the First World War. The war had transformed his own relationship to Catholicism: "Before ... I had lived up to all the rules and tried to believe what I was supposed to as a Catholic. Now I was personally religious, deeply so, but no longer a subservient soul. ... I had found God across all the suffering that I had seen." Shuster was heartened to see a compatible spirituality reflected in the American "Bishops' Program of Social Reconstruction" published on February 12, 1919, a Catholic faith committed to promoting justice and charity across the globe. Writing for *The Catholic World*, he reminded American Catholics that the best literature and art had been produced by Catholics, e.g., Cervantes, Thomas More, and Michelangelo, and challenged American Catholics to live up to the promise of their past.[4]

The time was not ripe for anything close to a full-blown revival within the American Catholic community amidst the nativism and materialism of the 1920s. There was much talk about it, however, among Catholic educators and literary types, notably Jesuits Francis X. Talbot, Daniel A. Lord, and Calvert Alexander. Lord, Director of the Sodality of the Blessed Virgin, was a formative influence upon generations of young Catholic men. Talbot was the literary editor of the Jesuit journal *America* (1923–1936). Alexander, a St. Louis University professor, was a founder and editor of *Modern Schoolman* (1925), which sought to propagate the philosophy of Thomas Aquinas among twentieth-century Americans. In the 1920s and early 1930s, these three Jesuits and others associated with Catholic colleges and journals sought to promote Catholic writing in an effort to rescue America from the impending moral and spiritual abyss.

---

[4]   George N. Shuster, *On the Side of Truth: An Evaluation with Readings* (Notre Dame, IN: University of Notre Dame Press, 1974), 20; George N. Shuster, "Soldiers of France," *The Catholic World* 111 (April 1920): 16–17; George N. Shuster, "Catholic Literature as a World Force," *The Catholic World* 111 (July 1920): 455.

This carefully organized initiative was not the revival that Shuster had envisioned. It contained an inherent contradiction, with its refrain "where are the Catholic writers?" and its tendency to dismiss successful American Catholic authors because they were not publishing (what some Catholic editors and educators considered) "Catholic" books. This became painfully apparent to F. Scott Fitzgerald (1896–1940), who was stung by the reaction of Catholic reviewers to his early, most explicitly Catholic, novel *This Side of Paradise* (1919). In his correspondence with a fellow Catholic author, Shane Leslie, Fitzgerald laments Catholic reviewers' misperceptions of his novel, especially the character based upon his spiritual advisor Father Cyril Sigourney Webster Fay. Fay, a trustee at Newman, the Catholic boarding school Fitzgerald attended from 1911 to 1913, worked strenuously to keep Fitzgerald in the fold by revealing aspects of Catholicism that would appeal to his identity as a fledgling writer. For example, he urged Fitzgerald to read Swinburne, Huysmans, Wilde, and Robert Hugh Benson.

Under Fay's influence, especially when shaken by his death in 1919, Fitzgerald considered becoming a priest. He was thinking of the cosmopolitan, aesthetically sophisticated, even worldly Catholic Church across the Atlantic, the one Father Fay had spoken of so passionately, not the "prim," bourgeois, defensive, barely postimmigrant church in America. To Fitzgerald, the difference was palpable. He wrote to Leslie: "It seems that an Englishman like Benson can write anything but an American had better have his works either pious tracts for nuns or else disassociate them from the church as a living issue."[5] By the mid-1920s, Fitzgerald had stopped practicing his faith, but he continued to write novels and stories informed by his Catholic experience and preoccupations. His story "Absolution" (also controversial among Catholic reviewers) was originally conceived as the prologue to *The Great Gatsby* (1925). His work continues to serve as a Rorschach test in discussions about what constitutes an American Catholic novel.

In the 1930s, clergy-led initiatives continued, bolstered by papal support of social and educational programs under the umbrella term lay apostolate. Frank Sheed and Maisie Ward had established Sheed and Ward in London in 1926 to publish works of Catholic history, popular theology, and fiction by the leading lights of the Catholic Revival and later authors who sought to continue their work. In 1933, they opened a

---

[5] F. Scott Fitzgerald to Shane Leslie, late January 1919; August 6, 1920; September 17, 1920 in *The Letters of F. Scott Fitzgerald*, ed. Andrew Turnbull (New York: Charles Scribner's Sons, 1963), 375–378.

branch in New York and lectured frequently at Catholic colleges and secondary schools. Bookstores such as St. Benet's in Chicago and St. Thomas More in Cambridge, Massachusetts, became hubs for informal networks of Catholic activists, especially students. By the end of the 1930s, an American Catholic Revival was taking its own unique shape, centered primarily in lay-led movements with a strong social justice component.

The American Catholic Revival was deeply grounded in life-writings ranging from memoirs and diaries to autobiographical fiction. This kind of literature helped an increasingly educated and self-conscious American laity to find their voices and claim their own Catholic experience. Thomas Merton's surprise bestseller *Seven Story Mountain* (1948), a memoir with a distinctly spiritual component, inspired a subgenre of Catholic spiritual writings, often by priests, monks, and women religious, which flourished from the 1960s onward. In *Color Ebony* (1951), Helen Caldwell Day (1926–2013), an African-American convert to Catholicism, found an opportunity to tell her story and publicly name the racism in her Catholic parish in Mississippi. In *Memories of a Catholic Girlhood* (1957), Mary McCarthy (1912–1989) explores class-consciousness and dysfunction within her prominent upper-middle-class Minneapolis family and closely scrutinizes her departure from the church in early adolescence. She also provides a lyrical account of why she is grateful *to have been* a Catholic. These memoirs contain features that would have troubled Catholic reviewers in previous decades because they described the actual lived experience of American Catholics in the twentieth century.

The writings of Jack Kerouac (1922–1969) hover on the boundary between memoir, confession, and fiction. They unsettled Catholic reviewers who wished to consider the immigrant church buried once and for all and had little stomach for Franco-American anti-Irish-clericalism, not to mention Beat vulgarity. They also disturbed non-Catholic critics for whom the reminiscences of Kerouac's childhood spirituality could only represent some form of pathology. Nevertheless, he is a canonical figure in the American Catholic Revival that reached its culmination just before Vatican II (1962–1965).

The undisputed central figure in the American Catholic Revival is Flannery O'Connor (1925–1964). She is a kindred spirit of the English and European authors of the Catholic Revival, yet distinctly American. In her novels *Wise Blood* (1952) and *The Violent Bear It Away* (1960) and the short stories in *A Good Man Is Hard To Find* (1955) and *Everything That Rises Must Converge* (1965), she examines the dynamics of what she calls "the Catholic sacramental view of life" within narratives set on her home turf, the evangelical Protestant world she saw from her farm near Milledgeville, Georgia. O'Connor's faith was rock-solid and traditional but infused with the insights of recent theologians like Teilhard de Chardin. Her essay, "The Church and the Fiction Writer" (1955), originally written for a LaSalle College symposium on the paucity of writers produced by Catholic colleges, addresses the popular notion that Catholic writers are brainwashed, not free to write what they see. She insists that since Catholic fiction writers start with the belief that human life "has been found by God to be worth dying for," this broadens, rather than constrains their vision, adding that only those with weak faith fear "an honest fictional representation of life."[6]

1960S–1980S: CHANGE AND REALIGNMENT

Flannery O'Connor's appeal to Catholic readers during her lifetime attests to the existence of an educated laity during the 1950s and 1960s that embraced the possibility of increased participation in their church and American society. The election of the first Catholic President, John F. Kennedy, in 1960 and highly publicized discussions of the role of the church in the modern world at Vatican II amplified the expectations of many American Catholics. After Kennedy's assassination in 1963, followed by that of his brother Robert and Martin Luther King, Jr., in 1968, the mood gave way to confusion and despair. The hopes of married people for a change in the church's prohibition of "artificial" birth control were dashed by Pope Paul's encyclical *Humanae Vitae* (On Human Life) in 1968.

The 1960s were barely over when Garry Wills published his evocative postmortem on the Catholic experience in that decade, *Bare Ruined Choirs: Doubt, Prophesy and Radical Religion* (1972). Wills, a former seminarian, has worn many hats: historian, journalist, public intellectual, classical scholar, and commentator on all things Catholic. Wearing several at once, he describes the feelings of loss that accompanied sudden change (or even talk of change) in Catholic life and liturgy, along with the exhilaration felt by those who were relieved not to pretend anymore. He reflects upon how the sense of Catholic identity and difference has been eroding since word got out that the

---

[6] O'Connor, "The Church and the Fiction Writer," 146, 151–152.

Catholic Church intended to join the modern world. Changes in the Mass and religious life were visceral: altars changing direction, hands suddenly touching the host, sisters altering their habits or leaving them behind. There were also theological and spiritual changes that would take much longer to sort out. Such moments inspire writers and artists seeking to make sense of it all.

In 1964, Sister Corita Kent, IHM, (1918–1986) captured the atmosphere of the changing church in her red, yellow, and orange screen-print entitled *the juiciest tomato of all*, an updated image of Mary intended for the post-Vatican II church. With this controversial – but to the artist, deeply spiritual – depiction of the mother of Jesus, Sister Corita, Professor of Art at Immaculate Heart College in Los Angeles, joined the pop art movement recently pioneered by Andy Warhol. The image was devout, but with an edge: this Madonna was clearly the enemy of all forms of commodification. Sister Corita's art became increasingly political, often in the service of peace and civil rights. It also spoke clearly, if implicitly, for women's and sisters' agency and their right to be heard. Her growing reputation brought unwanted fame and unintended conflict with her archbishop. In 1968, Sister Corita took a sabbatical and was released from her vows. By the 1980s, she had moved beyond Christianity and preferred to describe herself as spiritual but not religious – and still a believer in divine mystery.

The Jesuit poet Daniel Berrigan (1921–2016) also combined art and activism, moving in some of the same circles as Sister Corita. Starting in the 1960s, his poetry shifted from biblical and religious topics to moral and political themes. Travel to Paris, Eastern Europe, South Africa, and Latin America awakened Berrigan to pervasive institutionalized violence across the globe. He felt called to social activism and to more explicit and personal forms of poetic expression. His life as a poet dovetailed with his activism. Protests and other actions provided material for his poetry; writing poetry gave him a chance to reflect and a space in which to recover from stressful encounters.

In 1968, Berrigan and his brother Philip, a Josephite priest, were involved in burning draft files in Catonsville, Maryland, to protest the Vietnam War, and were arrested. The prose-poems in *The Dark Night of Resistance* (1971) bear witness to his experience as a fugitive, still protesting the war between his trial and his imprisonment. Writing *Prison Poems* (1973) about the men he knew while incarcerated at Danbury Prison constituted another form of protest, another action, as well as a needed sanctuary for the poet. Berrigan's productivity was prodigious. *And the Risen Bread: Selected Poems, 1957–1997* helps us to place his activist poems within the larger corpus of his work.

The 1970s and 1980s were decades of realignment for American Catholics. Concrete reforms that many had expected (approval of contraception, the ordination of women and married men, amnesty for divorced Catholics) did not materialize. Liturgical changes left Catholics in limbo, with a Mass that offered little comfort to the old and did not keep the young in the church. New forms of confession first felt awkward, and then seemed optional. Many laypeople and an alarming number of priests and sisters did what was formerly unthinkable and left the church. Two commercially successful first novels capture the atmosphere in the Catholic community immediately following the pivotal 1960s: Mary Gordon's *Final Payments* (1978) and Andrew Greeley's *The Cardinal Sins* (1981). Both are the literary equivalent of buddy films and tell stories of departure and return (on one's own terms). Both are serious explorations of American Catholic attitudes toward sexuality in the postconciliar years. These novels, which showed lay people and their priests grappling with religious and moral issues in a changing ecclesiastical landscape, helped Catholics to reflect upon what it meant to live their faith after Vatican II.

Final Payments established an audience for Gordon, primarily, but not exclusively, women considering new roles and choices that had previously been closed to them because of their sex or religion. It shows how female friendship can expose new answers to moral questions and replace or supplement the spirituality proffered by the parish priest. It takes an honest look at fundamental relationships that have always been the bedrock of Catholicism, e.g. father–daughter, pastor–layperson, and suggests realignments in the light of an emerging Catholic feminist movement. Its final chapter reexamines sin and guilt in ways that were especially helpful, even therapeutic, for women attempting to be feminists and still remain Catholics.

In *The Cardinal Sins*, Andrew Greeley, journalist, sociologist of religion, and dedicated pastor, applies what he has learned in a popular format. Greeley focuses on four characters, two young men who become priests, and two young women with messy personal lives, who came of age in the same Chicago Catholic circles on the eve of Vatican II. The plot allows Greeley to reiterate critiques of hierarchical power and clergy sexual abuse that he had already aired as a journalist. Greeley, the novelist, empowered his many readers to find their voices and lose their inhibitions when in the presence of priests and bishops. *The Cardinal Sins* and several of Greeley's subsequent novels made the

New York Times bestseller list. When criticized by conservative Catholics for writing "steamy novels" unbefitting a priest, he replied that his fiction was "the most priestly thing I have ever done."[7]

The evolution of American Catholic literature from the 1920s through the 1980s hinged upon a shift from clerical control and the search for a unified Catholic vision to a proliferation of voices and a clear demand by women (sisters and laity) to be heard. Even when acting as agents of social change, individual American Catholics remained aware that their faith made them different from other Americans, including fellow Christians. Speaking among themselves, however, they no longer agreed on the nature of Catholic difference. These same trends were visible when Catholics entered the new worlds of film and television.

FILM AND TELEVISION

The same war that convinced George Shuster of the church's potential to transform modern society became the occasion for the American Catholic bishops' first foray into film censorship. In 1917, the newly established National Catholic War Council mobilized members of Catholic organizations across America to protest showing *Fit to Fight*, a film about venereal disease, to troops. From this point on, the bishops considered film censorship part of their mandate and gladly entered into unprecedented collaborations with other Christians and moral reformers who had similar concerns about immorality in the movies. In 1922, they fought alongside Will Hayes, Presbyterian elder and Postmaster General, who did public relations work for the film industry, to defeat a Massachusetts film censorship bill. (Hayes wanted to preserve the studios' right to censor themselves; the bishops opposed state regulation boards as an invasion of the rights of the church and the family.)

In 1930, Daniel Lord, who reviewed films for the *Queen's Work*, built upon Hayes's guidelines for studios, the "Don'ts and Be Carefuls," in composing a Motion Picture Code. One of the premises of the code was that films appealed to a mixed audience, generally less educated, less mature, and more impressionable than the reading public, or those attending plays and art shows, and therefore they represented a more serious moral danger. Films must not provide instruction in criminal methods or glamorize crime. They should not make sin (e.g., adultery,

---

7   Peter Steinfels, "Andrew M. Greeley, Priest, Scholar and Scold, Is Dead at 85," *New York Times*, May 30, 2013.

theft, blasphemy, or acts of violence) look attractive, and they should never show disrespect for marriage, religious figures or rituals, the nation, or any kind of authority. In addition, films should treat relations between the sexes discreetly and respectfully and never feature nudity.

Since 1922, women of the International Federation of Catholic Alumnae had been publishing reviews of films they considered worthy, making no mention of the others. In 1933, American Catholic bishops assembled in Washington launched a more aggressive effort to distinguish acceptable films from objectionable ones: the National Legion of Decency, centered in New York, with branches in individual dioceses. The Legion worked closely with the Production Code Administration (PCA) in Hollywood, which reviewed scripts and sought to remove problem language and scenes proactively. The Legion in New York viewed films in (what studios hoped was) their final form and assigned one of three categories: A (morally unobjectionable, later divided to designate films only adults could see); B (morally objectionable in part); and C (condemned). If a film was condemned, the studio could revise and resubmit. Priests associated with the Legion engaged in detailed negotiations, which resulted in cutting or reshooting entire scenes and occasionally the inclusion of a prologue or epilogue. The Legion's lists were posted in church vestibules. Each year, through the 1950s, the Legion's oath (which included a promise to boycott condemned films and theaters showing them) was administered during Mass on December 8, the Feast of the Immaculate Conception.

This system was surprisingly effective during the 1930s and 1940s. Often studios anticipated the reactions of the PCA and the Legion and removed objectionable treatments of sex, crime, marriage, and religious or civil authority to avoid the expense of editing and reshooting later on. Films of this period closely reflected the values of the hierarchy. There are many myths about the Code, e.g., that it mandated twin beds and all kisses were limited to ten seconds in duration. The PCA's judgments concerning the overall moral impact of a given film, however, were more nuanced and ad hoc than these myths would suggest.[8] Starting in the late 1950s, studios, directors, and Catholic viewers who trusted their own consciences began to push back against the Legion and the PCA. Meanwhile, laymen working at the PCA, some of whom were sophisticated non-Catholics and ex-seminarians, increasingly found themselves at odds with the priests representing the Legion. The PCA,

---

[8]   See Jack Vizzard, *See No Evil: Life Inside a Hollywood Censor* (New York: Simon and Schuster, 1970), 111–120.

the Legion, and the Code were casualties of the enthusiasm for reform that preceded Vatican II.

Popular Hollywood films reflect American values: how they have depicted Catholics and their church helps us to gauge how others viewed Catholics. Catholic director Leo McCarey won nine Oscars for his sentimental film *Going My Way* (1944), including best picture. It was the first of two films in which Bing Crosby plays Father Chuck O'Malley, an all-American Midwestern musician-turned priest who makes Catholics proud to be different. The Academy's especially warm reception of the film derived in part from Catholic visibility in World War II. After the war, the Catholic church in the United States received an unprecedented number of converts, and this film hints at what some of them found attractive: a community grounded in an ancient tradition that knew what it believed but understood human finitude, cared for strangers and the elderly, forgave the truly penitent, and offered new beginnings.

Like their literary counterparts, directors from Catholic backgrounds often shunned the label "Catholic director" but there is a certain Catholic sensibility in their films.[9] It revolves around an awareness that God's grace and presence enter our world through humans and nature. It presupposes that humans have inherent dignity, and are never purely evil; they are always fallible and always redeemable. This comes through in explicitly religious films such as *The Last Temptation of Christ* (1988), which prompted scathing attacks from conservative Christians, Catholics included. Director Martin Scorsese, no longer a practicing Catholic, fired back: "I'm a lapsed Catholic, but I *am* a Roman Catholic—there's no way out of it."[10]

Traces of Catholicism in otherwise secular films often have their origins in a director's childhood experiences. Alfred Hitchcock's preoccupation with marginality and the underside of middle-class respectability was rooted in his boyhood experience in a working-class Irish Catholic enclave in England. John Ford's dogmatic views on the sanctity of the family and of all kinds of authority, inculcated by his Irish immigrant parents, made his films seem nostalgic and retrogressive to critics raised in a different America. Francis Ford Coppola, son of a

---

[9]   See Anthony Burke Smith, *The Look of Catholics: Portrayals in Popular Culture from the Great Depression to the Cold War* (Lawrence: University Press of Kansas, 2010).

[10]   Quoted in Richard A. Blake, *AfterImage: The Indelible Catholic Imagination of Six American Filmmakers* (Chicago: Loyola Press, 2000), 25.

professional flutist who became a music arranger for Radio City Music Hall, came from an Italian-American world where the sacraments were not primarily individual milestones, but bulwarks of the family, a vision that shines through his three *Godfather* movies. Catholic Hollywood, from the censors and the PCA to the lived faith of actors, directors, and studio employees, still awaits its historian.

The story of Catholics in television bears witness to an almost shocking revelation: Catholic difference can be very telegenic. This first became apparent in 1952 when Bishop Fulton J. Sheen (1895–1979), resplendent in his purple bishop's robes, launched his phenomenally successful television show "Life Is Worth Living" (1952–1957). That year, Sheen was watched by an estimated 5.7 million people from divergent religious backgrounds and walks of life. On television and in his many popular books, Sheen achieved what advocates of the Catholic Revival had dreamed of decades before. He packaged the natural law theology of Thomas Aquinas, the official Catholic theology, in ways that were attractive and interesting to heterogeneous audiences, and explained that our lives are only worth living when oriented toward the ends for which God created us.

His most memorable show, "The Death of Stalin," which aired on February 24, 1953, articulated Catholic opposition to communism, incorporated Sheen's dramatic reading from *Julius Caesar*, and predicted impending judgment upon Stalin, who died soon after on March 5. On every show, Sheen presented Catholic teachings clearly stated and carefully packaged, but never watered-down. He held them up against the generic, nondemanding, nondenominational "peace of mind" spirituality that had gained a substantial following after World War II. Sheen did not shrink from addressing controversial teachings associated with Catholics, such as Confession, which, he asserted, was far superior to Freudian analysis, or the Virgin Mary, whom he considered the answer to the Cold War. His sponsor, the Admiral Radio Corporation, considered Sheen's show well worth their million-dollar investment.

In 1981, another pioneer in Catholic broadcasting, Mother Angelica (1923–2016), a Poor Clare nun in a Birmingham, Alabama, monastery, took Catholic television to the next level and established the Eternal Word Television Network (EWTN). In the late 1970s, Mother Angelica, already a local celebrity on religious radio, began broadcasting on Christian cable television, taping her segments in the local studio of a secular network. In 1978, after a confrontation with the studio over its airing of a film she considered blasphemous, Mother Angelica established her own studio in her monastery's garage. This story about confrontation and Mother Angelica's preference for working within Catholic circles presages the rest of her career in broadcasting.

Sheen had sought to persuade outsiders, especially atheists and communists, to convert to Catholicism in an age in which the church's intellectual traditions and ancient rituals attracted unchurched Americans. In a very different Catholic moment marked by change and realignment, Mother Angelica trained her sights on fellow Catholics, hoping to reverse the erosion of Catholic orthodoxy that she believed came from a misinterpretation of Vatican II. She fought protracted battles against inclusive language in the catechism and promoted the Latin Mass, which she considered the true legacy of the liturgical reform movement at mid-century. Unlike Sheen, the theology professor, with his carefully structured arguments, Mother Angelica preferred a talk-show format, which allowed her to go wherever the Spirit took her. Her popularity with Catholic audiences confirmed and catalyzed a shift within the American Catholic community by the 1980s that paralleled the growth of conservative evangelical Protestantism at the same time. Her embrace of traditional Catholic morality and return to (what more progressive Catholics considered) a pre-Vatican II definition of the church as the hierarchy followed closely by the faithful coincided with the political migration of Catholics toward the Republican Party. In the spirit of Mother Angelica, the EWTN community gladly shares moral and political turf with conservative Protestants, but they remain firmly grounded in Catholic difference and spiritual superiority. At the time of Mother Angelica's death, EWTN reached 264 million homes in 144 countries.

A third major Catholic figure in American television is the comedian-commentator Stephen Colbert (1964–). Colbert, born during Vatican II, is not the only Catholic who has hosted on late-night television. Jimmy Kimmel, Conan O'Brien, and Jimmy Fallon have referred to their Catholic boyhoods from time to time. Colbert, a former CCD teacher, appears more comfortable going broader and deeper into Catholic topics than his counterparts. As the correspondent on *The Daily Show* (1997–2005) and *The Colbert Report* (2005–2014), he returned repeatedly to distinctive Catholic beliefs and spirituality. On September 14, 2012, he participated in a public dialogue on "Humor, Joy, and the Spiritual Life" with Cardinal Timothy Dolan at Fordham University. He has an inner compass concerning which aspects of the Catholic experience he can parody and which are off-limits. He steers clear of the sacraments and even sacramentals like the crucifix, for instance, but insists that Catholic involvement in politics and other kinds of social behavior is fair game.

Colbert's confidence, grounded in the common knowledge that he is a practicing Catholic, makes him comfortable jovially urging Bill Maher, self-proclaimed agnostic, to come back to the church and defending the real presence of Christ in the Eucharist against Catholic experts like Garry Wills. He quite naturally quotes Matthew 25 in response to Jeb Bush's contentions regarding refugees. These discussions are deadly serious, but they work within a larger matrix of humor. Catholics and post-Catholics, ranging from baby boomers to millennials, were used to getting their news from *The Daily Show* and found it was also a good place to receive upgrades in religious instruction.

Twenty-first century American Catholics were quick to recognize the promise of cyberspace. First in blogs, and later on Facebook and Twitter, Catholics of all ideological and theological stripes have found a platform for discussions of Catholic difference, identity, history, culture, and spirituality. The impact of clerical celebrities like Bishop Robert Barron (Word on Fire ministries), James Martin, SJ, and Pope Francis on Twitter has heartened those who have despaired of dwindling numbers in Catholic schools and parish Masses. Facebook and Twitter have made possible new kinds of community, amplifying the diverse voices of the laity. When diocesan teachers went on strike in Philadelphia in 2012, busy parents who had no time to meet shared responses and strategies on Facebook. Of course, the social media platforms have also exacerbated divisions within the church, giving rise to newfound mutations of the age-old Catholic tribalism.

EPILOGUE: *HEAVENLY BODIES*

On May 10, 2018, the Metropolitan Museum of Art in New York and the Met Cloisters opened *Heavenly Bodies: Fashion and the Catholic Imagination*, an unprecedented interdisciplinary exhibition on the influence of Roman Catholicism on dress and the fashion industry. The artworks included pontifical vestments and accessories displayed in the Anna Wintour Costume Center; Byzantine, medieval, and early modern religious costumes housed in the appropriate galleries; and the habits of religious orders at the Cloisters. Exhibits illuminated the influence of Catholic ritual and spirituality upon designer clothing, e.g., Dolce & Gabbana's silk organza gown which features a portrait of the Virgin and Child sewn with gold and silver thread and gold seed beads, and a seemingly endless array of costumes and accessories, each paired with original works of art. A blue silk Lanvin gown with gold and silver embroidery is displayed alongside Fra Angelico's *Saint Dominic and His Companions Fed by Angels* (ca. 1430–1432), in which an angel wears corresponding blue-and-gold robes.

Even viewed in the lavish catalog, the exhibition produces a strange combination of sensory overload and fervent desire for asceticism. It represents the combined efforts of devout Catholics, lapsed Catholics, and others who only wish to participate in the church through art. It also incarnates memories of sacramental experiences, when humans are graced with God's presence. Catholicism teaches that such encounters are everyday affairs, mediated through physical realities such as water, bread, wine, oil, human bodies, art – and perhaps finely wrought clothing. *Heavenly Bodies* is a twenty-first-century celebration of the sacramental imagination and a reminder that the future shape of American Catholic art and culture is wide open, and, due to its very nature, remains a mystery.

FURTHER READING

Black, Gregory D. *The Catholic Crusade against the Movies, 1940–1975*. New York: Cambridge University Press, 1997.

Blake, Richard A. *Afterimage: The Indelible Catholic Imagination of Six American Filmmakers*. Chicago: Loyola Press, 2000.

Giles, Paul. *American Catholic Arts and Fictions: Culture, Ideology, Aesthetics*. New York: Cambridge University Press, 1992.

Greeley, Andrew. *The Catholic Imagination*. Berkeley: University of California Press, 2000.

Messbarger, Paul R. *Fiction with a Parochial Purpose: Social Uses of American Catholic Literature*. Boston: Boston University Press, 1971.

Sparr, Arnold. *To Promote, Defend, and Redeem: The Catholic Literary Revival and the Cultural Transformation of American Catholicism*. New York: Greenwood Press, 1990.

Walsh, Frank. *Sin and Censorship: The Catholic Church and the Motion Picture Industry*. New Haven, CT: Yale University Press, 1996.

11 Anti-Catholicism in the United States

MARK MASSA, SJ

EXPLANATIONS FOR THE ANTI-CATHOLIC BIAS

The perception of Roman Catholic faith, practice, and polity as being either corrupt, superstitious, undemocratic, or somehow "un-American," dates back to the arrival of British Protestants in New England in the seventeenth century, and has morphed into newer shapes more recently in social media. It has been labeled "the deepest bias in the history of the American people" by historian Arthur Schlesinger, Jr.; others have termed it the "anti-Semitism of the intellectuals" and "the last acceptable prejudice."[1]

There are three large groupings of explanations that seek to explain why and how this bias emerged so early (and stayed so late) in US culture, usually labeled, respectively, the "cultural," "intellectual," and "sociological" explanatory narratives. Arguably the oldest and most widespread set of explanations can be categorized as *cultural.*

In the cultural set of explanations, American national identity was itself profoundly shaped by its Puritan founding, thus making anti-Catholicism part of an American value system marked by a distinctively *Protestant* ethos: a fear of unlimited government (and thus of the unlimited powers of the pope); a call for direct personal participation in democratic decisions, resting on the Congregationalist tradition of democratic church government polity and personal conversion as the basis for church membership (as opposed to a Catholic "top-down" model of church run by popes and bishops); a Protestant work ethic which bade believers to devote themselves soberly and diligently to their "calling" – an ethic that led to the kind of material prosperity that scholars like Max Weber argued provided the rich soil from which modern capitalism grew; a revered tradition of literacy and public education, as everyone was expected to encounter the Word of God directly

---

[1] James Martin, "The Last Acceptable Prejudice?" *America* 182 (March 25, 2000): 9.

by reading the Bible, and not be dependent on priests to explain what the Bible taught; and a deep suspicion of Catholic nations like Spain and France, both of which were marked by absolute monarchies that were the avowed political enemies of Protestant England.[2]

A slight variation on this explanation of the Protestant cultural origin of US public culture has been pressed by scholars of evangelical revivalism like William McLoughlin and Donald Mathews, who date the emergence of a distinctively American character to the nineteenth, as opposed to the seventeenth, century. In this version, the successive waves of "great awakenings" that shaped US political and cultural history during the first third of the nineteenth century gave rise to a resolutely *evangelical* Protestant understanding of culture that found in the Catholicism of Irish and Italian immigrants a rhetorical and institutional foil against which revivalist preachers could rail. In this accounting, the warm and intense religious societies that emerged from the Second Great Awakening offered the young republic the ready-to-hand model of small-scale congregations whose leaders were chosen, paid, and directly answerable to the individuals who comprised the local congregation – over against the model of unelected and distant Old World hierarchies who stirred the deepest suspicions of second-generation republican Americans.[3]

The second set of explanations for the long tradition of anti-Catholicism in US culture can be labeled "*intellectual*," in that it substitutes philosophical ideas in place of cultural traditions as the origin of anti-Catholicism in the United States. These ideas have been presented as arising variously from the English (Lockean) or Scottish ("Common Sense Realism") Enlightenments, the Whig tradition of political thought, or a combination of all of them. Further, this set of explanations emphasizes the ideas of religious liberty and the inviolability of individual conscience in making decisions (as opposed to waiting for the church to tell you what to do); the belief in the free expression of personal opinion in both speech and print; and, most importantly, the idea that religion should be kept separate from the protocols of the state, and a profound belief in "America's mission" as the universal beacon of democracy (presented either as "manifest destiny" or "millennialism") invariably show up as core ideas.

---

[2] William Haller, "John Foxe and the Puritan Revolution," in *The Seventeenth Century*, ed. Richard F. Jones (Stanford: Stanford University Press, 1951), 213–219.

[3] Donald G. Mathews, "The Second Great Awakening as an Organizing Process," *American Quarterly* 21 (1969): 24–28.

Arguably the single most important and influential scholarly voice behind this interpretation of the intellectual roots of US culture (and concurrently of Catholic "otherness") was Yale scholar Ralph Henry Gabriel, whose *The Course of American Democratic Thought* (1940) influenced several generations of intellectual historians and cultural commentators. Gabriel's history of "defining ideas" was organized around what he termed three "doctrines": a frank supernaturalism derived from Christianity; the belief in the "free individual ... derived from the moral order," which made the commitment to individual freedom a *religious,* as well as a political idea; and the belief in the "mission of America [because of] its unique origin and unique destiny" to lead the world to freedom, decency, and economic affluence – that is, a commitment to a universal national, as opposed to church, mission to "save the world."[4]

The third set of explanations for the anti-Catholic animus in US thought and culture is rooted in the social sciences, and are usually presented under the rubric of either "nativism" or "secularization." Nativism is most often defined as a fear of social "outsiders" by cultural insiders and rests on work done by sociology's founding father, Emile Durkheim. Durkheim argued at the dawn of the twentieth century that social deviance in all of its forms (the persecution of religious heretics, the hunt for political subversives, the oppression of ethnic and racial outcasts) performs an absolutely essential service in all human societies by establishing the boundaries that define the controlling group. Durkheim, therefore, argued (in one of the founding documents of the modern discipline of sociology) that all societies may be said to *invent* deviance – a property not inherent in any set of human actions or beliefs, but rather a designation *conferred on* certain kinds of religious, political, or social behaviors by the community to demonstrate where the line was drawn between behavior and values that define "us" and behavior and values that belong to "them."[5]

Generations of social historians have applied Durkheim's insights to the North American tradition of anti-Catholicism to argue that the animus was *not* primarily a cultural or intellectual inheritance from America's past, but rather a function of "boundary maintenance" throughout American history – defining and guarding the boundary

4   Ralph Henry Gabriel, *The Course of American Democratic Thought: An Intellectual History Since 1815* (New York: Ronald Press, 1940), 22–23.
5   Mark Massa, *Anti-Catholicism in America: The Last Acceptable Prejudice?* (New York: Oxford University Press, 2003), 14–15.

between the *real* American identity (white, Anglo-Saxon, Protestants), and the spurious hybrid forms crafted by "others" arriving (undigested) from abroad. Thus, John Higham, in a work that was regarded for decades as the most thorough and reliable study of nativism in the United States, argued that anti-Catholicism was "by far the oldest and the most powerful of the anti-foreign traditions," precisely because it allowed an odd assortment of fellow patriots – working-class laborers, evangelicals, southern "states' rights" conservatives, northern progressive reformers and Protestant social gospellers – to unite to repel "influences originating from abroad [that] threatened the very life of the nation from within." And those "influences" reflected the spectrum of threats nativists most feared among Catholic immigrants: "others" from nondemocratic, non-Protestant, and non-English speaking cultures who were perceived to pose a direct threat to how North American society understood itself.[6]

PATTERNS OF ANTI-CATHOLIC ACTIVITY IN THE UNITED STATES

The Colonial Era

Cavalier Anglicans in Virginia no less than nonseparating Puritans in New England had been cradled in a mother country that was more bitterly distrustful of Catholic faith and practice than at any other time, before or since. That distrust was based in part on what they perceived to be Catholicism's "anti-national character": Roman Catholicism's very "catholicity" – its claim to transcend mere "nationalistic" loyalties in its devotion to the Pope as the source of church unity regardless of language, ethnicity, or political beliefs – bred fear and suspicion of Catholic belief and practice not only as a theological system antagonistic to the Church of England's Thirty-Nine Articles and the Puritans' Westminster Confession, but just as importantly as a very real political and military threat to the English government itself. Nationalistic loyalties and fears, therefore, were so intertwined with theological beliefs in the colonial distrust of the Roman Catholic Church and its adherents that it is difficult to disentangle them in any clear-cut way.[7]

---

[6] John Higham, *Strangers in the Land: Patterns of American Nativism, 1850–1925* (New Brunswick: Rutgers University Press, 1955), 3, 4.

[7] Ray Allen Billington, *The Protestant Crusade, 1800–1860: A Study of the Origins of American Nativism* (New York: Macmillan, 1938), 1.

And while some of those nationalistic fears were the product of jingoistic hysteria, some of them were most assuredly not baseless. "Treasonous" Catholic attempts at overthrowing the British state was most famously embodied in the Gunpowder Plot in 1605, in which several dozen Catholics conspired to blow up Parliament (and the Queen to boot) by stockpiling barrels of gunpowder in the cellar under the House of Commons. The annual celebration marking the "foiling" of that plot arrived with the first settlers and was observed annually on November 5. Guy Fawkes Day (also called "Pope Day") was a yearly public holiday marked by the burning of an effigy of the pope on town commons up and down the eastern seaboard while children sang anti-Catholic ditties ("Remember, remember, the fifth of November") and adults drank rounds of toasts to the overthrow of the pope (more commonly referred to on these occasions as "The Beast" described in the Book of Revelation). Guy Fawkes Day was celebrated in both the northern and southern colonies from the mid-seventeenth century until 1775, when General George Washington issued an intercolonial order forbidding its continued observance, as part of a larger strategic effort to enlist the support of the French (Catholic) Province of Quebec in what was then emerging as a revolutionary war against the mother country. What had begun as a partly nationalistic celebration was thus ended for equally nationalistic concerns.[8]

This much-anticipated November 5th holiday served as an emblematic public ritual testifying to a much broader series of political and legal constraints on Catholics in most of the colonies: "papists" were forbidden from holding public office, carrying firearms, or serving on juries in both Virginia (by a 1641 act of the House of Burgesses) and in Maryland; indeed, in the latter colony (first settled by the Catholic George Calvert, Lord Baltimore), a 1654 law announced that "none who profess to exercise the Popish religion can be protected in this colony." But far more famous for its anti-Catholic virulence was the Puritan colony of Massachusetts Bay, whose General Court decreed in 1647 that "any Jesuit or priest coming within the colony was to be banished, and if he return, executed." That same Court enacted laws forbidding the December celebration of the "Popish festival of Christmas," and the "importation of any Irish persons whatsoever." "Break the Pope's Neck" was a popular fireside game for New England children, while the New England Primer – the "hornbook" on which children learned

---

[8]   Massa, *Anti-Catholicism*, 18–19.

their ABCs with little phrases to help memorize the alphabet – offered
as the phrase for remembering the letter A "abhor that abhorrent Whore
of Rome."[9]

The American Revolution is sometimes presented as the cultural
moment when colonial anti-Catholicism was put to rest, especially
after the entry of Catholic France into the conflict in 1778 on the side
of the colonists. This supposed demise of the animus is often presented
as one of the healthy byproducts of the triumph of Enlightenment
reason among colonial leaders like Washington, Jefferson, and
Madison, and the enshrinement of that devotion to reason in the
founding documents of the new republic. But scholars of the stature of
Carl Bridenbaugh, Nathan Hatch, and Alan Heimert have documented
with compelling evidence the continued importance of colonial
(Protestant) fears of Catholic designs on North America.

One of the most common pieces of evidence produced to witness
to the importance of anti-Catholicism in the ideology of the patriots
was the colonial response to the Quebec Act of 1774. That act, passed
by the British Parliament to pacify ever-fractious North American
colonists, granted religious toleration to Catholic citizens in the
British province of Quebec (who represented the vast majority of colonists in the province, and who had previously been forbidden by
British law from publicly practicing their religion). Far from celebrating that extension of religious toleration to citizens in a neighboring
British colony, revolutionary propagandist Samuel Adams argued that
the 1774 Act evinced an unholy alliance between an autocratic king
(George III) and an equally autocratic pope. Adams therewith drafted
the (in)famous "Suffolk Resolves" – the single most virulent and
inflammatory colonial petition against the British produced in the
years before 1776, which garnered widespread support in New
England and further afield.[10]

But more revealing in illustrating not only the continuance, but the
actual growth, of anti-Catholicism during the Revolutionary Era, has
been scholarly studies undertaken by historians like James Davidson
and Robert Handy, who along with a number of others, have documented the close tie between the "left wing" of colonial evangelicals
(who had vigorously supported the revivals of Jonathan Edwards in New
England and the Tennent brothers in New Jersey) and support for the

---

9   Billington, *The Protestant Crusade*, 7–8, 16.
10   Massa, *Anti-Catholicism*, 20–21.

revolutionary cause "on the ground" by nonelites.[11] In this "evangelical interpretation" of the American Revolution, while elites like the signers of the Declaration of Independence certainly knew well, and quoted often, the bright lights of the English and Scottish Enlightenments of the seventeenth century, the impulses that energized the vast majority of colonial soldiers – who had never heard of, much less read, John Locke – had been galvanized in the fires of evangelical revivals, which had denounced the "carnal Christianity" of the Catholic Church no less than the Church of England. For those soldiers of the cross reborn under revivalist preaching, the very idea that "hierarchies" (bishops no less than kings) could somehow mediate between believers and a direct and personal experience of the Holy One witnessed to a usurpation of the rights of believers that had to be fought against. That usurpation not only paralleled that of colonial rights by the British Parliament: it was part and parcel of it. In Handy's account of the meaning of the Revolution, therefore, the Christian soldiers who overcame the Mother Country at Yorktown proceeded to erect a "voluntary establishment" of Protestant Christianity that would provide the soul and ethos of the new nation. That establishment celebrated direct personal experience, equality in both church and state, and a deep suspicion of clerical elites. "While the means to effect this vision were to be voluntary and persuasive" (rather than legal) "the goal of a Christian [meaning evangelical Protestant] was as clear as it had been in the days of legal establishment – even clearer." As soon became evident by the opening of the nineteenth century, those who opposed this evangelical vision of a "voluntary establishment" of Protestant Christianity as the soul of the Republic – Catholics especially – became the brunt of nationalistic, theological, and political fears. Those fears had not been interrupted by the Revolution according to the evangelical account of the revolutionary cause; they were generated by it.[12]

More recently a number of revisionist historians have reframed the positive correlation between an evangelical Protestantism forged in the fires of the First Great Awakening and support for the patriot cause against old England, limning a more complicated understanding of the religious impulses fueling revolutionary fervor. Maura Jane Farrelly, for instance, has argued persuasively that "papist patriots" were more likely than their

---

[11] Robert Handy, *A Christian America: Protestant Hopes and Historical Realities* (New York: Oxford University Press, 1971), 56, 58.
[12] Massa, *Anti-Catholicism*, 21–22.

Protestant neighbors to enthusiastically support the independence movement. Farrelly's work, in addition to problematizing the older Heimert/
Handy thesis regarding the evangelical interpretation of the Revolution,
also adumbrates the colonial roots of a distinctively American "brand" of
Catholicism less devoted to hierarchy and more devoted to a voluntaristic
understanding of their faith. As Farrelly argues the case, the very constraints and indignities imposed on them during the colonial (British)
"Penal Period" made Maryland Catholics the most prepared colonists to
support the cultural and ideological implication of a break with the
oppressive Mother Country in 1776, and belies a narrative in which
evangelical Protestants comprised the most fervent supporters of the
"glorious cause."[13]

The Nineteenth Century

The rise of dramatic anti-Catholic activity in the early decades of the
nineteenth century coincided with the arrival of Irish Catholic
immigrants in steady but hardly overwhelming numbers in the ports
of Boston and New York in the 1830s – a fact that reveals the deepest
roots of anti-Catholic prejudice after the Revolutionary Era. For while
the pattern of anti-Catholic activity in the colonial era certainly
evinced nativist and nationalist impulses, theological concerns still
played an important role in the mix of motives for the animus.
Nativist fears emerged front and center as the leading source of anti-
papal activity after 1830.

The single most famous artifact in nineteenth-century American
popular culture witnessing to the virulence of this animus was the
publication in 1836 of Maria Monk's *Awful Disclosures of the Hôtel
Dieu Monastery in Montreal*. The (almost completely fictitious) "disclosures" narrated by Monk offered a deliciously salacious escape
account of a poor Protestant girl held captive against her will in a
convent full of secret doors to priests' bedrooms, buried bodies of nuns'
illegitimate children, and dark rituals in the convent chapel. Equal parts
pornographic depiction of priest and nun couplings and purple prose,
Monk's account was published by a dummy press in New York City
funded by several Protestant clergymen, the manuscript having been
prudently rejected by the Harper publishing house. It was, nonetheless,
one of the best sellers of the antebellum period, along with *Uncle Tom's*

---

[13]   Maura Jane Farrelly, *Papist Patriots: The Making of an American Catholic Identity*
       (New York: Oxford University Press, 2012), 236–240.

Cabin, if aimed at a somewhat less discriminating readership than the latter. Monk's work is still in print today.[14]

Readers of the *Disclosures* learned (along with the hapless heroine) that she "to her utter astonishment and horror was to live in the practice of criminal intercourse with [the priests]." The children born from these unholy unions were immediately baptized and strangled, which (in the words of the convent's mother superior) "secured their everlasting happiness ... How happy are those who secure immortal happiness in such little beings!" Monk's account, unsurprisingly, led to "convent investigating committees" in a number of cities, made up of outraged citizens concerned about the unholy doings going on in their neighborhoods under the guise of religion, which in turn led to other (equally salacious) convent exposes. Indeed, "escaped nun tales" comprise an interesting and important genre for understanding mid-nineteenth century popular literary culture – a surprisingly large genre with titles like *Six Months in a Convent, The Testimony of an Escaped Novice,* and *Rosamund.*[15]

Convent tales represented the "low culture" version of a vast anti-Catholic publishing tradition that flourished in the first half of the nineteenth century at every level of mainstream Protestant culture. Both the American Home Missionary Society and the American Tract Society – pillars of the evangelical empire that published literally hundreds of pamphlets to be read both at home and Sunday School – produced numerous titles "exposing" the crimes of the Jesuits and other assorted Catholic conspirators against American liberties. The title of one of the most famous of these works – written by Samuel F. B. Morse (of Code fame) – encapsulated the theme of most of them: *A Foreign Conspiracy against the Liberties of the United States.* Morse's book was serialized in the pages of the *New York Observer* throughout the fall of 1834 to sensational popularity, and was immediately picked up and reprinted by various denominational newspapers before being published in monograph form in December. Morse's "foreign conspiracy" posited a labyrinthine plot between the pope and the crumbling monarchies of the Old World: in order for the monarchies to survive they had to enlist the aid of "the other great foe of liberty, the Catholic Church." The concrete expression of affecting their aim was to inundate the United States with illiterate and drunken immigrants hatching unspeakable plots against the democratic liberties; and, of course, the

---

[14]   Massa, *Anti-Catholicism,* 22.
[15]   Massa, *Anti-Catholicism,* 23.

mastermind of all of this was the Jesuit order. Morse thus urged his fellow Protestants to rise above their denominational squabbles and unite in opposing the two greatest threats: parochial schools and Catholic officeholders.[16]

The single most famous anti-Catholic event of the nineteenth century was the burning of the Ursuline Convent in Charlestown, Massachusetts, on August 11, 1834. On the extraordinarily hot evening of August 10, 1834, Lyman Beecher (father of both Harriet Beecher Stowe and Henry Ward Beecher) delivered the last of three virulently anti-Catholic sermons, arguing that if the Catholics had their way, especially through the crafty ruse of running schools like the one in Charlestown, they would be quite successful in their aim of "subverting our free institutions and bring into disgrace all ideas of an effective government."[17]

The Ursuline Convent School was in fact an exclusive finishing school, many of whose students were the daughters of Boston's liberal Unitarian aristocracy. Thus, economic and class tensions played as significant a role in the events that followed as theological ones. But within hours of Beecher's third sermon, a working-class mob (composed largely of Scots-Irish Presbyterian bricklayers) attacked the school, outraged that Unitarian merchants and bankers could deliver their own daughters into the hands of Catholic nuns for their education. The misogynist fear and suspicion of nuns as self-sufficient women "living on their own" without husbands or fathers overseeing them likewise informed the motives of the working class mob. One rioter, interviewed a few days after the attack, defended his own role in burning down the convent by asserting that "bishops and priests *pretended* to live without wives, but the nuns were kept to supply this particular." The newspaper article reporting the rioter's defense went on to drily declare: "He said this in vulgar language."[18]

Despite the outcry against the burning made by Protestant city leaders like Harrison Gray Otis, all of the rioters who stood trial – save one – were acquitted by the sympathetic jury. Their defense attorney had baldly stated in his argument to the jury that his clients "cannot be convicted without Catholic testimony, and we will endeavor to show what that testimony is worth." The Charlestown convent school was in

16 Massa, *Anti-Catholicism*, 23–24.
17 Nancy Lusignan Schultz, *Fire and Roses: The Burning of the Charlestown Convent, 1834* (New York: Free Press, 2000), 182.
18 Schultz, *Fire and Roses*, 182.

fact the first in a series of attacks against Catholic property, flaring up a decade later when two Catholic churches in Philadelphia were destroyed by a mob on May 8, 1844.[19]

Local "No Popery" impulses became organized on a national level in May 1848, with the formation of the American and Foreign Christian Union, whose constitution announced the Union's dedication to "diffuse and promote the principles of religious liberty, and a pure and Evangelical Christianity both at home and abroad, wherever a corrupted Christianity exists." The new Union represented the merging of three separate evangelical Protestant voluntary societies that had been operating for a number of years: the American Protestant Society, which had dedicated itself to converting to "true Christianity" both unchurched Americans and recently arrived Irish and German Catholic immigrants; the Foreign Evangelical Society, which had been formed in 1839 to convert French Catholics to Protestantism; and the erstwhile Christian Alliance in Italy.[20]

These "missionary" manifestations of a vibrant anti-Catholic impulse in the years before the Civil War coalesced into more overtly political form in 1849 in the meteoric rise of the American Party, more generally known among students of American history as the "Know Nothings." Its founder, Charles B. Allen, sought to organize local chapters who would work to elect nativist candidates in order to keep Catholic political candidates out of office. Party members generally became known as Know Nothings in the 1852 elections because – when questioned about the purpose and aims of their political party – they professed to know nothing. In the elections of 1855, whole tickets of Know Nothing candidates in Massachusetts, Delaware, and Pennsylvania – not even listed on official voting ballots – won elections, and candidates running unopposed found themselves defeated by write-in candidates whose party affiliation was unknown.[21]

The Civil War represented a (momentary) disappearance of the anti-Catholic impulse, as sectional issues and the great moral crisis of slavery engaged popular and political debate. But with Reconstruction, a new crop of "secret societies" (many of them anti-Catholic) cropped up. One of the most visible of these postwar groups was the American Protective Association (A.P.A.), founded in Clinton, Iowa, in 1887. Its founder, Henry F. Bowers, blamed the deficiencies of

---

[19]   Massa, *Anti-Catholicism*, 26.
[20]   Billington, *The Protestant Crusade*, 265–266.
[21]   Massa, *Anti-Catholicism*, 27.

his own education on a "subversive Jesuit conspiracy against the public schools of Baltimore." He traveled widely in the Midwest, lecturing publicly on the Roman peril, and founding A.P.A. councils modeled on the Masons: new members swore a solemn oath never to vote for a Catholic, never to join one in a strike, and to avoid hiring one if a Protestant was available. By 1893, A.P.A. membership stood at 70,000, most in the larger towns of the Upper Midwest like Detroit and Chicago, where Catholics were beginning to rise in political power and economic prosperity. But the explosion in A.P.A. membership occurred just one year later, when leadership passed into the hands of a former saloonkeeper, "Whiskey Bill" Traynor. By the summer of 1894, the Association claimed half a million members nationally, with ten thousand members in Columbus, Ohio, and sixteen thousand in Buffalo New York. Riding on the coattails of the 1890s economic depression, A.P.A. speakers preached to crowds of unemployed Protestant workers that their jobs had been stolen from them by a flood of Catholic immigrants washing up on American shores.[22]

But the most famous – and perhaps the most violent – of nineteenth-century secret societies aimed at harassing American Catholics was the Ku Klux Klan. The "modern Klan" (as opposed to its Reconstruction Era parent organized to intimidate newly freed African Americans in former Confederate states) was revived in Atlanta, Georgia on October 16, 1915, by William J. Simmons, who proclaimed himself Imperial Wizard. "Colonel" Simmons (a rank not earned in military service but through membership in Masonic-like groups like the "Woodmen of the World") envisioned a broader range of targets than Yankee Carpetbaggers and the descendants of freed slaves. The Klan's improbable-sounding ranks of Kleagles, Cyclops, Geniis, and Goblins (all ordered according to its sacred scripture, the Kloran) attracted hundreds of small-town patriots concerned with a growing list of foreigners threatening American ways, a list that now included Jews from Eastern Europe, socialist radicals, and Catholics. D. W. Griffith's immensely successful film, *The Birth of a Nation* – the first blockbuster movie hit in American popular culture – had valorized the bravery of white-hooded ex-Confederate soldiers riding in the night to protect their womenfolk and children from the imagined horrors of African Americans "on the loose" during the final decades of the nineteenth century. Simmons' revived Klan flourished by tapping into the fears

[22] Massa, *Anti-Catholicism*, 29–30.

generated by the new cultural circumstance of the United States in the years after World War I.[23]

The Twentieth Century

For several years after its founding, Simmons' Klan achieved modest success with perhaps 5,000 members. But in the summer of 1920, a rapid expansion occurred in terms of both numbers and activities – an expansion certainly aided by the cultural upheaval unleashed by demobilization after World War I, but more directly by Simmons' hiring of a pair of hard-boiled publicity agents, Edward Clark and Elizabeth Tyler. In return for $8 on every $10 taken as initiation fees, Clark and Tyler launched a mammoth membership campaign in Masonic lodges throughout the country, bringing in 90,000 new Klansmen in sixteen months. They defined the Klan's mission as "protecting the interests of those whose forebears established the nation," a mission in which Catholics would emerge as an important focus of fear. Fear of the "New Negro" (which played a central role in Simmons' original vision) declined as American blacks either "accepted their place" or moved to northern industrial cities; that fear was now replaced by the sudden (and frightening) discovery that "others" were now in positions of cultural, political, and economic authority. Many working and middle-class Protestants now felt like strangers in their own land, and the Klan's denunciatory finger pointed at the growing ranks of Catholics.[24]

The much-weakened Klan had one last hurrah in the presidential election of 1928, which saw Al Smith, the Catholic "wet" governor of New York, running as the Democratic candidate against the Republicans' "dry" Herbert Hoover. Smith lost by a landslide, a defeat that fueled a cottage industry about what really happened in the most acrimonious political campaign of the first half of the twentieth century. Certainly, Smith's antiprohibition stance worried southern and Midwestern Americans dedicated to the campaign against alcohol as to a religious crusade. But it was Smith's religion that generated the most controversy, and the "Catholic issue" is now considered determinative among historians for explaining his crushing defeat. For both Republicans and Democrats looking for organizational networks to oppose Smith, the Klan appeared as a godsend.

---

[23] Massa, *Anti-Catholicism*, 30–31.
[24] Massa, *Anti-Catholicism*, 31–32.

The election of John F. Kennedy to the presidency in 1960 represented something like a coda to the defeat of Smith earlier in the
century, at the very least marking something like the disappearance of
overt forms of anti-Catholicism as permissible in national political
culture. Indeed, Kennedy's appearance before the Greater Houston
Ministerial Association (an evangelical Protestant clerical group) in
the final months of his presidential campaign witnessed the sense of
both the candidate himself and of his (largely non-Catholic) political
advisers that "the religion issue won't go away." In fact, Kennedy's
successful bid for the presidency did witness to the truth that overt
and crude forms of the animus were no longer acceptable in the public
square, even if subtler forms continued to flourish.[25]

CONTEMPORARY MANIFESTATIONS OF CATHOLIC "OTHERNESS"

By the outbreak of World War II, anti-Catholicism appeared to many to
have been pushed to the local culture of small southern and Midwestern
towns, becoming almost irrelevant to the larger national story. Several
explanations have been offered for the surprisingly evanescent postwar
fate of a once quite sturdy and respected prejudice. The most famous is
Will Herberg's spin on the secularization thesis in his classic 1955 essay
in religious sociology, *Protestant, Catholic, Jew*. In Herberg's estima-
tion, the labels identifying one as Protestant, Catholic, or Jewish had, by
the mid-1950s, become largely irrelevant in explaining the real religion
of the United States, a belief system that Herberg termed "the American
Way of Life." For Herberg, the once hard-and-fast boundary markers of
belief and cultural location between Protestants and Catholics were
now simply "three diverse representatives of the same 'spiritual values'
that American democracy is presumed to stand for: the fatherhood of
God, the brotherhood of man [*sic*], the dignity of the individual human
being, democracy as a spiritual undertaking, the 'mission of America,'
etc." An idolatrous kind of secularism had inverted ends and means in
postwar America so that the impressively high numbers of Americans
joining churches and synagogues were doing so less for theological
reasons than as a way of identifying themselves as dedicated to
American cultural values and beliefs. Under the large umbrella of this

---

[25]   Mark Massa, *Catholics and American Culture: Fulton Sheen, Dorothy Day, and the
Notre Dame Football Team* (New York: Crossroad Publishing, 1999), 128–147.

true "common faith," Catholicism was now a safely recognized expression of the underlying unity.[26]

Another explanation for the disappearance of Catholic otherness might be described as the "assimilationist account," arguing that by sheer dint of numbers, educational level, per capita income, political party affiliation, and self-described values, Catholics (along with other outsider groups like Jews and Mormons) had become so successfully embedded into the fabric of middle-class life by the mid-twentieth century (helped significantly by the G. I. Bill) that their perceived threat to the American Way of Life had largely disappeared. Thus, Finke and Stark, in their book *The Churching of America*, argued that Catholicism's ecological success in defining a distinctive niche in the national religious economy made its low-tension relation to the culture "safe for America."[27]

A variation on the Finke and Stark model is more overtly theological (or at least ecclesiastical) and tends to focus on the momentous "Americanizing" changes in US Catholicism after the Second Vatican Council. In the decade after the closing of the Council in 1965, the older theological and liturgical traditions of Tridentine Catholicism – traditions that had emphasized the hierarchical and "foreign" part of the Catholic tradition – changed at a dizzying rate. The mass in English, "democratic" parish councils, women giving out communion and serving as parish administrators, and a host of other reforms coming out of the Council seemed to dispel the "foreignness" of the tradition, and made other believers – especially old line Protestants – believe that Catholics were, at last, joining the American religious mainstream. The older fears of "Romanism" as the Mother of Harlots now appeared unfounded or even embarrassing.[28]

But in fact the death of the anti-Catholic impulse – much like the rumors of Mark Twain's death – would seem to have been somewhat exaggerated. Neoconservative public intellectual George Weigel was the first to label a late twentieth-century reappearance of the old animus "the New Anti-Catholicism" in a famous article published in *Commentary* magazine in 1992. In that much-read piece, he offered an application of the secularization thesis of Peter Berger to a newly

---

[26]   Will Herberg, *Protestant, Catholic, Jew: An Essay in American Religious Sociology* (Chicago: University of Chicago Press, 1955), 38–39.

[27]   Roger Finke and Rodney Stark, *The Churching of America, 1776–1990: Winners and Losers in Our Religious Economy* (New Brunswick: Rutgers University Press, 1992), 171, 262.

[28]   Massa, *Anti-Catholicism*, 38–40.

vibrant hostility to things Catholic, arguing that precisely because
secularization in North America took the form of the privatization of
religion rather than its disappearance, Catholicism as both the largest
denomination and as a "public voice" in the culture came in for especially vituperative denunciation in the media and academia. Weigel
argued that Catholic positions on abortion and reproductive rights, gay
marriage, and the role of women in the community were targeted for
public ridicule, media carping, and political litmus-testing so often and
so nastily (especially in comparison with other groups like Orthodox
Jews, African Americans, and white Fundamentalist Christians who
espoused analogous or identical positions) that a palpable but indefin-
able "something else" could be reasonably argued to be going on.[29]

A group of Catholic commentators as ideologically diverse as sociologist Andrew Greeley, journalist James Martin, and William
Donohue (founder of the pugnacious Catholic League for Religious
and Civil Rights) agreed with Weigel, and the evidence they presented
to substantiate their various claims is impressive when presented in
summary form: they variously offered evidence for their belief that a
"new anti-Catholicism" was afoot by pointing to sexually rapacious
and physically abusive nuns and priests as stock characters in Off-
Broadway shows like "Late Night Catechism" and on TV soap operas
like "Ally McBeal"; to tourist shops selling a – equal parts amusing and
disturbing – "Boxing Nun" wind-up toy (presumably to bring back
pugilistic memories of parochial school education); to Hollywood-
made movies like *Dogma* and *Stigmata*, probably more irreverent than
anti-Catholic, but which nonetheless consistently presented "religion" in the generic sense in ways that seemed quite consciously
targeted to highlight and offend Catholic practice and belief); to the
Easter issue of the *New Yorker* magazine which featured a crucifixion
scene on its cover with the figure of the Easter Bunny in the place of
Christ; to the fact that the San Francisco Board of Supervisors had
granted permission in 1999 to the "Sisters of Perpetual Indulgence" –
a Bay Area-based group of men parading in nuns habits with names like
Sister Homo Fellatio and Sister Joyous Reserectum – to hold a
"Condom Mass" on one of the streets of the city, during which a
Latex "host" was held up before the assembled worshippers to the
words "this is the flesh for the life of the world."[30]

---

[29]   George Weigel, "The New Anti-Catholicism," *Commentary* 93 (June 1992): 25–31,
       25.
[30]   Massa, *Anti-Catholicism*, 42.

But Weigel, Martin, and Donohue also pointed to examples in the realm of respected national media no less than to instances in popular culture: they noted that David Bolt, editorial page director of the *Philadelphia Inquirer*, opined in an op-ed piece in July 1990 that the US Catholic Bishops' Conference – in taking culturally unpopular stands on a range of issues – "risked reawakening old religious prejudices by giving them substance" (this in a city that had witnessed some of the worst anti-Catholic riots in the mid-nineteenth century). They likewise observed that *Washington Post* columnist Judy Mann penned a column during the confirmation hearings for Clarence Thomas for the Supreme Court in which she noted that "Thomas makes much of his education at the hands of Catholic nuns; and much should be made of it during his Supreme Court confirmation hearing." An "expert" on PBS's *Newshour with Jim Lehrer*, discussing mandatory DNA testing for criminals, identified all Catholic priests – along with homeless people and teenagers – as being a group "at serious risk for criminal behavior."[31]

The very randomness of these examples – spanning the spectrum from national newspapers of record to street theater in the Bay Area – offer a complex and ambiguous set of examples. Some Catholic observers have argued that it was as though Catholic iconography, leadership, and sensibilities were somehow perceived by important sectors of the culture as fair game for attack, in ways that the beliefs and practices of other religious groups are not. When *Newsday* columnist Jimmy Breslin wrote an editorial in 1993 entitled "The Old Men in Rome Don't Get It" (arguing that "unless the Catholic Church quickly changes its mind about abortion, celibacy, women in the priesthood, and the like, it will die") a number of pundits (not all of them Catholic) publicly commented that it was difficult to imagine analogous articles appearing with titles like "The Old Rabbis in Brooklyn don't Get It" or "Harlem Pastors Need to be Quiet About Gays and Women's Submission to Their Husbands." But what critics "on the outside" and Catholic commentators "on the inside" would agree on is that Catholicism somehow did not seem to "fit" into North American cultural values and presuppositions, while other religious groups (holding analogously countercultural positions) were somehow immune to public attack.[32]

But in addition to the anti-Catholic impulses found in the PBS *Newshour* and *The New Yorker*, the animus would appear to be alive

---

[31] Massa, *Anti-Catholicism*, 42–44.
[32] Massa, *Anti-Catholicism*, 42–44.

and flourishing in "popular" print culture as well, perhaps best evinced in Jack Chick's cartoons, known as "Chicklets." The comic book theology advanced in these Chicklets (estimated at four hundred million copies produced in seventy languages) always appears in two-by-four inch, twenty-four page booklets, purposefully left on buses, subways, and in diners. While the demonic forces contending against the "Bible Christianity" Jack Chick himself espouses are presented in a democratic kind of way as being pressed by Masons, rock musicians, Jews, gay people, and big-city culture generally, it is the Catholic Church that represents the very epicenter of the "Synagogue of Satan." In cartoon narratives with names like "The Thing" and "The Death Cookie" (a title blasphemously referring to the bread of the Eucharist), Chick presents a world in which the reader learns that Karl Marx, Stalin, Adolf Hitler, and the entire Nazi S.S. corps were actually secret members of the Jesuit order plotting to overthrow western democratic culture to set up in its place a "One World Government" under the control of the pope, who is himself the Anti-Christ.[33]

Chick's cartoon gospel empire might be termed the dark side of Fundamentalist Protestantism, proclaiming an extreme form of individualistic belief and biblical literalism, a more extreme (or at least a more offensive) form of a diffuse distrust of Catholics shared by a number of contemporary evangelical Christians in North America across the denominational spectrum.

Whatever the explanation(s) for this sense of Catholic "differentness" in the United States since World War II (and there are various explanations), many historians of American Catholicism would nonetheless argue that *that* perception is quite important for understanding the relation of Catholicism to US culture.[34]

FURTHER READING

Billington, Ray Allen. *The Protestant Crusade, 1800–1860: A Study of the Origins of American Nativism*. New York: Macmillan, 1937.

Gabriel, Ralph Henry. *The Course of American Democratic Thought: An Intellectual History Since 1815*. New York: Ronald Press, 1940.

Greeley, Andrew. *An Ugly Little Secret: Anti-Catholicism in North America*. Kansas City: Sheed, Andrews & McMeel, 1977.

Handy, Robert. *A Christian America: Protestant Hopes and Historical Realities*. New York: Oxford University Press, 1971.

---

33 Massa, *Anti-Catholicism*, 100–120.
34 Massa, *Anti-Catholicism*, 45–50.

Martin, James. "The Last Acceptable Prejudice?" *America* 182 (March 25, 2000): 9.

Massa, Mark. *Anti-Catholicism in America: The Last Acceptable Prejudice.* New York: The Crossroad Publishing, 2003.

McGreevy, John. "Thinking on One's Own: Catholicism in the American Intellectual Imagination, 1928–1960," *Journal of American History* 84 (June 1997): 97–131.

Schultz, Nancy Lusignan. *Fire and Roses: The Burning of the Charlestown Convent, 1834.* New York: Free Press, 2000.

12 Gender and Sexuality

JAMES P. MCCARTIN

INTRODUCTION: DEVIANCE AND PURITY – DUELING IMAGES OF US CATHOLICS

It was the culmination of a months-long legislative fight, not to mention some eighty years of swirling allegations about Catholic sexual deviance, when the local sheriff and health commissioner arrived at St. Joseph Academy in remote Mena, Arkansas, where Catholics represented a tiny minority of the population. The county officials entered the school under authority bestowed by the state's new Convent Inspection Act of 1915, designed to end the rumored practice of Catholic institutions harboring girls for the sexual gratification, as one enraged Arkansan put it, of a "lecherous bunch" of priests.[1] Discovering no evidence of crime or malfeasance among the several Sisters of Mercy and the small number of female students at the school, the sheriff, evidently impressed by his hosts, apologized to them and promised to return for a social visit with his wife. Meanwhile, elected officials in Georgia successfully installed a similar law aimed at routing out Catholic perversion, and legislators in seven other states – from Iowa to Oregon to Minnesota – debated their own versions of a convent inspection bill. Together, these largely forgotten efforts at policing sexual activity in Catholic institutions hint at how significant and controversial Catholicism has been in the history of gender and sexuality in the United States.

An enduring tension has characterized US Catholics' engagement with a full array of issues related to gender and sexuality. On the one hand, many non-Catholics have historically imagined their Catholic neighbors as marginal and aberrant, both because of their immigrant

---

[1] Otis L. Spurgeon quoted in Kenneth C. Barnes, *Anti-Catholicism in Arkansas: How Politicians, the Press, the Klan, and Religious Leaders Imagined an Enemy, 1910–1960* (Fayetteville: University of Arkansas Press, 2016), 38.

status or background and their consistently bad reputation when it came to issues of gender and sexuality. The 1836 release of *The Awful Disclosures of the Hôtel Dieu Nunnery*, a sensationally successful book which falsely claimed to chronicle a real-life story of serial rape and infanticide inside a cloistered convent, ensured that Catholics would, over the long haul, be branded as a fundamentally foreign, sex-obsessed threat to the public welfare. *Awful Disclosures* depicted priests as "unmanly" according to the prevailing standards of the day because they were irrational captives of their wild sexual appetites, and it suggested that religious sisters were "unwomanly" because, as murderers of their helpless offspring, they outrageously refused women's defining vocation of motherhood. In subsequent eras, the critique would shift in its particular details, but after *Awful Disclosures* critics persistently viewed Catholics as both distinctive and powerful in unnerving and dangerous ways. Even during the twentieth century, when US Catholics acquired a robust reputation as conservative defenders of traditional sexual mores and gender norms, critics continued to depict them as out of step with prevailing cultural and social values around gender and sex – this despite the pronounced distance of this view of Catholics from the lurid stereotypes advanced in *Awful Disclosures*.

On the other hand, US Catholics frequently viewed themselves as the very opposite of marginal and aberrant when it came to gender and sexuality. Indeed, by the end of the nineteenth century, lay and clerical leaders alike, the majority of them immigrants or the children of immigrants, took care to project an image marked both by an effusive American patriotism and by a heightened sense of virtue which privileged sexual "purity" and aligned closely with the gender ideals advanced by white Protestant majority elites. Both despite and because of their ongoing association with deviance, Catholics endeavored to cast themselves as paragons of sexual morality and as living models of gender ideals, exhibiting as they did so an often tribalistic sense of moral superiority over non-Catholic Americans. This sense of self-understanding, by which Catholics cast themselves as archetypes to be emulated, ultimately gave their leaders a platform from which to hold forth on an expansive array of issues. By the 1880s, for example, Catholics would become the most vociferous opponents of liberalized attitudes toward divorce, and more recently they would serve as central players in movements opposing legal abortion and same-sex marriage. During the intervening decades, Catholics would lead organized efforts to combat secular-minded sex education programs in public schools and to censor motion pictures to ensure they excluded sexually suggestive material. In their stridency to protect moral standards and bolster an array of gender and sex norms, Catholics struggled to overcome the enduring stigma of deviance with which they had long been marked. But in doing so, they only further emphasized their distinctiveness and thus, ironically, reinforced in the minds of many non-Catholics the notion that Catholics were out-of-step with American standards and norms around gender and sexuality.

This brief survey ranging from the early nineteenth century to the early twenty-first century highlights the persistent significance of these two contradictory assessments of Catholics – as agents of vice and repression, or as models of virtue and moral rectitude – and also aims to draw each of these assessments into a single narrative, thereby suggesting the true complexity of Catholics' place in the history of gender and sexuality in the United States. Too often, US historians interested in these topics have emphasized Catholic distinctiveness without recognizing or acknowledging how their scholarship may uncritically adopt and amplify views advanced by past critics of US Catholics. Consequently, in histories of gender and sexuality, Catholics routinely appear as opponents and foils of the central players who are generally cast as the agents of liberation and progress. Conversely, historians whose work focuses on US Catholicism have too often overlooked the powerful significance of gender and sexuality in Catholic life, though a flurry of recent publications indicate a positive and notable shift in this regard. Therefore, this essay not only advances the case that historians should develop duly complicated historical narratives, but it also highlights some of the significant themes and conclusions emerging out of recently published research.

FROM *AWFUL DISCLOSURES* TO *CASTI CONNUBII*: THE DEVELOPMENT OF A REPUTATION

Catholicism's contentious place in US history is intimately tied up with the story of the transnational migration of Catholic people and practices and how non-Catholics received and interpreted them. It should thus come as no surprise that the perception of Catholics as foreign and unassimilable outsiders became increasingly potent as the early nineteenth-century mass immigration of European Catholics inter-sected with important developments in the history of gender and sexu-ality in the United States. *The Awful Disclosures of the Hôtel Dieu Nunnery*, published amid an explosion of Irish and German immigra-tion in the 1830s, was but the most widely remembered example of a vigorous pre–Civil War trend of depicting Catholics as perverse deviants. In this era of rapid social and cultural transformation wrought by industrialization and urbanization, white American-born Protestants responded to change, in part, by elevating the value of the nuclear family and asserting a clear distinction between the male-directed public/political sphere and the female-dominated private/domestic sphere. Within this context, critics regularly disparaged vowed celibacy among Catholic clergy and religious sisters as a threat to marriage, family, and home: not only did the practice of lifelong sexual abstinence frustrate the purpose of the reproductive family unit, but the immigrant laity's purported deference to the church's celibate representatives – including celibate women – seemingly undermined the integrity of the private family sphere, subject as it was to these foreign-born celibates' coercive powers.

This view of Catholic celibacy as fundamentally opposed to American values provided the foundation for ongoing critiques advanced over a series of decades. *The Awful Disclosures'* duplicitous priests who publicly feigned sexual abstinence but clandestinely forced themselves upon adult female victims would become stock figures in the American popular imagination, fueling a drive for convent inspections not only in the 1830s and 1840s but also several decades later. For many nineteenth-century white Americans, such images placed priests in a league with African-American men whose allegedly uncontrollable sexual appetites transformed them into rapists who both threatened the well-ordered nuclear family and challenged whites' hold on racial supremacy. Likewise, non-Catholic commentators often contended that religious sisters, whose freedom from domestic responsibilities enabled them to take up rapidly expanding work among immigrants in social service and education, rejected their maternal vocation in the private realm and usurped masculine privilege in the public. In the post–Civil War era, after a multinational assembly of bishops at the First Vatican Council (1869–1870) endorsed the dogma of papal infallibility, critics denounced celibacy on still different grounds, depicting it as one of multiple tactics deployed by Roman authorities to exert their control around the globe. By depriving the growing legions of vowed celibates in the United States of the physical and emotional comforts of heterosexual partnership and the morally elevating experience of family life, the pope and his curia rendered them psychologically fragile and intellectually docile, thus lacking in the independent judgment and stability of character that was the necessary foundation for democratic life.

Amid a proliferation of such unflattering perspectives, Catholics, both laity and clergy, endeavored to install themselves and their progeny as the quintessential models of American sexual morality and gender propriety. On the one hand, these largely working-class and poor Catholics often did so by adopting the values of their middle-class white Protestant contemporaries, affirming the prevailing gender ideals of the self-sacrificing and nurturing woman and the self-restrained and industrious man while translating them into terms that would particularly appeal to Catholics. Ultimately, Catholic leaders' perennial insistence that young people embrace the demands of sexual continence, and their particular interest in reforming the ranks of "fallen women" who transgressed the boundary between virtue and vice, mirrored that of their Protestant counterparts – and just as they did among Protestants, transgressions triggered serious consequences for those deemed wayward by their family and their community. On the other hand, Catholics cast themselves as the foremost defenders of marriage and the fiercest enemies of divorce – asserting as they did so, that this differentiated them from Protestants who neither acknowledged the sacramental nature of the marriage bond nor accepted that civil divorce was simply contrary to divine mandate. As instances of divorce rose annually across the United States after 1880, Catholics' vocal disapproval nourished a reputation for self-righteousness and superiority that would die hard and have important consequences over the long haul.

Late nineteenth-century interventions on divorce laid the groundwork for future forays into a variety of controversies. In the 1910s and 1920s, as local public school boards introduced sex education programs to curb a reported rise in sexual activity among youth, objections arose from multiple quarters. Catholics often led the fight, however, charging that school districts trampled on the parental right to educate children about delicate matters related to reproduction, and objecting to the "secular" presentation of sex merely as a physiological phenomenon while overlooking its essential moral and spiritual dimensions. At the same time, Catholic leaders became embroiled in debates sparked by the advocates of eugenic science whose idealization of white Anglo-Saxons and support for state-sponsored "racial hygiene" initiatives (including restrictive laws regarding marriage, reproduction, and immigration) made them instant adversaries of Catholics who increasingly hailed from Latin American and southern and eastern European backgrounds. Catholic voices also notably intervened on the issue of women's suffrage – though, significantly, they openly disagreed about the propriety of extending the vote through the Nineteenth

Amendment, ratified in 1920. While opponents deployed well-worn arguments about maintaining separate spheres, advocates of women's right to vote invoked Catholic teaching and suggested that women's participation would have a purifying and elevating effect in political life and public morality.

Early twentieth-century Catholics' most consequential public interventions, however, came in the form of vocal opposition to a burgeoning movement to legitimize birth control and ensure legal access to artificial contraception. Some Catholics flatly drew a moral parallel between contraceptive heterosexual intercourse and murder, thereby ensuring that their anti-birth control crusade surpassed in stridency the moralistic tones of earlier denunciations of divorce. Though most employed more tempered rhetoric, leaders among the clergy and laity so regularly and confidently denounced contraception that they nurtured a powerful stereotype of Catholics as unrelentingly conservative and unsparingly vigilant in sexual matters. Such developments were predicated, in part, on the profound influence exercised by ethnically Irish leaders within the broader US Catholic community: over the course of the nineteenth century, Ireland would become home to a famously restrictive sexual culture, and as Irish clergy and religious sisters – along with Irish laity – imported their sexual mores into the United States, they promoted, and at times even imposed, their values within a Catholic community comprised of a variety of ethnicities and sexual subcultures.

Yet nothing was more effective than Pope Pius XI's highly publicized encyclical letter of 1930, *Casti Connubii*, in bolstering the image of Catholics as self-appointed guardians of sexual morality. In response to a dramatic and widespread softening of moral and legal objections to contraception across the Western world, the pope depicted the Roman Catholic Church as holding the moral line against the advance of immorality and declared artificial birth control to be, without exception, "shameful and intrinsically vicious" and "an offence against the law of God and of nature."[2] For Catholics, he concluded, the only legitimate means of family limitation was for a married couple to abstain from intercourse during the wife's fertile period – a declaration that would spur a particular interest in the "rhythm method," which US Catholic doctors and theologians would thereafter endeavor to hone and proffer in the service of public morality.

[2] Pope Pius XI, "Casti Connubii" in *The Papal Encyclicals, 1903–1939*, ed. Claudia Carlen, IHM (Hays, KS: McGrath Publishing Co., 1981), 399.

In the wake of *Casti Connubii*, many US Catholic leaders embraced the notion that they bore a special responsibility for protecting sexual morality and traditional gender norms within a fast-changing society. Such was the impulse that undergirded the Legion of Decency, an organization founded in 1933, which for decades exercised a powerful cultural influence by rating Hollywood films for their moral content and sponsoring boycotts of productions deemed morally offensive because they included, for example, divorce, extramarital relations, or suggestive dialog. Amid profound social changes unleashed by US involvement in World War II, the Pre-Cana and Cana movements, founded to assist young engaged and married couples across the country in fulfilling their vocations as spouses and parents, reproduced and promoted well-worn ideals of the typical husband as "protector and provider ... calm, calculating, logical" and the typical wife as desiring "nothing more than to have someone worth while whom she can serve, to whom she can subject herself, to whom she can be loyal."[3] When concerns about a rise in homosexuality spiked in the early postwar United States, Catholic moral theologians eagerly dove into the issue and, echoing the prevailing assessment among secular authorities, declared those who desired same-sex sexual relations to be "immature" and "self-indulgent" egoists who threatened the stability of the nuclear family and of the American nation.[4]

THE WAGES OF POLARIZATION AND THE ENDURANCE OF A REPUTATION: FROM BIRTH CONTROL AND ABORTION TO CLERICAL SEX ABUSE AND SAME-SEX MARRIAGE

It is important to remember, however, that the church's hierarchy never achieved universal influence and ordinary Catholics never marched in lockstep. During the mid-twentieth century, this was notably so in the case of birth control. Amid the Great Depression and in the shadow of *Casti Connubii*, birthrates among Catholics declined in tandem with birthrates among the wider population, such that one excessively alarmed priest, writing in 1934, declared that "the trend of our

---

[3] "A Chicago Pre-Cana Conference Outline, 1950" in *Gender Identities in American Catholicism*, ed. Paula Kane, James Kenneally, and Karen Kennelly (Maryknoll, NY: Orbis Press, 2001), 7–8.

[4] James P. McCartin, "The Church and Gay Liberation: The Case of John McNeill," *U.S. Catholic Historian* 34 (Winter 2016): 131–132.

Catholic people is toward extinction."[5] In fact, a substantial percent-age – as many as 43 percent of middle-class US Catholic wives surveyed in 1940 – testified that they used methods of family limitation declared illicit by church authorities. In 1960, leaders at the National Catholic Welfare Conference, the official organization of bishops from across the United States, ruefully admitted that laypeople employed artificial birth control at rates roughly equivalent to non-Catholics. For their part, ordinary parish priests, who occupied the pastoral front lines and whose responsibility it was to dispense private counsel in the sacrament of Confession, struggled to reconcile official church teaching with the testimony of anguished spouses on the subject of the unreliability of the rhythm method and the economic and psychological burdens of caring for large families. Over the course of the 1950s, laypeople grew more vocally restive toward official church teaching on the matter, and as scientists (including the Catholic physician, John Rock) experi-mented with early prototypes of oral contraceptives, theologians and laity alike waded into a prolonged debate about whether pharmaco-logical methods of birth control could be acceptable under Catholic teaching, since (like the rhythm method) they did not alter or impede the physical act of intercourse.

Despite such complexities, the popular notion that Catholics were distinctive – either sexually excessive or repressive, depending on the point of view – persisted throughout the post–1945 era. Indeed, rapid movement into the middle class and increasing entrance into interfaith marriages, often cited as evidence of Catholics attaining American mainstream status, had limited impact on such perceptions. During the immediate postwar years, the glorification of very large nuclear families in Catholic circles reinforced the sense of difference. Even amid the baby boom, during which American mothers generally bore two or three offspring, the families of eleven or twelve children celebrated nationally as the official "Catholic Family of the Year" placed Catholics in a separate category. At the same time, critics promoted the view that Catholics represented a dual threat: both as fervent pro-moters of an "anti-sexual code" that cast a pall over all sexual desire and activity, and as reckless pro-natalists who hastened the "unspeak-able horrors" to be triggered by immanent global overpopulation.[6]

---

[5] Rev. Msgr. John A. Ryan quoted in Leslie Woodcock Tentler, *Catholics and Contraception: An American History* (Ithaca, NY: Cornell University Press, 2004), 76.

[6] Paul Blanshard, *American Freedom and Catholic Power* (Boston: Beacon Press, 1949), 132, 148–149.

As movements for women's liberation and gay and lesbian liberation gathered momentum in the 1960s and 1970s, activists fashioned the notion of Catholic difference into a potent symbol in their assault on restrictive sexual mores and gender ideals. Though critics primarily directed their ire toward the church's hierarchy, the effect of critiques leveled from multiple sources on a sustained basis over a series of decades was ultimately to undermine a more textured sense of on-the-ground complexity and promote the perception of Catholics as united in their sexual conservatism.

Of course, the 1960s represented a pivotal decade for two principal reasons: first, it was a period of swift and lasting transformation in sex and gender norms within the United States; and second, it saw a tradition-bound US Catholic community enter into an era of dramatic change, thanks to the Second Vatican Council (1962–1965). Within this context, an array of distinct groups within the Catholic community raised challenges to official church teaching and discipline around sex. Taken together, these challenges amounted to a specifically Catholic iteration of the broader sexual revolution. The spirit of reform gave rise, for example, to an organized effort among clergy from across the United States to rescind the age-old requirement that men must renounce sex and marriage before ordination – an effort that temporarily buoyed the hopes of clerical activists, but received a profoundly cool reception from Roman authorities. Further, amid the exuberant sense of new opportunities that pervaded the immediate post-Council years, thousands of US priests, as well as thousands of religious sisters, joined an unprecedented exodus from church-sponsored ministry, frequently citing dissatisfaction with vowed celibacy and a desire to pursue relationships which frequently led to marriage and parenthood. At the same time, Catholic women, many with ties to secular women's rights initiatives, organized around the goals of women's equality and women's ordination, cultivating growing support among both clergy and laity even as they publicly clashed with US bishops and Vatican officials. Likewise, an organization called Dignity, founded in 1970, along with a small but significant cadre of scholars, gave voice to gay and lesbian Catholics who challenged official church teaching about the immorality of homosexual relations and even ventured the theological argument that committed same-sex partnerships could be the moral equivalent of heterosexual unions.

Yet the most striking evidence of revolt among US Catholics came in the wake of Pope Paul VI's 1968 encyclical letter, *Humanae Vitae*, which reaffirmed *Casti Connubii*'s judgment against artificial birth control.

Prior to his death in 1963, Pope John XXIII launched a commission to reevaluate church teaching on birth control, and when that commission privately reported back to his successor, Pope Paul VI, in 1966, a total of sixty-four of the sixty-nine commissioners recommended reversing the church's teaching against artificial contraception. News of that recommendation soon leaked to the press, fostering a widespread expectation – one nourished by the experience of a range of other significant changes after the Second Vatican Council – of an imminent reversal of the church's official teaching. When the encyclical instead reaffirmed that teaching, large numbers of laity and clergy reacted with bitter disappointment. In a manner unprecedented among earlier generations of US Catholics, many publicly proclaimed their rejection of the encyclical's teaching on birth control, while a still larger number seemingly regarded *Humanae Vitae* as a watershed after which they quietly opted to disregard church officials' moral authority on sexual matters. One sign of such disregard was the precipitous decline of lay participation in the sacrament of Confession. Although older generations frequently went to confess the sin of using artificial contraception, within a few years after the promulgation of *Humanae Vitae*, participation in the sacrament plummeted. In time, it would become clear that the encyclical would serve as an enduring source of discord and division: supporters of *Humanae Vitae* regularly deployed it as a yardstick by which to measure commitment to the Catholic faith, while opponents persistently pointed to the encyclical as evidence of the church hierarchy's outmoded and ill-founded approach to a full range of questions regarding sexual morality. Over fifty years later, laypeople's widespread rejection of church officials' authority to make moral judgments about sex and the persistent tensions the encyclical has nourished among Catholics confirm that the issuance of *Humanae Vitae* was an event of lasting consequence.

It was in the immediate post-*Humanae Vitae* years that abortion emerged as a major issue in US politics, drawing Catholics into an increasingly acrimonious national debate that, over subsequent decades, would foster only further polarization. Church authorities had long condemned as mortally sinful the procurement of an abortion, and though it was not the central focus of *Humanae Vitae*, the encyclical restated the traditional teaching against abortion without provoking substantial opposition on that issue. Indeed, public opinion surveys suggested that in the late 1960s and early 1970s, US Catholics were widely opposed to abortion. But after the US Supreme Court's *Roe v. Wade* decision in 1973, lay people's support for abortion rights slowly expanded (to roughly 51 percent in 2018), even as Catholic mobilization against abortion became both increasingly organized and strident in its tone and tactics. In the aftermath of *Roe*, US Catholic bishops, along with lay leaders of a theologically and politically progressive stripe, endeavored to advance a "consistent ethic of life" that linked Catholic opposition to abortion with other public policy concerns, including opposition to capital punishment, assisted suicide, and nuclear war, as well as support for civil rights, antipoverty programs, and expanded access to health care. In fact, throughout the 1970s and 1980s US Catholic leaders' positions on an array of public policy issues regularly aligned with the priorities of political progressives, despite persistent disagreement with them over abortion rights. Yet by century's end, the dominant image of Catholics became for many synonymous with fierce opposition to legalized abortion – this, thanks to the emergence of theologically and politically conservative lay activists, as well as a new generation of clergy, who elevated opposition to abortion above all other issues of political and moral significance. Despite ongoing disagreement among US Catholics over abortion rights, such an image bolstered the perception of the faithful as a united conservative front against abortion, even as it reaffirmed Catholics' status as out-of-step within a society where abortion was decreasingly stigmatized.

Amid the prolonged debate about abortion, women's increasing willingness to give voice to their anger and frustration over experiences of inequality within the church further elevated the significance of gender issues among US Catholics. In response, the National Conference of Catholic Bishops began a consultation in 1983 that generated input from some 75,000 US Catholic women, a process designed to inform a major pastoral letter – a first of its kind – in which bishops would directly address women's interests and concerns. When a draft of the letter prompted Roman authorities to complain that US church officials were insufficiently firm in their opposition to women's ordination, the bishops found themselves caught between honoring the perspectives of US Catholic women and those of the ordained males who occupied the hierarchy's uppermost ranks, and they ultimately jettisoned the entire project. By the early 1990s, polling indicated that two-thirds of US Catholics supported women's ordination and, especially among younger generations who came of age in the wake of the women's movement of the 1960s and 1970s, theological arguments for an all-male clergy often came off as a disingenuous cover for church officials' unremitting commitment to patriarchy. Nevertheless, amid a prolonged decline in the number of priests and religious sisters, laywomen, often with advanced theological and pastoral training, flooded into leadership positions in parishes, schools, and other Catholic institutions during the final decades of the twentieth century. Despite their exclusion from ordination and from the exercise of authority within the church's highest echelons, laywomen at the local level attained elevated status and visibility within church-sponsored institutions, increasingly delivering pastoral care and assuming responsibilities previously reserved for ordained men.

The divisive issues of birth control, abortion, same-sex sexual relations, clerical celibacy, and women's ordination triggered reactions of such volume and intensity that matters pertaining to gender and sexuality became critical fault lines in the US Catholic community over the last quarter of the twentieth century. Whereas previous generations of the faithful tended to segregate according to ethnicity, race, and class, now attitudes about gay rights and women's ordination often became key indicators by which Catholics determined affinities and alliances among themselves. Those of a more conservative stripe emphasized to an unprecedented extent the importance of wholehearted assent to official church teachings on sexual morality. Among such Catholics, the practice of Natural Family Planning (NFP), a scientifically advanced version of the church-approved rhythm method, became an acknowledged marker of conservative orientation, as did a view of gender that was tied to the genital sex bestowed on the individual by God and characterized by distinct but complementary roles for women and men. Yet for those who identified as theological and social progressives, regular and, at times, vocal dissent from official church pronouncements on sex and gender signaled their commitment to an alternate variety of Catholicism.

Humanae Vitae's pronouncement against contraception continued to serve as a lingering source of disaffection among many who disagreed with church teaching. But amid the devastating impact of human immunodeficiency virus (HIV)/acquired immunodeficiency syndrome (AIDS) among gay men during the 1980s and 1990s, a growing number of liberal Catholics went beyond mere disaffection and echoed non-Catholic critics who decried church leaders for denigrating sexual minorities by describing their relationships as "intrinsically disordered" and by characterizing even loving and long term same-sex partnerships as the product of a "moral evil."[7] Indeed, alongside

7   Congregation for the Doctrine of the Faith, "Declaration on Certain Questions Concerning Sexual Ethics," *Origins* 5 (Jan. 22, 1976): 489; and Congregation for the Doctrine of the Faith, "Letter to the Bishops of the Catholic Church on the Pastoral Care of Homosexual Persons," *Origins* 16 (Nov. 13, 1986): 379.

women's inequality within the church, younger generations cited official teaching against same-sex sexual relationships as a source of
profound alienation – and increasingly, a reason to depart – from the
church in which they were raised.

Alongside these developments, instances of the sexual abuse of
minors by clergy became an issue of growing concern in the mid-
1980s, eventually exploding into a scandal of cataclysmic consequence
and reviving the powerful old image of priests as virulent sexual preda-
tors. The first major criminal prosecutions covered in the national
media – the notorious cases of Gilbert Gauthe of Louisiana and James
Porter of Massachusetts – provided initial clues later recognized as a
common pattern: serially predatory priests whose religious superiors
kept secret their abusive behavior and knowingly reassigned them to
new locations where the abuse continued. Though a trickle of new cases
became public throughout the 1990s, it was only in 2002, after abuse
victims came forward and testified that local church officials in the
Boston Archdiocese regularly reassigned abusive priests, that revelations of clerical sex abuse quickly became a tidal wave crashing upon
the US Catholic community. Subsequently, media outlets in every
region of the nation reported thousands of stories of clerical sex abuse
and its coverup by church officials over the course of several decades.
The result was widespread outrage, forcing US bishops to remove scores
of credibly accused priests from ministry and paving the way for financial settlements paid out to thousands of victims and amounting to
more than $3 billion. In time, a rash of similar revelations would spread
around the globe, demonstrating that clerical sex abuse and its cover-up
in the United States was no aberration. Critics of the church thus lost
no time in condemning the hypocrisy of church officials who serenely
passed judgment on others' sexual behaviors even as their actions
allowed abusive priests to inflict untold psychological damage and
evade legal consequences. Some who identified as theological liberals
drew upon parallel controversies and asserted that only women's ordination and an end to mandatory clerical celibacy could ultimately solve
the problem of clerical sex abuse. Others of a more conservative variety
tendentiously blamed gay clergy for the problem and supported Vatican
efforts to discourage gay men from seeking ordination. Among ordinary
laity in the pews, such arguments never gained traction, but cynicism
about the moral authority of ordained leaders became entrenched, and
especially in locales where some of the most egregious abusers served,
many invoked clerical sex abuse as they suspended donations or cut
their ties with the church.

If revelations of clerical sex abuse revived old associations with sexual deviance and thus reinforced the enduring perception of Catholic distinctiveness, debates over same-sex marriage further confirmed that perception by drawing on the image of Catholics as agents of unrelenting conservatism and enemies of sexual liberation. When the Massachusetts high court issued a 2003 ruling making it the first state in the union to legalize same-sex marriage, officials from the commonwealth's four dioceses summoned the faithful to exercise their "moral obligation" to oppose same-sex unions, launching a losing campaign to overturn the court ruling by constitutional amendment.[8] Thereafter, the Boston Archdiocese announced that its social welfare agency, long responsible for facilitating adoptions, would suspend its work in this area rather than treat prospective same-sex parents on an equal footing with heterosexual couples. Such developments, notable for their origin at the epicenter of clerical sex abuse revelations, predictably elicited a renewed round of outrage from advocates for lesbian, gay, bisexual, transgender (LGBT) rights who charged the hierarchy with advancing an "ugly political agenda" rather than promoting the dignity of oppressed sexual minorities and the needs of vulnerable children.[9] Still, as the fight for marriage equality became increasingly organized across the nation, members of the church hierarchy persisted in their vocal opposition, denouncing same-sex unions as "detrimental to human life" and an attack upon "the very cornerstone of our society."[10] Yet by the time that the US Supreme Court intervened and legalized same-sex marriage in the 2015 case of *Obergefell v. Hodges*, the gulf between outspoken church officials and ordinary Catholics in the pews was pronounced: among US laity, some 57 percent approved of same-sex marriage, while among those under age 30 such approval spiked to 75 percent.

8   Catholic Bishops of Massachusetts quoted in Maurice T. Cunningham, "Catholics and the ConCon: The Church's Response to the Massachusetts Gay Marriage Decision," *Journal of Church and State* 47 (Winter 2005): 31–32.
9   Human Rights Campaign press release (Mar. 11, 2006) quoted in Colleen Theresa Rutledge, "Caught in the Crossfire: How Catholic Charities of Boston Was Victim to the Clash between Gay Rights and Religious Freedom," *Duke Journal of Gender Law and Policy* 15 (Jan. 2008): 313.
10 Bp. William Weigand and Bp. Jaime Soto, "Sacramento Bishops," *Origins* 38:8 (July 3, 2008): 119; and Card. Timothy J. Dolan quoted in "Catholic Leaders Object as Public Attitudes Shift," *America* (May 28, 2012): 6.

CONCLUSION: OLD THEMES, NEW CHALLENGES

The substantial and longstanding distance between church authorities and laypeople, alongside the persistent popular perception of Catholics as agents of sexual deviance and sexual repression, virtually guarantees that the place of US Catholics in the history of gender and sexuality will remain both complex and divisive into the immediate future. Throughout the past two centuries, tensions about appropriate gender norms and approaches to sexual morality have shaped the relationship between Catholics and their neighbors, and more recently such tensions have generated increasing discord and fracturing within the US Catholic community. Certainly, as issues of gender and sexuality become increasingly complicated with the rising prominence of transgender and non-binary communities in the United States, old themes will continue to inform how new challenges play out. Likewise, as abortion rights maintains its place as a perennial issue in American politics and as US Catholics grapple with the ongoing fallout from revelations of clerical sex abuse, established themes of Catholic distinctiveness in matters of sexuality and gender will remain powerful and continue to shape public debate.

FURTHER READING

Cummings, Kathleen Sprows. *New Women of the Old Faith: Gender and American Catholicism in the Progressive Era.* Chapel Hill: University of North Carolina Press, 2009.

Henold, Mary J. *Catholic and Feminist: The Surprising History of the American Catholic Feminist Movement.* Chapel Hill: University of North Carolina Press, 2008.

Leon, Sharon K. *An Image of God: The Catholic Struggle with Eugenics.* Chicago: University of Chicago Press, 2013.

Massa, Mark S., SJ. *The Structure of Theological Revolutions: How the Fight Over Birth Control Transformed American Catholicism.* New York: Oxford University Press, 2018.

Tentler, Leslie Woodcock. *Catholics and Contraception: An American History.* Ithaca, NY: Cornell University Press, 2004.

Vander Broek, Allison. "Rallying the Right-to-Lifers: Grassroots Religion and Politics in the Building of a Broad-Based Right-to-Life Movement." Ph.D. dissertation, Boston College, 2018.

Yacovazzi, Cassandra L. *Escaped Nuns: True Womanhood and the Campaign against Convents in Antebellum America.* New York: Oxford University Press, 2018.

13 American Catholics in a Global Context

ANGELYN DRIES, OSF

The *multidimensional* nature of American Catholicism requires attention to mission and evangelization as one lens through which to understand the global dynamics of the American Catholic experience. Evangelization and mission were more nuanced than simply "converting" or "civilizing" people. Mission encounters in diverse local contexts transformed those on both sides of the relationship. This chapter will explore briefly three themes: mission *to* America ("transplanting," or handing on the faith); the growth of an evangelization/mission impetus *within* the United States; and the effect of mission engagement *from* the United States. These mission encounters involved much more than simply learning a catechism. Missionaries effected social change, religious development, and humanitarian responses to injustice in many countries, even while at times carrying on practices that sometimes had a negative effect on the people they came to serve.

MISSION TO THE AMERICAS

American Catholicism was affected by *global* Catholicism from the start. Catholic evangelization in the first four centuries in the Americas focused on a multifaceted "transplanting" or handing on the Catholic faith and mission outreach to indigenous people and to those who came to American shores. Pope Alexander VI's line of demarcation (1493) on the Atlantic side of the world set parameters for control of lands west (Castile/Spain) and east (Portugal) of the meridian. These countries reflected the Catholicism that eventually developed in Florida, the Caribbean islands, a good portion of mid to southern California and the Southwest, and much of Central and South America. Catholic Portugal gained Brazil and areas especially around the coasts of West Africa. Pope Alexander VI's papal bull, *Inter Caetera* (1493), further indicated that governments were to take responsibility for the religious instruction of aboriginal people in those lands.

As commerce and colonization, mainly from Spain, Portugal, France, and England, shaped the first three centuries of American Catholicism, missionaries often demonstrated that they were capable of taking on many roles beyond evangelization of indigenous people or other spiritual tasks. They were explorers, cartographers, geographers, artists, negotiators, and intermediaries between tribal leaders and colonial governors. While the colonial government had its goals, missionaries had a different aim: to understand the life of the people to whom they were sent and to work toward their conversion to Catholic life. Some also became advocates for native peoples as they witnessed the cruelty and hardship inflicted upon them. Living in New Spain for almost a half-century, Bishop Bartolomé de Las Casas (1484–1566) saw the devastating impact soldiers had on the native population, and traveled back and forth to Spain to apprise the Court and the King of the situation. Las Casas's *Destruction of the Indians of North America* (1552) sought to persuade the Spanish King to take punitive action against soldiers for their adverse treatment of indigenous people.

Franciscans and Jesuits were the first missionaries to the Americas in the colonial era. Working alongside Spanish explorers, Franciscans from Mexico arrived in St. Augustine, Florida, in 1587. They served the Indians and people of mixed races in their existing villages in La Florida Missions until 1763, when the English invaded that part of the eastern seaboard. The friars also began missions in Alta California. Perhaps the best known of the Franciscan friars of the time, Junipero Serra (1713–1784), founded nine missions from San Diego (1769) through Mission San Buenaventura (1782). Although Serra strongly opposed forced conversions of indigenous people, the mission was to be a site where potential converts lived as a community apart from the Spanish and other natives in order to keep the neophytes away from the bad example of the Spaniards.[1] At the same time, some Franciscans served as chaplains for the soldiers.

In the Southwest, Jesuit missionary Father Eusebio Francisco Kino (1645–1711) was multitalented, working as a mathematician, royal cosmographer (his explorations determined that Baja California was not an island but a peninsula), ethnographer, and rancher. He wrote and demonstrated that a missionary should excel in tolerance and patience, maintain personal contact with the Pima Indians, and look for goodwill

---

[1]   For an overview of Franciscan work in colonial America, see Timothy J. Johnson and Gert Melville, eds., *From La Florida to La California: Franciscan Evangelization in the Spanish Borderlands* (Berkeley, CA: Academy of Franciscan History, 2013).

among them. Kino also defended the Pimas against the aggression and faults of the Spanish, and his journal described numerous Pima ceremonies to which he was invited. He founded Mission San Xavier del Bac (1692), which continues as an active Catholic community located south of Tucson, Arizona.

The French also joined the missionary enterprise. When French traders began a settlement in Québec led by Samuel Champlain (1608), four French Recollet Franciscans sailed with him to instruct French boys and evangelize indigenous people. Jesuits arrived in New France in 1611 (Port-Royal) and in Québec in 1625. They opened Mission Sainte-Marie among the Huron in 1639. The Company of One Hundred Associates who settled in Ville-Marie (Québec) proposed a model of evangelization: a family environment fashioned after the early Jerusalem apostolic community. One Associate, Ursuline Sister Marie de l'Incarnation (1599–1672), opened the first school for French-speaking and indigenous girls in Canada (1639).[2] Marguerite Bourgeoys (1620–1700), foundress of the Sisters of the Congregation of Notre Dame in Canada, opened the first school in Montréal in 1658, the first of many educational and human services systems. French Sulpicians, whose mission was to train men for the priesthood, opened Le Séminaire de Saint-Sulpice in Montréal (1657).

In northern New York, Jesuit Father Isaac Jogues (1607–1646) worked among the Huron, moving with them during their seasonal hunting migrations.[3] When the Mohawks, the enemy of the Huron, attacked them, several Jesuits living among the latter tribe were martyred. In 1642 Jesuit lay brother René Goupil and Jogues were killed near Auriesville, New York (1642); Jesuit lay brother John de Lelande was murdered in the same location several years later (1649). Five additional Jesuit priests were martyred in Canada (1649). The stories of their hardship and heroic suffering circulated widely in France, inspiring others to provide financial support to the missions or contemplate a missionary vocation of their own. Probably the best-known indigenous convert of the time was Algonquin–Mohawk Kateri Tekakwitha (1656–1680), who was canonized in 2012.

Subsequent generations of Jesuits mapped the Mississippi River and its tributaries, influenced higher education in North America, and

---

[2] See, Mary Dunn, *translation, notes, From Mother to Son: Selected Letters of Marie de L'Incarnation to Claude Martin* (New York: Oxford University Press, 2014).

[3] See Micah True, *Masters and Students: Jesuit Mission Ethnography in Seventeenth Century New France* (Montréal: McGill-Queen's University Press, 2015), for analysis of the interactions the French Jesuits had with the Huron and the French.

continued mission among Native Americans. Belgian Jesuit Pierre de Smet (1801–1873), leader of a band of six Jesuits that opened a mission among the Salish people in what is now British Columbia, took care to observe and write about the life of the tribes he met along the way. French-born Nicolas Point (1799–1868) provided watercolor paintings and sketches of tribal activities as he and de Smet traveled with fur traders from the area around St. Louis, Missouri. In contrast with the Franciscans, who gathered converts into communities, the Jesuits during this period tended to follow Native Americans as they moved throughout the area.

Another factor in global developments underlying American Catholicism during this era was the initiative of Propaganda Fide (Congregation for the Propagation of the Faith). Founded in Rome in 1622, the Congregation oversaw the transmission and dissemination of the faith in those places where Catholicism was in a "mission" status. Propaganda Fide authorized jurisdiction over mission territories and missionary cooperation while emphasizing cultural and scientific pursuits related to mission. Under this authority, Bishop François de Montmorency Laval (1623–1708) opened a "foreign missions" seminary in Québec.

English Catholics came to the New World primarily for commerce and with an emphasis on civic harmony. Three Jesuits arrived among other English (Protestant) passengers on the *Ark* and the *Dove* that anchored on a small island in the Potomac River (1634) on land that would be named Maryland. Shortly after St. Mary's City was founded, Jesuit missionary Andrew White (1579–1656) went among the Piscataway people of Chesapeake Bay. Eventually White learned enough of their language to compose a grammar, dictionary, and catechism in Piscataway. Other Jesuits worked among the Indians even though continued hostility from tribal people toward the English settlers made missionary travel difficult. Captain Richard Ingle's Rebellion (1644–1647) ended the Jesuit mission in that area.

After papal suppression of the Jesuits in 1733, the members of the society remained to serve the relatively small number of Catholics in the Maryland area. John Carroll (1735–1815), born at a large plantation in Marlborough Town, Province of Maryland, was appointed the Superior of the Missions in the thirteen United States of America (1784); in 1789 Carroll was named the first bishop in the United States. In the years that followed, the church's missionary focus would shift and begin to focus on the large number of European immigrants and enslaved Africans arriving in the United States.

NINETEENTH AND TWENTIETH CENTURIES: MULTIPLE DIRECTIONS WITHIN AND FROM THE UNITED STATES

During the nineteenth century, the Catholic population grew immensely as streams of immigrants arrived from Europe. Parishes formed, often along ethnic or language lines. In time, communities of women religious responded *en masse* to the need for evangelization within that setting. To ensure the continued development of the immigrants' faith, priests conducted missions (a type of retreat) in parishes. The Redemptorist Fathers, for instance, had arrived in 1832 to work among Native Americans, but discovered that – because they lived in a community house – their lifestyle was not compatible with the migratory life of indigenous people. As a result, they turned their attention to immigrant groups, especially German, Irish, and Slavic Catholics. Jesuit and Franciscan mission to Native Americans continued from Alaska through Arizona, and at the same time, missions opened overseas, sometimes because the territory became part of the United States.

While the US was still a young nation, US Catholics were invited to mission overseas. The first bishop of Charleston, South Carolina, John England (1786–1842), visited Pope Pius VIII in 1830 to draw attention to the composition of his diocese. The diocese (the Carolinas and Georgia) was comprised, 11,000 Catholics, including about 1,000 enslaved people of African descent. England, who raised money for a mission to Liberia, cited the spiritual and physical needs of American Black Catholics who had returned to western Africa and noted there was no pastoral presence among them. A decade later, Propaganda Fide responded to England's concerns and requested that US Bishops send missionaries to Liberia. Two priests and a lay catechist from New York and Philadelphia arrived there in 1842. Edward Barron, vicar general in the Archdiocese of Philadelphia, was appointed vicar apostolic for Upper Guinea, an area that spanned Liberia south to Angola. When the missionaries were affected by poor health and could no longer continue their work, Barron eventually appealed to French missionary priests who continued the mission into the mid-1880s.

Other congregations focused on the Caribbean and Latin America. Sisters of St. Francis of Allegany, New York, sent three sisters to begin a Jamaica mission (1879) and opened the first government-chartered Catholic teachers college in that country in 1897. Sisters of Mercy from Louisiana were missioned to Belize (British Honduras) in 1883, as were Jesuits from the Missouri Province (1894). Henriette DeLille (1812–1862), born a free woman of color in New Orleans, founded the

Sisters of the Holy Family (1842) in spite of local ecclesiastical and public opposition. Having ministered to Yellow Fever victims in New Orleans, the sisters opened their first mission among the Garifuna in Stan Creek, British Honduras, in 1897.[4] Some European mission congregations started US Provinces, and from this base took on overseas missions. The Redemptorists, for instance, opened St. Thomas mission, St. Croix, Antilles (1857), their first mission outside Europe and the United States. The Passionist Fathers started a foundation in Mexico City in 1865.

American missionaries also journeyed to Pacific and Asian nations to conduct missionary work. Marianne Cope (1838–1918) was two years old when she arrived in the United States with her family from the grand duchy of Hesse-Darmstadt. After working in a factory in Utica, New York, she joined the Sisters of St. Francis in Syracuse. Initially assigned to teach, Cope was elected the community's major superior. When missionary Father Leonard Fousnel wrote to Cope requesting sister nurses for Hawaii, she was immediately attracted to the mission but came to her final decision after Fousnel visited her in Syracuse. As part of the agreement, Cope stipulated that the sisters would be in charge of and manage the hospital, but would also be able to open schools. Along with six sisters, Cope arrived in Hawaii in October 1883, and became known for work among those afflicted with Hansen's disease (leprosy). In 2012, Pope Benedict XVI declared her a saint.

After the cessation of the Spanish American War in 1898, Cuba was granted independence and Guam, Puerto Rico, and the Philippines were entrusted to the United States. Propaganda Fide was especially concerned about American Protestant activity in those former Spanish possessions. The US church was charged with responsibility for Catholic Filipino schools, for instance, because of fears that students attending Protestant schools would weaken Catholic life in that country. As a result, Dennis J. Dougherty (1865–1951) was named a bishop in the Philippines (1903–1915) and Jeremiah J. Harty (1853–1927) was appointed Archbishop of Manila (1903–1916). Harty valued the importance of education for the Filipino people and worked to procure the Christian Brothers to teach high school boys. Both bishops continued to pay attention to overseas missions when they were appointed to US archdioceses. Dougherty encouraged Dr. Anna Dengel's and Dr. Joanna Lyons's foundation of the Medical Mission Sisters outside of Philadelphia – the first

---

4   Edward Brett, *New Orleans Sisters of the Holy Family: African American Missionaries to the Garifuna* (Notre Dame, IN: University of Notre Dame Press, 2012).

Roman Catholic congregation of women to work as obstetricians, surgeons, and physicians – and Harty authorized the Irish-founded Missionary Society of St. Columban to open a mission seminary in his diocese of Omaha.

American Catholic missionaries also continued to reach out to the underserved at home. Born into a wealthy Philadelphia family, Mother Katharine Drexel (1858–1955) was attuned to the needs of poor people and the plight of Native Americans from a young age. She traveled extensively to visit various Native American and African-American communities in order to learn of their situation firsthand. When she traveled to Rome to ask Pope Leo XIII to send a missionary priest for this purpose, he responded, "Why don't you yourself become a missionary?" In addition to financial support for the work, Drexel founded the Sisters of the Blessed Sacrament to work among these two groups.[5] With a grant from Katharine Drexel, the Divine Word Missionaries opened a seminary in Mississippi to educate Black men who desired to become priests and brothers.

GROWTH IN MISSION IMPETUS: 1900–1950

Until 1908, the United States was considered a "mission country" (i.e., under the jurisdiction of the Office of Propaganda Fide in Rome). During Pope Pius X's pontificate, the Catholic Church in the United States received "regularized" status. That meant the local church (i.e., the Catholic Church in the United States) could support itself financially, had adequate clergy, and was capable of educating American Catholics about mission. It was also expected to repay its debt and support missionary activity. Evidence of rising interest in mission among US Catholics was reflected through the growth in mission seminaries, and the establishment of congresses and mission organizations for laity. These mission venues also evidenced a Catholic community that was educated and involved in its church on both a local and national level. Some ethnic groups – the Germans, for example – had a strong tradition of supporting overseas missions. German Catholics continued to send money to mission groups who settled in the United States well into the twentieth century. Women particularly saw mission-focused activities

5   See Raymond Pace Alexander, "A Tribute to Mother Katharine Drexel," *Negro History Bulletin* 29(8) (1966): 181–191; and Amanda Bresie, *By Prayer and Petition: Sisters of the Blessed Sacrament's Mission of Evangelization and Americanization, 1891–1935* (Ph.D. diss.: Texas Christian University, 2014).

as a kind of "religious entrepreneurship." The Ladies' Catholic Indian Mission Association, along with two other groups, brought the needs of Native Americans to the bishops assembled at the Third Plenary Council of Baltimore (1884). Clara Westropp (1886–1965), a cofounder of the Women's Federal Savings Bank in Cleveland, along with her sister, began Mission Circles that provided financial assistance to Jesuit missions in Patna, India, where their brother was missioned. She was also influential in the formation of the Cleveland Diocesan Mission Office.

Paulist Fathers Walter Elliott and Alexander Doyle formed a Catholic Missionary Union (CMU) of priests whose focus was on home missions, especially in the southern part of the United States. They also established a seminary for this purpose. The Apostolic Mission House opened officially in 1903 on the campus of the Catholic University of America in Washington, DC. The CMU missionaries gathered in periodic conferences for support and to share their experiences. In addition, American Catholic Missionary Congresses were held in Chicago (1908) and Boston (1913) under the leadership of Father (later Bishop) Francis C. Kelley, founder of the Catholic Extension Society (1905). The congresses, attended by laity and clergy, highlighted several dimensions: mission to non-Catholics, home missions, especially in the southern United States, and missions overseas. Several Propagation of the Faith offices, especially in New York and Boston, raised large amounts of money for the society's overseas missions.

CMU member Father Thomas F. Price, who was recognized by bishops for his evangelization work in the South, joined the Director of the Boston Propagation of the Faith Office, Father James A. Walsh, to inaugurate the Catholic Foreign Mission Society of America, popularly known as Maryknoll, in 1911. Part of the Society's attraction was that it was "American," not "foreign"; i.e., it was not founded in Europe. A large seminary building, Chinese-themed in architecture, was built in Westchester County, New York, and the society began admitting candidates for the priesthood and brotherhood. The architecture reflected the location of the first Maryknoll missions to China. Under the guidance of foundress Mother Mary Joseph Rogers, women entered the Maryknoll Sisters of St. Dominic. The sisters became doctors, nurses, educators, and pastoral care personnel, and assisted the poor on several continents. The Maryknoll Society published a popular magazine, *The Field Afar*, later called *Maryknoll Mission*, that brought China to its readers. The magazine was listed as having the most subscriptions of any US-based mission magazine.

The participation of the United States in World War I broadened America's global scope and influence. One reflection of Catholic America's realization of increased international status in the post–World War I era was the formation of the Catholic Students' Mission Crusade (CSMC), which began among seminarians at the Divine Word Fathers' Provincial House near Chicago in 1918, and quickly spread across the country. The CSMC became one of the most extensive and successful national movements to raise mission awareness among seminary, college, and high school students.[6] Not only was this a time for America to "save" some of the missions (the French and German missionaries in China, for example, were expelled after the Boxer Rebellion, 1899–1901), but the Crusade's magazine, books, study guides, and national conferences brought the people, customs, and global mission interaction to a younger generation of Catholics.

Two international events in the 1920s provided opportunities to showcase American missions. Angelo Roncalli (later Pope John XXIII), then national director in Italy of the Society for the Propagation of the Faith, organized a Vatican Mission Exposition in 1925.[7] Missionaries sent artifacts, books, maps, and other materials that exemplified the religious and cultural contexts where they served throughout the world. "America" was represented through items related to Native American missions. The second global event was the International Eucharistic Congress (1926), which concluded at Chicago's Mundelein Seminary. Missionaries from China attending the Congress traveled to US convents to request sisters' assistance for their missions, and several communities with no prior overseas experience sent their members on this new venture. Increased Catholic interest, financial support, and publications surrounding missions were seen by American Catholics as a sign that they had come of age in a global church.[8] By the 1930s, forty mission magazines published in the United States were avidly being read by American Catholics.

Missionaries to China would become the first of a long line of US missionaries who interpreted global realities and situations to Americans. Missionaries suffered along with their people when catastrophic floods,

---

6   David J. Endres, *American Crusade: Catholic Youth in the World Mission Movement from World War I through Vatican II* (Eugene, OR: Pickwick Publications, 2010).

7   Angelyn Dries, "The 1925 Vatican Mission Exposition and the Interface between Mission Theory and World Religions," *International Bulletin of Mission Research* 40 (April 2016): 119–132.

8   Angelyn Dries, OSF, The Missionary Movement in American Catholic History (Maryknoll, NY: Orbis, 1990) 304.

internal wars, and the rise of Communism in the 1920s disrupted their lives. Mission magazines informed Catholic Americans of these conditions and appealed for help for the suffering Chinese. Not only were children invited to rescue a "pagan" (unbaptized) baby through sending their nickels and dimes to the Holy Childhood Association, they also became "missionary children" by helping to spread the gospel. They saw a world beyond their neighborhood and received an introduction to social justice through engagement with children in need. The social justice element underlying mission would strengthen in the 1960s and 1970s.

War II and the Korean War (1950–1953) adversely affected missions in China and other Asian countries. Many American soldiers stationed in Korea and the Philippines would see missionaries "in action" for the first time and witness Catholic life and mission beyond the United States. American troops sometimes participated in missionary work as they reconstructed bombed Catholic churches, schools, and hospitals for the people in Korea and the Philippines. In a post-war divided Korea, the Wisconsin Province of Jesuits opened Sogang University, Seoul, in 1960. In addition, American involvement in the protracted and contentious Vietnam War eventually resulted in the arrival of five "waves" of Vietnamese immigrants to the United States. The church in the United States was now receiving the "fruits" of mission overseas.

By the 1940s, US Catholics were becoming aware that missionaries were needed in other parts of the world, especially Africa and Latin America. The encyclical of Pope Pius XII, *Fidei Donum* (1957), directed Catholics to respond to the needs of Africa in terms of the development of local church leadership.[9] Prior to the pope's encyclical, five US Spiritan Fathers had worked with their European confreres in Tanganyika, Nigeria, and Sierra Leone in 1923, and received their own vicariate in Kilimanjaro and Tanganyika in 1932. The congregation opened an Institute of African Studies at Duquesne University in Pittsburgh in 1957. The institute taught North Americans about African life and the people with whom the Spiritans worked while preparing institute attendees to serve in African countries.

---

[9]   Pius XII's *Evangelii Praecones* (1951) updated Catholics on the consequences of World War II upon missions and the need to relook at missions globally. A movement to increase indigenous, rather than "foreign," ecclesial leadership in China and elsewhere had been emphasized in the mid-1920s under Pope Benedict XV. The first four Chinese bishops in modern times were ordained at St. Peter's Basilica in 1926, a fitting close to the Vatican Mission Exposition.

Other congregations were also active in African missions. The Maryknoll Society arrived in Tanganyika (Tanzania) in 1946 after being invited by the Vicar Apostolic of the Musoma-Maswa district to continue mission work begun there in the 1920s. The Society of Mary (Marianists) opened schools and skills-training centers in East Africa, and Divine Word Missionaries worked in Ghana in the education of seminarians and in parish ministry. The Tamale Institute of Cross-Cultural Studies, begun by Father Jon Kirby, SVD, introduced missionaries to the language and cultures of Ghana and fostered the process of inculturation through teaching, research, and publications. Salvatorian sisters joined their European priest colleagues in Tanzania, and the New York Jesuit Province was invited to open a new university center in Lagos, Nigeria. In the 1950s, the Women Volunteers for Africa worked alongside the White Sisters of Africa as teachers and medical personnel.

MISSION TO LATIN AMERICA IN THE POST–WWII ERA

Prior to the 1950s, the Catholic Church in the United States was aware of Latin American governments' anticlericalism, religious persecution, and appropriation of church properties. The US bishops had issued a "Resolution on Guatemala" (1925) in support of and in solidarity with Catholics who experienced religious persecution under President Jorge Ubico. The ban against the Catholic Church in the 1930s in Mexico, as well as the murder of local priests in that country, led the US bishops to respond to a call from their Mexican counterparts and open a seminary in the United States devoted to educating priests from that country. The Montezuma Seminary outside of Las Vegas, Nevada, educated hundreds of Mexican priests until 1971 when the seminary was no longer needed.

In 1955, Latin American bishops formed a regional conference (CELAM)[10] to address the religious situation and growing political and social unrest in their dioceses. After the conference, Bishop Juan Francisco Larraín of Talca, Chile, emphasized, "We must pass from a plane of national isolation to one of inter-American cooperation. Goals must be determined in terms of human need." Identifying "shocking" social inequality, inhumane conditions, and land ownership monopolies, Larraín noted, "With us or without us social reform is going to take place." It was time for the Catholic Church to "take a definite

---

[10] CELAM: *Consejo Episcopal Latinoamericano.* More recently, bishops of the Caribbean countries are part of CELAM. The conference was formed among the bishops for collaboration and reflection on common pastoral issues.

stand."[11] CELAM's agenda addressed both the need to strengthen local church leadership and speak to the sociopolitical realities ordinary Latin Americans faced.

That same inter-American connection extended from the United States. By 1958, 33 percent of US Catholic missionaries (1,192 men and women) were in South and Central Latin America. The US bishops opened a Latin America Bureau in 1959 with Cardinal Richard Cushing of Boston as the first chairman. Maryknoll Father John Considine served as director of the bureau from 1960 to 1968. The bureau gathered information from missionaries and church personnel about the social, political, and religious dimensions of life in Latin America for US bishops and other Catholic groups. Given the rise of Marxist Communism, the loss of church members, and attacks on the Latin America church, the Vatican urged US Catholic leaders to assist the church in the Southern hemisphere. Several factors underlay the request: the Americas are contiguous geographically; there had been interaction historically between Iberian and Indigenous Catholics; and US Catholics had strong financial, personnel, and institutional bases from which to draw.

In May 1959, Archbishop Antonio Samore, who had been the main organizer of the first General Council of Latin American Bishops (1955) and later vice president of the Papal Commission on Latin America, addressed the major superiors of religious orders and urged religious communities to send priests and sisters to confront the success of Protestantism and Communism in Latin America. The message became stronger when Samore put the topic on the US major superiors' agenda for their meeting in August 1961. Arriving on behalf of Samore, Agostino Casaroli, who also had attended the 1955 Latin American Bishops' Conference, offered nine considerations for members sent to Latin America. The topics ranged from cultural and linguistic preparation to an emphasis on the idea that Latin Americans needed to take responsibility for rebuilding the church in Central and South America. This meant that ecclesiastical personnel from outside Latin America should not move into public leadership positions.[12]

Through the Sister Formation Conference, women religious in the United States had successfully advocated for adequate spiritual,

---

[11]   Larraín quoted in Leonardo Bacigalupo, OFM, *American Franciscan Missions in Central America* (Andover, MA: Charisma Press, 1980), 166.

[12]   For Casaroli's speech, see Gerald M. Costello, *Mission to Latin America. The Successes and Failures of a Twentieth Century Crusade* (Maryknoll, NY: Orbis Books, 1979), 273–281.

intellectual, educational, and social formation for their sisters before they were sent to their ministry. Aware of this, Archbishop Romolo Carboni, Apostolic Delegate to Peru, approached the conference to invite them to work with Latin American sisters in order to achieve a similar well-rounded formation program. Sisters Annette Walters, CSJ, and Ritamary Bradley, CHM, visited several countries to explore possible locations where this work could take place. They met resistance on the part of some major superiors, whose focus was to get their sisters as quickly into teaching positions as possible because of their fear that Catholics would enroll in Protestant schools. In addition, although US women religious were used to working across congregations, that was not the case in the Latin American locations the sisters visited. Nevertheless, a counterpart to the US Sister Formation program, Regina Mundi, was started in Lima (1963) under the direction of Sister Gretchen Berg, a Rochester, Minnesota, Franciscan. The program lasted until 1967. Years later, clergy who worked with Regina Mundi faculty and students noted that in retrospect they could see the program as a "bright light" of the church in Peru.[13]

With a growing sense that North and South America were geographically, historically, and religiously connected, several other US mission groups sent their members to Latin America. Some dioceses opened a local office of Papal Volunteers for Latin America (PAVLA), a lay group approved by the Pontifical Commission for Latin America (1960). Others received training from Father Ivan Illich at the Center for Intercultural Formation in Cuernavaca, Mexico.[14] Illich, who emphasized intercultural communication and the experience of "identification with" the people, raised key questions about mission itself, such as: Why send missionaries at all? Were missionaries simply replicating an unjust system? Participants were forced to confront their cultural blindness and recognize the considerable differences between Catholicism in the United States and its Latin American counterpart.

Mission experience opened US Catholics' eyes to different cultures and contexts. Not only did they see extreme poverty, disease, and inadequate housing, but missionaries also began to observe the deleterious effects of dictatorships and the negative impact of foreign

---

[13] Information about Regina Mundi obtained from author interview with Gretchen Berg, OSF.

[14] For an analysis of this controversial priest and Director of the Center, see Todd Hartch, *The Prophet of Cuernavaca. Ivan Illich and the Crisis of the West* (Cary, NC: Oxford University Press USA, 2015).

corporations that took advantage of land and resources without considering the consequences for either people or the earth. A better understanding of "development," especially in relation to justice, seemed the new word for mission. The US Catholic Bishops' pastoral on mission activity (1971) noted the "alleged conflict" between those who emphasized development over that of evangelization.[15] In the meantime, the United Nations had declared a Decade of Development (1960–1970), and continued to reiterate that theme for the next three decades. For many missionaries, development meant not only public projects centered around health, running water, and better roads, but identification of and respect for people's local and indigenous cultures. Mission and evangelization now included more than teachings about God; there was also a focus on relationships that are just, peaceful, and loving.

The US government supported authoritarian regimes in Latin America during the 1960s and 1970s, with some moderation during the presidency of Jimmy Carter (1977–1981). Missionaries and others spoke out against US foreign policy in the southern hemisphere especially during Ronald Reagan's administration (1981–1989). Theologians from Latin America shared the struggles facing the people in their countries with the entire church. A new term, Liberation Theology, came to the fore shaped by the experience of Latin American religious leaders, such as Bishop Helder Câmara, José Comblin, and Leonardo Boff (Brazil), Gustavo Gutiérrez (Peru), and Archbishop Oscar Romero (El Salvador). Even more powerful was the message of missionaries who gave their lives in service to mission. Between 1959 and 1990, eleven Catholic missionaries sent from the United States were killed, all of them, with a few exceptions, in Central America. They include laywoman Jean Donovan and Sisters Maura Clarke, MM, Ita Ford, MM, and Dorothy Kazel, OSU, El Salvador (1980), Brother James Miller, FSC, Guatemala (1982), Sister Maureen Courtney, CSA, Nicaragua (1990), and clergy William C. Kruegler, MM, Bolivia (1962), Raymond Herman, Bolivia (1975), Conventual Franciscan Casimir Cypher, Honduras (1975), William H. Wood, MM, Guatemala (1976), and Stanley Rother, Guatemala (1981). The group that galvanized the United States the most were probably the four women murdered in El Salvador. When news of their deaths was announced, vigils were held in their honor throughout the country. When the circumstances surrounding their death were reported – the women had been sexually assaulted

---

[15]   Hugh J. Nolan, ed., *Pastoral Letters of the U.S. Catholic Bishops*, vol. 3 (Washington, DC: U.S. Catholic Conference, 1987), 293–297, here 293.

and murdered – groups, many of them ecumenical, called for an investigation and demanded the arrest of those responsible.

Missionary involvement in Latin America also exposed American Catholics to new views and vocabulary. North Americans heard and sometimes used terms such as, "preferential option for the poor," "Base Christian Communities," and "sinful structures," perspectives that began south of the Rio Grande.[16] Archbishop Jorge Bergoglio, president of the Argentine Bishops Conference, was elected president of CELAM when the Latin American and Caribbean bishops promulgated their 2007 Aparecida document, the theme of which was "Disciples and Missionaries of Jesus Christ, so that our peoples may have life in him." All Catholics, they proclaimed, are called to a life of mission and service among the poor. Bergoglio, elected to the papacy in 2013, was the first pope from the Americas. He took the name Francis, carrying forward some of the same emphases he learned in CELAM. While American Catholic focus in the 1920s had begun when Catholic structures and institutions in Latin America were denounced, the mission of the 1960s and beyond paid attention to attacks on people, especially the poor, and to structures that kept people and the earth impoverished.

CONCLUSION: AMERICAN CATHOLICS AND GLOBAL CATHOLICISM

Geographically, "America" is a continuous continent. As we look back at mission in the American context, we see that the terms *global* and *diverse* are present from the start, beginning with sixteenth-century Spanish and indigenous people, the French, and the English. It wasn't until the early nineteenth century that Catholics from other European countries arrived in the United States in significant numbers. During the twentieth century, the papacy drew the attention of Catholics in the Americas toward issues related to people in other parts of the world. By 1960, for instance, papal offices sanctioned lay mission and expected US religious congregations to send members to Latin America. Meanwhile, the Latin American Catholic Church's social justice agenda was reflected in periodic but significant meetings of CELAM that challenged and inspired North American Catholics to address systemic injustice.

[16] Mark Noll, *New Shape of World Christianity: How American Experience Reflects Global Faith* (Downers Grove, IL: InterVarsity Press, 2009), though directed toward an Evangelical audience, argues that missionary influence abroad did not necessarily produce an "American" experience on local cultures in mission countries. Such a position denies the fact that believers have agency.

Over the last thirty years, people from so-called mission countries (Chile, Fiji, Korea, India, and Vietnam, for example) are now themselves missionaries elsewhere, including the United States. "Sister parishes" or "parish twinning" groups connect local US parish communities with those in other parts of the world, particularly Latin America or Africa. In their local churches, US Catholics meet new African immigrants who reflect a contemporary "Africa." Sunday Masses in the Archdiocese of Los Angeles, for example, are celebrated in forty-two languages. The interface between US mission/evangelization and geographic, political, and ethnic backgrounds from around the globe has led to a rich, variegated Catholic experience in the United States. An overview of *mission* to, within, and from the United States, and interaction with pertinent papal offices, has provided a lens to explore the constant pulse that mission has contributed toward the complex dynamics of a Global Catholicism. We are continually being "missioned."

FURTHER READING

Bingemer, Maria Clara L. *Latin American Theology: Roots and Branches.* Maryknoll, NY: Orbis, 2016.

Dries, Angelyn, OSF. *The Missionary Movement in American Catholic History.* Maryknoll, NY: Orbis, 1990.

Markey, Eileen. *A Radical Faith: The Assassination of Sister Maura.* New York: Nation Books, 2016.

McGlone, Mary, CSJ. *Sharing Faith Across the Hemisphere.* Maryknoll, NY: Orbis, 1997.

McGreevy, John T. *American Jesuits and the World: How an Embattled Religious Order Made Modern Catholicism Global.* Princeton, NJ: Princeton University Press, 2016.

Part III

The Many Faces of Catholicism

14 American Catholic Laywomen and Feminism

PAULA M. KANE

This chapter charts laywomen's experiences within and contributions to Roman Catholicism in the United States from the late nineteenth century to the present, with particular focus on their relationship with and response to the broader women's rights movement and modern feminism. It addresses the roles that women have played in building up the church and passing on the faith, while also recognizing the struggles they have faced in making their voices heard in an institution governed by patriarchal structures and attitudes. Three distinct eras in Catholic women's history help illustrate their contributions: the Progressive era, roughly 1890–1920, with the building and flourishing of an organizational network of women's organizations; the Vatican II era, 1960–1980, including the updating of the church through the Council, as well as the American feminist movement, and the controversy surrounding birth control; and finally, the present moment, 1990–2020, characterized by cultural challenges posed to religions by issues of gender identity and human rights.

In each era, Catholic women embodied the religious and cultural influences of their times. Overall, modern gender norms resulted from nineteenth-century industrialization, which produced a doctrine of "separate spheres" for men and women, prescribing women's roles as secondary in church and society, but with primacy over the domestic sphere of hearth and home. After establishing the nineteenth-century's impact on Catholic womanhood, we turn to the early twentieth century when greater access to higher education and the activity of laywomen as fundraisers, charity workers and social activists, and career professionals, drew them outside the home. Women's orientation changed again in the 1960s and 1970s, following theological changes wrought by Vatican II and American social upheavals around gender and race. These events did not produce a linear path toward women's liberation, but they have produced dissenting voices that reject the "essential woman" arguments of the past and who trust their own consciences to guide them rather than the institutional church. Ongoing cultural conflicts have paved the way in recent decades for the consideration of new topics such as gay rights and lesbian, gay, bisexual, transgender and queer (LGBTQ) identities; women's participation in theological fields formerly reserved to men; and the pursuit of women's rights as human rights.

MIDDLE-CLASS DOMESTICITY IN THE PROGRESSIVE ERA

For centuries prior to 1920, Catholic dogma represented an essentialist and binarist approach to gender. This meant that church teaching rested upon what it assumed were fixed scriptural and theological principles that established clear cut identities and duties for only two sexes: men and women. The process of industrialization in the nineteenth century promoted similar notions of separate roles for men and women. The so-called cult of domesticity spoke of Protestant women's sphere as defined by four traits – purity, piety, submission, and domesticity – in which religion played a principal role to sheltering women from the dangers of commerce and industry.[1] This ideology worked to enshrine a static and submissive role for Catholic women as well. Catholics spoke of the complementary nature of the sexes, a pairing in which women were cherished for being self-sacrificing, destined for motherhood or the convent, but not paid for their labor. The model of Catholic womanhood drew inspiration from Biblical texts and centuries of male scriptural interpretation that defined proper feminine behavior as though divinely ordained and eternal. As Catholic women began to volunteer in service to children, the poor, and new immigrants, these activities seemed to fit this formula.

Print culture contributed greatly to spreading the ideals of Catholic womanhood in the latter decades of the nineteenth century. As Catholic newspapers and magazines emerged in the United States, they fostered traditionalist norms of gender and reinforced the notion of complementary gender roles. Etiquette books also taught these notions, admonishing Catholic girls to be moral and chaste before marriage by avoiding behavior or clothing that might "inflame his passions." Prescriptive manuals characterizing femininity, such as Father Bernard O'Reilly's *The Mirror of True Womanhood* (1876–1892), show Catholic clergy

---

[1] Barbara Welter, "The Cult of True Womanhood: 1820–1860," *American Quarterly* 18(2) Part 1 (Summer 1966): 151–174.

sharing Protestant notions of the self-sacrificing, home-centered mother. In this vein, woman's contribution was to serve her family and the church as the "keeper of her children's hearts." These religious norms of womanly propriety, shared by Victorian culture, helped patriarchy to remain uncontested.

The idealization of women, highlighting virginity and nobility, flourished in Catholic journals such as *Ave Maria* and *The Queen's Work*. These same themes appeared in articles, book reviews, poems, and short stories in magazines produced for the general public, like *Catholic Digest*, or the more intellectually inclined *Catholic World*, published by the Paulists from 1865 to 1996. *Catholic World's* offerings could range from a summary of women's addresses at the Columbian Exposition in 1893 to "Hints on Housekeeping," a grandmother's warning that only in the household can women "find profitable and legitimate exercise"; and to poems like "Motherhood," where God ordained to make "woman's heart the agent of His power."[2]

Around 1900, when female roles seemed sharply defined and limited, Catholic women began to create an organizational culture to perform charitable service outside the home. In part, this was a response to the unwelcoming attitude of Protestant benevolent agencies, which treated Catholics with condescension and targeted them with evangelization. Catholic immigrants were regarded by white Protestants as in need of both hygiene and Christian conversion. Catholic women's associations, therefore, often began as efforts within parishes and dioceses where they were welcomed and needed. From the parish core, women served many functions in the larger Catholic community. But their public activities also followed upon the expansion of educational opportunities. The late nineteenth century witnessed a dramatic growth of Catholic academies, many of which later developed into Catholic colleges for women, beginning with the College of Notre Dame (now Notre Dame of Maryland University) in Maryland in 1895.

In addition to sodalities (lay associations promoting prayer and spiritual works, often ethnically based) and altar guilds that had enrolled the majority of Catholic women in the nineteenth century, women soon created an impressive new set of charities to aid orphans, children, and the sick. Over time, these organizations grew into national and international programs. Sparked by the bishops, an era

---

[2] "The Woman Question among Catholics: A Round Table Conference," *Catholic World* 57 (August 1893): 668–684; "Hints on Housekeeping," 10:59 (February 1870): 610–614; "Motherhood," 47 (April 1888): 58.

of consolidation and coordination of Catholic charities occurred throughout the United States in the decades after World War I, when the church's war mobilization effort, the National Catholic War Council, was transformed into the National Catholic Welfare Council (NCWC). Through the NCWC, Catholics created a range of social agencies. The gendered outlook of Catholic charities can be seen in their emphasis on prevention (of sin) and rehabilitation (of the sinner) as a Catholic resolution to the "girl problem" that likewise preoccupied Progressive reformers in the 1920s.[3]

The Boston archdiocese exemplified how organizations for Catholic women evolved over time. Its League of Catholic Women was established in 1910, and eventually federated more than forty women's societies in the region "to unite Catholic women for the promotion of spiritual, cultural, and educational work." Leagues of Catholic Women (LCWs) soon formed in many American dioceses, culminating in the founding of the National Council of Catholic Women (NCCW) in 1921. The LCWs illustrate the growth of middle-class associationism among Catholic laywomen, a strategy that combined good works with cultural events and educational lectures, and Americanization classes with language and job training for immigrant and working women. Catholic women's groups served varying socioeconomic levels but nonetheless were limited by the church from receiving professional training in social work and cooperating with secular agencies.

As Catholics helped shape national policies during and after the Great Depression (1929–1939), their work was often in tension with public welfare agencies, as they sought to avoid entanglements that might force them to be subjected to laws or regulations that undermined the autonomy of the church. Because the approval of women's benevolent associations rested with each bishop, the waves of consolidations of diocesan charities in the 1920s and 1930s meant that clerical control did tend to subvert women's leadership. Women needed to work doubly hard to manage charities on their own, in order to escape direction from either the Catholic hierarchy or from Protestant or public oversight. The Depression, however, also gave rise to a unique model of charity, the Catholic Worker movement, founded in 1933 by Dorothy Day (1897–1980), a convert. Her model of lay activism, which supported

---

[3]   Dorothy M. Brown and Elizabeth McKeown, *The Poor Belong to Us: Catholic Charities and American Welfare* (Cambridge, MA: Harvard University Press, 1997), 134.

pacifism, nonviolent resistance, and care for the poor through urban settlement houses, combined with her personal asceticism, remains a countercultural challenge to all Americans.

Over the course of the twentieth century, the upward mobility of Catholics permitted them financially to support their own philanthropic activities. Throughout the twentieth century, Catholic women continued to work on behalf of the child, the immigrant, and the poor, following patterns of voluntarism already a century old. In 1919, NCCW purchased the National Catholic School of Social Service (NCSSS) (1918–1947) and helped to support it financially even after it affiliated with the Catholic University of America in Washington, DC, in 1923. The goals of the NCSSS were to train professional women as social workers because the church did not want them to attend non-Catholic institutions. Eventually, the school merged its faculty, students, and curriculum with its male counterpart at Catholic University in 1939.

Despite their success in social welfare fields, the distancing of Catholic women from asserting their own rights was evidenced in the cause of woman suffrage. Before passage of the Nineteenth Amendment in 1920, rather than joining suffrage campaigns, Catholic women emphasized their devotional activity, their care for infants, the poor, and the sick, and their voluntarism. Even career woman Katherine Conway (1853–1927), first woman editor of Boston's archdiocesan paper, opposed woman suffrage. She typified a certain Catholic who regarded men as legitimate public leaders, as she cautioned women to avoid an unhealthy emphasis on women's causes. Those Catholic women who agreed with her preferred an indirect role in society and claimed that they did not need to vote or hold waged jobs because men would provide for them.

But even among Catholic women, rebellious and diverse voices emerged to defy the separation of spheres, notably as advocates for the rights for working-class people, for suffrage, and for birth control. Labor activists, such as Irish-born Mary Harris "Mother" Jones (1837–1930), rejected demure behavior: "No matter what the fight, don't be ladylike!" Admittedly, Mother Jones's relationship to the Catholic Church was complicated. She condemned its inertia in helping wage-workers, and yet she received a Catholic funeral. Jones is best remembered for aiding the coal miners of Pennsylvania and West Virginia in 1873 during the nation's worst financial panic, and railroad workers in 1877. Other Catholic women labor activists included Irish-born Leonora Barry (1849–1923), the first woman to hold national office in the Knights of Labor, and Mary Kenney O'Sullivan (1864–1943), a bookbinder who became the first female organizer for the American Federation of Labor.

Spanning the first two eras in Catholic women's history was another activist, the defiant Margaret Sanger (1879–1966), daughter of an Irish-born freethinker stonemason and an American Irish-Catholic mother. Since the early 1900s, Sanger was targeted by Catholic Church leaders due to her defense of birth control and her efforts to expand sex education to women who were ignorant of basic biological processes. The Comstock Laws, which were in effect during her lifetime, had been enacted by conservative Protestants in the 1870s to make it illegal to send birth control information through the mails by defining it as obscene. But Sanger vented her anger at Catholics in a speech in New York City in 1921:

> The church has ever opposed the progress of woman on the ground that her freedom would lead to immorality. We ask the church to have more confidence in women. We ask the opponents of this movement to reverse the methods of the church, which aims to keep women moral by keeping them in fear and in ignorance, and to inculcate into them a higher and truer morality based upon knowledge … If we cannot trust woman with the knowledge of her own body, then I claim that two thousand years of Christian teaching has proved to be a failure.[4]

DIVISIONS AND REFORMULATIONS IN THE VATICAN II ERA

Women were leaders in two lay initiatives that preceded Vatican II by decades: the Grail, a women's movement, and the Christian Family Movement for married couples. The Grail, which flourished from the 1940s until the mid-1970s, originated in the Netherlands in 1921 in response to papal calls for the laity to participate in "Catholic Action." As such, the Grail provided an alternative culture for laywomen interested in the lay apostolate, but not necessarily convent life. Janet Kalven (1913–2014) of Chicago, a pioneer in feminist spirituality, joined the Grail in 1942 and went on to found Grailville in Loveland, Ohio, in 1944 as an educational and retreat center. In her memoir, she recalled: "Personally, I ground my hope for the world and for the Grail chiefly in

---

[4]   Margaret Sanger, "The Morality of Birth Control," November 18, 1921, accessed at www.nyu.edu/projects/sanger/aboutms/

the strength of women, women who develop all of their gifts and talents, women who act together generously and in hope to bring into reality their vision of a world where difference does not connote domination."[5] Their focus upon the liturgy was one striking aspect of the Grail, as was the way in which it weathered the challenges posed by Vatican II and the social conflicts of the 1960s to reemerge, as did many orders of women religious, with a greater emphasis upon justice and peace.

Also prior to Vatican II, the Christian Family Movement (CFM) strove to increase lay ministry within the Catholic Church, and by doing so helped grow an emerging feminist consciousness. While the documents of the Council would welcome and uplift lay ministry, when the CFM was organized in 1949 by several married couples, some bishops criticized it for taking on too much decision-making authority or of usurping the work of the clerically controlled Catholic Family Bureau. In the postconciliar era, other lay-led groups endured the same complaints from priests and bishops – that laypersons were acting without deference to the authority of the hierarchy.

Pat and Patty Crowley served as the first national presidents of CFM from 1949 to 1968. The movement encouraged small groups of five to seven adult couples to meet once or twice a month in each other's homes to discuss how to live a Christ-centered marriage and how to enact their faith in everyday situations, using the See-Judge-Act method promoted by Cardinal Joseph Cardijn of Belgium. Their discerning observations were to lead couples to social action, which led CFM members to foster parenting, prison ministry, and refugee work. The movement's membership peaked in 1964 with about 50,000 couples.

Among nuns and sisters, the Leadership Conference of Women Religious organized the first meeting in 1974, nine years after the close of the Second Vatican Council, to consider women's ordination. In Detroit in the following year, some 1,200 Catholics met for the Women's Ordination Conference (WOC). The Vatican did not endorse these efforts, and firmly rejected women's ordination in a 1976 document, which stated that the sex of the priest must embody literally the maleness of Jesus. This "Declaration on the Question of the Admission of Women to the Ministerial Priesthood" disappointed Catholic feminists and demonstrated a surprising detour around the church's rich tradition of metaphorical and symbolic language, but still led to calls for reconciliation and dialogue with the Catholic hierarchy. The church

---

[5] Janet Kalven, *Women Breaking Boundaries: A Grail Journey, 1940–1995* (Albany, NY: State University of New York Press, 1999), 303.

reaffirmed its position in 1994 when Pope John Paul II declared there would be no further debate on women's ordination and no change to Canon Law 1024, which restricted the priesthood to men.

Vatican II is often heralded as the liberation of the modern laity, fully supporting women in redefining their roles. Differing interpretations of the Council, however, have led to deepening divisions between traditionalists and progressives on many issues, especially gender. The documents of Vatican II have been brandished by Catholics on opposite sides of social issues, and the Council itself has been unevenly integrated throughout American dioceses. On one hand, women benefited from the postwar shift in political discourse about Catholics, who began to be accepted as loyal citizens rather than criticized as immigrant subversives. As Catholics enjoyed social and economic integration, women's agendas changed as well, leading charities and children's welfare ministries to extend their efforts to the general population. Yet as the American suburbs expanded in the1950s and 1960s, they drew white women back into domestic roles, creating a scenario allowing women to be better educated, but not career-minded. Few Catholic women put gender identity first to embrace what would be called radical feminism, and most were content to work within the church, despite misgivings. The rule governing Catholic women's organizations for decades, including those that required that their agendas be approved by church authorities and their groups headed by male chaplains, also limited the spread of feminist ideas.

An unexpected development among laywomen that upheld traditionalist gender outlooks in postconciliar America was a series of reported Marian apparitions. Beginning with Mary Ann van Hoof in Wisconsin in 1949, the roster of visionaries accelerated in the 1980s and 1990s to include Veronica Lueken, Nancy Fowler, Estela Ruiz, and others. These visionaries were typically adult women whose revelations often called for prayer, sacrifice, rejection of materialism, and conversion. They also encouraged renewed devotionalism to the Virgin Mary, using her to promote a restoration of traditional gender roles. Their message tended to emphasize "family values," the phrase enshrined by the conservative American political factions emerging in the 1970s. Whether these apparitions are real or fraudulent, the predominance of laywomen in the Marian movement suggests that it has provided a venue for concerned conservatives and less elite Catholics to voice their fears of the waning of devotional practices.

Radical laywomen, a small percentage of Catholics during the 1960s and 1970s, learned from the philosophic arguments leveled against

Christian patriarchy, sexism, and its rhetorical devices, especially as inaugurated by feminist philosopher Mary Daly (1928–2010) in *The Church and the Second Sex* (1968), a Catholic equivalent to Simone de Beauvoir's *The Second Sex* (1949). De Beauvoir had declared that "one is not born, but rather becomes, a woman," a rebuke to essentialist theories. In 1985, Daly revised her own thinking about how the church shaped gender in a "Feminist Postchristian Introduction" to the book's third edition, emboldening women to leave the church, advising that they had nothing to lose "since the Church has given us precisely Nothing."[6] While most American Catholic women stayed in the church, Daly's salvos posited a stark choice between belonging and "Be/Leaving," and her provocations to women to stop participating in their own spiritual oppression continued for the next quarter-century, now finding echoes in Catholics' responses to the clerical sexual abuse scandals. As her philosophy evolved, Daly was accused by critics of positing innate traits for women that made them superior to men.

Other female activists have urged women's ordination, not new statements, as a solution to problems within the church. Following the example of the "Danube Seven" – Catholic women from the United States, Austria, and Germany who were ordained by consenting bishops on the Danube River in 2002 – more women were ordained on the St. Lawrence Seaway in Canada in 2005, and eight Catholic women became Roman Catholic Womenpriests (RCWP) on the Ohio River at Pittsburgh in the summer of 2006. The Catholic Womanpriest movement (CWP) organized these events, later ordaining some of the womanpriests as bishops, despite the church's insistence that their actions were invalid (because the ordaining bishops were not in communion with the church) and illicit (because canon law forbids women to become priests). The church subsequently excommunicated all ordained women in a general decree of 2008. Nevertheless, the RCWP has ordained more than 150 women and continues its quest. As one anthropologist notes, "At root, of course, remains the problem of how Catholic women can be Godlike but not priestlike."[7]

While most Catholic women did not align themselves with Daly or with women's ordination activism, they did show opposition to the

---

[6]   Mary Daly, "New Archaic Afterwards," *The Church and the Second Sex* (Boston: Beacon Press, 3rd ed., 1985), xiii.

[7]   Maya Mayblin, "Containment and Contagion: The Gender of Sin in Contemporary Catholicism," in Kristin Norget, Valentina Napolitano, and Maya Mayblin, eds. *The Anthropology of Catholicism: A Reader* (Berkeley: University of California Press, 2017), 147.

church on the issue of contraception. Despite church teachings, the use of birth control increased among Catholic women from a rate of about 30 percent in 1955, to 51 percent in 1965, to present rates of more than 90 percent. In 1930, Pope Pius XI had issued *Casti Connubii*, an encyclical on "chaste marriage," prohibiting the use of all types of contraception – even for married Catholics – as part of the church's defense of the procreative goal of the sacrament of marriage. This document, in tandem with *Humanae Vitae*, the 1968 encyclical of Pope Paul VI, has defined the Catholic position on contraception as unique among the other Christian churches. Yet judging by the rapid rise in the use of birth control among laywomen after 1968, *Humanae Vitae* failed to convince couples to rely upon the church-approved rhythm method of regulating family size. The first hormonal birth control pill appeared in 1960, in part as an attempt to permit family planning and prevent poverty in the wake of the Depression. A Catholic obstetrics professor at Harvard University, John Rock, conducted the pill's first clinical trials and intentionally described it as similar to the rhythm method, which the church approved in 1951.

In the final quarter of the twentieth century, the US Supreme Court in the 1973 decision, *Roe v. Wade*, legalized abortion rights. Rather than focusing on fighting racism or gender inequality, Catholic women's political engagement turned to antiabortion activism. In the *Roe* decision, the Court held that the constitutional right to privacy includes a woman's right to end her pregnancy and affirmed the right of a woman to choose abortion as a method to do so. Hence, the Court's majority opinion rested on the issue of privacy of married couples to be free of unwarranted government intrusion rather than on the constitutional principle of equal protection. Since *Roe*, the church has maintained its long-standing opposition to abortion, whereas the feminist movement enlisted women's support for reproductive freedom as a gender right. (A dissenting group, Catholics for Free Choice, was established in 1973, whose very claim as a Catholic organization was rejected by the American Catholic bishops.) Many Catholic women, as defenders of the pope and bishops who guarded tradition, tended not to regard the issue as one of women's rights, but rather one of defense of the vulnerable fetus.

Two careers of two women reveal the complex and conflicting status of Catholic women's political activism during the 1970s and 1980s. On the conservative side was activist Phyllis Schlafly, "the sweetheart of the silent majority," who mobilized antifeminists to defeat the Equal Rights Amendment. Schlafly (1924–2016) might be the first Catholic woman whose activism, in this case for conservative political and moral issues, was not identified primarily with her religion. Her opposition to feminism, abortion rights, the Equal Rights Amendment, same-sex marriages (despite having one gay son), immigration reform, and communism made her a mainstay on the Republican right through her national organization, the Eagle Forum, founded in 1972. In contrast, many Catholic women embraced a leftward move in politics. Among them were figures like Geraldine Ferraro, who defied the gendered expectations placed upon her by her family and society. Dissatisfied with her career as an elementary school teacher, she earned a law degree and later entered politics, getting elected to the House of Representatives in 1978. The abortion debate had negative consequences for Catholic women in politics, as Ferraro soon learned: when she ran for Vice President in 1984, Ferraro was repeatedly denounced by the Archbishop of New York and allied priests because of her support for abortion rights. Catholics for Free Choice placed an advertisement in the *New York Times* signed by 100 Catholics supporting Ferraro's position in defense of freedom of conscience, which led to church reprisals against some of the signatories, including nuns.

How did national and international organizations involving Catholic women fare in the postconciliar era? The NCCW continued to profess a "modest" variety of feminism, and yet consistently opposed the Equal Rights Amendment (ERA) since it was first proposed in 1956. Their position stemmed from unfounded fears among members that the ERA would impose abortion rights throughout the United States. Nevertheless, in the pages of its journal, *Word Magazine* (1963–1971), and its successor, *Catholic Woman Magazine*, launched in 1975, NCCW members could gain considered information on social issues, learn about diocesan council activities around the country, and get advice on implementing new programs at the local level.

NCCW's early antifeminist stance contrasted with the more global-minded members of its umbrella affiliate, the World Union of Catholic Women's Organizations (WUCWO), established in 1952 in order to organize women internationally to embrace Catholic social action. WUCWO grew from a 1910 French initiative to unite Catholic women's organizations around the world. In the postwar era, WUCWO members have been affiliated with commissions at the United Nations as delegates of nongovernmental organizations (NGOs) and thus have gained exposure to an international perspective on issues affecting women. Among the more successful outcomes of the 1995 International Conference on Women that have been embraced by Catholic women was opposition to human trafficking, a modern form of slavery and criminality that targets women and children. Since 1995, fighting the sex trade has become a major focus for laywomen and women religious. Along with their participation at UN forums, American Catholic women have lobbied their Congressional officials to pass anti-trafficking legislation and have created safe houses and shelters for victims, often staffed by Catholic sisters.

WUCWO's global outlook on women's issues contrasts with the two most traditionalist Catholic women's groups of the second half of the twentieth century – the Catholic Daughters of the Americas and the Daughters of America – who fashioned themselves as crusaders against threats to American Catholic life, namely abortion, communism, feminism, and immodest clothing for women.

FROM GENDER RIGHTS TO HUMAN RIGHTS

Gender issues particularly affecting women dominate the current moment, and reflect the irregular diffusion of Vatican II principles nationally and the backlash against them during the papacies of Pope John Paul II and Pope Benedict XVI. At the forefront is the impact of Catholic feminism and antifeminism; debates over family, fertility, and new expressions of gender identity; and efforts to secure women's spiritual and personal equality within the church.

Despite the goodwill engendered by Vatican II, support for women from the American hierarchy was not forthcoming in the subsequent decades. Because the council documents had said little about women or about sexism, the US bishops decided to draft a pastoral letter on the topic. The ill-fated project was scuttled in 1992, when progressive bishops argued that the traditionalist tone of the document, now in its fourth draft, would only alienate women, in the same way that *Humanae Vitae* had by issuing a blanket prohibition without weighing the advice given to the Vatican commission on birth control by the invited married Catholics. The proposed women's pastoral letter failed to gain the necessary two-third majority of votes, marking the first time since 1966 that the US bishops had opposed their own document. Notably, though, the "no" votes did not indicate that those bishops favored the more radical strategy of women's ordination.

A forward-looking approach to uplifting women has come from Call to Action, a progressive reform group for Catholics established in 1976 that has focused in recent years on training future lay leaders for the church through young adult outreach in a program called Re/Generation. Its cohort of millennial and Generation X Catholics includes persons who feel marginalized in the church but do not plan to leave it. Similar goals are represented by Future Church, a coalition founded in Ohio in 1990 committed to "changes that will provide all Roman Catholics the opportunity to participate fully in Church life, ministry, and governance." It seeks to prepare for the coming priest shortage by supporting male and female leadership in the priesthood and regular access to the Eucharist, and it supported the Leadership Conference of Women Religious against Pope Benedict's XVI's order for the Vatican Congregation for the Doctrine of the Faith to investigate American nuns and sisters between 2009 and 2014.

The emergence of electronic media has created new opportunities for Catholic women to voice their own opinions about gender issues. Innovative uses of technology to address and expand Catholics' views of gender include podcasts and blogs, such as Catholic Women Preach, inspired by Pope Francis's call for laity to participate more fully in the church. Its weekly videos and web reflections by female students and scholars follow the liturgical calendar and discuss the weekly readings for Mass especially from a woman's perspective. Since 2010, a shared blog called Women in Theology offers the perspectives of Catholic women trained in theology as well as those of Orthodox and Protestant Christians. On the opposite end of the spectrum, the Eternal Word Television Network, based in Alabama and once led by Mother Angelica (1923–2016), a Poor Clare nun, promotes traditionalist Catholic messaging.

As national women's service agencies like NCCW reach their centenary in 2020, few younger women are joining. Still, the NCCW continues to provide up-to-date information on contemporary social crises on its website, including climate change, human trafficking, and domestic violence. International agencies like WUCWO, concentrating efforts upon economic development, education, and protection of human rights, have endured and expanded their focus to accommodate global concerns affecting women. NCCW remains one of WUCWO's five affiliates in North America and collaborates with other international groups like Catholic Relief Services and with various Catholic sisterhoods. Effective recent initiatives of the NCCW include food banks, care for the poor and elderly, and especially, the Respite program, in which trained volunteers help primarily female caregivers of the elderly to get temporary relief from their burdensome labor.

If contemporary Catholic women are no longer joining sodalities or organizations such as LCW, NCCW or WUCWO, where do they go? In the arenas of education and scholarship, the assimilating effects of increased affluence and acquisition of advanced professional degrees have produced well-educated women within academia and ministry who teach and publish in canon law, liturgy, philosophy, religious studies, and theology. In the late twentieth century, groundbreaking theological reflection has come from the pens of sisters Joan Chittister, Elizabeth Johnson, Ilia Delio, Joyce Rupp, and Christine Schenk, and from laywomen Mary Daly, Elizabeth Schüssler Fiorenza, Diana Hayes, Ada Maria Isasi-Diaz, Catherine LaCugna, Pheme Perkins, Rosemary Radford Ruether, and Mary Jo Weaver, among many others. Women's expanded roles in education and ministry have compensated in part for their exclusion from the priesthood and permanent diaconate. The vocation shortage in America has also unexpectedly placed women in leadership roles in parishes and in faith formation programs. Between 1966 and 1984 the number of active diocesan priests declined by about 20 percent, opening places for women to serve as chaplains, spiritual directors, and pastoral administrators. This trend has only increased in the last thirty years as seminary classes continue to shrink. At present, about 80 percent of paid lay ministers in American parishes are women.

As noted above, the decline in younger women's engagement in the Catholic Church may be the most significant Catholic trend. Beyond the determination to care for others, many women today find little to draw them into the church or to return to it, and lament the paths of ministry that are closed to them. Data from the *America* magazine survey of 2018 conducted by the Center for Applied Research in the Apostolate (CARA) at Georgetown University found that among millennials, those Americans born around 1982 and after, only 17 percent of women attended Mass weekly. Of women born during and after Vatican II (1961–1981), the total was only 18 percent. This contrasts with women respondents born between 1943 and 1960 (31 percent) and before 1943 (53 percent). Less than a quarter of women surveyed in 2018 attended Mass a few times a year, and only 20 percent attended weekly. Most surveyed women did not feel obliged to participate in parish life, the historic locus of women's participation. Still, despite their grievances, a high percentage of women (82 percent) did not consider leaving the church. Exposure of clerical sexual abuse, however, which stemmed from journalists' investigations in the Boston archdiocese in 2002, has yet to have its full impact. To date, the mothers of the abused and the victims of abuse have raised their voices in criticism of the hierarchy and clergy accused of the crimes and their cover-up, noting the hypocrisy of the bishops in promoting the family while in fact, destroying it. As the abuse scandal continues to unfold, affecting more and more dioceses and Catholic institutions, women's rejection of the institution for its failure to protect the innocent may lead to further disaffiliation and disengagement.

Among contemporary Catholic laywomen, no single voice dominates, and no single political cause identifies them as a unified cohort. Grouped by political party affiliation, data indicate that Democratic women tend to favor helping the poor, whereas Republican women tend to prioritize opposing abortion rights. Among those surveyed, Democratic Catholic women are more likely to support female deacons, the ordination of women, and aid to migrants and refugees. What remains constant across age groups of American laywomen is a commitment to helping the poor and promoting social justice. One recent development among laywomen is the nonprofit group known as Ladies of Charity USA, who have started a home care service, staffed by paid employees, to patients in need of light housekeeping, help with food preparation, bathing, and other personal tasks. The pioneering program began in 2018 in Pittsburgh, Pennsylvania, where the Ladies of Charity is well established. Its efforts indicate the continuities between twentieth and twenty-first century women's service, as well as women's innovative responses to the needs of an aging demographic.

In response to being kept in a secondary position in church governance, American women are pursuing other fields and vocations, with the probable result that the church will be made less diverse by their absence and lose its strongest allies and low-wage/volunteer labor force. The clerical sexual abuse scandal has increased pleas for women's ordination and presence in leadership and oversight positions in the church. The lay initiative, Voice of the Faithful, founded in 2002 in response to the Boston abuse revelations, offers a positive motto of "Keep the Faith, Change the Church." Because of the Vatican's intransigence on gender issues, the VOTF supports victims of clerical abuse, and also encourages women preaching in a church and acting as parish life coordinators. A version of Catholic feminism exists now in the United States, but even Pope Francis, regarded as more progressive on social justice and environmental issues, links the church's opposition to abortion with the ordination of women. Francis also wrote that "A woman's role in the Church must not end only as mother, as worker, limited," but he has yet to detail what he means by women's ability to contribute a "profound theology." As feminist-minded Catholics have noted, popes endorse women's service roles rather than their empowerment and leadership. So far, Pope Francis has not made progress on discussions opened in 2019, for including women in the permanent diaconate.

CONCLUSION

The preceding pages have outlined contours of the lives of Catholic laywomen in the United States since the late 1800s. Several persistent themes emerge to show that Catholic women's strategies differed from those of labor agitators, radical politicians, and secular feminists. First, Catholic women have defended the church's ideal of gender complementary for much of their history, even while joining in public activism during the Progressive era. Second, they have vigorously supported immigrants, orphans, and the poor in the charitable organizations that emerged in the early twentieth century. They have also ably served as managers of Catholic institutions and organizations that support women, until recently standing a bit apart from national and international secular organizations.

Yet, in the wake of the cultural revolutions of the 1960s and 1970s, Catholic women have not agitated for "freedom of choice" in religion or of conscience in a way that modern rights-oriented Americans would recognize, or readily embraced the aggressive tactics of second-wave feminism. The majority chose to remain within the church to reform it from within, and when necessary, working behind the scenes. Thus, American Catholic women have been less likely to publicly agitate for abortion rights, access to ministerial roles, and feminism than their counterparts in Protestant or Jewish traditions. They have engaged gender roles as defined by ecclesiastical documents and tradition rather than using their shared gender identity to address their own experiences of inequality, sexism, and second-class status. They have, however, supported women's higher education and now, their theological training. The clerical sexual abuse scandal may turn out to benefit supporters of women's ordination, and of admission to the permanent diaconate and preaching ministries, as critics of the church blame male clericalism for the abuses that have occurred, and regard women as a corrective. Finally, following the path of many religious organizations in the past fifty years, from ethnically defined or sectarian projects to an emphasis upon protecting women's rights and then human rights, Catholic women now work more closely with Orthodox and Protestant Christian groups and with international agencies, such as the World Health Organization, United Nations International Children's Fund (UNICEF), and environmental protection organizations, a trend that may continue to flourish. In these discussions, evolving notions of gender identity as fluid will continue to play a major role, offering a direct challenge to the binary or complementarity view of two stable genders promoted for centuries by the Catholic Church.

FURTHER READING

Brown, Dorothy M. and Elizabeth McKeown. *The Poor Belong to Us: Catholic Charities and American Welfare.* Cambridge, MA: Harvard University Press, 1997.

Campbell, Debra. *Graceful Exits: Catholic Women and the Art of Departure.* Bloomington: Indiana University Press, 2003.

Hayes, Diana L. "Faith of Our Mothers: Catholic Womanist God-Talk," in *Uncommon Faithfulness: The Black Catholic Experience,* ed. M. Shawn Copeland, with LaReine-Marie Moseley, SND and Albert J. Raboteau. Maryknoll, NY: Orbis Books, 2009.

Henold, Mary J. *Catholic and Feminist: The Surprising History of the American Catholic Feminist Movement.* Chapel Hill: University of North Carolina Press, 2008.

Isasi-Diaz, Ada Maria. *Mujerista Theology: A Theology for the Twenty-first Century.* Maryknoll: Orbis Books, 1996.

Kane, Paula M. "Marian Devotionalism since 1940: Continuity or Casualty?," in *Habits of Devotion: Catholic Religious Practice in Twentieth-Century America,* ed. James M. O'Toole. Ithaca: Cornell University Press, 2004.

Kane, Paula, James Kenneally, and Karen Kennelly, eds. *Gender Identities in American Catholicism.* Maryknoll, NY: Orbis Press, 2001.

Raab, Kelley A. *When Women Become Priests: The Catholic Women's Ordination Debate.* New York: Columbia University Press, 2000.

Ruether, Rosemary Radford. *Sexism and God-Talk: Toward a Feminist Theology.* Boston: Beacon Press, 1983.

Spruill, Marjorie J. *Divided We Stand: The Battle Over Women's Rights and Family Values that Polarized American Politics.* New York: Bloomsbury USA, 2017.

Tentler, Leslie Woodcock. *Catholics and Contraception: An American History.* Ithaca: Cornell University Press, 2004.

15   Black Catholics

CECILIA A. MOORE

On Easter Sunday in 2010, nineteen elementary and middle school students in the District of Columbia awoke to find themselves featured in *The Washington Post*.[1] These children had captured the newspaper's attention because the previous night they became members of the Catholic Church. During the Easter Vigil at St. Augustine's, "the mother church of Black Catholics" in the nation's capital, these girls and boys received the sacraments of baptism and holy communion. All of these new Catholics attended St. Augustine parochial school where non-Catholic children constituted the majority. However, on their first day back at school after the Easter Vigil, the number of Catholic students enrolled at St. Augustine's rose from 51 to 70 out of a total of 185.

Critical in creating the environment in which children, who ranged in age from five to thirteen, would feel drawn to this ancient faith was the push at St. Augustine's to promote a vibrant Catholic identity. St. Augustine's pastor, Father Patrick Smith; the school's principal, Sr. Emanuella Ladipo, HHCJ (Handmaid of the Holy Child Jesus); the faculty, composed of lay teachers and Nigerian sisters; and the staff all invested in the mission to deliver messages central to Catholicism. St. Augustine's students had regular opportunities to participate in Catholic rituals such as the Mass and daily prayers, and to learn about aspects of Christianity that are particularly important to Catholics such as devotion to the Virgin Mary.

The story of the new Black Catholics at St. Augustine School offers some insight into the values and aspirations that have animated Black Catholics in America from colonial times to the present. Their feelings of power, community, commitment, difference (both the reality of being treated differently from other Catholics and the determination to be different from other Catholics), and their desire to be Catholic have

[1]   Michelle Boorstein, "A Big Step beyond Catholic Schooling," *Washington Post*, April 4, 2010, C1.

been shared by Black Catholics in every age of their experience in America. One can see the history of Black Catholics in St. Augustine Catholic School from its name that evokes the history of Africans in the Catholic Church to the African sisters who, along with African Americans, administer and staff the school, to the Black Catholic priest who pastors this historic Black Catholic parish that was founded soon after the conclusion of the Civil War, to its mission to be a Catholic presence in the Black community.

WHO ARE BLACK CATHOLICS?

Today, there are approximately seventy million Catholics in the United States, with Black Catholics making up about three million of that number. The majority of Black Catholics today are descended from Africans who arrived in the Americas (North, South, Central, and the Caribbean) either in the colonial period or from the early republic period through the antebellum era. For the most part, these persons were enslaved, but there were also some who arrived in the United States as free persons. From the end of the nineteenth century through the middle of the twentieth century, the US Catholic Church gained additional Black members through concerted efforts to evangelize African Americans, particularly in cities most changed by the Great Migration and in places in the American South that attracted the efforts of various Catholic missionary communities from the late nineteenth century through the 1960s. More recently, the Black Catholic community has grown through the immigration of Catholics from various African and Caribbean nations.

PRESENT FROM THE BEGINNING

When Spanish conquistadors and colonists arrived in the New World in the early sixteenth century to claim, explore, exploit, survey, and colonize all lands "granted" to them in papal treaties from the latter part of the fifteenth century, Blacks were in their company. Given the charge that the Spanish had to bring the people of the New World into communion with the Holy Roman Catholic Church, in all likelihood the Blacks who accompanied the Spanish were already Catholic and they were also free persons. However, tens of thousands of enslaved Blacks from African nations soon arrived in the Spanish colonies. Spanish colonists opted to engage the labor of enslaved Africans when the practice of *encomienda*, the right of the Spanish to take the free labor of the indigenous Americans in exchange for evangelizing them, failed due to a massive number of deaths of indigenous Americans from the harsh treatment they experienced at the hands of Spanish colonists and by exposure to diseases to which they were introduced.

The French, the second major Catholic power to arrive in the New World, also turned to slavery to promote their economic interests. Like the Spanish, they too determined that it was necessary for enslaved persons in their colonies to become members of the Catholic Church. They established this requirement in the *Code Noir* (1724), which mandated that all slaves be baptized and instructed in the Catholic faith, that provisions such as freedom from work on Sundays be made to so that they could attend to their religious duties as Catholics, and that they be treated humanely by their masters. Although this law did not intend to advantage enslaved Blacks by providing for their right to take a place in cultural, political, and spiritual institutions of the colony, an unintended consequence was that it did allow them to build a spiritual world and community among themselves that would prove liberating in generations to come. And though the *Code Noir* levied harsh and inhumane punishments, including death, for Blacks who transgressed the law, it contained legal pathways for enslaved persons to gain their freedom. When the Spanish took control of French Louisiana in 1763, they enacted a more liberal code of laws governing the enslaved called the *Siete Partidas*, which gave more rights to enslaved persons than the *Code Noir*. During Spanish rule in Louisiana, the number of free persons of color grew rapidly, particularly in New Orleans, which would become a vital center of African-American Catholicism. By the 1730s, there were three distinct Black Catholics communities in colonial America in lands governed by the Spanish, the French, and the English. Although some Black Catholics had become free people by this time, the majority were enslaved persons.

Spanish concern about the English threat to their colonial power in North America likely inspired a royal edict in 1693 that granted fugitives from slavery sanctuary and freedom in Spanish Florida.[2] Encouraged by this chance for freedom, many Blacks from English colonies risked their lives to make it to Florida. Those who succeeded

---

[2]   Kathleen A. Deagan and Jane Landers, "Forte Mose: Earliest Free African-American Town in the United States," in *"I, Too, Am America": Archeological Studies of African American Life*, ed. Theresa A. Singleton (Charlottesville: University of Virginia Press, 1999), 266.

in this quest converted to Catholicism and took up arms in defense of Spain in America. In exchange, they gained freedom and land. This essentially created a Black Catholic military community in Florida, Fort Mose, that by 1738 was large and strong enough to establish a city and military garrison two miles north of St. Augustine.

One justification for enslaving Africans was to give them hope for the salvation of their immortal souls by exposing them to Christianity. Some, however, were already Christians in Africa. This was particularly true of enslaved persons from the Kongo and Angola where Catholicism had been introduced by Portuguese slave traders. One of the most popular Catholic spiritual practices among Blacks in the Americas, enslaved as well as free, were confraternities and sodalities dedicated to the Virgin Mary.[3] Through these societies, Blacks professed their devotion to Mary and also created opportunities for offering mutual material, social, and emotional support to one another. And, in the case of enslaved persons, sodalities and confraternities also offered avenues to obtain freedom.

The largest slave uprising in North America before the American Revolution happened in South Carolina in 1739. It was led by Black Catholic enslaved persons who may have been members of a Marian sodality or confraternity. Called the Stono Rebellion, this uprising involved Catholic Portuguese-speaking enslaved men from the Kongo. Inspired by the promise of freedom in Florida, these men rose up against white slaveholders on September 9, 1739, the day after the feast of the birth of the Blessed Virgin Mary.[4] The rebellion raged for nearly a week before it was put down, but not before an equal number of enslaved Blacks and white colonists were killed and the leaders of the rebellion were caught and executed. The rebellion prompted the passage of laws to prevent such an event from ever happening again. In particular the Negro Act of 1740 restricted slave assemblies, education, and movement, and sought to ban the importation of slaves directly from Africa.

The creation of Fort Mose and the Stono Rebellion offer insight into the multivalent relationship between Catholicism, slavery, and Black people in colonial America. Holding fast to their mission to build a new Catholic world in America, the two conditions the Spanish set for Blacks to meet to attain freedom were conversion to Catholicism and

---

[3]   Patricia A. Mulvey, "Slave Confraternities in Brazil: Their Role in Colonial Society," *The Americas* 75 (2018): 39–68.

[4]   Mark M. Smith, "Remembering Mary, Shaping Revolt: Reconsidering the Stono Rebellion," *Journal of Southern History* 6 (August 2001): 513–534.

military service. As Fort Mose attests, the Spanish deal appealed to many Blacks and thus a new Black and Catholic community in America was born. At Stono, enslaved Catholics in an English colony with few white Catholics were inspired by their faith to rise up to take their freedom by force; their attempt failed and this led to punitive laws and practices that spread throughout slaveholding America.[5]

SLAVERY, BLACK CATHOLICS, AND THE BUILDING OF THE AMERICAN CATHOLIC CHURCH

Following the American Revolution, the relationship of the Catholic Church to slavery became even more complex as the church planted itself in the cultural, social, and political life of the newly established United States and welcomed more members from various European countries. Certainly, from the end of the eighteenth century through the end of the Civil War, a significant amount of the money used to care for the temporal, educational, and spiritual needs of Catholic immigrants was gained from the labor of enslaved Black Catholics and sometimes from their sale as well. Nearly all religious communities of men and women in the US South prior to the Civil War owned slaves whose labor both produced financial resources that supported the ministries of these priests, brothers, and sisters and that freed up their time to engage in direct and intensive work with the Catholic immigrant community. Indeed, enslaved Black Catholics were such an important part of the early US Catholic community, that in one of his first reports to the Holy See, then Father John Carroll noted that in this country there were about 3,000 enslaved persons who were Catholic in a total Catholic population of about 25,000.

In the years leading up to the Civil War, while many Black Catholics in the United States continued to be enslaved persons, a growing community of free Black Catholics also emerged through immigration and through various forms of manumission. Among them were those who began arriving in the United States in the 1790s as a result of the Haitian revolution that gave birth to the second democracy in the Americas. Although a minority in the US church, Black Haitians proved to be some of the most enterprising, socially conscious, and devout Catholics of the immigrant era. Among them were Pierre Toussaint and Mary Lange.

---

[5]   See Albert J. Raboteau, *Slave Religion: The "Invisible Institution" of the Antebellum South*, Updated Edition (New York: Oxford University Press), 2004.

Pierre Toussaint was busy giving New York City socialites the latest hairstyles when he received word that his master, Jean Berard, had lost both his fortune and his life in the wake of the Haitian revolution. When the revolution began, Toussaint had been living with his master's family in New York for about four years. He could have easily left his master's widow, Madame Berard, alone to face her future without a husband, a home, or an income, but instead he stayed and provided for her and the whole household, which included two of his sisters and an aunt who were also slaves of the Berards. Because his skills were in such great demand, Toussaint was able to keep the household in good order. Before her death in 1807, Madame Berard freed Toussaint. As a free man, Toussaint purchased the freedom of his sister, Rosalie, and Juliette, the woman he loved and married.

Gladly and generously, Toussaint gave money and time to serve the needs of others. He was a benefactor of the Sisters of Charity in New York City who ran an orphanage for white children, of a Catholic school for Black children at the Church of St. Vincent de Paul, of the Oblate Sisters of Providence in Baltimore, and to countless individuals who presented their needs to him. He also nursed victims of epidemics that plagued the city during his long life. After his death he was remembered in this way: "his heart was not only kind and affectionate, but gay and cheerful; it was filled with trust and confidence and gave him the happy power of dispelling gloom and anxiety in others ... He truly was an African."[6]

Born in Cuba but reared in Haiti, Mary Lange was one of the thousands of Haitian émigrés who came to Baltimore in the late eighteenth and early nineteenth centuries. Sulpician Father James Joubert, also a Haitian refugee, worked among the Black Catholics who worshipped in the basement of St. Mary's Seminary and met Mary Lange and her friends who were already conducting a school for girls out of Lange's house.

By 1828, Lange and her friends were living a religious life together informally. Their commitment to teaching children and their desire to live for God prompted them, with Joubert's assistance, to found the first successful community of Black Catholic sisters in the United States. While the archbishop of Baltimore approved the foundation of this order that was called the Oblate Sisters of Providence, many white Catholic Baltimoreans opposed them, believing they did not have the qualifications to teach or the morals to live lives of holiness.

---

[6] Quoted in Cyprian Davis, *The History of Black Catholics in the United States* (New York: Crossroad Publishing, 1990), 93.

Nevertheless, they persisted. The Oblate Sisters of Providence, led by Mother Mary Lange, regarded their mission of providing education, particularly to Black girls, to be a manifestation of God's care for Black people. Aside from the racism that they had to negotiate on a daily basis in order to meet their mission, financing their ministries and community was a constant challenge. Though the local Black community ardently supported the Oblates, the sisters did not enjoy the patronage of the wider Catholic Church or its leaders as many white orders of sisters did. To pay their bills and finance their schools, Oblate sisters did embroidery work, made vestments, and worked as domestics. When Mother Lange agreed to provide sisters to do domestic work at the Sulpician seminary in 1835, she made it clear in a letter what her expectations of their treatment would be:

> We do not conceal the difficulty of our situation a[s] persons of color and religious at the same time, and we wish to conciliate these two qualities in such a manner as not to appear too arrogant on the one hand and on the other, not to miss the respect which is due to the state we have embraced and the holy habit which we have the honor to wear. Our intention in consenting to your request is not to neglect the religious profession which we have embraced . . . .[7]

Free Blacks in antebellum America were acutely aware of the strangeness of their situation. Although they certainly enjoyed greater privileges than Blacks who were enslaved, very few of them could exercise voting rights. In addition, their status as citizens was not universally accepted, and it was not always easy to find work to support themselves and their families. All of these factors inspired them to create communities within communities where they could experience a sense of belonging and agency.

Antebellum Black Baptists, Presbyterians, and Episcopalians all established their own denominations as a response to white racism, but Black Catholics did not. Nineteenth-century Black Catholics did not wish to break away from the church, but even if they had desired to do so it would have been very impractical as there were no known Black men ordained priests in the United States before the Civil War, neither was there a critical mass of free Black Catholics anywhere in the United

---

[7]   Quoted in Diane Batts Morrow, *Persons of Color and Religious at the Same Time: The Oblate Sisters of Providence, 1828–1860* (Chapel Hill and London: University of North Carolina Press, 2002), 27.

States that could have financially supported the creation of a separate church and affiliated institutions.

Yet, Black Catholics did experience a great deal of rejection from their white coreligionists. For example, in antebellum Baltimore Black Catholics were usually relegated to worshipping in the basement of the cathedral, St. Mary's Seminary Chapel, and the Jesuits' St. Ignatius Church. Black Catholics in New York City were told that their children were not welcome in the parochial schools. And in New Orleans, the second order of Black sisters founded in the United States, the Sisters of the Holy Family, were not allowed to wear formal religious habits in the city until well after the Civil War because some white Catholics were offended by the thought of Black women as sisters. Attitudes and actions such as these did not make the Catholic Church a very welcoming place for Blacks, yet they believed the church was a place of power that was worth fighting for.

BLACK CATHOLIC PARISHES

Among the ways that Black Catholics found a way to remain within the Catholic Church and make it as welcoming and comfortable for themselves as possible was through the creation of parishes. During the nineteenth century, Black Catholic parishes were either created by Black Catholics themselves, meaning they requested permission to have their own churches and provided the labor and financial resources for the construction of such churches, or they were created by members of the clergy who either believed that Black Catholics would only flourish in parishes of their own, or who assented or conceded to principles and practices of racial segregation based on white supremacy and Black inferiority. In between these two pathways was the occasional creation of parishes that came about both through the ingenuity of Black Catholics themselves and the activism of white priests who believed that Black Catholics could in fact marshal the social and financial capital necessary to have their own parishes. A few examples of the development of early nineteenth-century parishes reveal these dynamics.

Before the Civil War, New Orleans was home to the largest community of free Blacks in the United States with the majority living in the Faubourg Tremé. In Louisiana, and in New Orleans in particular, free Blacks were called free people of color. As the offspring of mothers of African descent and fathers of French or Spanish descent, the majority of free people of color were Catholic. They regularly attended mass, received the sacraments, and generously supported the church and its institutions. Free Catholics of color who lived in the Tremé requested permission from Bishop Antoine Blanc to create a parish in their own neighborhood. He agreed, and by the early 1840s, they began the construction of St. Augustine's church. Ursuline Sisters, who had a complex relationship with the free and enslaved Black populations of New Orleans because they were slaveholders as well as educators of the free and enslaved Black communities, donated the land for the church.

Even though Blacks, free and enslaved, were the primary founders of this parish, it was not for them alone; it was for the people of the Tremé, open to all people without racial distinction. At the same time, however, the racial hierarchy of New Orleans still asserted itself in the antebellum parish through its seating arrangements. The parish used a system of pew rentals that divided the parish along class and racial lines. Pews along the sides and in the back of the church were reserved for enslaved persons, while free people of color and whites occupied pews in the front and center of the church.

According to the tradition of the Sisters of the Holy Family, the second order of Black sisters founded in the United States, their foundress, Mother Henriette Delille, made her first vows as a religious at St. Augustine's in 1842. From St. Augustine's the Sisters of the Holy Family served the various educational, material, and spiritual needs of enslaved Blacks, elderly Blacks, and the poor in general. Their charitable work established St. Augustine as a place where the poor could find support and compassion, a reputation that it maintains to this day. But St. Augustine also became known as a place of radical dissent and racial resistance as Black parishioners fought for the Union during the Civil War, organized to oppose the implementation of Jim Crow laws in Louisiana following the end of Reconstruction, and cultivated a generation of Black Catholic civil rights leaders. St. Augustine's, like most New Orleans parishes, remained integrated until after the Civil War when the Archbishop of New Orleans decided in the 1890s that segregated parishes would better serve the needs of all New Orleanians, particularly those who were Black.

St. Francis Xavier Church in Baltimore, Maryland, is an example of a Black parish that was created specifically for Black Catholics. Black Catholics who lived in antebellum Baltimore were barely tolerated in the city's Catholic churches outside of the Oblate Sisters of Providence motherhouse chapel. Briefly in the 1840s, Black Catholic Baltimoreans formed the Society of the Holy Family, which met regularly on Sunday evenings in the basement of the Baltimore cathedral. There they prayed, sang, studied, and enjoyed each other's company until they were told they could no longer meet there. Clearly desiring a way to be together, Baltimore's Black Catholics likely rejoiced in 1863, when the Jesuits purchased a building for the purpose of creating a mission for Blacks; the church was dedicated in 1864. The Jesuits were in charge of the parish until 1871, when the Society of St. Joseph, otherwise known as the Josephite Fathers, took over the mission.

St. Augustine Catholic Church proclaims itself to be the "Mother Church of Black Catholics in the Nation's Capital," yet even before they had a parish in Washington, DC, antebellum Black Catholics had already founded a Catholic school and a chapel under the patronage of Blessed Martin de Porres. At the time, Washington, DC, neither mandated nor provided free education for Blacks, so Black Catholics determined to provide educational opportunities for their community by starting a school in 1858.[8] The parish of St. Augustine grew out of their school. Black Catholics did the fundraising and the planning for the parish's building, and in 1876, they dedicated their parish to St. Augustine in the Northwest section of the district.

THE CATHOLIC RESPONSE TO EMANCIPATION

In 1863, the same year that President Lincoln issued the Emancipation Proclamation, Bishop Martin J. Spalding of Louisville, Kentucky, sent his "Dissertation on the American Civil War" to the Congregation of the Propagation of the Faith in Rome. His purpose was to explain to the Holy See that although slavery was indeed a terrible institution, its abolishment in the United States would be even worse for Black people. According to Spalding, one need only look at the lives of free Blacks to see that freedom was detrimental to Black people, leading them to vices that threatened body and soul. On the other hand, enslaved Blacks were protected from such dangers by their masters.[9]

A year later, in 1864, Spalding was elected Archbishop of Baltimore. Born into a slaveholding family and a slaveholder himself, Spalding was quite public and firm in his defense of slavery, but once the Civil War was over, unlike so many of his peers, he seems to have accepted that that way of life was over and it was time to devise a plan for ministering

---

[8] See Morris J. MacGregor, *The Emergence of a Black Catholic Community: St. Augustine's in Washington* (Washington, DC: The Catholic University of America Press, 1999).

[9] Davis, *History of Black Catholics in the United States,* 117.

to the newly freed Black Americans. So, as he had once written to Rome to defend slavery, he now wrote to seek approval to gather the bishops of the United States together in order to create a national evangelization plan for Blacks. Spalding felt a certain urgency to have this decided and implemented quickly because he was well aware that Black and white Protestant denominations were already sending missionaries to teach and to preach to newly freed Blacks. With the support of the Holy See, Spalding convened the Second Plenary Council of Baltimore in 1866 to propose a plan that included special churches for Blacks, support for Black vocations to the priesthood, and an "ecclesiastical man" who would have charge of overseeing Catholic evangelization of Blacks throughout the United States.[10]

According to historian Cyprian Davis, the bishops' discussion of the plan was "long and bitter," and most of Spalding's proposals were roundly rejected. The only proposals the majority of bishops were willing to pursue were parishes designated for Blacks, and initiatives to secure the assistance of religious orders who would commit to doing missionary work among Blacks in the United States. They also agreed to do what they each deemed best for Blacks in their dioceses, but practically speaking that did not amount to much.

BLACK PRIESTS

One concrete result of Spalding's proposals emerged in 1886, when a former slave, Augustus Tolton, was ordained to the priesthood. Rejected from every diocesan seminary in the United States, Tolton, his mother, and his priest mentors in Quincy, Illinois, refused to give up on finding a way for him to answer his vocation. His opportunity came in 1880 when he was accepted to study for the priesthood at the Urban College in Rome. Tolton was admitted to the college with the understanding that he would become an "international" priest who would serve an African nation. On the eve of his ordination, however, he learned that plans had changed, and he was assigned to minister to the Black community of his hometown, Quincy, Illinois.

For three years, Tolton pastored a mission church in Quincy that served the town's small group of Black Catholics, and also worked to evangelize the rest of the Black community. The church thrived with a small number of Black parishioners and with some local white

---

[10]   Davis, *History of Black Catholics in the United States*, 117.

Catholics of Irish and German descent who chose to worship there. In addition to his work at home, Tolton accepted as many invitations as he could from Black Catholics around the country who asked him to visit, say mass, and speak to them.

Tragically, Tolton's popularity aroused the anger of some white priests in Quincy who resented that there were members of their parishes who preferred the Black priest over them. They unleashed a campaign of harassment directed at Tolton. One of the German priests was so relentless in his harassment that Tolton thought it was best to leave Quincy because he feared for his safety. In 1889, he began ministering to Black Catholics in Chicago who had appealed for Tolton to be invited to establish a parish in the city. He began this new Chicago ministry in a storefront in 1891. Two years later in 1893, he and his parishioners, who numbered about 600, broke ground for the first Black Catholic Church in the city, which was dedicated the next year in 1894.

Tolton showed that indeed it was possible for Black men to represent Christ to the people of God, but while he was defying ecclesiastical, racial, and cultural gravity, America was becoming a smaller and more oppressive place for its Black citizens as anti-Black laws, customs, and practices became common throughout the country. In an officially Jim Crow America, Father Tolton, a priestly transgressor of the color line, died in Chicago at the age of forty-three in 1897. He was mourned in Chicago, Quincy, and throughout the United States.

As groundbreaking as Father Tolton's priesthood was, he was not the first American priest of African descent. James, Sherwood, and Patrick Healy were the sons of an enslaved mother, Mary Eliza Healy, and an Irish immigrant planter father, Michael Morris Healy.[11] As soon as the children were of an age where they could be separated from their mother, they were sent north to study in boarding academies. Their experiences at these schools helped foster the religious vocations of at least six of the ten Healy children. Three daughters entered religious life and three sons became priests. Their ability to do this hinged on their ability to pass for white, which some were able to do better than others.

James Augustine Healy was the first to be ordained. In 1854, he became a priest of the Archdiocese of Boston, and in 1875 was ordained bishop of Portland, Maine. Like his brother, Alexander Sherwood Healy was a priest of the Archdiocese of Boston. Ordained in 1858, he was a seminary professor and canon lawyer, and also served as a theologian for

[11]   James O'Toole, *Passing for White: Race, Religion, and the Healy Family, 1820–1920* (Amherst: University of Massachusetts Press, 2002).

the American bishops at the First Vatican Council in 1869. Because of his intellectual and pastoral gifts, he was a candidate for the position of rector of the North American College in Rome but was eliminated when it was pointed out that his Black heritage was too apparent in his features.[12] A member of the Society of Jesus, Patrick Healy was ordained in 1864. He taught philosophy at Georgetown, and by 1876 was president of the university. Roundly regarded as a path-breaking Jesuit leader in education, Father Patrick Healy deliberately kept his racial identity hidden throughout his life.

When Father Tolton died in 1897, only one more African American had been ordained to the priesthood. Ordained in 1891 for the Society of St. Joseph, more commonly known as the Josephites, Father Charles R. Uncles was a native of Baltimore. In joining the Josephites, Uncles committed himself to serve exclusively in the Black apostolate. Father Uncles was followed by two more Black Josephites, Father John A. Dorsey in 1902 and Father John Plantvigne in 1908. All three of the first Black Josephites experienced a great deal of pain and derision as they tried to fulfill their vocations. As a result, Josephite leaders decided not to recruit African Americans for the priesthood. There would be no significant growth in the number of Black Catholic priests in the United States until well into the 1950s and 1960s. Racism proved to be a very difficult hurdle to clear when it came to welcoming and supporting Black men on the altars of America's Catholic churches.[13]

CATHOLIC EVANGELIZATION IN THE BLACK COMMUNITY

Despite the indifference of some bishops and the outright hostility of others to pursue a unified plan for evangelizing African Americans, including the ordination of Black men to the priesthood, other avenues for Catholic outreach to African Americans emerged at the end of the nineteenth century. One of the most consequential paths was created through the determination and philanthropy of Katharine Drexel and her sisters, both of blood and religion. Born in Philadelphia a few years before the beginning of the Civil War, Drexel grew up with great privilege and wealth but also with a mandate from her parents that wealth and status were to be used in service for those with less. When their

---

[12]   Davis, *History of Black Catholics in the United States*, 149.
[13]   See Stephen J. Ochs, *Desegregating the Altar: The Josephites and the Struggle for Black Priests, 1871–1960* (Baton Rouge: Louisiana State University Press, 1990).

father died in 1885, Katharine and her sisters Elizabeth and Louise were left an enviable fortune. The Drexel sisters decided to devote much of their inheritance to building schools and churches and to endow and support projects and programs designed to improve the lives of Native Americans and African Americans. In 1891, Katharine took a further step, founding a new religious community, the Sisters of the Blessed Sacrament for Indians and Colored People, and devoted not only her money but her life to service among these two communities.

Through the work of their religious order, Katharine Drexel and her sisters founded, built, and taught at Catholic schools and missions throughout the United States. Drexel also gave money to other Catholic schools in Black communities that were staffed by laypeople and other religious communities to pay the salaries and stipends of the teachers. Her single largest educational endeavor was the founding of Xavier University of Louisiana in New Orleans in 1925, which was and continues to be the only historically Black Catholic college or university in the United States; it was one of the first coeducational Catholic universities that had a focus on science, medicine, and pharmacy. In their work of education and other ministries, Drexel and the Sisters of the Blessed Sacrament believed that if children of color, Native American and African American, enjoyed excellent, creative, and spiritually enriching educational opportunities, there were no limits to the contributions they could make later in life. When these children flourished, the benefits would redound to themselves, their families, the Catholic Church, and the United States.

THE RISE OF BLACK CATHOLIC LAY LEADERSHIP

A contemporary of both Father Tolton and Mother Drexel, Daniel Rudd was born into slavery in Bardstown, Kentucky, in 1854. As a young free man, Rudd moved to Ohio to obtain an education that would lead him in 1886 to found the *American Catholic Tribune*, the first Black Catholic newspaper in the United States. Rudd used his paper to support the antilynching crusade, advocate for civil rights for Blacks, promote a positive self-understanding for the Black community, and promote the Catholic Church as the greatest hope African Americans had for justice in the United States, as well as for their eternal salvation.[14] Through

---

[14] See Gary Agee, *A Cry for Justice: Daniel Rudd and His Life in Black Catholicism, Journalism, and Activism, 1854–1933* (Fayetteville: University of Arkansas Press, 2011).

original and wire articles, he shared the events and interests of Black and Catholic communities and highlighted aspects of Catholicism that he hoped would convince skeptical Blacks that the church's social teaching was the key to dismantling racial prejudice and discrimination in the United States.

In 1889, Rudd led a group of Black Catholic laymen in hosting the first of five Colored Catholic Congresses. In his call for Black Catholics to gather, Rudd declared, "Colored Catholics ought to unite. Let the Colored Catholics gather together from every city in the Union to some suitable place, under the blessing of Holy Mother Church, they may get to know one another and take up the cause of the race."[15] Working on the model of European lay Catholic congresses that were also happening at this time, Rudd advanced his plan as a way to build a national sense of community among Black Catholics who, outside of the few densely Black Catholic sites in the United States, were scattered in every section and corner of the country. In order for the gathering to be representative of the entire Black Catholic population, the Congress called for each parish in the United States to send a delegate. At the very first Colored Catholic Congress, Father Tolton celebrated the opening Mass.

At the first congress meeting in Baltimore, and in all of the five subsequent Colored Catholic Congresses, the delegates pledged to work for social change and racial justice in the wider society and in the church. Living under the specter of Jim Crow, a focus on education recurred in all meetings because of its liberative power for Blacks. In particular, the Colored Catholic Congress called for industrial and vocational education, catechetical education, more Catholic schools in Black communities, and greater opportunities for Black Catholics to gain admittance to Catholic high schools and institutions of higher education. They even opined that leakage of young Black men from the Catholic Church was directly related to the lack of opportunity for Catholic education.[16] With every meeting of the Colored Catholic Congress, the leaders became clearer in their purpose and vision. While they always expressed their fidelity to the church, they also were forthright in rejecting racist accretions because they believed they harmed their ability to evangelize effectively in the Black community.[17]

---

[15] Davis, *History of Black Catholics in the United States*, 171.
[16] Davis, *History of Black Catholics in the United States*, 178.
[17] Davis, *History of Black Catholics in the United States*, 187.

The last meeting of the Colored Catholics Congress happened in 1894, the same year that it produced a report documenting specific examples of racial discrimination in US Catholic churches and institutions. In a bold move, they sent the report to the American bishops and planned to deliver it to Pope Leo XIII, as well. This may have been too radical a move. Historian Cyprian Davis suggested that the 1894 Congress may have been the last because some American church leaders felt Black Catholics were becoming too militant in their demands and approach, and the Holy See was becoming "wary of the activities of lay Catholic congresses in general." According to Davis, the end of the Colored Catholic Congress movement did not mean it was a failure. Instead, it demonstrated that by the end of the nineteenth century there was a definite Black Catholic community that had real leaders who were intellectuals and activists. Rather than failing, they laid the groundwork for "future black Catholic movements."[18]

Following in the tradition of Black Catholic activism for racial justice in the church, Dr. Thomas Wyatt Turner founded the Federated Colored Catholics (FCC) in 1924. This lay Black Catholic organization had three primary goals. First, it sought to foster a national Catholic conversation about ways in which racism practiced in the Catholic Church injured all of its members. Second, the FCC intended to develop methods to make Catholics more conscious of racism in the church so that they could work together to change racist policies and practices. The FCC's third goal was to improve and extend Catholic educational opportunities to African Americans. In a deeply ironic and racially charged turn of events in 1932, the FCC was ruptured when two white priests, Father John LaFarge, SJ, and Father William Markoe, SJ, engineered a takeover of the organization from Dr. Turner. The priests alleged that the FCC under Turner's administration was a "Jim Crow" organization because it insisted that its leadership must remain Black. About one-half of the members of the FCC left the organization and joined the newly created Catholic Interracial Council that LaFarge led, while the other half remained with Turner. The FCC continued its work into the 1950s. Using some of the goals of the FCC, the Catholic Interracial Council and Father LaFarge became the public face and voice of Catholic work for racial justice well into the 1960s.

[18]   Davis, *History of Black Catholics in the United States*, 187.

WORKING FOR RACIAL JUSTICE IN THE CHURCH
AND SOCIETY

Raising white Catholic consciousness about racism was a principle of the FCC adopted by the Catholic Interracial Council. Evidence of the effectiveness of raising white Catholic awareness of racism in self, church, and society was best seen in the activism of American Catholic college students. In 1933, Catholic women attending Manhattanville College in New York published "The Manhattanville Resolutions," which declared that their Catholic education obliged them to work to ensure that African Americans experienced "the full measure of social justice." The first promise these women made in the Resolutions was to see the humanity of African Americans and recognize that they had the right to "life, liberty, and the pursuit of happiness." They also promised to be respectful of and kind to Blacks, to not use demeaning language when speaking to or about Blacks, to use principles of Catholic social teaching to work for justice for African Americans, to see African Americans as part of the Mystical Body of Christ, to financially support Catholic endeavors in Black communities, and to simply care about Black people.[19] The students' promises produced positive changes. In 1938, Manhattanville's president, Mother Grace Dammann, RSCJ, announced in a speech entitled "Principles vs. Prejudices," that the school would begin admitting African-American women, making Manhattanville one of the first Catholic colleges to integrate its student body.

Beginning in the 1940s, New Orleans black and white Catholic college students banned together to work for the integration of Catholic institutions in the city through the Southeastern Regional Interracial Commission (SERINCO). Members met regularly, usually on the campus of either Xavier University of Louisiana or Loyola University of New Orleans, to discuss race and justice, and to work on strategies for integrating Catholic institutions in the city, including their own schools. By conversing regularly, attending lectures by Catholic leaders on racial justice issues, and attending Mass and having breakfast together, these students intended to make Catholic individuals and institutions seriously consider questions of race and racism, and ultimately join forces with them to dismantle racist practices in the

---

[19]   "All Men Are Created Equal: A Brief for the Black Man," Joint Report of a Committee of Catholic College Graduates and Undergraduates and the Interracial Committee of the Brooklyn Catholic Action Council, Brooklyn, NY, 1933.

church and its manifold institutions.[20] One of the victories that came out of this Catholic interracial work in New Orleans was the admission of Norman Francis, a Xavier graduate who was also a member and leader of SERINCO, and Ben Johnson, another Xavier alumnus, to Loyola's law school in New Orleans in 1952. As the first African Americans to attend Loyola Law, Francis and Johnson became part of an integrating force that had been running through American Catholic education since the 1930s. For example, in 1938, Bishop Joseph Ritter integrated Catholic schools in the Diocese of Indianapolis. When called to serve as the archbishop of St. Louis, Ritter desegregated Catholic schools in that diocese beginning in 1947. Cardinal Patrick O'Boyle of Washington, DC, integrated its schools in 1948, followed by Bishop Vincent Waters desegregating all Catholic institutions in the Diocese of Raleigh, North Carolina, in 1953. In an acute but subtle manner, Catholic schools that integrated before *Brown v. Board of Education of Topeka* in 1954 demonstrated to Americans that it was indeed possible for Blacks and whites to learn in a shared environment without disadvantaging either.

Catholics, black and white, showed up in quiet and prominent ways throughout the 1950s and 1960s as the modern civil rights movement commenced. The most prominent instance occurred in 1965, when over nine hundred Catholics, laywomen and laymen, religious sisters and brothers, and priests demonstrated and showed their support for voting rights in Selma, Alabama. Among the many sisters who went to Selma were two African Americans, Sister Mary Antona Ebo, FSM, and Sister Barbara Moore, CSJ. In public remarks, Sister Mary Antona said that she, as an African American, had the right to vote where she lived in Missouri and was there to witness for the civil rights of Blacks and all people. Catholics who came to Selma did so in defiance of Bishop Thomas J. Toolen of Mobile-Birmingham, who had forbidden Catholic priests and religious in his diocese from having anything to do with the demonstrations, and had pleaded with his fellow bishops to tell their people to stay home. This was easier said than done, however, especially since the Second Vatican Council the year before had promulgated the Decree on Ecumenism that encouraged Catholics to become involved with other Christians working for justice. One concession that Toolen did grant was for the City of St. Jude in Montgomery to provide hospitality to the Selma demonstrators on the night before they were due to march to the courthouse in Montgomery with Dr. King.

[20] See R. Bentley Anderson, *Black, White and Catholic: New Orleans Interracialism, 1947–1956* (Nashville: Vanderbilt University Press, 2006).

Responding to the message of Dr. King, as well as the growing calls for Black Power and liberation, would bring Black Catholic priests and sisters together in revolutionary ways in the coming years. A few weeks after Martin Luther King, Jr.'s assassination in April 1968, a group of Black priests met for the first time as a body while attending the Catholic Clergy Conference on the Interracial Apostolate (CCCIA) in Detroit. The priests issued the "Statement of the Black Catholic Clergy Caucus – April 16, 1968." Reading like a manifesto, its first sentence revealed the anger of the priests in attendance: "The Catholic Church in the United States is primarily a white racist institution, has addressed itself primarily to white society, and is definitely part of that Society." It asserted that the Catholic Church had lost its moral authority or role in "the ghetto." No longer could the church and its white ministers be spokesmen and teachers. It was time for them to be supporters and learners. The Black community's attitude in America was "changing," and these changes required "meaningful and realistic adjustments." Black people were ready to make their own decisions about themselves, and were ready to assume leadership roles "throughout the entire gamut of ecclesial society."[21]

The expression "Black Power" is not to be found in the Caucus's statement, but definite allusions to it are. The priests spoke, for instance, of "Black militancy" and why it was an important and powerful concept to grasp. These Black priests wished it to be duly recorded that militant protests were real, that Black people were no longer willing to practice nonviolence in hopes that white brutality would eventually die, that it was legitimate for Blacks to practice self-defense and "just warfare" in response to white violence, and that responsible, positive militancy against racism was in fact Christian. They warned that because of these factors, the official channels and institutions of the Catholic Church in the United States were in an "extremely weak position in the Black Community."

Sister Martin DePorres Grey – the only woman present at the historic meeting of the Black priests in 1968 – left that assembly determined to host a similar gathering for Black sisters later that same year. With the consent and support of her superior, letters were sent to over 600 major superiors around the country asking for their help in bringing

---

[21]   "A Statement of the Black Catholic Clergy Caucus," in *Stamped with the Image of God: African Americans as God's Image in Black*, ed. Cyprian Davis, OSB and Jamie Phelps, OP (Maryknoll, NY: Orbis Books, 2004), 111–114.

the Black sisters together. These letters went to the historically Black orders – the Oblate Sisters of Providence, the Sisters of the Holy Family, and the Franciscan Handmaids of Mary – and also to predominately white communities that had Black sisters. About 200 superiors answered, and on August 18, 1968, 155 Black sisters from around the United States, as well as the Caribbean and Africa, gathered at Mount Mercy College (today Carlow University) in Pittsburgh, Pennsylvania. There they promised "to work unceasingly for the liberation of black people." Their meeting was covered in *Ebony* magazine replete with beautiful photographs of Black sisters purposely assembled to get to know each, build relationships, learn, and make positive changes in their community. According to M. Shawn Copeland, for "an entire week, the sisters, along with invited members of the clergy and laity, listened to, argued with, and affirmed interpretations of black power activists, educators, students and social workers on the condition of black America." They prayed, shared meals, and enjoyed informal conversations in which they considered how they might move forward with ideas that were surfacing at this first meeting.[22]

Members of the National Black Sisters' Conference (NBSC) were committed to promoting a positive self-image for Black people using Black history and culture, engaging in community action to achieve "social, political, [and] economic black power," and helping Black sisters deepen their own spirituality and sense of solidarity as women religious. Members of the NBSC also pioneered non-Eucharistic rituals, litanies, chants, and dances that placed African customs and symbols at the center. As Copeland explained, "the women were forging new theological and ministerial understandings of the Christian life with regard to the task of black liberation."[23]

From the 1970s through the 1990s, finding ways to achieve "black liberation" while remaining a part of the Catholic Church was the mission to which Black Catholics – lay and religious, women and men – dedicated themselves. Looking to the experiences, accomplishments, failures, and struggles of their Black Catholic American ancestors, they returned to familiar themes and strategies and created new ones to make the Catholic Church again a place of hope for Black

---

[22] M. Shawn Copeland, "A Cadre of Women Religious Committed to Black Liberation: The National Catholic Sisters' Conference," *U.S. Catholic Historian* 14 (Winter 1996): 129.

[23] Copeland, "A Cadre of Women Religious Committed to Black Liberation," 134, 138.

people, as well as a place where they could share their particular gifts. With this in mind, Black Catholics commenced a new Black Catholic Movement to address many of the problems, and to exploit the opportunities the Black clergy and sisters had identified during their 1968 meetings. The movement included the creation of a panoply of new Black organizations including the National Black Catholic Clergy Caucus, the National Black Sister's Conference, the National Black Lay Caucus, and the National Office of Black Catholics. The Black Catholic Movement embraced the Second Vatican Council's promotion of the inculturation of liturgy by bringing gospel sounds, the spirituals, and jazz into liturgies, and created *Lead Me, Guide Me*, an African-American Catholic hymnal as a resource for inculturation. The movement also supported the development of the Black Catholic Theological Symposium that was created to promote Black Catholic scholarship, as well as the Institute for Black Catholic Studies, which was designed to prepare women and men to do excellent culturally competent ministry in the Black community. Out of the Black Catholic movement came initiatives to support the spiritual development of Black Catholics such as the Lyke Conference and Rivers Institute, Unity Explosion, and Black Catholic women's and men's retreats. During the Black Catholic Movement, Black Catholics also celebrated the elevation of Black priests to the hierarchy and reveled in hearing them speak as a body in the pastoral letter, "What We Have Seen and Heard." While the Black Catholic Movement did not solve all the problems Black Catholics faced in their church or society, it did revive Catholicism in the African-American community at a pivotal point in American history and equipped Black Catholics with tools, attitudes, and convictions to use on their path to survive, grow, and fight new battles.

CONCLUSION

Three years before the *Washington Post* reported on the large number of young Catholic converts at St. Augustine School, the school was slated to be turned over to the charter school system in Washington, DC, along with seven other Catholic schools in the city. Regarding his decision, Archbishop Donald W. Wuerl declared, "We have attempted to educate as many people as possible, and have done so beyond our means ... We can't continue to be an alternative to public schools in the District." These schools primarily served Black children. Turning these schools over to the charter system would make the schools eligible for funding from the city and also might generate rent that would benefit the archdiocese.[24]

But the people of St. Augustine's, from the priest to the parishioners to the parents, banded together to keep their school out of the charter system. They presented a comprehensive plan to the archdiocese that would make St. Augustine's a parish-funded school not dependent on the archdiocese. The ability and determination of Black Catholics to preserve parochial education in the Black community no matter the religious makeup of the students was a testament to the historical sensibilities of its people and their sense of Black Catholic identity. They remembered that their parish was born out of the school in the first place, and as Black Catholics they acknowledged and acted on their privilege and their responsibility to maintain a positive, powerful, and liberative Catholic presence in the heart of the Black community. Because they persisted, they prevailed, and St. Augustine Catholic School lives on today. Surely, the children educated now at St. Augustine's will one day add new chapters to the unfolding story of African-American Catholics.

FURTHER READING

Brown, Joseph A., SJ. *To Stand On the Rock: Meditations on Black Catholic Identity*. Maryknoll, NY: Orbis Books, 1998.

Copeland, M. Shawn, ed., with LaReine-Marie Mosely, SND, and Albert J. Raboteau, eds. *Uncommon Faithfulness: The Black Catholic Experience*. Maryknoll, NY: Orbis Books, 2009.

Cressler, Matthew. *Authentically Black and Truly Catholic: The Rise of Black Catholicism in the Great Migration*. New York: New York University Press, 2017.

Davis, Cyprian. *The History of Black Catholics in the United States*. New York: Crossroad Publishing, 1990.

Morrow, Diane Batts. *Persons of Color and Religious at the Same Time: The Oblate Sisters of Providence, 1828–1860*. Chapel Hill: University of North Carolina Press, 2002.

Ochs, Stephen J. *Desegregating the Altar: The Josephites and the Struggle for Black Priests, 1871–1960*. Baton Rouge: Louisiana State University Press, 1990.

[24] "Parents Protest School Closures," *The Washington Times*, October 1, 2007.

16 Latinx Catholicism

LAUREN FRANCES GUERRA AND
BRETT C. HOOVER

PROLOGUE: CONTESTED TERMS AND IDENTITY

For a community as diverse as those of Latin American and Caribbean descent living in the United States, finding an appropriate term that encapsulates all of its members is a tremendous challenge. The terms *Hispanic* or *Latino/a* are often used interchangeably for this community, yet they do not fully reflect the complicated history of the population. Two additional terms, important to reflections on community identity, include *mestizaje* and *mulatez*. *Mestizaje* refers to the mixing of Spanish and indigenous heritage, while *mulatez*, the mixing of Spanish and African heritage, which is also part of the Latin American story. Both terms remain contested and have been explored in detail by community theologians such as Virgilio Elizondo, Michelle Gonzalez, Jorge Aquino, Nestor Medina, and Miguel De La Torre. Markers such as race and class play a critical role in understanding the history and intricacy of these terms, too much to tackle in this space. To complicate matters further, many people forgo the terms Hispanic or Latino all together and self-identify by particular nationality, calling themselves "Mexican," "Puerto Rican," or "Ecuadorian," or by variations born in the US context such as "Guatemalan-American," "Chicana," or "Nuyorican."

The term *Latinx* first appeared in 2004 and has increased in use since 2014.[1] While Latinx has found more acceptance than Hispanic or Latino/a among academics and on college campuses, it is less common to find in churches or among grassroots communities. The term was created in response to the gendered nature of the Spanish language. Latino refers to a man while Latina refers to a woman. The use of Latinx seeks to disrupt the gender binary with a new, gender-neutral

---

[1] For a discussion of this contested term, see Catalina M. de Onís, "What's in an 'x'? An Exchange about the Politics of 'Latinx,'" *Chiricú Journal* 1 (Spring 2017): 78–91.

term. While we recognize that no term will be perfect, we have chosen to utilize the term Latinx throughout this essay.

STUDYING LATINX CATHOLICISM

For many students of US Catholicism, studying Latinx Catholicism may feel like a new branch or area of study, especially as they observe the quickened pace of contemporary demographic change and the emergence of a Latinx majority among US Catholics. Yet Latinx Catholicism has long been present, from Spanish colonial origins in Florida, Puerto Rico, and the Southwest, to the considerable share of immigrant Catholics who arrived in the late nineteenth and early twentieth centuries from Latin America and the Spanish Caribbean. Greater recognition of that presence brings trajectories of both challenge and continuity to the study of US Catholic history. Latinx Catholic history, for example, contextualizes Catholicism in the United States as an expression of Catholic life among others in the Americas, rather than perceiving it only in relationship to a European colonial center. Studies of African-American Catholicism, Native American Catholicism, and Asian-American Catholicism have similar decentering effects, inviting us to consider Catholicism across the African diaspora, in global indigenous contexts, or as a minority faith in Asia and Asian America. These approaches join with the study of Latinx Catholicism to draw necessary attention to the ambiguous racial and ethnic history of both the United States as a nation and Catholicism as a historical faith community.

At the same time, in continuity with long-established trends in Catholic Studies and US Catholic history, Latinx Catholicism affirms the necessity of attention to immigrants and an immigrant church. The majority of Latinx Catholics remain immigrants or their recent descendants, and many parts of their stories echo those of other groups. Like Italian Catholics of earlier generations, Latinx immigrant Catholics have often struggled economically, have devoted themselves to Catholic life in the absence of resources and native clergy, and have faced nativist opposition. Like German Catholics of old, attachment to language has proven a beloved element of the Catholic faith for Latinx Catholics. Such continuities, however, also bring into relief certain discontinuities. By the 1920s, immigration from Europe came to a relative standstill, and this led to a declining prominence for European ethnicities. Irish and German-American Catholics, for example, "assimilated," both because no new immigrants arrived to keep them acquainted with the mother country, and because they "blended in" racially with the white mainstream. In contrast, migration from Latin America (as well as East and Southern Asia) continues, "replenishing" a complex sense of ethnic identity, even as racial barriers to complete social and economic acceptance persist.[2]

In the following pages, we will draw attention to these continuities and discontinuities, intending to provoke a fuller appreciation of the richness and depth of US Catholicism in all its diversity. We begin with a brief exploration of Latinx Catholic history in the United States, from colonial origins through various waves of immigration (and the nativist resistance they provoked). Our historical section concludes with an account of the late twentieth-century immigration that formed today's Latinx Catholic community, as well as various struggles over Latinx empowerment in church and society up to the present moment. The essay continues with an exploration of key themes in contemporary Latinx Catholicism, including popular religion, transnationalism, Latinx Catholic theology, and ecumenism, as well as language complexities and the way in which the pastoral style of Pope Francis has proved familiar to Latinx Catholics. The essay concludes with a consideration of how an emerging Latinx Catholic majority will impact the future of US Catholicism.

PART ONE: AN ALTERNATIVE HISTORY

Even a brief review of Latinx Catholic history challenges some old and deeply embedded narratives of US and US Catholic history. Many American Catholics have been taught that our history, like the history of the United States itself, began "back east," often in colonial Maryland, and that history then moved inexorably westward with the frontier. Yet the different strains and vectors of Latinx Catholicism tell a more complicated story. Puerto Rico, a US commonwealth, contains the oldest Catholic diocese in the Americas. The oldest European settlement in the lower forty-eight states, at St. Augustine, Florida (1565), included a Spanish-speaking Catholic church. Texas, New Mexico, and California were originally part of the *northern* frontier of New Spain or Mexico, long before they formed the southwestern *frontera* (border) of the United States. During that era and even into the early US period, the real *immigrants* of Latinx Catholic history were Euro-Americans,

---

[2]   See Tomás Jiménez, *Replenished Ethnicity: Mexican Americans, Immigration, and Identity* (Berkeley: University of California Press, 2010).

including famous immigrants like James Bowie, who died at the Alamo, and the explorer Kit Carson. Many of these immigrants accepted Catholic baptism as a condition of their settling in Mexican lands or marrying into Mexican families.[3]

Latinx Catholic history also upends and complicates the popular "migrant to mainstream" narrative of US Catholic history, in which European migrants assimilated and over the generations blended into a white-dominant American middle class. As already noted, the Latinx Catholics of the Southwest were not migrants; the border crossed them when the United States invaded Mexico in 1846, and the latter surrendered half its territory. Spanish remained one of the official languages of the new state of California in 1850, and parts of Texas, New Mexico, and southern California remained primarily Spanish speaking and Latinx in culture for decades to come, even to the present day. In addition, while Spanish colonial attitudes toward racial differences privileged European heritage and Latin American social structures matched the resulting *casta* distinctions, interracial mixing among Europeans, indigenous, and Africans, both forced and voluntary, was more common and less hidden than in English North America. The resulting "mainstream" was a much more fluid racial and cultural mix, summarized in terms like *mestizaje* and *mulatez*. In short, the racial and ethnic backgrounds of Latinx Catholics, whether immigrants or the descendants of original settlers, confound the persistent racial and ethnic classification systems of US and US Catholic history.

Finally, Latinx Catholic immigration narratives challenge any version of the "migrant to mainstream" narrative that idealizes the United States as an immigrant destination. Latinx Catholic history brings into relief the way US political, military, and economic involvement in Latin America spurred migration to the United States. Postwar immigration from Mexico increased dramatically due to the recruitment of Mexican *braceros* to do industrial and agricultural labor in the United States from 1942 to 1964, and a great deal of undocumented immigration occurred when the program ended, as robust demand for Mexican labor endured. Waves of Nicaraguan political dissidents and other immigrants arrived in the United States during periods of economic dominance by the United Fruit Company and other American economic

---

[3]   Timothy Matovina, *Latino Catholicism: Transformation in America's Largest Church* (Princeton, NJ: Princeton University Press, 2012), 1–7.

interests in Central America.[4] The North American Free Trade Agreement (1994) created agricultural competition than helped to make subsistence farming untenable in Mexico, and thousands of farmers flocked to major Mexican cities or to the United States looking for work. In terms of military incursions into Latin America throughout the twentieth century, there were too many to count, and each cemented asymmetrical ties that brought Dominicans, Cubans, Central Americans, and others to the United States as immigrants. These immigrant accounts serve as a catalyst for what the Protestant theologian Justo Gonzalez calls "a non-innocent view of history," a view that refuses to romanticize the ambiguous, sometimes oppressive, and complicated history of this country.[5]

THE COLONIAL ORIGINS OF SOME LATINX CATHOLICS

Though they constitute a small percentage of the Latinx Catholic population today, one can still find descendants of the Spanish colonial presence in the Southwest. There are still *Tejanos* in Texas, although in common parlance the word now indicates all Mexican-American Texans; *Hispanos* still ranch in northern New Mexico and southern Colorado, with their distinctive bilingual Hispanic culture; fewer descendants of the *Californios* remain, in part because of the great inundation of settlers and migrants during the Gold Rush. Yet even where very few of the descendants of the original settlers remain, a great deal of Spanish Catholic material culture endures. We could include, for example, the artifacts of the Franciscan missions in Texas and California; the ruins of Spanish settlements on Florida's northern coast; *La Placita* church in Los Angeles that still baptizes the children of Mexican immigrants; and the early retablos – devotional folk art originally found behind altars – of saints in colonial New Mexico, whose work continues among *santeros*, that is, those local "saint-maker" folk artists who create contemporary New Mexican images of saints. This material culture tends toward a colorful, popular aesthetic distinct from both the spare style of Northern European (and Anglo-American) religious art and the baroque splendor of religious art in Latin America, Spain, and Italy.

---

4   John Powell, *Encyclopedia of North American Immigration* (New York: Facts on File Publishers, 2005), 211–212.
5   Justo Gonzalez, *Mañana: Christian Theology from the Hispanic Perspective* (Nashville: Abingdon Press, 1990), 38–41.

Historical scholarship of the last few decades has documented previously underappreciated elements of this colonial story, including the African heritage of many prominent *Californio* families, such as that of the last Mexican governor of California, Pío Pico. In a pattern perhaps familiar to African Americans during the Great Migration, descendants of African slaves in Mexico abandoned discrimination in the large metropolises for relative freedom on the northern frontier.[6] Contemporary scholars have also disrupted both "Black Legend" stereotypes that vilified the Spanish as well as the romanticized visions of Spanish colonial California that emerged in the wake of Helen Hunt Jackson's romantic epic *Ramona*, whose trajectory eventually led to innumerable Zorro books and films. The Tongva insurrectionist Toypurina, for example, who participated in a rebellion at the San Gabriel Mission in Los Angeles in 1785, was neither a defiant shaman cursing the Spanish nor an evil witch challenging the rural idylls of colonial California. Instead, like many other indigenous persons, she was fed up with the spread of European diseases and attempts to eradicate her culture. Defeated and banished to Monterey, she married a soldier from Puebla, a fellow exile far from home, and bore three *Californio* children.[7]

After the American invasion of 1846–1848, the Treaty of Guadalupe-Hidalgo ceded half of Mexico to the United States, guaranteeing US citizenship as well as land, cultural, and religious rights to the Spanish-speaking persons in the region. In practice, Anglo and European immigrant settlers often pushed these locals off the land or acquired their land through expensive court battles. Pio Pico of Los Angeles became one of the richest men in California in the late Mexican and early American periods by selling beef to Gold Rush miners, but he lost everything in protracted court proceedings by the time of his death in 1894. Many of the Catholic bishops sent to preside over the Southwest, such as Jean Baptiste Lamy of Santa Fe and Thaddeus Amat of Los Angeles, attempted to impose the uniformity of nineteenth-century Catholicism on the region, hoping to stamp out Hispanic popular religious customs and practices, such as the penitential processions of the *Penitentes*, a fraternal order of men dedicated to hymn-singing and ascetical practices like flagellation. Other pastoral leaders, however, such as Bishop Joseph

---

6   Damany M. Fisher, *Discovering Early California Afro-Latino Presence* (Berkeley: Heyday Press, 2010), 8–24.

7   See Steven W. Hackel, "Sources of Rebellion: Indian Testimony and the Mission San Gabriel Uprising of 1785," *Ethnohistory* 50 (Fall 2003): 643–669.

Alemany of San Francisco, Jean Marie Odin of Galveston, and a sizeable cadre of Mexican priests worked hard to preserve Latinx Catholicism as a distinctive expression of the faith in the Southwest.[8] While pushes toward assimilation, along with newer waves of immigration from Latin America, essentially replaced these older strands of Latinx Catholic piety and practice in many places, they still endure in not a few communities of faith, especially those in northern New Mexico and southern Colorado.

IMMIGRANT CHURCH

By the early twentieth century, the majority of Hispanic Catholics in the United States were no longer the descendants of those whom the border had crossed but of those who had crossed the border. The late nineteenth century saw the recruitment of railroad workers from Mexico, and the chaos of both the Mexican Revolution (1910–1917) and the Cristero War (1926–1928), an uprising against anti-Catholic measures by the government of Mexican President Plutarco Elías Calles, instigated a great deal of movement to the US Southwest. At the time, US labor markets suffered shortages due to tight limits on immigration from southern and Eastern Europe as well as Asia, but these quotas did not apply to the Western Hemisphere. By 1930, for example, Chicago had as many Mexicans as many of the cities of the Southwest.[9] Yet Latinx Catholics remained thoroughly marginalized in both church and society. Pastoral negligence and church segregation were often the norms; small mission churches were built away from more affluent Anglo churches, the missions sometimes staffed by priests who were Cristero refugees. Catholic bishops emphasized *Americanization*, a rapid push toward assimilation that involved the forced adoption of Euro-American customs inside and outside of church. During the Great Depression, a combination of economic pressure and ethnic prejudice resulted in the deportation of hundreds of thousands of Mexicans and even Mexican Americans.

Only in the 1940s and 1950s did some overall momentum build among church leaders to address Latinx Catholic poverty and marginalization, in part under pressure from Mexican bishops. Even a confidential US government report lamented that Catholic pastoral negligence

---

8   Matovina, *Latino Catholicism*, 15–25.
9   David A. Badillo, *Mexican Americans and the Catholic Church, 1900–1965*, ed. Jay P. Dolan and Gilberto M. Hinojosa, (Notre Dame, IN: University of Notre Dame Press, 1994), 252.

of Latinx people hindered the war effort. San Antonio Archbishop Robert Lucey formed the US bishops' Committee for the Spanish Speaking, which pushed for accurate information about Hispanic people and their culture and needs. The committee drew attention to the problems faced by agricultural workers, worked to recruit priests from Mexico during the 1950s, and established local councils throughout the country. Though Lucey himself opposed any kind of forced assimilation and encouraged agency among Hispanic priests and laity, many of those who followed his lead were less conscientious. The era is replete with insulting ecclesial portraits of Latinx cultures as "primitive," as well as paternalistic obsessions with Protestant proselytizing and Latinx ignorance of the faith.[10] Around the same time, Cardinal Francis Spellman of New York sent seminarians and priests to Puerto Rico for language and culture training and founded an Office of Spanish Catholic Action. Yet many parishes still relegated Puerto Rican communities to the basements of churches.[11]

EMPOWERMENT AND OPPOSITION

The 1960s brought an explosion of movements in church and society where Latinx people took the lead. Precipitating factors included the disappointment of Latinx soldiers returning from World War II and finding that sacrifices made for their country made little difference in terms of their rights at home. Younger generations resolved to push back. In 1965, Cesar Chavez and Dolores Huerta joined with Filipino farmworkers in launching the Delano Grape Strike. The strike led to an international boycott that drew many allies in church and society. Chavez famously kept Latinx Catholic popular religion, especially a devotion to the Virgin of Guadalupe, at the center of the struggle. During the summer of 1966, striking farmworkers in Texas marched from the Rio Grande Valley to the state capitol in Austin, supported by Mexican-American Catholic clergy. In 1968, Puerto Rican Catholics in the Bronx began organizing for better housing conditions.[12] In that same year, an emerging Chicano student movement gained attention with a series of high school walkouts

[10]   Badillo, "The Catholic Church and the Marking of Mexican American Parish Communities," 297–307; Matovina, *Latino Catholicism*, 71–72; and Roberto R. Treviño, *The Church in the Barrio: Mexican-American Ethno-Catholicism in Houston* (Chapel Hill: University of North Carolina Press, 2006), 81–102.
[11]   David A. Badillo, *Latinos and the New Immigrant Church* (Baltimore: Johns Hopkins University Press, 2006), 73–83.
[12]   Badillo, *Latinos and the New Immigrant Church*, 170–173.

in Los Angeles protesting against profound educational inequality; other walkouts in Texas followed. Activist students also inspired Latinx priests to organize, and by 1969 fifty Mexican-American priests had formed an advocacy group known as PADRES, *Padres Associados por los Derechos Religiosos, Educativos y Sociales* (Associated Priests for Religious, Educational, and Civil Rights). A year later, a similar group of Catholic women religious founded Las Hermanas, with an explicit agenda to push church leadership to be more responsive to Hispanic Catholics.[13]

This proliferation of leadership and confidence had an increasing impact on the Catholic Church in the United States. Inspired by the development of pastoral training centers in Latin America after the Second Vatican Council (1962–1965), Latinx Catholic leaders worked to create regional pastoral institutes in the United States, including the Mexican American Cultural Center in Texas, the Northeast Hispanic Catholic Center in New York, and the Southeast Pastoral Institute in Miami. These centers and institutes promoted the development of Latinx leadership development, provided cultural study and training for non-Latinx pastoral ministers, and maintained pastoral networks with the church in Latin America. The transformative meetings and pastoral thinking of the Latin American bishops conference, *la Conferencia Episcopal Latinoamericana* (CELAM), inspired Latinx pastoral leaders, especially as news spread of the 1968 meeting in Medellín, Colombia, with its focus on the concerns of the poor and their liberation. Three national meetings of Latinx Catholic leaders (called *Encuentros*) ensued from 1972 to 1985, each meeting more grassroots in its process and involving more laity. Not all of the meetings' recommendations went as far as participants hoped, such as a call for more national or ethnic parishes, the promotion of base communities, the empowerment of women to leadership, and greater integration of Latinx pastoral leaders in church structures. In retrospect, the greatest successes of the *Encuentros* were: (1) the spread of the grassroots see-judge-act methodology appropriated from Catholic Action via liberation theology; (2) the US bishops' commitment to a pastoral plan for Hispanic ministry, promulgated in 1987 (though never significantly funded); and (3) the development of a generation of Latinx Catholic leaders across the country, as well as national organizations to support them.[14]

---

[13]   Treviño, *The Church in the Barrio*, 182–194; and Matovina, *Latino Catholicism*, 73–74.
[14]   Matovina, *Latino Catholicism*, 74–97; Treviño, *The Church in the Barrio*, 201–205.

The *Encuentros* formed a generation of Latinx pastoral leaders through the early 1980s, but ecclesial changes already afoot portended new directions for both Latin American and Latinx Catholicism. Pope John Paul II was elected in 1978, and he brought with him from Poland a profoundly negative experience of Marxist thought and rule. Under the direction of Cardinal Joseph Ratzinger, the future Pope Benedict XVI, the Congregation for the Doctrine of the Faith took steps to critique and limit the influence of liberationist ideas in Latin America, and John Paul II sought to discipline priests involved in politics and replace bishops perceived as having leftist sympathies. In 1983, John Paul II first proposed to Latin American bishops gathered in Port-au-Prince, Haiti, a "new evangelization" for Christian nations, and a theology of the new evangelization took root in Latin American seminaries and ecclesial institutions. This theology began to shape both immigrants and younger Latin American priests who came to serve in the United States, and Latinx Catholicism came under its influence. This approach to Catholic life and practice de-emphasized political participation and liberation, though it maintained a commitment to the preferential option for the poor. In addition, it raised alarms about the success of Pentecostal and Evangelical missionaries and prioritized a more in-depth and doctrine-centered approach to religious education, in part to defend against proselytism.[15]

POSTWAR IMMIGRATION AND LATINX CATHOLICISM

As the political and theological winds shifted back and forth during the postwar years, immigration from Mexico and other parts of Latin America to the United States grew exponentially. World War II labor shortages had led to the *bracero* program, which recruited contract agricultural and industrial workers, mainly from Mexico. Some found ways to stay, and the program was extended several times. Even when it finally ended in 1964, many employers continued to recruit and employ Mexican workers; a flow of immigrants without legal papers also emerged to meet the demand, often agreeing to work for lower wages that led to a protest by the nascent farmworker movement (they later made common cause with undocumented workers). Postwar economic hardships in Puerto Rico increased migration to the mainland in the 1950s and 1960s, often to New York City and its environs. US economic

---

[15]   See Anna L. Peterson and Manuel A. Vasquez, "The New Evangelization in Latin American Perspective," *Cross Currents* 48 (Fall 1998): 311–329.

involvement in Cuba and Fidel Castro's turn toward the Soviet Union led to a large exodus of Cuban refugees to Miami and other parts of the United States. The Hart-Cellar Act of 1965 ended immigration quotas and established an immigration system based on family reunification and special skills, which helped family members of those from earlier waves to come. Political and military interventions in the Dominican Republic (1965) and Central American countries during the 1980s created larger, though often precarious, pathways for migration from those countries.

These waves of migration have never completely ceased, energizing what the sociologist Tomás Jiménez calls "replenished ethnicity," where even third or fourth generation English-speaking Latinx people must grapple with the language and culture brought by newcomers.[16] This process marked a contrast to earlier waves of European migrants, who accepted assimilation (or lighter, more symbolic forms of ethnicity) in part because there were few or no newcomers with a more proximate sense of language, culture, and strong ethnic identity. Jiménez observed the phenomenon of replenished ethnicity in cities with a long history of Latinx settlement. By the 1990s, however, Latin American immigrants moved beyond traditional enclaves and gateway cities to cities and towns across the country. By the 2010s, only a handful of states had very few Latinx residents.

As has often happened in US Catholic history, waves of immigration met with waves of nativism, in this case particularly antagonistic toward Latinx Catholic Americans. The anthropologist Leo Chavez speaks of a "Latino threat narrative," propagated on talk radio or the internet, made up of old nativist tropes that depict Latinx people as threatening, eternal outsiders. Latinx families are said, for example, to be unwilling to learn English, to isolate themselves from other Americans, intent on abusing social services, unreasonably fertile, disproportionately criminal, and determined to take advantage of *jus soli* citizenship privileges for their children (the so-called anchor babies), all claims easily refuted or at least complicated by research.[17] Since the 1990s, the narrative has undermined more rational public policy discourse and has gained traction among white Americans, including Catholics, surprised or worried by demographic

---

[16]   See Tomás Jiménez, *Replenished Ethnicity: Mexican Americans, Immigration, and Identity* (Berkeley: University of California Press, 2009).

[17]   Leo R. Chavez, *The Latino Threat Narrative: Constructing Citizens, Immigrants, and the Nation* (Stanford, CA: Stanford University Press, 2008), 1–18.

changes. A number of restrictionist state laws and initiatives have become public policy as a result, though these have also created political backlash, most famously in the rapid decline of the California Republican party after the passage of Proposition 187, which included provisions to limit access to social services and education for undocumented immigrants and their families. The threat narrative became a large part of the election campaign of Donald J. Trump in 2016, who won with a majority of white Catholic support. Subsequent efforts by the restrictionist Attorney General Jeff Sessions to reduce legal immigration and to punish and deter undocumented immigrants have created fear in many Latinx Catholic families and communities, and have exacerbated tensions and distrust between Latinx and Euro-American Catholics, who very often share the same parishes.

PART TWO: KEY THEMES IN CONTEMPORARY LATINX CATHOLICISM

Religion of the *Abuelitas*

Despite these renewed waves of nativism in response to demographic changes, the long history of Latinx Catholics in the United States affirms that Latinx people are not newcomers. Yet Latinx Catholics do express their faith in unique ways measurably different from the cultural expressions of the dominant Euro-American Catholic culture. Latinx Catholicism, for example, is a more home-based and grassroots form of religiosity. Euro-American Catholicism also has its devotional history of novenas and other forms of popular religion, but most developed under clerical direction, as the myriad rules and guidelines indicate, and many such devotions were deemed passé in the wake of the Second Vatican Council's rapprochement with modernity. Rooted in the homes and villages of Latin America, Latinx popular religion focuses on rituals and practices passed down from generation to generation, often with women as the primary teachers and practitioners. For this reason, popular religion among Latin Americans and Latinx Catholics is termed the religion of the *abuelitas* (grandmothers). Theologian Orlando Espín argues that this practice of women teaching popular religion within their families constitutes part of the Catholic process of "traditioning," of reanimating and handing on Christian faith. Powerful examples of Latinx popular religion include devotion to Our Lady of Guadalupe (so beloved by Cesar Chavez), the celebration of *Día de los Muertos* (Day of the Dead), and the popular *Via Crucis* or living Way of the Cross processions of Holy Week. Popular religion makes an important contribution to Latinx Catholic ecclesiology, as it reaffirms the agency of the laity through the power of the Holy Spirit. One result is that Latinx Catholics often see home or neighborhood as the center of Catholic life, while parishes and shrines serve more as the beloved location for the sacraments and *ceremonias* of the life cycle, including baptism and confirmation, as well as the *Quince Años* celebration for *quinceañeras* (fifteen-year-old girls).[18]

The popular religious practices of Latinx Catholics cannot be understood without addressing the colonial history of Latin America and the Caribbean. Many practices show signs of influence from or symbolically represent the three cultural strands intertwined throughout the Americas. During the colonial period, a people of Indigenous, African, and European descent began to form, and religious expressions developed that combined elements of Iberian Roman Catholicism with African or indigenous elements. For example, in stories about the image of *La Virgen de la Caridad de Cobre* (Our Lady of Charity of Cobre, the national patroness of Cuba), two indigenous men and an African boy, all named Juan, uncover a statue of Our Lady of Charity floating in the Bay of Nipe, presumed to have been lost from a Spanish vessel. More controversially, it is not unheard of for a Roman Catholic to also practice *Santería*, a Caribbean religion with Catholic and African roots, or *curanderismo*, a loose set of healing and herbal practices with indigenous roots. The ability to navigate among multiple worldviews and cosmologies is a gift bestowed on the Latinx community by its tripartite origins. This type of moving betwixt and between is a defining characteristic and aesthetic of the Latinx community, and it does not produce cognitive dissonance.

COMMUNITIES WITHOUT BORDERS: GIFTS AND CHALLENGES

Yet another layer of cultural mixing is inaugurated by the movement and migration of peoples. From the US perspective, migration appears a unidirectional movement but, in reality, culture and faith migrate back and forth across borders. Indeed, it is impossible to speak of Latinx Catholics in the United States without speaking of their ongoing transnational connections to Latin America and the Caribbean. This reality disrupts the notion, implicit in theories of assimilation or

---

[18]   See James Empereur and Eduardo Fernández, *La Vida Sacra: Contemporary Hispanic Sacramental Theology* (Lanham, MD: Rowman & Littlefield, 2006).

Americanization, that immigration severs the connection between Latinx Catholics and their loved ones back in Latin America. Those who immigrate to the United States often financially support family members in Latin America (the support termed *remittances*), cementing ties back home. It is not unusual to encounter homes, churches, or town plazas rebuilt or refurbished with funds from the United States, and we have already noted how movements like liberation theology and the new evangelization in the Latin American church have strongly shaped Latinx Catholicism. Migration can make the Catholic material culture from Latin America ever more precious, as when rosary beads or prayer cards are all that undocumented migrants bring with them on their dangerous journeys to the United States. A grandmother in Central America may give her grandson a *Virgen de Guadalupe* or Christ of *Esquipulas* prayer card to carry with him for protection on his journey to the United States. These seemingly insignificant items hold sacred significance. They serve to provide hope in times of struggle or hardship and as priceless and powerful symbols of family, faith, and culture. Indeed, the transnational faith of the people cannot be constrained or defined by borders. It moves back and forth across the Americas along with the community.

With transnationalism emerges questions about immigration status and citizenship. As Leo Chavez' account of the "Latino Threat Narrative" demonstrates, racism and nativism continue to afflict Latinx Catholic immigrants. The impact goes beyond just immigrants, however, as Latinx Catholic families and communities usually present a mix of permanent residents, citizens, and undocumented immigrants. The staggering number of mixed-status families makes any clear, morally tinged distinction between "legal and illegal," such as that made by many Euro-American Catholics, less tenable. As a practical matter, opposition to illegal immigration often operates as a blunt instrument, targeting not only undocumented immigrants but Latinx people in general. Economic and social inequalities that disadvantage the Latinx community exacerbate the situation so that Catholic parishes themselves can become spaces of disenfranchisement. On average, 43 percent of parishioners at a parish with Hispanic ministry are Euro-Americans.[19] Many of these "shared parishes" showcase inequalities between communities. For example, Euro-American pastoral leaders are often revealed to be paid employees with access to parish

---

[19] Hosffman Ospino, *Hispanic Ministry in Catholic Parishes* (Boston: Boston College, 2014), 14.

resources while Latinx leaders are volunteers who purchase their own supplies. White Catholics outnumber Latinx Catholics on parish committees, even when Latinx Catholics form a clear majority in the parish. These inequalities perpetuate tensions and resentments back and forth, even as other Catholic communities age and suffer disaffiliation among the young. In contrast, as a much younger population less prone to disaffiliation, Latinx Catholics continue to contribute to the lifeblood of the church.

TEOLOGÍA EN CONJUNTO

As the Latinx population in the United States has grown, Latinx theology has emerged as a recognized and distinct movement in Catholic theology. Two key methodological contributions to theology by US Latinx theologians include a more intentional focus on the everyday, *lo cotidiano*, and a theology and pastoral life developed *en conjunto*, that is, collaboratively. Regarding the latter, Latinx academics feel a responsibility to be accountable to their communities by researching and giving voice to community concerns. They work *en conjunto* on behalf of *la comunidad* through scholarship and advocacy work that is not always easy to distinguish. Professional organizations like the Academy of Catholic Hispanic Theologians in the United States (ACHTUS), the Hispanic Theological Initiative (HTI), and La Comunidad of Hispanic Scholars of the American Academy of Religion promote such collaboration and monitor accountability. While an academic publication by a Latinx theologian may list one author, if one looks just beneath the surface, a team of conversation partners emerges, including colleagues and grassroots community members. Scholarly work is never done alone. Checking in with communities of accountability serves as a hallmark of Latinx theological method. Ethicist Ada-María Isasi-Díaz, for example, interviewed working-class Latina women as part of her work in developing theological ethics attuned to the everyday life of Latinas, which she termed *mujerista* theology. Collaboration in Latinx Catholic theology also goes beyond denominational lines; the Hispanic Theological Initiative and La Comunidad are, and have always been, ecumenical organizations.

This ecumenical collaborative work refutes the misconception that every Latinx is by culture and right a practicing Roman Catholic. While Iberian Roman Catholicism had a significant impact on Latin American and Caribbean cultures, the extensive presence of and active missions of Protestant churches cannot be overlooked. Evangelical and Pentecostal communities have grown exponentially throughout Latin America as well as in the United States, and more recently a growing number of Latinx young people have chosen "no religion." Yet despite identifying as disaffiliated, many second and third-generation Latinx young adults continue to revere cultural-religious icons such as Our Lady of Guadalupe, understood to transcend the limitations of the Catholic Church as an institution. Such reactions emerge naturally from the home-based traditions of Latinx Catholicism, the faith of the *abuelitas*. There also seems to be a growing interest among the younger generations in a return to indigenous and African spiritual practices. A deep affinity toward ancestral wisdom and ritual can be seen in the popularity of healing circles, sweat lodges, and *botanicas* (folk medicine shops).

LANGUAGE AND APOSTOLIC MOVEMENTS

An important interpretive key to Latinx Catholicism is the Spanish language. While not every Latinx person in the United States speaks Spanish, it remains a common thread that carries elements of culture and tradition, and which unites Latin American and US Latinx communities. Attending Mass in Spanish and praying in Spanish remain a deep source of empowerment for Latinx Catholics. The pressure to assimilate and discriminatory practices in the US educational system have conspired to rob many second and third-generation Latinx young people of fluency in Spanish, introducing rifts with Spanish dominant immigrant elders as a result. While bilingualism and bilingual education appear to be reemerging as accepted practices in some parts of the United States, they remain contentious. Like twentieth-century German Catholic families before them, many Latinx Catholic families do not teach their children their native language for fear of discrimination. Because a large number of church ministry programs are aimed at immigrants, there remains a lacunae of programming geared toward English-speaking Latinx Catholics. Yet the situation can be far worse for Latinx Catholics who primarily speak indigenous languages or Brazilian Portuguese, languages that rarely even appear when the question of language is introduced. To complicate the question of language even further, the phenomenon of Spanglish – a mix of Spanish and English – has developed in many parts of the United States. As Latinx theologian Carmen M. Nanko-Fernández argues, Spanglish can be considered a language unto itself.[20]

[20]   See Carmen M. Nanko-Fernández, *Theologizing En Espanglish: Context, Community, and Ministry* (Maryknoll, NY: Orbis, 2010).

Prominent Latinx Catholic ministries in the Spanish language have included a flowering of apostolic movements in the United States. Apostolic movements are para-ecclesial organizations oriented to lay-people that emphasize distinct spiritualities and a focus on lay leadership. Thus, while the Catholic Charismatic Renewal, for example, has largely faded among those Euro-American Catholics who brought it into mainstream US Catholicism, it has become ubiquitous in many Spanish-speaking Catholic communities.[21] Other apostolic movements have emerged over time as well, including several with roots in Spain, such as the Cursillo retreat movement and the Neo-Catechumenal Way, and more recent homegrown movements such as the media-savvy *El Sembrador* movement in Los Angeles, which broadcasts liturgy and programming across Latin America. The apostolic movements' parallel structures have sometimes led to tensions or even open conflict with church authorities, and some are accused of a lack of attention to justice concerns. As nativist pressure has grown, some Latinx Catholic communities have gotten deeply involved in advocacy for immigrants and activism for immigration reform, usually with the explicit though sometimes tepid support of bishops and clergy.

A POPE FOR LATINX CATHOLICS

A focus on immigrant justice and other concerns of the marginalized have of course characterized the papacy of Jorge Bergoglio, the former Archbishop of Buenos Aires often seen ministering in the slums of his city. As the first Jesuit pope and the first pope from Latin America, Pope Francis demonstrates a pastoral approach familiar to Latinx Catholics. Welcoming lost sheep with open arms, Pope Francis takes a more grass-roots approach to pastoral ministry, urging church leaders to respond to the concrete wounds and needs of the people. Envisioning the church as a field hospital and calling all Catholics to a "missionary discipleship" that draws them to the margins and peripheries in service of others, the pontiff from Argentina recognizes the significance of popular religion and honors martyrs of the church in Latin America, such as Archbishop Oscar Romero of San Salvador. Yet Pope Francis' pastoral emphasis does not in any way negate or lessen his theological acumen. His actions resound with theological clarity. For example, with the papacy of Francis, we see a renewed focus on the rich theological tradition of the

---

[21] Ospino, *Hispanic Ministry in Catholic Parishes*, 17–18.

preferential option for the poor. In *Laudato Si'*, his encyclical on the ecological crisis, the pope not only draws attention to the theological significance of our human relationship to the physical environment, "our common home," but he probes how environmental destruction (including climate change) disproportionately impacts the living conditions of the majority poor of the world, increasing their sense of being forgotten and dehumanized by those who reap the benefits of resource depletion. In short, Pope Francis' teaching and ministry emerge out of his context in the majority Global South; he serves as a symbol of historic shifts in Global Catholicism, including the emergence of a Latinx majority church in Catholic America.

WHITHER LATINX MAJORITY CATHOLICISM?

Having considered a complex history of conquest, immigration, empowerment, and resistance, and having examined prominent themes in contemporary Latinx Catholicism, we conclude with a few ruminations on the long-term impact of a Latinx Catholic majority on US Catholic thinking and practice. For example, even as popular religion has waned in importance among Euro-American Catholics, its central importance among Latinx (and many Asian-American) Catholics will likely propel it back to the center of American Catholicism. We can expect that devotional practices oriented to the Virgin of Guadalupe will continue to grow not only among Latinx Catholics, but among non-Latinx Catholics as well. While many Euro-American Catholics speak of the importance of family in church and society, US politics from both ideological wings has generally emphasized the importance of individual work rather than family support. Latinx focus on families and extended families may challenge that ethos over time. A burgeoning Latinx Catholicism may also bring greater attention to the needs of the poor, making the preferential option for the poor as central an aspect of US ecclesial identity as attention to sexual ethics has been since the 1990s.

The emerging majority status of Latinx Catholicism may work its biggest change by altering some of the dominant narratives of US Catholic identity. The "migrant-to-mainstream" story that has dominated US Catholicism through the postwar period could give way to broader acceptance of US Catholicism as a multicultural, multiethnic, and multiracial communion. Non-European strains of immigrant Catholicism – Mexican, Central American, Korean, Vietnamese, Filipino – will undoubtedly occupy ever more of the attention of

Catholic leadership. In addition, the children and grandchildren of immigrants will require more attention from church leaders, as the church discerns what it means to form and sustain a young church with a proud, bicultural, and bilingual identity. Euro-American Catholics will have to leave behind a self-conception of themselves as a dominant culture within the church and become simply one "cultural family" among others. All this might evoke significant struggle, as demonstrated in the rise of white backlash against immigrants in the early twenty-first century, even among fellow Catholics. Catholic leadership must be attentive and strong to help midwife US Catholicism into a new multicultural creation.

FURTHER READING

Badillo, David A. *Latinos and the New Immigrant Church*. Baltimore: Johns Hopkins University Press, 2006.

Casarella, Peter and Raúl Gómez, eds. *El Cuerpo De Cristo: The Hispanic Presence in the U.S. Catholic Church*. New York: Crossroad Publishing, 1997.

Elizondo, Virgilio. *Galilean Journey: The Mexican Promise*. Maryknoll: Orbis Books, 1983.

Espín, Orlando, ed. *The Wiley Blackwell Companion to Latino/a Catholicism*. Oxford: John Wiley and Sons, Ltd., 2015.

Isasi-Díaz, Ada María. *En la Lucha/In the Struggle: Elaborating a Mujerista Theology*. Minneapolis: Fortress Press, 1993.

Matovina, Timothy. *Latino Catholicism: Transformation in America's Largest Church*. Princeton: Princeton University Press, 2012.

Nanko-Fernández, Carmen. *Theologizing in Espanglish: Context, Community, and Ministry*. Maryknoll: Orbis Books, 2010.

Rodríguez, Jeanette. *Our Lady of Guadalupe: Faith and Empowerment Among Mexican-American Women*. Austin: University of Texas Press, 1994.

17 Asian-American Catholics

ROBERT E. CARBONNEAU, CP

In November 2000, the United States Conference of Catholic Bishops (USCCB) issued a pastoral letter, *Welcoming the Stranger Among Us: Unity in Diversity*, which reiterated the fact that the growth of the Catholic Church in the United States was greatly dependent upon immigrants from "many races and cultures."[1] In looking at the changing face of the US Catholic population, it recognized the increasing presence of Asian and Pacific Island Catholics, a community that has been largely invisible within the history of American Catholicism. Awareness of the growing Asian Catholic population prompted the bishops the following year to issue *Asian and Pacific Presence: Harmony in Faith*, a statement that more clearly acknowledged their presence in the church. Noting that "Christ Was Born in Asia," the document encouraged a fuller appreciation of the gifts and contributions of Asian and Pacific peoples to the life of the church and acknowledged the need to respond with a "welcoming spirit."[2] A companion statement in 2018, *Encountering Christ in Harmony: A Pastoral Response to Our Asian and Pacific Island Brothers and Sisters*, laid out a national pastoral plan for Asian and Pacific Island Catholics in the United States. The product of the work of the bishops' Subcommittee on Asian and Pacific Island Affairs, the report recognized the "richness of the spiritual and cultural backgrounds" that Asian and Pacific Island Catholics bring to the church and their contributions to the faith.[3] Taken together, these pastoral statements draw attention to two key themes, *presence* and *faith*, that have been central to the Asian-American Catholic experience.

[1] *Welcoming the Stranger Among Us: Unity in Diversity* (Washington, DC: USCCB, 2000).

[2] *Asian and Pacific Presence: Harmony in Faith* (Washington, DC: USCCB, 2001).

[3] *Encountering Christ in Harmony: A Pastoral Response to Our Asian and Pacific Island Brothers and Sisters* (Washington, DC: USCCB, 2018), 3.

This chapter will focus on the history and experience of Asian Catholics in the church in the United States.[4] The first part of this article describes developments during the early twentieth century, focusing on Chinese and Japanese Catholics who lived primarily on the West Coast. Evangelization and outreach ministry undertaken at this time by religious congregations in conjunction with ecclesial leadership and laity were sometimes limited by existing prejudices. The second section of the chapter concentrates on the post–1965 period, a time marked by changes in immigration law, civil rights law, and Catholic renewal amid the reforms of the Second Vatican Council (1962–1965). This period was also characterized by increased diversity within the Asian-American Catholic population as evidenced by the growth of the Filipino, Korean, and Vietnamese communities. These new arrivals gave rise to diversified faith experiences witnessed in parishes and dioceses, where they also began to cultivate networks and establish leadership roles. Asian-American Catholicism today is the subject of the third section of the chapter and will include a discussion of devotional life, cultural practices, and new theological ideas. Across these three periods, the history of Asian-American Catholics calls attention to transnational influences within Catholicism and the ongoing struggle to recognize and respect diversity within the multicultural church.

CHINESE AND JAPANESE CATHOLICS BEFORE 1960

When histories of Catholicism in the United States speak of the era of the "Immigrant Church," the discussion tends to focus almost exclusively on Irish, German, Italian, Polish, and other European arrivals who flocked to American shores from the mid-nineteenth century through the opening decades of the twentieth. The Catholic historical narrative rarely acknowledges the presence of Asian immigrants and their encounters with or contributions to the church in the United States during this period. Although their numbers were small, an accurate account of immigrant-era Catholicism needs to recognize the experience of Asian Americans, who worked to establish themselves in the United States despite obstacles and hardship, including those they faced

---

4   In all three statements, Asian and Pacific Islanders was the inclusive population. From the start, however, an editorial decision was made that this article should concentrate on Chinese, Japanese, Filipino, Vietnamese, and Korean Catholics in the United States.

within the church that lacked the experience and personnel needed to minister effectively to them.

As Chinese immigration to the United States surged in the wake of the California Gold Rush and the lure of jobs related to the construction of the transcontinental railroad, church leaders on the west coast made some limited effort to provide for their spiritual care. During the early 1870s, the archbishop of San Francisco, whose diocese covered the northern half of the state at that time, wrote to the Jesuits and other religious orders in an effort to procure a priest who could care for the spiritual needs of the Chinese community. At the same time, however, many Catholics, including members of the clergy, viewed the Chinese as an inferior race and joined in the growing chorus of anti-Chinese nativism. They expressed little confidence in the prospect of converting the Chinese to Christianity.[5] Such views helped fuel the anti-Chinese backlash that led to the passage of the Chinese Exclusion Act in 1882, a federal law that severely limited further Chinese immigration. The law was renewed in 1892 and made permanent in 1902.

Since very few nineteenth-century Chinese immigrants were Catholic and most lacked previous encounters with the faith, ministering to them proved a challenging prospect. When efforts began to take shape during the early twentieth century, church leaders often relied on the efforts of religious orders with experience in missionary work. In San Francisco, the Missionary Society of St. Paul the Apostle, known familiarly as the Paulists, made an effort to reach out to the large Chinese population living in the vicinity of the parish they staffed, Old St. Mary's. There, in 1903, they established the first Catholic mission in the United States, which later grew to include a parochial school and a Chinese language school. In New York, the Salesians assigned to the Church of the Transfiguration in lower Manhattan likewise worked to minister to the Chinese within the district. They replaced the former pastor who railed against the "Oriental" invasion of his parish and complained about being "kept awake at night ... by the noise of these Mongolians ... [and] the clatter of their tongues."[6] While not all shared his intemperate views, there remained a common

---

5   "Father James Bouchard, SJ, 'White Man or Chinaman – Which?' 1873" and "Archbishop Joseph S. Alemany Requests Assistance with the Chinese Apostolate in San Francisco, 1871, 1874," in *Keeping Faith: European and Asian Catholic Immigrants*, ed. Jeffrey M. Burns, Ellen Skerrett, and Joseph M. White (Maryknoll, NY: Orbis Books, 2000), 232–235.

6   Peter P. McLoughlin, *Father Tom: Life and Lectures of Rev. Thomas P. McLoughlin* (New York: G. P. Putnam's Sons, 1919), 83.

sentiment within the church that ministry to the Chinese remained difficult "on account of the[ir] dissimilarity of race, the natural reticence of the Chinese character, the persistence of the age-long Oriental customs, and finally, or rather principally, because of the indifference of white people."[7]

Gradually, as early ministerial efforts bore fruit, converts within the Chinese community joined in the work of evangelization. At St. Mary's Chinese Mission in San Francisco, lay catechists helped to meet the demands of any who, in the words of the pastor, sought to have "the truths of our Church explained in his native tongue." In addition to providing religious instruction to recent converts and serving as an interpreter for the pastor as he made sick calls and conducted home visits, lay catechists also assisted at liturgies by "preach[ing] our messages, announcements and Gospel sermons to the assembly and to the congregation."[8] By the 1950s, growing lay activism brought visibility to the Chinese Catholic community, which began to establish organizational networks and host regional gatherings so that individuals could come together to address common concerns and promote greater understanding of their shared faith.

In many ways, Japanese Catholics followed a trajectory very similar to that of their Chinese counterparts during the late nineteenth and early twentieth centuries. Very few were born into the faith, and it was only through missionary outreach that their numbers began to increase. The first official missions to the Japanese were established in San Francisco and Los Angeles during the early 1910s, partly in response to demands from the handful of Japanese Catholics living in those regions. In 1912, Francis Risaburo Hami, a convert, sent a letter to Archbishop Patrick W. Riordan of San Francisco asking him to address the neglect of the more than 80,0000 Japanese souls in California, noting that many of them were being lost to Protestantism. The following year, a small Japanese Mission Center was established in the city through the efforts of Father Albert Breton, a French-born missionary who had served in Japan for several years following his ordination in 1905. Breton later turned the mission over to the Jesuits, so that he could concentrate on the one he had established the preceding year in Los Angeles. Although the mission shared many of the same hallmarks as regular parish life – from sacramental ministry and religious education to

---

7   "Father Bradley's Mission among the Chinese," *The Monitor*, November 20, 1915.
8   "Chinese Ministry in San Francisco, 1945," in *Keeping Faith*, 237–238.

fundraising events and social and cultural activities – to outsiders it could seem like a decidedly foreign enterprise, one more akin to the church's work in the overseas missions. One article from 1918, for instance, noted the strangeness of finding "a mission to the heathen established in the very heart of a great city like San Francisco."[9] Such views indicate that in the eyes of many observers, it would take time for the Japanese to come to be seen as either fully Catholic or fully American.

As Catholic missionary activity among the Japanese developed in the 1910s and 1920s, concerns about assimilation and acculturation became a potential source of friction. In Los Angeles, for instance, Bishop John Cantwell actively promoted the Americanization of his diverse flock and insisted that Japanese converts "conform to American ways in religious matters." He invited Maryknoll sisters to replace the Japanese women that Father Breton had recruited to work among the Japanese population, believing the American-born sisters were better suited to the task of assisting Japanese Catholics in assimilating to their new American environment. As historian Michael Engh has written, Cantwell's actions reveal how "prevailing American attitudes of superiority over Asians manifested itself in the assumptions of who was best suited to lead and to make decisions, as well as what activities constituted a 'truly American Catholic Church.'"[10]

No degree of assimilation, however, would protect Japanese Catholics from scrutiny during World War II, when they and other Japanese Americans on the Pacific coast were forcibly removed to internment camps. In some cases, pastors found their entire congregations relocated to distant camps. Among them was Father Leo Tibesar, a Maryknoll priest, who moved near to the camp in Minidoka, Idaho, to minister to the internees. He was one of many Maryknoll priests and sisters who engaged in such activity, helping to ensure that those in the camps continued to receive the sacraments, religious instruction, and spiritual care. Those interned also did their part to maintain the rhythms of religious community by conducting catechism classes for their children, hosting evening study groups for adults, and organizing meetings of the Holy Name Society, Legion of Mary, and other associations.

9   Pius Moore, SJ, "Catholic Japanese in California," *Catholic Missions* 12 (January 1918): 3.
10 Michael E. Engh, SJ, "'Japanese Trimmings on Our American Catholicity': Contested Ministry to Japanese Immigrants in Los Angeles, 1912–1925," *U.S. Catholic Historian* 31 (Spring 2013): 75–94, quotes on 88 and 76.

Recognizing the injustice of the government's action, a handful of church leaders spoke out in defense of Japanese Americans. Most notably, Bishop Gerald Shaughnessy of Seattle, in a pastoral statement that he ordered to be read at all masses, urged Catholics to "embrace our fellow American citizens of Japanese extraction in a special bond of charity," emphasizing that they are "no less claimants of true American citizenship and of all rights thereunder."[11] Overall, however, the Catholic response to internment was muted. Most church members failed to recognize that fellow Catholics were among those affected, a reality that reflected the fact that Japanese and other Asian-American Catholics remained largely invisible to their coreligionists at this time.

THE POST–1965 ERA

The 1960s ushered in a new era in the history of Asian-American Catholicism. The passage of the Immigration and Naturalization Act of 1965 (also known as the Hart-Cellar Act) ended discrimination based on national origin and thus effectively abolished the restrictions that had been put in place by the 1924 Immigration Act and other exclusionary immigration policies. This legislative reform opened the nation's doors to a new wave of Asian immigration from more diverse national origins. Among these newcomers were large numbers of Filipinos, Vietnamese, and Koreans, each of which had sizable Catholic populations. Their growing presence in the United States would coincide with the implementation of the reforms of the Second Vatican Council, which encouraged greater respect for cultural-religious customs and authorized liturgical renewal that would invigorate the public expression of Asian-American Catholicism in the decades ahead.

While the growing diversity of the Asian-American Catholic population made them a more visible presence within the church, it also drew attention to the differences present within and among these communities. Taken as a whole, Asian-American Catholics during this period experienced many of the same collective challenges, including the struggle to establish communities of faith in their new country and to gain recognition from church officials. Yet their experiences were also shaped by their own unique national circumstances and distinctive histories. A closer examination of the Filipino, Vietnamese, and Korean experience reminds us of the need to avoid lumping these groups

---

[11]   "Catholicism at Minidoka Internment Camp," in *Keeping Faith*, 256–262.

together indistinguishably, yet also helps us understand the various trends and transformations common to the wider Asian-American Catholic population.

Within this new wave of Asian immigration, Filipinos comprised the single largest group of arrivals, adding to a presence in the United States that dates back to the late nineteenth century, with vibrant communities in California, Hawaii, and other states. Although they faced many of the same barriers to immigration as other groups, their colonial history distinguished them from other Asian populations in two significant ways. First, they came from a country that was predominantly Catholic, a legacy of Spanish colonial rule and missionary activity dating back to the sixteenth century. Second, they had established ties to the United States dating back to the end of the Spanish-American War, when the Philippines came under US control. Their post–1965 migrations built upon these earlier pathways that had been put in place by the United States, including opportunities for citizenship granted to those who enlisted in the military.

As their numbers increased in the post–1965 period, Filipinos struggled against earlier patterns of discrimination. During the 1920s, for instance, newly arrived Filipino Catholics in greater Los Angeles found themselves labeled as part of the "immigrant problem" that was being voiced locally and across the nation.[12] They also faced neglect within the church. Only when confronted by government reports of the civil rights abuses and economic injustice that Filipinos suffered did bishops like San Francisco's Archbishop John J. Mitty take heed of their plight. Responding in 1956 to Vatican concerns that the spiritual needs of Filipino immigrants were being ignored, he surveyed his priests to determine what efforts were being made to minister to Filipinos in the diocese, finding pockets of vibrancy like the outreach being done by the Franciscans among Filipinos and other Spanish-speaking farmworkers in the area around Stockton. Unfortunately, such efforts were relatively rare. They also tended to be guided by paternalist assumptions and be dismissive of traditional devotions and other folk practices.[13]

[12]   Kathleen Garces-Foley, "From the Melting Pot to the Multicultural Table: Filipino Catholics in Los Angeles," *American Catholic Studies* 20 (Spring 2009): 27–53.
[13]   "Report on Filipinos in San Francisco, 1941–1942" and "Report on Filipinos in Stockton, California, 1956," in *Keeping Faith*, 266–272. See also Dawn Bohulano Mabalon, *Little Manila Is in the Heart: The Making of the Filipina/o American Community in Stockton, California* (Durham, NC: Duke University Press, 2013), ch. 5.

Recognition of Filipino presence in the church increased as they gained a stronger foothold in parishes and pressed for greater recognition and respect from pastors and other church leaders. Drawing upon strong social connections rooted in the historic legacy of the *barangay*, or village association, they came together to advocate for their needs. While some looked to Filipino priests to speak on behalf of the community, they also cultivated lay leadership. In Los Angeles, the missionary Columban Fathers working in Los Angeles boasted in 1951 that their parish possessed the "most successfully run organization of any kind among Filipinos in the US, whether religious, civic, or political."[14] But with the growth of the Filipino population, questions arose over how best to minister to their needs. While some advocated for separate parishes or dedicated Filipino ministries, others, including some Filipino leaders themselves, argued that efforts should be made to enter the mainstream of American Catholic life and that "special ministry to Filipinos or ... [the] formation of a Vicariate for Filipinos ... would only serve to foment a spirit of isolationism, perpetuate differences, and delay the day when the Filipino Catholic will feel at home in an American Catholic community."[15] As a result, many Filipinos have chosen to become active in existing parishes, where they are one group among many joining together in worship. Others, though, have chosen deliberately to seek out "destination" parishes that serve their spiritual needs. In Philadelphia, for instance, Filipinos from across the region began flocking in the 1970s to two downtown parishes, St. Augustine and St. Peter, that welcomed them with special liturgies and an embrace of traditional Filipino devotions.[16]

The growth of the Vietnamese Catholic population in the United States was directly connected to the history of the Vietnam War (1955–1975), a conflict that resulted in massive internal displacement and a series of refugee crises. The Communist victory in Vietnam in 1975 set in process a series of relocations that would swell the ranks of Vietnamese Americans from 130,000 in 1975 to more than 600,000 in 1990. In addition to those who were evacuated in the immediate aftermath of the war, the United States also accepted a large number of "boat people," the peak number of whom

---

14   Angelyn Dries, OSF, *Be Centered in Christ and Not in Self: The Missionary Society of Saint Columban: The North American Story (1918–2018)* (Bloomington, IN: Ex Libris Corporation, 2017), 282–292.
15   "Inquiry and Response on Filipino Ministry, 1980," in *Keeping Faith*, 273–274.
16   Vivienne S. M. Angeles, *Filipino Catholic Communities in Philadelphia* (Harvard University Pluralism Project, 1998) at http://pluralism.org.

fled the country between 1978 and 1982.[17] Many came to the United States after enduring temporary homes in refugee camps in Thailand, the Philippines, and Hong Kong. Though initially scattered across the country by these resettlement efforts – many of them coordinated by local Catholic Charities organizations working in cooperation with the federal government – the Vietnamese gradually clustered in a number of major population centers, including Southern California, Louisiana, and Texas.

The legacy of war and displacement had profound implications for Vietnamese-American Catholics in the United States. As historian Tuan Hoang has written, it fostered an "exilic identity" that informed their beliefs and practices. They looked to their faith to cope with national loss and family separation, often through an emphasis on traditional devotions, obedience to papal authority, and other defining features of Catholic life in Vietnam. Their wartime experience also fueled a fervent anti-Communism that aligned them with Cold War Catholic attitudes in the United States.[18] While some integrated into American parishes, many Vietnamese Catholics sought to carve out religious space where they could preserve their language, culture, and traditions, advocating for their own parishes at a time when many dioceses in the United States had moved away from establishing ethnic parishes. In these efforts, members of the laity often took the lead in petitioning for rights and recognition and organizing local support. Such was the case in Port Arthur, Texas, when members of the refugee community petitioned the bishop of the Diocese of Beaumont for a parish of their own in 1976. Such actions marked a notable shift in the Vietnamese-American Catholic experience, sparking a movement toward "greater and more active involvement in church life" than was customary in Vietnam, where church affairs were "generally initiated, managed, and directed by the clergy."[19]

Yet even as lay involvement has grown among Vietnamese American Catholics, the community has gained distinction for the large number of religious vocations it has generated. In 2009, the US bishops reported that 6 percent of those ordained to the priesthood that year

[17] Peter C. Phan, *Vietnamese-American Catholics* (New York: Paulist Press, 2005), 66–67.
[18] Tuan Hoang, "Ultramontanism, Nationalism, and the Fall of Saigon: Historicizing the Vietnamese American Catholic Experience," *American Catholic Studies* 130 (Spring 2019): 1–36.
[19] Carl L. Bankston, III, "Vietnamese-American Catholicism: Transplanted and Flourishing," *U.S. Catholic Historian* 18 (Winter 2000): 45.

were Vietnamese. Though estimates vary, some surveys indicate that by the early 2010s, more than 800 Vietnamese priests were serving in the United States, some as members of the diocesan clergy and others as part of religious communities like the Redemptorists and the Society of the Divine Word. In some dioceses, Vietnamese clergy, whether immigrant or first generation, comprise a significant portion of the priestly personnel, staffing Vietnamese and non-Vietnamese parishes alike. Catholic sisterhoods have also benefitted from these Vietnamese vocations, though most of these women tend to gravitate toward Vietnamese congregations, some of whom have sent sisters to the United States to receive their education. Some observers have even gone so far as to refer to the Vietnamese as the "New Irish," noting how their disproportionate number of vocations today parallels that of the Irish in the nineteenth and early twentieth centuries. Questions remain, however, whether these vocational trends will continue in subsequent generations as members of the Vietnamese community assimilate more into the secular American mainstream.[20]

The issue of generational change has similarly been one of central concern to the Korean-American Catholic community, the third group that stands out as part of the post–1965 wave of Asian-American immigration. Although there had been waves of Korean immigration to the United States dating back to the start of the twentieth century, the influx would peak in the period between 1976 and 1990. A disproportionate number of these Korean immigrants were Christian, with Protestants substantially outnumbering Catholics, a trend reflective of Korea's overall religious demography. Many of these newcomers were seeking greater educational and economic opportunities, assisted by US immigration policies that promoted family reunification. Upon arrival, Korean Catholics tended to cluster in a handful of major metropolitan areas, including San Francisco, Los Angeles, and New York, where they were ministered to by members of religious orders who had prior missionary experience in Korea. The Columban Fathers, for instance, were instrumental during the 1970s in establishing Korean ministries in Chicago, Seattle, and Southern California. As Korean parishes were

---

[20]   On vocation trends, see Jonathan Wiggins and Sr. Thu Do, "Shelter from the Storm: The Parish's Role in the Faith Life of Vietnamese American Catholics in the United States" (Center for Applied Research in the Apostolate, August 2019), https://cara .georgetown.edu/VietnameseAmericanCatholics.pdf. See also Tuan Hoang, "The Resettlement of Vietnamese Refugee Religious, Priests, and Seminaries in the United States, 1975–1977," *U.S. Catholic Historian* 37 (Summer 2019): 99–122.

formed, many came to rely on priests from Korea sent to the United States on temporary assignment. As Mi-Kyoung Hwang explains, this arrangement has led to an interesting dynamic, in which "visiting priests stay for a few years before returning to their [home] dioceses, while parishioners continue to live in the United States and must navigate their faith journey while interacting with American culture and society."[21]

As the Korean-American Catholic population has grown, one of the most pressing pastoral concerns has been ensuring that the faith is passed down from one generation to the next. Members of the immigrant generation worry about declining rates of church membership among the American-born generation, which can result from either secularization or the shifting of religious affiliation to Protestant Korean congregations, many of which boast vibrant youth ministries.[22] Another source of generational tension emerges as church leaders debate whether ministerial efforts should focus on serving recent immigrants or catering to the needs of earlier arrivals who have become more settled in the United States. Efforts to adhere strictly to religious culture and practices from the homeland may appeal to the former group more than the latter. Priorities will vary depending on whether the population identifies as being an *immigrant* community or an *ethnic* community, and whether the goal of parish ministries is to support cultural distinctiveness or to help integrate newcomers into regular parish life. As part of the process of religious adjustment, these concerns speak to the realities faced by many other Catholic immigrant groups, both Asian and non-Asian alike.

With Asian Americans and other recent arrivals bringing greater diversity to the Catholic Church in the United States, their presence in parish and diocesan life has forced church leaders to reenvision how "ethnic ministries" operated. In the post–Vatican II era, dioceses moved away from the older models that emphasized the creation of distinct parishes or apostolates to serve each group, shifting instead toward the creation of multicultural ministry programs. As Kathleen Graces Foley explains, the multicultural model of parish ministry, which gained ground in the 1980s and 1990s, "emphasizes 'unity in diversity' and

[21] Mi-Kyoung Hwang, "Passover to Crossover," in *Reconciling Cultures and Generations: Reflections on Today's Church by Korean American Catholics*, ed. Simon C. Kim (Chicago: Paul Bechtold Library Publications, 2018), 64.

[22] Simon C. Kim, *Memory and Honor: Cultural and Generational Ministry with Korean American Communities* (Collegeville, MN: Liturgical Press, 2010), 21.

rejects the cultural pluralist tendency toward separate ethnic ministries." Among the rationale has been a desire to counteract the insular-
ity of ethnic ministries, with each group speaking narrowly for its own
members, and promote "a voluntary encounter of cultures that leads to
mutual appreciation and greater integration" at both the parish and the
diocesan level. In Los Angeles, for instance, the archdiocese sponsored
workshops on intercultural communication and cultural appreciation,
and has held annual conferences on "Building Inclusive Communities"
that seek to move individuals "beyond 'awareness' of the diversity in
the community and develop an understanding and appreciation of culture, ethnicity, and other differences."[23] Although this shift has not
been without its critics, it signals a rejection of the view that diversity
is somehow a "problem" to be overcome. Rather, such efforts seek to
promote integration across ethnic lines and foster greater respect for
pluralism within the church.

LEADERSHIP AND ADVOCACY

The growing Asian-American Catholic presence within the church in
the United States has led to a demand for greater recognition within the
institutional church and a formal voice in its decision-making structures. At the parish level, Asian-American Catholics often confront the
stereotype that they are passive or reserved, and can sometimes feel like
a "forgotten group." They recognize the need to cultivate leadership
within the community to advocate for their interests and make parishes
more sensitive to their traditions and practices, and see involvement in
parish ministries as a way to raise cultural awareness and make their
presence felt. Yet feelings of inclusion can vary dramatically across
parishes and groups, depending on the size of the particular Asian-
American population relative to the community as a whole. Filipinos,
for instance, while often still minorities within their parishes, tend to
possess greater visibility within the community and its ministries
because of their relatively larger numbers.[24]

Asian-American clergy have similarly recognized the need to organize collectively to amplify their voice and influence within the church.

[23]   Garces-Foley, "From the Melting Pot to the Multicultural Table," 48–49.
[24]   Tricia C. Bruce, Jerry Z. Park, and Stephen M. Cherry, "Asian and Pacific Island
        Catholics in the United States: A Report Prepared for the United States Conference
        of Catholic Bishops Secretariat for Cultural Diversity in the Church" (October 2015),
        quotes on 61 and 45.

In 1983, the US bishops supported the formation of the North American Conference of Priests for Korean Ministry, a group dedicated to promoting "the grassroots ministries of clergy and lay leaders in nourishing the spiritual and cultural needs of Korean immigrants and subsequent generations of Korean American Catholics."[25] More recently, in 2011, the National Assembly of Filipino Priests Serving the Church in the USA was established to support Filipino priests in their ministry and promote greater collaboration among them. Such organizations mirror the formation of groups like the National Black Catholic Clergy Caucus, founded in 1968, or PADRES, an association for Mexican-American priests, founded in 1969, which sought to combat discrimination and influence policymaking within the church.

Other national organizations, conferences, and gatherings have likewise worked to promote pastoral and educational initiatives. Founded in 1978, the North American-Chinese Catholic Clergy, Religious, and Laity Association, for instance, has since 1981 coordinated the North American-Chinese Apostolate Convention. In 1989, representatives of American religious orders that had previously been involved in overseas missions to China founded the US Catholic China Bureau (later renamed the US-China Catholic Association), which works to educate American Catholics about the needs of the church in China and to promote rapport between the Catholic community on both sides of the Pacific. Another source of intercultural engagement has occurred as a result of the growing number of vowed Asian members within American Catholic religious congregations of men and women. Religious communities with international membership, in particular, have become advocates for cultural diversity within the church. The Society of the Divine Word, for instance, a missionary order founded in 1875, has in recent decades consciously incorporated respect for Asian-American culture as integral to the religious formation of its members. The Maryknoll Sisters, who accepted their first Asian vocation in 1927 and later established novitiates in China and the Philippines, have similarly come to embrace intercultural Catholicism as part of their community identity.[26]

One of the clearest signs of growing Asian-American presence within the US church and confirmation of their importance to the faith

---

[25] *Harmony in Faith: Korean American Catholics* (Washington, DC: USCCB, 2015), 27–30.

[26] Cindy Yik-yi Chu, *The Maryknoll Sisters in Hong Kong, 1921–1969: In Love with the Chinese* (New York: Palgrave Macmillan, 2004), 26.

has been the appointment of Asian Catholics to positions of episcopal leadership. With his appointment as auxiliary bishop of San Francisco in 2003, Ignatius Wang became the first Asian-American member of the church hierarchy in the United States. That same year, Vietnamese-born Dominic Luong was named an auxiliary bishop for the Diocese of Orange, in Southern California. One year later, Oscar A. Solis became an auxiliary bishop of Los Angeles and the nation's first Filipino bishop. In 2017, he was named the bishop of Salt Lake City, making him the first Asian American to lead a diocese. Their presence in episcopal leadership has had a direct impact on the pastoral messaging and activities of the US bishop's conference. Bishop Solis, for example, as chair of the US bishops' Subcommittee on Asian and Pacific Island Affairs, has worked to implement the pastoral priorities laid out in the bishops' statements on Asian and Pacific Island Catholics of 2001 and 2018. The increased presence of members of their own communities within the clergy and hierarchy offers a hopeful sign for greater cultural understanding and sensitivity within the US church, especially in light of Asian-American Catholics' concern that the US church "forces them to be like everyone else" or that it judges them according to a romanticized view of Asians as "model minorities."[27]

DEVOTIONAL LIFE AND CULTURAL PRACTICES

As their presence in the United States has grown, one way that Asian-American Catholics have added a richness and vibrancy to the church has been through their strong devotional life and distinct cultural practices. In an effort to preserve and celebrate their heritage, they have brought to parish life a range of religious rituals and customs that celebrate the union of Catholic and Asian culture in unique and distinctive ways. But their practices have also reawakened debate within the church over the nature and limits of religious inculturation. As a result, the degree to which eastern and western religious cultures are compatible has become one of the major themes taken up by Asian-American theologians and pastoral leaders.

Across these groups, many maintain a fervent devotion to Mary, a figure who functions as a source of Catholic unity and identity for Asian-American Catholics, not only linking them together across their

---

[27]   On these concerns, see Linh Hoang, OFM, "The Asian American Experience and Catholic Studies," in *The Catholic Studies Reader*, ed. James T. Fisher and Margaret M. McGuinness (New York: Fordham University Press, 2011), 295–296.

ethnic and national lines, but also connecting them spiritually to the universal church and to the local church in their homelands. For those who came to the United States as immigrants and refugees, the memory of Marian prayers, rituals, and symbols from their respective homeland has often provided a source of solace, strength, and inspiration amid relocation and adaptation. Chinese-American Catholics, for instance, honor Our Lady of China, who is said to have appeared along with a fiery horseman (believed to be St. Michael) in Donglu village in Hebei, China, amid the Boxer Uprising (1899–1901) to protect local Christians from the soldiers. In thanksgiving, the local Chinese pastor commissioned a painting of Mary with the Christ Child dressed in golden imperial robes, a sign of her embrace of Chinese culture.

Marian devotion is equally strong among Filipino and Vietnamese Catholics, who have embraced her in various forms, both those of European origin – such as Our Lady of Fatima – and those distinct to their own native countries. For Filipinos, great honor is given to the Virgin of Antipolo, a wooden statue of Mary that accompanied the Spanish Governor-General Don Juan Niño de Tabora in 1626 on his voyage from Acapulco, Mexico, to the Philippines. Convinced that the Marian statue enabled him to survive storms and fire onboard, henceforth, as a sign of protection all ships traveling the route carried the Marian statue, which also became known as Our Lady of Peace and Good Voyage. Among Vietnamese Catholics, distinct honor is given to Our Lady of La Vang, named for the site north of Huế, in Quaüng Tri province, where Mary is believed to have appeared to the local population. Persecution led the Catholics to seek safety in the La Vang jungle, where under a banyan tree, while reciting the rosary, there occurred an apparition of a beautiful and radiant woman in white holding a baby. She announced her name as Blessed Mother, or *Đức Me* in Vietnamese, and consoled them and made known she would answer their prayers.

While this devotional culture helps Asian-American Catholics maintain transnational connections and sustain distinctive national identities in a multicultural US Church, it has also helped to integrate them into American parish life. Like immigrant Catholics of earlier eras, Asian Catholics have worked to secure places of honor within their parishes for their statues, icons, and other religious symbols, and have established confraternities, sodalities, prayer groups, and other organizations to promote their own particular devotions. These efforts also foster a more intimate sense of community and belonging within parishes, helping members overcome the isolation and loneliness many encounter in an American church that can come across as cold and unwelcoming. Some of these groups are highly organized, and have helped Asian-American Catholics cultivate lay leadership and gain a voice in parish affairs. Devotional practices have also helped make Asian-American presence known on a national level, as can be seen with the Marian Days celebration in Carthage, Missouri. First held in 1978, this annual summer pilgrimage now brings together tens of thousands of Vietnamese Catholics from across the United States for four days of prayer and devotion, accompanied by a celebration of Vietnamese culture and heritage.

As the Asian-American Catholic population has grown, their religious practices have increasingly become an established part of the liturgical and devotional calendar in American parishes. Those with a strong Filipino presence, for instance, will often perform passion plays during Lent and gather on Easter morning for *Salubong*, a procession that commemorates when the resurrected Jesus met Mary, his mother. Religious preparation for Christmas includes *Simbang Gabi*, a nine-day series of masses, traditionally held at dawn or in the predawn hours. A few weeks later, on the third Sunday of January, Filipinos celebrate *Sinulog*, a popular cultural festival that celebrates the feast of the Santo Niño, or Christ Child. A growing number of American parishes have also come to celebrate the lunar new year alongside their Asian-American members, who view the holiday as an important time of family celebration.

At times, however, the growth of Asian-American presence within the church has rekindled debates over whether certain Asian cultural practices are compatible with Catholicism. Most prominent among them is the question of ancestor worship, an issue that can be traced all the way back to the Chinese Rites Controversy of the late 1600s, when missionaries and church officials argued over whether Confucian rituals were religious or secular in nature and whether their practice could be tolerated without compromising Catholic teaching. Chinese, Vietnamese, and other Asian-American Catholics continue to grapple with the issue, which has led to ongoing negotiation between their cultural and religious identities. Despite objections on the part of some church leaders, defenders of these rituals of respect and gratitude for one's ancestors maintain that they mirror long-standing Catholic practices, like the honor given to the dead on All Souls' Day.

As they straddle East and West, Asian-American Catholics have brought an important voice to debates over interreligious dialogue and religious pluralism. One of the most prominent figures has been the Vietnamese-born priest and theologian, Peter Phan, a member of the faculty of Georgetown University, who has served as past president of the Catholic Theological Society of America. He immigrated to the United States with his family in 1975 as part of the wave of wartime refugees. In his writings, he has drawn on his cultural background to advance arguments affirming the belief that the Holy Spirit is at work in non-Christian religions. But the concern that such views were at odds with official church teachings on the nature of salvation prompted doctrinal investigations by both Vatican officials and the US bishops.[28] While controversial, his work reflects a larger effort on the part of Catholic theologians and pastoral leaders to recognize the fluid dynamics of faith within and across cultures.

CONCLUSION

While it may be too soon to gauge the full impact that Asian-American growth has had on US Catholicism, the example of the Basilica of the National Shrine of the Immaculate Conception in Washington, DC, points to the transformations that are already underway. A place of spiritual and symbolic importance for Catholics in the United States and host to many important national Catholic gatherings, the basilica pays tribute to Mary as she is known and honored by the many peoples who have made a home in the United States. While many of the images located throughout the space depict Mary as she is known to Catholics of European descent, several recent additions call attention to Asian-American presence in the church. In 2012, the Basilica blessed panels depicting Our Lady of Korea at Cana and Our Lady of the Korean Martyrs, which were received as gifts from the Korean-American community. That same year marked the tenth anniversary of the dedication of a mosaic honoring Mary, Our Lady of China, which depicts her in traditional Chinese attire. In the lower church, there are chapels to Our Lady of Antipolo and Our Lady of La Vang, which draw thousands of Filipino and Vietnamese visitors per year.

These sacred images and the space they claim are a testament to the faith and presence of Asian American in the US church. Like the statements issued by the US bishops cited at the start of this chapter, they remind us of the need to include Asian Americans more fully into the story of US Catholicism, one that recognizes their long-standing presence in the nation and their immense contributions to the faith. Our

---

[28] Peter C. Phan, *The Joy of Religious Pluralism: A Personal Journey* (Maryknoll, NY: Orbis Books, 2017).

narratives need to be enriched through a greater appreciation for how hope, endurance of faith in local circumstance, leadership, and piety and devotion have been, and will remain into the future, a core experience for Chinese, Japanese, Filipino, Vietnamese, Korean, and other Asian-American Catholics. Their story of confident presence and deep faith is essential to understand American Catholic history.

FURTHER READING

Burns, Jeffrey M., Ellen Skerrett, and Joseph M. White, eds. *Keeping Faith: European and Asian Catholic Immigrants.* Maryknoll, NY: Orbis Books, 2000.

Cherry, Stephen M. *Faith, Family, and Filipino American Community Life.* New Brunswick: Rutgers University Press, 2014.

Hoang, Linh, OFM. "The Faith and Practices of Asian American Catholics: Generational Shifts." *New Theology Review* (February 2010): 48–57.

Kim, Simon C. and Francis Daeshin Kim. *Embracing Our Inheritance: Jubilee Reflections on Korean American Catholics (1966–2016).* Eugene, OR: Pickwick Publications, 2016.

Phan, Peter C. *Vietnamese-American Catholics.* New York: Paulist Press, 2005.

18 Cultural Catholicism

TOM BEAUDOIN

AN ERA OF CHANGE AND CRISIS

In the opening decades of the twenty-first century, the matter of who stays Catholic, and how, has become one of the most important questions in American Catholicism. Research about Catholics going their own way captured the attention of the public in general and Catholic leadership in particular, and focused on the notable drop-off in participation in Catholic ritual life, an increasing political independence of the laity from the wishes of Catholic bishops, a widespread abhorrence at the continuing revelations of clerical sexual abuse and episcopal cover-up, and enduring resistance toward active church involvement from post–Vatican II generations.

In addition to a raft of widely reported social research, social media amplifies voices of cultural influencers who leave active affiliation or depart the church altogether, peopling public awareness of slippage from Catholicism. What is distinctively "Catholic" about this crisis of affiliation is a matter of debate. Cultural Catholicism refers to a widespread downturn in Catholic Church participation. Part of the responsibility for the expansion of cultural Catholicism in recent decades seems to belong to the action or inaction of the Catholic hierarchy, while a considerable amount has to do with broader cultural changes affecting established mainline religious institutions well beyond the Catholic Church. Understanding the reasons that baptized Catholics create a form of life and faith at some remove from the Catholic Church is crucial for a church that has historically presumed and encouraged obedience and affiliation, whether in traditionalist or progressive forms. What neither traditionalist nor progressive twentieth-century models of Catholic identity imagined or encouraged, however, was that large proportions of baptized Catholics would not find the church itself compelling enough to stay connected. Far from being just a matter of a temporary adolescent "vacation" from church practice, what the rise of cultural Catholicism opens up is the prospect of baptized Catholics never returning to active or even modest practice and not supporting the church's political aims, however much these Catholics might respect individual Catholic leaders and love their own Catholic forebears.

Perhaps the greatest contemporary concern on the part of Catholic leaders, older-generation Catholics, and recent-immigrant Catholic parents, is the willingness of great numbers of teenagers and young adults to dispense with what has been considered the richly complex, universal, and indeed "salvational" heritage of Catholic tradition. A great deal is at stake in acknowledging and understanding cultural Catholicism, including families' and communities' capacity to stretch to include a range of affiliations, and the Catholic Church's viability and attractiveness as a credible and vital public presence. New terms are in widespread circulation for young Catholics who do not find official church rituals or teachings compelling, including "Dones" (done with Catholicism) and "Nones" (claiming no religious affiliation regardless of baptism or upbringing). Catholic high schools, colleges, and universities struggle to respond creatively to what feels like a spreading sea change in students' spiritual lives and a major decline in everyday Catholic "buy-in." For the middle classes, these matters stay a part of familial deliberation, and sometimes debate, into adulthood, as college students increasingly "boomerang" back home for years after graduation. A growing "cultural Catholicism" represents both change and crisis for American Catholicism.

A COMPLEX DEVELOPMENT

That most people in the United States who are baptized Catholic do not regularly participate in the officially specified acts of the faith is one of American Catholicism's open secrets. Catholicism is a religion, in the main, of modest affiliation. As a simple measure, in many urban and suburban areas, the majority of persons baptized Catholic attend Mass infrequently at best.

This widespread demurral might be unremarkable – after all, earlier eras saw marginal involvement by large numbers of Catholics in official church life – and yet it is important, for at least three reasons.

First, it matters because it marks a change from an earlier, more consolidated Catholic culture, a divergence that illustrates transitions in the US Catholic Church and in the society of which it is a part. This dramatic shift betokens a crisis for a church built on expectations about participation by, and control of, people that are officially presumed to be baptized members. This crisis has been met by a variety of creative though relatively ineffective responses by Catholic institutions.

Second, fracturing affiliation matters because it has been unassimilable to the story the church tells about itself; it has been an "open secret." While various brokers of Catholic identity (church leaders, clergy, Catholic intellectuals) have over time increasingly acknowledged the affiliational rupture, institutional Catholic efforts to learn from marginally affiliated or disaffiliated persons have been rare. Cultural Catholics are frequently treated as "fallen away," their lack of assent or involvement interpreted as a loss for themselves and the Catholic Church. A minor vocabulary has sprung up, uniformly derogatory: "bad Catholics," "nonpracticing," "fallen away," "lost," "inactive," "lapsed."

The third reason cultural Catholics matter is because paying attention to them tells something about American Catholicism – what it is and where it is going. This point is what authoritative brokers of Catholic identity have resisted. To admit it would require reimagining Catholic identity as something more pliable, porous, and pragmatic than was thinkable when Catholicism was socially ascendant, administratively governable, and given to cultural and religious consolidation in earlier centuries.

Despite this open secret, most Catholic families include "cultural Catholics," which for the purposes of this entry means those who were baptized Catholic and do not make official Catholic teaching or practice a central part of their lives. "Cultural Catholics" may or may not refer to themselves as Catholic. They may or may not participate in other spiritualities, religions, or ways of life. They may or may not engage in what they were taught were essential Catholic beliefs or practices. What joins them together, however, is that they were baptized as Catholics, and as adults they make other things the center of their lives than what brokers of Catholic identity would consider the marks of a "good Catholic" to be. Those marks might be weekly Mass attendance, active participation in official or local sacramental life, or avowal of certain beliefs and customs.

In other words, cultural Catholicism is not a clear and stable set of practices or beliefs. It is always relative to what people have been *taught* is central to the faith. There is not one single definition of Catholic identity taught by brokers of the faith (such as popes, bishops, priests, religious educators, and academic theologians.). Yet it has been typical of American Catholicism that a cluster of beliefs and practices are presented as normative, as defining "good Catholics." What that is can be described in general to some degree (belief in God as Trinity, weekly reception of Eucharist), but is always rooted in the local varieties of Catholic knowledge that has helped create what counts as a good Catholic in a particular context.

Few people are neutral about cultural Catholicism because the phenomenon essentially embodies conflict about who has the right or authority to tell whom how to live. But even the label "cultural Catholicism" itself introduces biases, ruling certain persons and experiences in and out, suggesting that we should remain skeptical of and curious about whom any Catholic labels serve – including this one. Such caution is especially the case because religious labels have a history of excluding some classes of persons from dignity or legitimacy. Indeed, religious labels frequently assist in creating and perpetuating disadvantage. The deeply ambiguous record of American Catholic treatment of the church's ethnic and sexual minorities, as well as of women, should chasten any embrace of a new term for marginally affiliated or disaffiliated persons. The ways that shifts in Catholic practice are labeled reflect specific Catholic discourses and have real-world effects: not just effecting exclusion, but providing an identity in which people can reside to make sense of their lives. It is fair to ask: Is "cultural Catholicism" the most adequate term? Is it even coherent?

"Cultural Catholicism" is helpful insofar as it opens awareness to the ways that the larger culture qualifies and modifies Catholic practice and belief. In other words, whatever one does with one's Catholic heritage and identity, it must be made to fit the world in which one lives. The introduction of the notion of "culture" into Catholic identity usefully questions the inherited universalizing of European, male, white governance that has been so determinative for US Catholicism. At the same time, the label "cultural Catholic" is also negative and marginalizing because of the way that it paints nonnormative affiliates – cultural Catholics – as less than "pure," "true," or "real" Catholics. Everyone knows that Catholic leaders do not aspire to make "cultural Catholics" in the sense of relative detachment from the circuit of assents and activities of "the faith" as prescribed. At a deeper level, however, "cultural Catholics" are ostensibly what American Catholic leaders want, in-depth: adherence to the essentials of the faith – in local terms. In other words, "cultural Catholicism" can be a way of talking about strengthening the church's mission and energizing its structures when it means that people are living broadly shared, officially endorsed, or tolerated Catholic values, in ways that are highly local, suitable to their families, work environments, and society. A further drawback of referring to nonnormative affiliates as "cultural Catholics" is that the name draws attention away from the way in which *all* baptized Catholics are necessarily cultural Catholics: no one lives outside a culture or cultures.

Another popular term is "Nones," who exceed but include substantial numbers of baptized Catholics who claim adherence to no religion. This term emphasizes that refusal of religious allegiance is a live modern option, motivating large numbers of people. "Nones" direct attention to the variety of ways that people find what is significant about life, living with integrity without recourse to established religious traditions. At the same time, a normative way of life still shadows the concept of "Nones," because the implied contrast to "None" is "Some" or "All." In other words, to be a "None" is to lack something otherwise well-established and sustaining: a religious identity. The term "Nones" does little to question how baptized Catholics might decelerate or even retire their affiliation while actually retaining aspects of their religious upbringing (thereby remaining a "some"), or how a Catholic upbringing might include space for becoming "none." Just as the term "cultural" can romanticize "pure," so too can the term "none" perpetuate fictions that there are people who are by contrast "some" Catholic or "all" Catholic.

What are we talking about, then, when we talk about "cultural Catholics" or similar labels? We should understand that the practice of assigning a name like "cultural" or "none" to oneself or others is part of the experience of an available "parking space" in and from which to manage cultural shifts today. Such an available space comes with a ready-made armature of words to give provisional anchor – words like "diversity," "journey," "spirituality" – in which many take refuge for holding life together.

In the long run, "secular Catholic" may prove a useful alternative label. The obvious analogy is to secular Jews, who like Catholics also came from a strongly ethnically-bounded immigrant heritage and who over time have landed largely in the middle class, decelerated official religious participation, and have substantial rates of intermarriage, in part by redefining and detaching in some measure from what used to count as religious and ethnic heritage. For many European-descended secular Catholics, there may also be parallels to the privilege of being counted as white like many secular Jews. Invoking a "secular Catholicism" also points to contemporary debates over the nature of secularity. Its defenders characterize secularity as freedom from outdated religious worldviews and freedom for new ways of making life matter. Secularity's critics see secular culture as a Western export meant to legitimize market values and capitalist violence. Nevertheless, "secular Catholic," too, has limitations. For one thing, there is not one kind of secularity. Moreover, while marginally affiliated and disaffiliated baptized Catholics tend to fall on the more progressive end of the political spectrum, not all would agree that secularity describes what has become of their Catholicism.

These scholarly labels should never be held so tightly that the experiences of real people are lost. The concepts we use for understanding American Catholicism, like "secular Catholics," must answer to lived experience even as it "organizes" what counts as Catholic experience. Indeed, how many cultural Catholics would rather not think of themselves as Catholics at all? Likewise, in naming nonnormatively affiliated Catholics, scholars must be careful of uncritically repeating doctrinal assumptions, such as that once one is baptized, that baptized identity can never be undone or modified.

Whether "cultural" or "secular" Catholicism is the more fitting descriptor for persons baptized Catholic, it is evident that one sanction culture is collapsing – and for many it has already fully cratered. "Sanction culture" refers to both the penalties (a sanction imposed) and benefits (a sanction granted) for showing one's good standing in a religious community.

American Catholicism used to broadly punish those who broke with its norms and reward those who participated in its prescriptions. From familial and congregational censure or even ostracism to a deeply felt sense of guilt, shame, and sin, penalties were effective. Equally motivating were benefits such as finding a marriage partner, job connections, maintenance of ethnic livelihood and connection to country of origin, and assurance of salvation. All of these sanctions, "debits" and "credits," have eroded and they are no longer motivating for many Catholics, especially those whose families have been in the United States for more than a few generations.

In its place, another sanction culture (call it "secular") has arisen for those baptized Catholic. Here, the penalties pertain to being seen and treated as backward for having parochial beliefs or practices, where parochial means blocking relational bridges with others who are "different." The benefits include being seen and treated as mature for having beliefs and practices that bridge well to "others," not judging them, with each person having the right to their own moral compass so long as it does not infringe on others' right to navigate their lives.

A lack of fit between Catholicism as taught by its identity brokers (priests, teachers, bishops, popes, parents), and the new sanction culture creates a space for cultural Catholics. Into this space flood a number of baptized Catholics who have substantially revised their commitment relative to the expectations of the church of their baptism, whether decelerating involvement in expected Catholic practices or avowing significant other-than-prescribed beliefs.

In the first and second decades of the twenty-first centuries, the Pew Research Center reported that leaving the church is something that half of all baptized US Catholics have done at some point in their lives and that around 40 percent exit for good (whether by no longer thinking of themselves as Catholics or by identifying as Catholic but not practicing). In recent decades, the Catholic Church has fared the worst among US denominations, or religious traditions, in attrition. People who leave Catholicism outnumber people who join the church by a ratio of four-to-one. More than 10 percent of all Americans are former Catholics, and this percentage is slightly higher for teens and young adults.

Other studies found that the decision to decelerate involvement in, or step away entirely from, practice or affiliation comes early for many Catholics. One large study of young adults revealed that three-quarters of those surveyed had decided to leave the church in their teens. Pew calculated that were former Catholics to be considered their own religion, they would be the third-largest community in the United States. Indeed, in the United States and many other countries, adults reporting "no religion" are overall the second-largest "religious" category, conspicuous by nonaffiliation.

Baptized Catholics are leading the way to nonaffiliation in many of these countries, especially in the Americas and Europe. Numbers of Catholics receiving sacraments of baptism, communion, confirmation, and marriage are in decline in the United States relative to the Catholic population, and for the last few decades the sacrament of penance or "confession" has virtually disappeared in practice in many places. Mass attendance shows a downward trend, with commonly one-quarter at most being regular attenders. As is well known, the number of men receiving the sacrament of ordination has been in a downward trend for decades. American Catholicism has not yet seen the bottom of these rates of affiliation and sacramental participation.

Despite large numbers of immigrant Catholics in recent decades, the Catholic population has not grown accordingly due to the large numbers of cultural Catholics. The relationship between Catholic advocacy for immigrants and the church's substantial losses of cultural Catholics is a complex phenomenon. The Catholic Church has historically been a vigorous and effective protector of immigrants as part of its social teaching commitments. Without substantial numbers of immigrants, the Catholic Church would be in more open free-fall. Yet these immigrant families are likely to see their second or third generations decelerate Catholic participation. It may well be that a ceiling on the proportion of cultural Catholics relative to the "normatively practicing" Catholic population will eventually be reached due to their lower birth rates.

Cultural Catholics are not, *ipso facto*, a representative cultural sample of the overall baptized Catholic population. Research indicates that they are more likely to be white, middle class, moderate to progressive, and not first-generation. This represents the more secure, less at-risk, and more privileged plurality of Catholics. It also happens to be the most de-ethnicized segment of the church. Will this change as demographics of baptized Catholics continue to change?

Cultural Catholicism as a public stance seems as casually open as ever in popular culture. The list is extensive and includes, for example, comedian Paul Rodriguez ("I'm not practicing, but I've made a commitment to the jewelry"), author Joyce Carol Oates ("You're born Catholic and you're baptized, then you become a lapsed Catholic for the next 90 years"), and the lead singer of Soundgarden, Chris Cornell (who described himself as a "freethinker" and ended up in marriage joining the Greek Orthodox Church). For all three artists, their early Catholic experience has proven influential for their adult creativity, but like many baptized Catholics, their relation to Catholicism eventually hit escape velocity.

Frank public confessions of leaving the church, which run the gamut from reactive to sophisticated, are notable public displays, indicating and furthering widespread acceptance of Catholic disaffiliation. On the internet, Wikipedia maintains a site listing "former Roman Catholics" that, while extensive, is but a small list of notable names. Such internet lists must be read carefully for what is meant by "former Catholic."

The effect of these public "defections" from normative Catholicism, apart from the opprobrium they receive from a vocal minority of traditionalist Catholics, is to help clear space in ordinary Catholic life, especially among younger generations, for a wide range of ways of relating to what Catholicism is "supposed" to be. This multiplication, and cultural-spiritual legitimation, of wider Catholic "subject positions" is one of the most effective causes and consequences of the emerging "cultural Catholicism."

Becoming a cultural Catholic, while a challenge and even a threat to the flourishing of the tradition as it has recently been imagined by its official brokers, does not necessarily spell the demise of Catholicism as a rich, long-standing tradition. Rather, it betokens the dispossession of an older Catholic culture and the artful embrace of, or inelegant backing into, new ways of living how Catholicism comes and goes. What are these new ways of living the Catholic heritage? They include deepening intercultural relationships and marriage within and outside of Catholicism, which will pose new questions about what still "works." New ways of living the heritage will also legitimate treating Catholic rituals as elective events, to be used as necessary, and the tradition as a social good insofar as it actually helps people hold their lives together in American society. Overall, these new ways are a looser tether to official Catholic authorities, more self-consciously pliable, porous, and pragmatic, while interest in the aesthetic, mystical, and to some degree intellectual and activist resources of the heritage will remain. So long as the major ordinary ethical discovery of a multireligious/nonreligious world continues to prevail – that one does not need to be "religious" to be a good person – these new ways of living the heritage are likely to continue. Perhaps the new forms of Roman Catholicism that are being lived by "cultural Catholics" will solicit genuinely new forms of official Roman Catholicism in the United States. It is not clear whether the brokers of Catholic identity can prudently facilitate such a transition.

KEEPING CULTURAL CATHOLICS CONNECTED TO CATHOLICISM

Priorities of the modern papacy have been shaped by the emergence of cultural Catholicism, in turn influencing American ministry and theology. From a different direction, the liberal Catholic theological tradition in the United States has operated as an ongoing acknowledgment of the fissures cultural Catholicism has opened up.

Catholic institutions generally recognize cultural Catholicism as a crisis, actively or passively influencing what goes on in churches, schools, and leadership structures (from the diocese to the Vatican). For the most part, baptized Catholics who notably decelerate their church participation, in belief or practice, are seen as threats to the future of American Catholicism. This has to do with how Catholic institutions imagine what American Catholicism might be and become, of how those who are charged with supervising Catholic identity conceive of the "spaces" in which baptized Catholics might "park."

In Catholic theology and ministry, there have been numerous attempts to identify and to recuperate those whom Catholic institutions tend to think of as "nonpracticing," "inactive," or "fallen away." In Catholic theology, the primary mechanism has been through invoking a distinctively Catholic way of being, called variously the "Catholic imagination," the "analogical imagination," or the "sacramental imagination."

This notion was the successful creation and elaboration of three white Irish-heritage American priests, each of them major figures in twentieth-century Catholic intellectual life. It was elaborated by theologian David Tracy (University of Chicago) in the 1980s in academic theology. It was given social-scientific buttressing and initial pastoral dissemination by sociologist, novelist, and church commentator Andrew Greeley (University of Chicago). Finally, it became instantiated in Catholic education by inclusion as the coda to theologian Richard McBrien's (University of Notre Dame) widely used survey of the faith titled *Catholicism*, an essential *vade mecum* for Catholic educators and ministers for decades.

The "Catholic," "analogical," or "sacramental" imagination is thought to be fostered by participating in Catholicism's liturgical, intellectual, and justice traditions, confirmed and concretized through innumerable everyday minor sacraments, or "sacramentals." This formation is said to shape a distinct sensibility: the sacred is experienced as present in and through everyday experience, such that the material world manifests the transcendent, and the finite shows forth the infinite. This imagination is thought to be curated when Catholics are nurtured in their faith amidst saints and icons and crucifixes, imbibing rich architectural aesthetics, and experiencing the stuff of the world, bread and wine, become body and blood on the altar. It is strengthened when these Catholics grow up knowing of the works of mercy and their witness to God's preferential presence in the poor. It is confirmed when Catholics learn of the trust in reason and confidence in humanism that is asserted to undergird the Catholic intellectual tradition.

The well-formed Catholic thus, according to this theory of the imagination, learns that the world is more like God than unlike God. The divine hovers startlingly, consolingly near in all things. In response, Catholics should address the world in a critically realistic way, simultaneously testing and trusting nature and sense experience, and the cultural practices in which they are caught up, as clues to divine origins and purposes. This imagination then is said to go forth from Catholicism's curative cradle into public art and thought, which can then be viewed in Catholic artists from musicians Bruce Springsteen and Madonna to novelists Flannery O'Connor and Walker Percy, and even to controversial artists Andres Serrano and Andy Warhol.

By the 1990s, this notion became part of the presumptive world by which most US Catholic theologians interpreted Catholic beliefs and practices inside the church and Catholic activities in the larger world. A substantial part of its power is that it purports to describe a deep structure inherent in Catholicism in its diverse eras, creative expressions, rituals, and cultures. It functions as an organizing concept for the extraordinary diversity of Catholic life around the world and within the United States.

The Catholic imagination is often used as a way of making sense of, and theologically embracing, cultural Catholics, including persons who are marginally affiliated with or disaffiliated from the Catholic Church. The idea is that no matter how far one strays from the Catholic cradle, one cannot but act on an analogical/sacramental disposition: you can take the person away from the church, but you cannot take the church out of the person. All Catholics, no matter how distant from their baptized origins, can potentially be included in this vision for Catholic identity, which is more existentially encompassing than assent to doctrines or participation in this or that ritual.

The idea of a Catholic imagination has been successful at least in part because it aggregates various data in a way that creates a positive space for continued affiliation for questioning Catholics in secularizing cultures. At the same time, it works because it is impossible to falsify. The notion of the sacramental imagination can positively incorporate endless amounts of contradictory, and potentially contrary, data. The notion works to make every possible contradiction into a positive confirmation so as to include people, no matter how far afield, in the Catholic sacramental project. For example, some persistent negative Catholic practices that contribute to decelerating affiliation are not included in the Catholic imagination, such as an all-male celibate clerical culture, white privilege in church governance, and clerical sexual abuse of minors. However, these can easily enough be assimilated to "sacramental imagination" by a negative mechanism when they are taken to be evidence for the incomplete hold that this imagination has on Catholics. More Catholic imagination would thus presumably solve whatever is causing the deceleration of affiliation.

It may be that the analogical imagination is a creative but ultimately unsuccessful twentieth-century attempt to create an adherence structure, a way of imagining membership that would keep people connected to the church. The analogical imagination tried to keep

Catholics, especially educated "modern" Catholics, connected by making a progressive notion of "mediation" part of the definition of being Catholic. To be Catholic, according to the articulators of the Catholic imagination, is to experience God through the richness of the world as such. In other words, God is encountered not only or primarily through obedience to the church hierarchy or reception of official sacraments, but through the full natural-nurtural environment of human life: for example, the body and natural human capacities, Christian and human community, Jesus Christ, and the church. This wide notion of "mediation" helped many American Catholics find a parking space for themselves. In the process, Catholics who subscribe to the analogical imagination were encouraged to develop modern interpretations of church authority, giving them room to question and live as thinking Catholics. Catholics learned to embrace ways of living and forms of thinking about authority that made contextual sense in American culture. Such a critical interpretive approach, a unique kind of Catholic hermeneutics, was then seen as central to being Catholic itself.

"Catholic imagination" and its proposal of a broadly mediated reality in which the Catholic is necessarily entangled has, on the whole, failed to keep most Catholics in most places actively affiliated with the church. Of course, no single imaginative idea could do so. Rather than succeeding at adherence to the church and Catholic tradition, "Catholic imagination" became a language for educated and active progressive-minded Catholics to understand themselves. It allowed Catholics to distinguish between an inclusive and an exclusive Catholicism. And it allowed Catholics to distinguish themselves from mainline Protestants denominations. (However, there is no similar "Protestant imagination" discourse among American Protestants.)

In elaborating this distinctive identity, Tracy, Greeley, and McBrien were not only perspicaciously advancing a way of understanding Catholicism for the United States, they were also creatively rehearsing the grounds for their own Catholic identities and those of a generation. They built on the Second Vatican Council's advocacy of conscience, dialogue, and justice as hallmarks of modern Catholic life. "Catholic imagination" is a founding conviction of Catholic Studies centers in Catholic higher education and other progressive Catholic sites where a Catholic vision cannot be presumed and must now be valorized. It continues to find new adherents and provides a welcoming "parking space" for those struggling to understand how they are both Catholic and committed to the "secular" world and its best values.

A conservative counterpart to the liberal advocacy of a distinctive imagination is the "New Evangelization." This was a church-wide attempt to reengage persons baptized Catholic, to teach them about the faith and invite them back to active affiliation. First articulated in the 1970s, it was broadly pronounced in the 1980s by Pope John Paul II, and emphatically programmed by Pope Benedict XVI in the 2000s. It was a multipronged effort to communicate the gospel, not to non-Christians, but to baptized Catholics. It was to be "new in ardor, methods, and expression." In other words, the New Evangelization would manifest vibrant faith in Christ and the church, would innovate new forms of communicating the gospel, and would find new language and images for gospel truth that spoke to the cultural Catholics of the day.

Extraordinary ecclesial resources were devoted to technologies, conferences, and ministries to fuel this attempt at a renewed Catholic vibrancy within churches and in society more broadly. John Paul II devoted himself tirelessly to youth around the world in service of such evangelization, staging huge masses and rallies meant to renew and solidify the faith. He shared a stage with American musician Bob Dylan and interpreted his song "Blowin' in the Wind" for modern searching Catholics. Benedict XVI emphasized the threat that the loss of the Christian moral and intellectual tradition represented for the West and sped up efforts to institutionalize the New Evangelization at the ground level. Pope Francis has emphasized some elements of the approach and muted others, eschewing didacticism and moralizing to emphasize a compassionate face of the church as evangelizing.

The New Evangelization was born from affiliation crisis. As the Second Vatican Council's liberalizing effects broke across the international church, some raised the alarm that an approach to Catholic identity and practice emphasizing ecumenical inclusivity, cultural accommodation, and local control were insufficient to counter social forces that were peeling Catholics away from formerly culturally and religiously uniform settings. Some of this peeling was "cultural Catholicism" in the sense of claiming Catholic identity but not practicing and believing what the hierarchy propounded, some of it was a melt into casual affiliation or disaffiliation in favor of "secular" pluralistic values and ways of life, and some of it was the loss of Catholics to evangelical and Pentecostal traditions.

The New Evangelization pictured these migrations of baptized Catholics away from prescribed belief and practice as a crisis of evangelization. By this was meant that baptized Catholics in formerly strong

Catholic communities had not been sufficiently "catechized," or taught the faith, and that a renewed personal encounter with Christ in the sacramental life of the church was required. The New Evangelization thus thought of the rise of cultural Catholicism after Vatican II as a problem of pedagogy and sought to change religious education, preaching, liturgy, and other forms of ecclesial formation to respond. According to the world's Catholic bishops, the church faced an "educational emergency."

Moreover, forays into the public square were taken to engage Catholics in need of evangelization by bringing Catholic teaching to the great matters of the day, such as the dignity of life, the erosion of morality, the challenge of secularization and erosion of Christian heritage, the limits of consumer capitalism, and the fragility of the environment. Over time, a range of forces was blamed for tempting Catholics away from the faith or making Catholic practice difficult. These included popular media, consumerism, individualism, and secularism. Pope Benedict XVI famously decried the "dictatorship of relativism" that countered the gospel taking root.

Cultural Catholics thus are at the center of the most deliberate international pastoral program of the Roman Catholic Church in the last fifty years. Dioceses and archdioceses around the United States have hosted evangelization trainings and made evangelization a focus for liturgy, religious education, retreats, and home and work spirituality. On the national scene, motivational speakers such as Matthew Kelly and Scott Hahn address concerns of youth and showcase the witness of recent converts; Colleen Carroll Campbell writes about the beauty of Catholic saints and material practices for young adults; Bishop Robert Barron offers accessible Catholics answers to American cultural questions; theologian Robert Imbelli teaches renewed Eucharistic commitment for a Christ-centered spirituality; and the Fellowship of Catholic University Students brings together Catholic college students as an intended contrast to the relativizing forces in higher education. The "Rebuilt" movement from the leaders of the Church of the Nativity in Timonium, Maryland, has become a model for a more centrist approach. (As in the American episcopal hierarchy, and in the articulation of the Catholic imagination, white men are substantially overrepresented as leaders.) These New Evangelization approaches typically emphasize personal piety, fidelity to the church and its hierarchy and teachings, the importance of lay initiative, and making Catholic faith effective in both daily life and in the face of the ills of American culture. Like the Catholic imagination, the New Evangelization has provided a "parking space." In this case, it has been a refuge for Catholics who experience American culture's pluralism of values as a challenge to the vitality of the Catholic faith. Despite the effort in the United States, however, there is little evidence for increased participation in the church. To the contrary, several decades into the New Evangelization, parishes have closed and consolidated around the country and Catholic participation (measured according to official rubrics) stands near record lows.

Cultural Catholicism in its many forms is strikingly robust and persistent. Despite its persistence, Catholic education, theology, and ministry in the United States have struggled to integrate its perspectives into official versions of Catholic self-understanding. Resistance to deep rethinking is widespread; the sexual abuse and cover-up crisis has not led to a thoroughgoing rethinking of Catholic identity, teaching, and governance; and the recent invention of an official "lay ecclesial ministry" by the hierarchy in the United States did not place lay Catholics in positions of ecclesial authority. Taking cultural Catholicism seriously on these fronts might have assisted (and might yet assist) in reconstructing ministry, theology, and teaching.

THE FUTURE OF CULTURAL CATHOLICISM

The challenge that cultural Catholicism poses to American Catholicism is similar to challenges faced by mainline Protestantism as well as branches of Judaism – in other words, long-standing religious traditions whose adherents gained widespread class status and whose public face and image have come to be counted as predominantly white in the American racial landscape.

However, the picture is considerably more nuanced than this. Generations of Latin American immigrants have often resisted performing Catholicism in ways that fit the expectations of leadership, for example in choosing worshiping communities beyond the local parish and blending Pentecostal and Catholic beliefs and practices. While nonwhite Latinx persons in the United States who were baptized Catholic do not disengage affiliation at the same levels as white non-Latinx persons baptized Catholic, recent studies suggest that appellations of "no religion" are rising steadily among Latinx persons, rivaling if not exceeding the number who identify as Pentecostal or evangelical. Attempts to recuperate and organize the faithfulness of Latinx persons baptized Catholic frequently invoke the sacramental imagination (in Latinx Catholic theology) and the New Evangelization (in Latinx and culturally mixed parishes). Insofar as "cultural Catholic" betokens a deceleration of belief and practice relative to leadership expectations, a variety of racial and ethnic heritages in the United States should be given attention in coming years to better understand dynamics of changing affiliation in the US Catholic Church.

Catholic institutions are reluctant to acknowledge the presence of widespread nonnormative affiliations. Beyond acknowledgment, however, is the difficult question of whether and how Catholic institutions might intentionally promote what is necessary and worthy about cultural Catholicism. This is no imposition of a foreign phenomenon. The plurality or majority presence of cultural Catholics has already effectively made many institutions that call themselves "Catholic" into "Catholic-heritage" institutions. The question is, then, what to do in response to remain vital and make the mission genuinely new while retaining the best of the past. Catholicism has become a "legacy" identity due to the rich variety of affiliations to which it gives rise, and due to Catholic leaders' inability to control the definition of identity in the emergence of a diverse cultural Catholic diaspora.

This fundamental shift in mindset to consider American Catholicism as constituted by "heritage" or "legacy" institutions (schools, hospitals, churches) will probably be resisted until this transition can be sufficiently grieved. Indeed, sponsoring creative mourning processes will be central to the vitality of American Catholicism as it navigates its future and as the "insider" brokers of its identity prepare to imaginatively acknowledge cultural Catholicism as an enduring and common outcome of American Catholicism. Mourning includes taking stock of what was noble about the earlier ways American Catholics understood themselves and also includes a respectful but determined process of handing over whatever it is about communal self-understanding, mission, and identity that are not sufficient yeses to a genuinely new future grounded in the lived experience of people today. If Catholic institutions can work through grief at the possible permanent loss of control over defining and managing a center for Catholic identity, and move to a more polycentric model, then they will be on the way toward being able to fulfill the charge of Vatican II to "preserve and promote" everything that is good in "other" religions, including presumably "other" worthy Catholic outcomes than those officially specified.

A further bridge to the future will be the recognition that thinking with and about cultural Catholics reveals the contingency and invented character of *all* Catholic designations. Such an understanding would move Catholic identity categories beyond binary options of "practicing" and "nonpracticing," "faithful" and "lapsed," and "normative" and "non-normative." As Richard Rodriguez has argued, Catholicism must and will become more "brown." This will happen with or without the Catholic Church's promotion of it, and it will be so not only with respect to continued immigration, intermarriage, and multiculturalization, but with respect to conceptions of who is "in" and who is "out" of Catholicism. One of the furthest theological horizons may prove to be official reconsiderations of what baptism means. Older theologies of baptism as a permanent mark, of "once Catholic always Catholic," may need to be rethought given the diversity of "parking spaces" being claimed by baptized Catholics.

In such reconsiderations occasioned by the presence of cultural Catholics, it is not a matter of the Catholic Church and allied institutions paternalistically deciding to "include" nonaffiliated persons, of exercising some religiously motivated largesse, in articulating the mission of Catholic institutions, but of coming to terms with the religious and nonreligious "other" who is always already "within," and what is more, coming to terms with the ways that religious and secular forms of construing reality create and maintain insiders and "the others" – with real-life effects for all in Catholic-heritage places.

Given the prevalence and complexity of cultural Catholicism, future interpretations of Catholicism in the United States will need to stand in the "wake" of Catholicism, with "wake" understood in three ways: as a *water trail*, as a *memorial*, and as an *awakening*: first, as a reverberative *water trail* created by a traveling watercraft, to acknowledge the wake will require coming to terms with what Catholicism has left behind; second, as a *memorial*, to articulate the wake will be to name what is passing away, to celebrate the life of the Catholic tradition by recollecting and celebration, including permission for mourning what has been lost. Finally, *awakening* suggests fearless attention to the styles of Catholicisms that go their own ways within and without normative expectations, as church leaders and all with a stake in the Catholic heritage sponsor ways of staying open to what affiliation or nonaffiliation can mean, in ever-new situations.

FURTHER READING

Bullivant, Stephen. *Mass Exodus: Catholic Disaffiliation in Britain and America Since Vatican II*. New York: Oxford University Press, 2019.

Carroll, Colleen. *The New Faithful: Why Young Adults Are Embracing Christian Orthodoxy*. Chicago: Loyola Press, 2002.

Dillon, Michele. *Postsecular Catholicism: Relevance and Renewal*. New York: Oxford University Press, 2018.

Greeley, Andrew. *The Catholic Imagination*. Berkeley: University of California Press, 2001.

John Paul II. *Redemptoris Missio: On the Permanent Validity of the Church's Missionary Mandate*, www.vatican.va

McCarty, Robert J. and John M. Vitek. *Going, Going, Gone: The Dynamics of Disaffiliation in Young Catholics*. Winona: St. Mary's Press, 2018.

Smith, Christian, Kyle Longest, Jonathan Hill, and Kari Christoffersen. *Young Catholic America: Emerging Adults In, Out of, and Gone from the Church*. New York: Oxford University Press, 2014.

White, Michael and Tom Corcoran. *Rebuilt: Awakening the Faithful, Reaching the Lost, and Making Church Matter*. Notre Dame: Ave Maria Press, 2013.

Part IV

Conclusion

19 US Catholicism in the Twenty-First Century

MARY L. GAUTIER

Sociology is not an exact science and sociological trends cannot be used with high confidence to predict the future of the Catholic Church in the United States. It is possible, however, to study the trends that lie in the data collected by the Center for Applied Research in the Apostolate (CARA) and other social scientists and to use those trends to formulate some educated forecasts of what may lie ahead for US Catholics in the near future. The research consulted for this chapter is organized into three broad areas: trends in Catholic population, trends in Catholic practice and beliefs, and trends in pastoral leadership. This should help to discern what may lie ahead for the twenty-first century.

TRENDS IN CATHOLIC POPULATION

In general, the Catholic population has kept up with overall US population growth over the last half of the twentieth and into the twenty-first century. Throughout that time, Catholics have comprised roughly one-quarter of the US population. Modest projections suggest that the number of US Catholics could approach 100 million by the middle of this century. Currently, the self-identified Catholic population in the United States is around 75 million. As such, Catholics are the largest single faith body in the United States[1] and their influence in US popular and religious culture is outsized. For example, when the Pew Research Center proclaimed "1 in 10 Americans is a Former Catholic," the headline made it appear that Catholics were suddenly leaving the faith in droves.[2] In actuality, the Catholic retention rate remains higher than

---

[1] Protestants outnumber Catholics in the United States and account for about half the total US population, but Protestants are comprised of close to two hundred discrete denominations.

[2] Russell Heimlich, "America's Former Catholics," June 13, 2008. http://pewresearch .org/fact-tank/2008/06/13/americas-former-catholics.

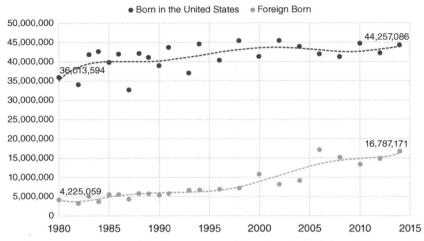

Figure 19.1

any single Protestant denomination.[3] But the sheer size of the Catholic population is such that former Catholics (i.e., those who were baptized Catholic but no longer identify themselves as Catholic), if they were counted as a separate denomination, would be larger than the most numerous Protestant denomination, Southern Baptists.

While some of this growth in Catholic population continues to be a result of immigration of Catholics from other countries, as was the case in previous centuries, most of it is due to natural increase. Nevertheless, about one in four adult Catholics now living in the United States is foreign-born, compared to about one in ten in 1980 (see Figure 19.1).

Immigration, particularly since the 1980s, has also increased the ethnic diversity of the Catholic population in parishes. Unlike the earlier nineteenth and twentieth-century waves of Catholic immigrants who came predominantly from western and southern Europe, much of Catholic growth at the end of the twentieth century and into the twenty-first century has been through immigration from other Catholic populations around the world, such as Latin America, Vietnam, the Philippines, southern India, and the French- and English-speaking

---

3   Mark M. Gray and Joseph C. Harris, "A Phantom Crisis: Are Catholics leaving the church in droves? Not really." *America* (July 21, 2008), https://americamagazine.org/issue/662/article/phantom-crisis.

countries of Africa. Just over one-half of all Catholics in the United States are non-Hispanic white, about four in ten are Hispanic/Latino, and the other 10 percent are non-Hispanic black, Asian, or Native American.[4] Increased racial and ethnic diversity is most pronounced in regions of the country where the Catholic population is growing most rapidly, in the South and in the West.

Regional Distribution

The Catholic population growth described above is not evenly distributed around the country, which is another important population trend of this century. Previous generations of Catholics, who arrived in the United States around the same time as the Industrial Revolution, tended to concentrate where the jobs were – in the cities of the industrial Northeast and the Midwest portion of the country that was later known as the Rustbelt. Large numbers also immigrated to the upper Midwest farming communities where they found opportunities in agricultural labor. The late twentieth- and twenty-first-century migration and immigration has been away from the Catholic ethnic neighborhoods in urban areas and into the suburbs, and away from the Rustbelt and into the Sunbelt states of the South and the West where jobs in technology, manufacturing, and the service economy are flourishing. Thus, Catholics are now nearly equally distributed in each of the four US Census regions instead of being concentrated mainly in the Northeast and the Midwest, with greater ethnic diversity in the South and the West (see Figure 19.2).

As a result, Catholic parishioners in different parts of the country experience very different realities; so much so that we can talk of "A Tale of Two Churches." The experience of Catholics in the Northeast and Midwest is one of decline and diminishment, with large numbers of under-utilized urban parishes closing to free up resources for funding and staffing parishes in the suburbs. Many parishes in the rural parts of those two regions are also being merged or closed to compensate for the declining number of priests available to administer parishes in areas where the population has diminished.

In contrast, Catholics in the South and West regions are dealing with explosive growth and must find ways to cope with chronic shortages.

---

[4]   Charles E. Zech, Mary L. Gautier, Mark M. Gray, Jonathon L. Wiggins, and Thomas P. Gaunt, *Catholic Parishes of the Twenty-First Century* (New York: Oxford University Press, 2017).

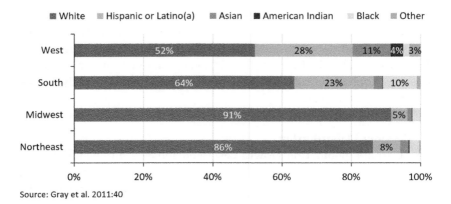

Source: Gray et al. 2011:40

Figure 19.2

Those parts of the country have never had a sufficient number of parishes or priests, and the surge in the numbers of Catholics moving into the Sunbelt over the last thirty or forty years has exacerbated those shortages. Particularly in the suburbs surrounding major population centers in the South and the West, it is quite common to find newer Catholic churches that seat 1,000–1,500 at a time, served by one priest and a large lay staff. Those parishes regularly offer multiple Masses over the course of a weekend, often in several languages in addition to English.

In fact, a 2013 CARA study located over 6,500 parishes – roughly one-third of all US Catholic parishes – that self-identify or are known to serve at least one particular racial, ethnic, cultural, and/or linguistic community. Some of these parishes serve two or even more distinct communities. They tend to be vibrant, active communities of faith, with many opportunities for involvement in parish and community activities outside of the regular worship services. These parishes, already the norm in most American suburbs, are likely to become increasingly common across the nation and into the future.

TRENDS IN CATHOLIC PRACTICE AND BELIEF

As mentioned above, the Catholic Church in the United States is increasingly a "tale of two churches." The near-empty pews in inner city ethnic parishes of the Northeast and abandoned rural parishes of the Midwest lead many Catholics in those areas to speculate about an apparent abandonment of the faith. They wonder why so few are at

Mass these days and express concern that Catholics in general – and young people in particular – must be leaving the church in large numbers. They worry that faith must be losing ground amid all the distractions of an increasingly complex and materialistic culture that presents religion as a commodity to be selected or rejected at will.

At the same time, parishioners in large suburban parishes in the South and the West also struggle with a shortage of resources. Their churches are too small and they have too few priests to handle the surging growth in Catholic population they have experienced in the last fifty years. They juggle the Mass schedule to deal with "parking lot paralysis" – when the cars leaving one Mass jockey with the cars entering the parking lot for the next Mass. They find creative ways to accommodate all the activities that come with a vibrant, growing parish – such as converting an old convent or rectory to meeting space, nursery space, youth group room, or senior center. They learned long ago that priests cannot possibly fill all the roles, so they recruited and formed lay people to serve as parish staff, catechists, leaders of sacramental preparation, and many other ministries that were formerly reserved for priests and religious sisters. At the same time, they worry whether churches have grown too large and impersonal so that people see the parish more like a "sacramental service station" than as a "community of the faithful."

Both of these realities – the shrinking church of the Northeast and Midwest and the flourishing church of the South and the West – worry about passing on the faith. They fear that younger generations of Catholics appear to be less committed to the faith than the generations before them. While a decline in commitment or attachment to the church is always a serious and valid concern, today's Catholics appear to have little cognizance that this concern was also expressed by previous generations. In fact, while each generation worries about passing on the faith to the next, Catholic identity remains strong and the absolute number of Catholics continues to grow. What is changing over time is the notion of what it means to be a Catholic.

Being a Catholic in the 1940s, 1950s, and even 1960s revolved around parish life. Catholics "belonged" to the parish in whose boundaries they lived. They derived most of their Catholic identity from their parish, with its expectation of regular attendance at weekly Mass, social events organized by the parish and its associated lay organizations, and even sports clubs organized by and for parishioners. Nearly every aspect of a person's life outside of secular employment was connected to the parish in some way.

This relationship has changed over time, however, as increased mobility has eroded the connection to a local parish and as increased assimilation into American culture has made Catholics more individualistic and less likely to identify with a particular community. Being Catholic today, therefore, is somewhat less a core identity and more just one of several characteristics (e.g., American, Washingtonian, Independent, baseball fan) that make up one's identity. This gradual shift in identity, where being Catholic is but one aspect of what makes you who you are, also affects many aspects of Catholic practice. We explore some of the important trends in Catholic practice in the next sections of this essay.

Mass Attendance

There has been some shift in Catholic practice over the past fifty years. Gallup poll data demonstrates a gradual decline in the percentage of Catholics who report attending services *in the past seven days* – from a high of about three in four in 1955 to a low of about four in ten in recent years.[5] Regardless of the methodological issues inherent in those data,[6] it is a fact that Catholics are less likely to place as much emphasis on attending Mass daily or even weekly than those who grew up in the church before Vatican II. This shift in Catholic culture occurred fifty years ago, however, and the decline in regular Mass attendance has been much more gradual since that time. Compared to pre–Vatican II Catholics (those born in 1940 or earlier), more than half of whom report attending Mass weekly or more often, members of each of the generations following them are less likely to report weekly attendance but more likely to report attending monthly or a few times a month. In other words, "monthly has become the new weekly" for Catholics. Catholic exceptionalism, then, may be slipping away as Catholics are as likely as their Protestant coreligionists to consider regular attendance to be less than weekly but more than occasionally.

Far from the perception that young Catholics are exiting the pews at alarming rates, however, recent CARA research shows that millennials, the youngest generation of adult Catholics (born 1982 or later), comprise one in every ten Catholics sitting in the pew on any given Sunday.

---

5   Lydia Saad, "Catholics' Church Attendance Continues Downward Slide," April 9, 2018. https://news.gallu.com/poll/232226/church-attendance-among-catholics-resumes-downard-slide.aspx.

6   See Mark M. Gray, "Sunday Morning: Deconstructing Catholic Mass attendance in the 1950s and now," March 21, 2011. https://nineteensixty-four.blogspot.com/2011/03/sunday-morning-deconstructing-catholic.html.

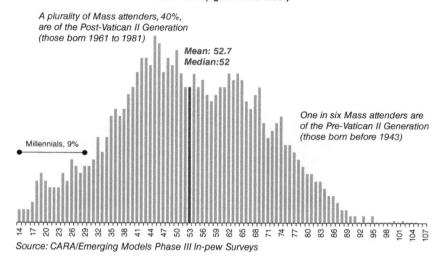

Age Distribution of U.S. Catholic Parishioners Surveyed In-pew, 2011–2012 (ages 14 and older)

A plurality of Mass attenders, 40%, are of the Post-Vatican II Generation (those born 1961 to 1981)

Mean: 52.7
Median:52

One in six Mass attenders are of the Pre-Vatican II Generation (those born before 1943)

Millennials, 9%

Source: CARA/Emerging Models Phase III In-pew Surveys

Figure 19.3

About one-half of Mass-attending Catholics ages fourteen and above are younger than age fifty – and the median age of Catholics in the pews is fifty-two (see Figure 19.3).

Core and Peripheral Catholics

Are the Catholics who are practicing the faith as committed as were previous generations? Father Joseph Fichter, SJ, a priest-sociologist of the last century, conducted one of the most thorough sociological studies of Catholics of the 1950s, the mythological "golden age," when Gallup was reporting that three in four Catholics were attending Mass weekly. What Fichter found, when he classified the Catholics he studied according to their level of participation in parish life, was that four in ten Catholics in the early 1950s were what he termed "Dormant Catholics." In his words, these individuals "have in practice 'given up' Catholicism but have not joined another religious denomination." Another 12 percent he classified as "Marginal Catholics," those who "are conforming to a bare, arbitrary minimum of the patterns expected in the religious institution." The largest group of Catholics he called "Modal Catholics" and described them as "normal 'practicing' Catholics constituting the great mass of identifiable Catholic laymen." Finally, Father Fichter named the most active Catholics he studied as

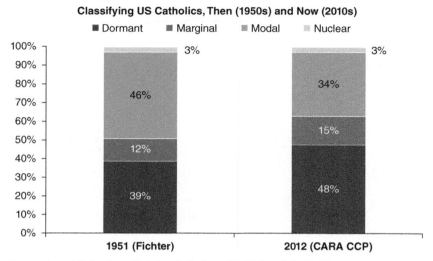

Figure 19.4

"Nuclear Catholics," and described that 3 percent as "the most active participants and the most faithful believers." In other words, perhaps the perception of a decline in attachment to the church is just that – a perception more than a real decline.

With data from CARA's national survey of self-identified adult Catholics conducted in 2012, we classified Catholics according to their self-reported Mass attendance to see how closely they conformed to Fichter's scale of Catholic participation. As Figure 19.4 shows, participation in Catholic parish life has not changed as much as some may think. The core, nuclear Catholics, who attend Mass weekly and say they are "very involved" in their parish, are still just 3 percent of Catholics. Modal Catholics, who attend Mass at least monthly, are 34 percent of all Catholics. Marginal Catholics, who attend Mass at Christmas and Easter but otherwise do not participate, are 15 percent of all Catholics, and those who still call themselves Catholic but do not attend Mass are 48 percent of all self-identified Catholics.

This comparison is not intended to provide comfort to lapsed Catholics, but to serve as a corrective to our common tendency to view the past through a rosy lens. Certainly the fact that nearly half of all self-identified Catholic adults never darken the doors of a church is no matter for celebration. But recognizing that four in ten Catholics were similarly alienated in the 1950s, when three in four were telling the Gallup pollsters that they had attended Mass in the past week, helps to paint a more realistic picture of the situation – then and now.

Other Sacramental Practice

Although Mass attendance has now stabilized at a somewhat lower rate than was customary fifty years ago, there is a more disturbing trend appearing in other sacramental practices. Fewer Catholics are getting married, fewer Catholic babies are being baptized, and the number of Catholic funerals has also been declining.

The number of infant baptisms fluctuates with the overall birth rate, and the effect of the post–World War II baby boom is readily apparent in Figure 19.5. Note, however, that the number of infant baptisms remained relatively consistent at around one million per year from 1970 through 2000, but has dropped steadily since that time to a low of just over 600,000 in 2018. Some of this drop is related to fewer Catholics marrying and fewer Catholics having children, but comparisons between US Vital Statistics for this same time period indicate that this trend may be more serious than just fewer Catholic babies. At its peak in the early 1960s, about one-third of all births resulted in a Catholic baptism. The number of baptisms roughly matched the proportion Catholic in the population from the mid-1970s through the end of the twentieth century, but since that time the rate of infant baptisms

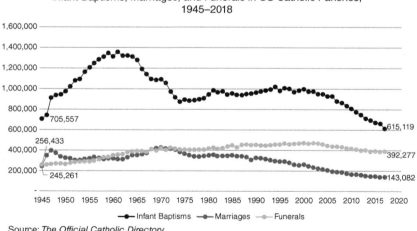

Infant Baptisms, Marriages, and Funerals in US Catholic Parishes, 1945–2018

Source: *The Official Catholic Directory*

Figure 19.5

to all US births has dropped below the proportion who are Catholic in the overall population. In other words, while Catholics are roughly a quarter of the US population today, only about one in five US births results in a Catholic baptism.

The number of Catholic funerals also increased very slowly between 1945 and 2000, from just about a quarter-million to nearly half a million. Funerals have been declining each year since 2000, though, at about 1 percent per year. Since Catholics are no more or less likely than non-Catholics to die, the decline in the number of Catholic funerals is another negative trend, suggesting that Catholics are a little less likely now than they were in previous generations to select a Catholic funeral for their loved ones.

Perhaps the most disturbing trend in this figure is the number of sacramental marriages, which has declined by 64 percent from its high point in 1970. Marriage rates in general have been declining throughout this time period, but the trend remains concerning because it points to the reality of a weakening institutional commitment among Catholics at a critically important stage in their life. The data suggest that in recent decades, Catholics who marry are increasingly likely to marry outside a Catholic setting, even when they marry another Catholic. In 1970, three in four Catholics who married got married in the church. Through the 1980s and 1990s, about half of Catholics married in the church. After 1996, a slow decline began and by 2016 only three in ten Catholic marriages were sacramental marriages.

This weakened attachment to the church at the time of marriage has a ripple effect throughout the lifecycle as well. Fewer marriages in the church between Catholics and non-Catholics result in fewer adult entries into the faith, since the most common reason given by non-Catholics for switching their religion is that they are married to (or marrying) a Catholic. And Catholic parents who have had their first child are less likely to bring that child to the church for baptism if they are not married in the church. Children who are not baptized are less likely than those who have been baptized to live in families who have a strong attachment to their local parish, so they are less likely to receive religious instruction or to take part in the other sacraments of the church.

Catholics are no less likely than non-Catholics in the United States to have children, to marry, or to die. The fact that they are electing to commemorate each of these lifecycle milestones outside the structures of the institution is a cause for consternation among those who are concerned about passing on the faith.

Many studies have been done and many programs have been developed to try to address the popular perception that Catholics are becoming less "Catholic" over time and losing their Catholic values in an ever-secularizing and materialistic popular culture. People lose sight of the reality, though, that this perception of an ever more diluted faith in a historically Protestant culture has always been the case. In fact, the Catholic parochial school system was developed in the mid-nineteenth century as a way to preserve the Catholic faith in the midst of a relatively hostile anti-Catholic culture. While US culture is perhaps less overtly anti-Catholic than it was in the past, Catholic schools (especially Catholic high schools) have proven to be effective transmitters of Catholic values and Catholic identity. Unfortunately, fewer than one in seven Catholic children of high school age are enrolled in Catholic high schools now, compared to about one in four in 1950.[7] This trend suggests that passing on the faith to new generations could be an increasing challenge for the church into the future.

Former Catholics

One of the major concerns among Catholics of the twenty-first century is whether those who have been baptized Catholic and perhaps even raised Catholic will continue to adhere to the faith in the future. The number of Americans who do not identify with any religion – identified in popular culture today as the "nones" because this is the option they select when asked about their religious affiliation – has been increasing throughout the twenty-first century, from a sixth of the population in 2007 to roughly a quarter of the population now.[8] Right now, due in part to the fact that the Catholic population is so large, the population of former Catholics is also disturbingly high. According to Pew Research, some 13 percent of US adults are former Catholics.[9] Unlike their Christian brethren, however, Catholics who leave the faith are unlikely to switch to another religion. Even Catholics who switch to an Evangelical church are unlikely to stay there. Therefore, most of the Catholics

[7] Bryan T. Froehle and Mary L. Gautier, *Catholicism USA: A Portrait of the Catholic Church in the United States* (Maryknoll, NY: Orbis Books, 2000), 73.

[8] Michael Lipka, "A Closer Look at America's Rapidly Growing Religious Nones," May 13, 2015. www.pewresearch.org/fact-fank/2015/05/13/a-closer-look-at-americas-rapidly-growing-religous-nones/.

[9] David Masci and Gregory Smith, "Facts about American Catholics," September 4, 2018. www.pewresearch.org/fact-tank/2018/09/04/07-facts-about-american-catholics/.

who leave the faith end up as agnostics, atheists, or "cultural Catholics" who no longer practice the faith.

Catholic Beliefs and Identity

Research has shown that there is something particularly resilient about being a Catholic. Catholics are more likely than any other Christian group, with the exception of Greek Orthodox and Mormon, to remain in the faith in which they were born (see Figure 19.6).

Even when Catholics are not actively practicing their faith, they still tend to self-identify as Catholic – occasionally referring to themselves as "fallen away" Catholic, "non-practicing" Catholic, "lapsed"

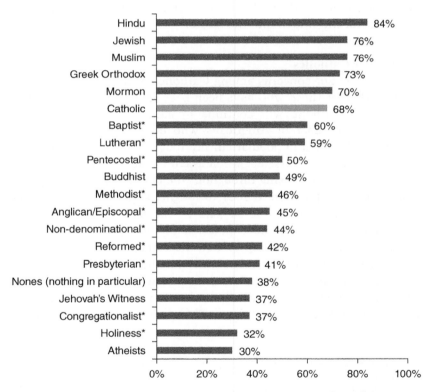

US Religious Retention Rates: Percentage of those raised in a faith who remain affiliated with that faith as an adult

Hindu	84%
Jewish	76%
Muslim	76%
Greek Orthodox	73%
Mormon	70%
Catholic	68%
Baptist*	60%
Lutheran*	59%
Pentecostal*	50%
Buddhist	49%
Methodist*	46%
Anglican/Episcopal*	45%
Non-denominational*	44%
Reformed*	42%
Presbyterian*	41%
Nones (nothing in particular)	38%
Jehovah's Witness	37%
Congregationalist*	37%
Holiness*	32%
Atheists	30%

'*' are Protestant denominations. Source: Pew Forum on Religion & Public Life (2008), U.S. Religious Landscape Survey, weighted data, including all respondents in continental U.S., Alaska, and Hawaii.

Figure 19.6

Catholic, or "cultural" Catholic. And at any given time, about one in eight Catholics now attending Mass has come back to the faith after falling away for a time.

In general, Catholics of all levels of commitment tend to agree on several different, but important, aspects of Catholic belief. The church's foundational theological beliefs and its sacraments are seen as core to their Catholic identity.[10] Three in four agree that belief in the resurrection of Jesus Christ is very important to them personally. Two in three agree that helping the poor is a very important part of their identity as a Catholic. About the same proportion agree as strongly that church teaching about Mary as the mother of God and the sacraments, such as the Eucharist, are important to their Catholic identity.

So just what does "fallen away" Catholic really mean? When CARA surveyed self-identified Catholics about their Lenten practice, Catholics who attend Mass at least monthly but less than weekly are only slightly less likely than weekly attenders to observe Lenten practices.[11] Even among Catholics who say they attend Mass a few times a year or less, four in ten say they abstain from meat on Fridays during Lent (a common Lenten practice). One in five Catholics who attend Mass a few times a year or less still pray the rosary at least a few times a year. Four in ten Catholics who attend Mass a few times a year or less say they are proud to be Catholic and strongly agree that they can be a good Catholic without going to Mass every Sunday.

In fact, one of the things that Catholics find most meaningful about the faith is the elasticity of this institutional bond. Almost nine in ten Catholics find personal meaning in the fact that they can disagree with aspects of church teaching and still remain loyal to the church. Even though they may not be attending Mass regularly, which they know the church teaches that they should be doing, they still feel confident in their identity as Catholics. They may disagree with other aspects of church teaching, such as the inadmissibility of contraception or gay marriage, but still feel comfortable identifying as Catholic. While they may elect to distance themselves from the

---

[10] See William V. D'Antonio, Michele Dillon, and Mary L. Gautier, *American Catholics in Transition* (Lanham, MD: Rowan and Littlefield, 2013).

[11] See Mark M. Gray and Paul M. Perl, *Sacraments Today: Belief and Practice among U.S. Catholics* (Washington, DC: Center for Applied Research in the Apostolate, 2008).

church for a time, Catholics still find comfort in the knowledge that the church is waiting for them, whenever they feel ready to return to more regular practice.

TRENDS IN PASTORAL LEADERSHIP

The third key trend that is affecting the Catholic Church in the United States now and into the future concerns changes in pastoral leadership. This trend intersects with the trend in the movement and growth of the Catholic population to exacerbate the tale of two churches that began this chapter.

The principal factors affecting this trend include an aging population of clergy, which has been declining in numbers since its peak in the late 1960s, the restoration of the diaconate as a permanent and stable order of ministry in the early 1970s, and a renewed understanding of the role of the laity in pastoral ministry, which came about as a result of Vatican II. We'll examine each of these factors in turn here and then describe how they have changed our understanding of pastoral leadership.

Aging and Diminishing Priest Population

The total number of Catholic priests ministering in the United States kept up with and even outpaced Catholic population growth during the first half of the twentieth century. There are many historical and socio-logical reasons for this growth, which occurred at a unique period in American history that was affected by waves of Catholic immigration, anti-Catholic prejudice in American society, modernism, and societal disillusion over a world seemingly mired in endless war and conflict. Many Catholic immigrant families considered a priest or a religious sister or brother to be a measure of social standing and they pressured their children to look for signs of a vocation in their lives. Likewise, the children and grandchildren of these Catholic immigrants also held the priesthood and religious life in a favorable light, believing it offered them an education and a much more comfortable lifestyle than the blue-collar life of an immigrant.

One outcome of this confluence of circumstances was an abun-dance of clergy and religious available to minister to the rapidly growing Catholic population. By 1950, the US ratio was one priest for every 650 Catholics, and there were so many parishes with multiple priests on staff that virtually all of the pastoral leadership was handled by priests and religious. Many religious sisters also ministered in parishes, often as directors of religious education or of liturgy. Laypeople helped out with various tasks when asked by the pastor, but virtually always in a voluntary, short-term capacity and always at the will of the pastor.

This abundance was short-lived, though, and the total number of US priests has dropped every year from its peak in the late 1960s. Some of this decline is due to a sizeable number of priests who left the priesthood in the decades immediately following the Second Vatican Council, but most is due to much smaller numbers of men entering seminaries to prepare for the priesthood. The number of men enrolled in theology in US seminaries declined by one-half between 1965 and 1985, but has tapered off since that time and has been quite stable for the last twenty years. The good news is that there is a steady supply of future priests in the pipeline, between 3,000 and 4,000 men in formation in US seminaries each year at the graduate level. This is only about a third of the number needed, however, to compensate for the very large numbers of priests who were ordained in the 1960s and 1970s, and who are now mostly retired from active ministry or even deceased.

Parish Reconfiguration Options

What this change in clergy demographics means for parish life is that now it is unusual for a parish to have more than one priest in residence. In fact, one in five parishes has no priest in residence and must share a priest with one or more other parishes, in a relationship that is known by various names (e.g., shared, twinned, yoked, linked, clustered) but always means that one priest has administrative and canonical responsibility for more than one parish. Another option that some bishops have tried is to share responsibility for several parishes among a team of priests, such as three priests pastoring five parishes. Each priest in the team has the obligations and responsibilities of a pastor in each parish, and one priest serves as the team moderator to coordinate the group's activities.

Another option is to merge parishes, creating a new parish out of the territory of two or more existing parishes that have been closed for this purpose. Alternatively, one parish is closed and its territory is consolidated with an existing parish.

The diocese also has the option of recruiting priests from other areas. Although it is not common practice to share priests across diocesan boundaries, bishops do sometimes recruit or accept priests from outside the United States to minister here, for a defined period or permanently. It was not uncommon in the nineteenth century for immigrant Catholics to bring with them a priest from their home country to provide for their sacramental needs in their home language. Today, bishops accept priests and seminarians from many other countries – not typically to meet the ethnic and language needs of US parishes, but to fill in for a shortage of priests. In fact, priests that were born outside the United States are now a quarter of all US diocesan priests, and the greatest numbers are from India, the Philippines, and Nigeria. This practice comes with its own set of challenges, however, as it is not at all uncommon for friction to develop as parishioners struggle with the accented English and different cultural practices of these nonnative clergy.

A final option, used when no priest is available, is for the bishop to entrust the pastoral care of a parish to a permanent deacon, a religious sister or brother, or a layperson, most typically referred to as a parish life coordinator (PLC). The PLC is not the pastor; the bishop or his delegate always serves as the canonical pastor of a parish. The PLC manages the day-to-day operations of the parish, oversees all minis-tries, and presides at services in the absence of a priest on weekends when no priest is available.

Even with all these options, the total number of parishes in the United States has declined from a high point of nearly 20,000 parishes in the mid-1990s to about 17,000, the same number of parishes that existed in the mid-1960s. The days of an abundance of priests in pastoral leadership are over. This new reality, however, has made room for a flourishing of new models of pastoral leader-ship, which include married men being ordained to the diaconate as well as laypersons trained and hired as pastoral staff, known as lay ecclesial ministers.

Permanent Deacons

The bishops and cardinals at the Second Vatican Council called for the renewal of the diaconate as a stable and permanent order of ministry, and the US Bishops' Conference was one of the early adopters of this order. The first US permanent deacon was ordained in 1969 and the numbers of men responding to this opportunity grew rapidly. Although the order was never intended to supplant the priesthood or to serve as a backup for declining numbers of priests, this restored ministry has played an important role in redefining and broadening our understand-ing of pastoral leadership. Deacons are, in fact, ordained clergy but they do not have all the faculties of an ordained priest. They can perform baptisms and funerals, and they can witness marriages. They cannot hear confessions, administer the last rites, or confect the Eucharist. Nevertheless, they have cushioned some of the impact of fewer priests by their sheer numbers (see Figure 19.7). Today, there are more than 18,000 permanent deacons, nine in ten of them serving in active

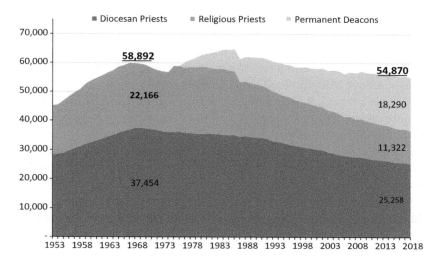

Figure 19.7

ministry, and 98 percent of them carrying out at least some part of their ministry in parishes.[12]

Deacons have a three-fold ministry of word, liturgy, and charity, and they carry out many of the responsibilities that were formerly the ministry of associate priests or parochial vicars. They provide catechetical instruction, sacramental preparation, and faith formation for adults and children. In addition, they serve on the altar alongside the priest, proclaiming the Gospel at Mass and occasionally preaching the homily. When a priest is not available, they can also preside at Word and communion services so the faithful can have access to the sacraments.

Deacons also perform a broad range of charitable service at the parish level and beyond. Because deacons, like priests, are ordained for service to a diocese, much of their charitable work takes place outside the parish. In many cases, the only ones aware of these acts of charity are the bishop, the deacon, and the people he serves. Nearly all deacons provide ministry to the sick and elderly in homes, hospitals, and hospices. Deacons also provide direct outreach to the poor and organize coordinated outreach to the poor through St. Vincent de Paul societies and other outreach efforts. They are involved in social justice ministry and in community organizing

---

[12]   See Center for Applied Research in the Apostolate, *Word, Liturgy, Charity: The Diaconate in the U.S. Catholic Church, 1968–2018* (Lanham, MD: Lexington Books, 2018).

and advocacy for social justice. Many deacons are involved in prison or jail ministry, in counseling and spiritual direction, in campus ministry and youth ministry, and in evangelization. In fact, there is likely no aspect of charitable ministry in which the church has a presence that does not have a deacon engaged in some way.

What makes all this service noteworthy for the purpose of this chapter is the fact that nearly all deacons are married (more than nine in ten) and the majority are not compensated financially for the work they do as deacons. They do not receive a stipend, a car or housing allowance, or a pension, as many priests do. If they are employed in a secular job, they perform their ministry as deacons outside of work hours and in addition to their other family responsibilities. On average, deacons pay a third of the cost of their education and formation for the diaconate, and their wives are typically required, or at least encouraged, to participate fully in their diaconate formation. Many wives of deacons also share in the ministry in a voluntary capacity or are otherwise very involved in charitable works of their own.

This level of commitment and investment by married couples in voluntary service to the church is striking. With well over 18,000 deacons (and their wives) now ministering in this capacity, our notion of pastoral leadership is evolving in new and interesting directions. Four in ten parishes have at least one deacon on staff, and nearly all of those deacons assist at liturgies and at least occasionally preach homilies. Catholics are gradually becoming accustomed to the presence of married men serving in pastoral ministry. They are increasingly open to the idea of a married priesthood, an idea that is endorsed by two in three Catholics. Lay Catholics are even more favorably disposed to the idea of women deacons, a role that many deacons also support. In fact, in a recent CARA survey of bishops and directors of the Office of Deacons in US dioceses, over half of responding bishops, and close to two in three deacon directors, said they thought their diocese would implement the sacramental ordination of women as deacons if the Holy See authorizes this change.

Lay Ecclesial Ministers

One final factor effecting change in pastoral leadership is an increase in lay ecclesial ministers, primarily in parish leadership positions. The Second Vatican Council called for increased awareness among laypeople of their co-responsibility with the clergy for parish life. Few could imagine, however, just how prophetic and successful this call would prove to be. As the numbers of women religious declined, from a high in the late 1960s of about 170,000 to less than 50,000 by 2015, their numbers have been replaced, particularly in parishes and parochial schools, by lay women.

Although laypeople have always been an important source of volunteer service in parishes, they did not commonly serve in paid positions as parish pastoral staff until after Vatican II. The definition of lay ecclesial ministers outlined by the US Conference of Catholic Bishops in their 2005 document "Co-Workers in the Vineyard of the Lord," describes these individuals as adequately formed and prepared laypersons, authorized by the hierarchy to serve publicly in leadership for a particular area of ministry, in close mutual collaboration with clergy. There are now more lay ecclesial ministers serving in US parishes than there are total priests in the United States (see Figure 19.8). While one does not supplant the other, much like deacons these lay ecclesial ministers support and extend the pastoral ministry of priests by assuming many of the responsibilities of parish life that were formerly the domain of associate priests, parochial vicars, or religious sisters and brothers. In this way, priests are freed up to devote more time to sacramental responsibilities and to share some of the administrative, catechetical, and evangelical aspects of pastoral ministry with qualified laypersons.

According to a 2013 CARA survey of Catholic parishes, the average parish in the United States has nearly six paid ministry staff. Nearly

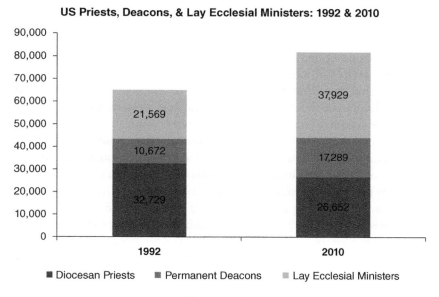

Figure 19.8

eight in ten parishes have a diocesan priest on staff and one in six has a religious priest on staff. In addition, more than seven in ten have at least one laywoman on paid staff and a majority employ at least one layman. Three in ten parishes indicate that they have a deacon on staff who is paid for his ministry but, as mentioned above, most deacons are not compensated for their ministry and many more parishes have deacons serving who are not included among paid staff.

Eight in ten lay ecclesial ministers are women, and they serve alongside priests, deacons, and laymen in pastoral leadership positions. They bring an added dimension to parish life that was absent in parishes where all decisions and all power were reserved to male clerics. While some would opine for a return to the old days of a pre–Vatican II church, the vast majority of priests see the need for sharing responsibility for parish life with others. They recognize that laypeople have high expectations for parish life and that a single priest cannot possibly do it all alone. Most priests agree that the church should allow women greater participation in all lay ministries and would encourage it to move faster in empowering lay persons in ministry. These lay ecclesial ministers are changing the way parishes relate to parishioners and are expanding our understanding of what it means to be a pastoral minister. The implications of this change are far-reaching for the future of the church.

CONCLUSION

The trends described here suggest several changes that may be on the horizon for the Catholic Church in the United States. Population trends suggest that the church will continue to grapple with decline and diminishment in the Northeast and Midwest as it struggles to match available resources of people and property to the population shifts within those regions. Dealing with diminishment is never pleasant or easy, and the increased burden of clergy sexual abuse settlements within many dioceses makes the process even more onerous and urgent. But this process has been underway now for several decades and many dioceses are exploring new ways that parishes can be restructured to form new and vibrant communities of faith without necessarily creating winners and losers among parishes being restructured.

Churches in the suburbs around major cities in the South and in the West are dealing with a chronic shortage of resources by building ever larger parishes and staffing them with lay pastoral ministers to provide for the abundance of parishioner needs. Pastors are learning to rely on a strong team of dedicated and trained lay staff to extend their ministry effectiveness in ways that would be impossible for just one person.

Increasing diversity of ethnicity, culture, language, and age is another population trend that is both a challenge and an opportunity for the church. Rather than creating national parishes to serve the needs of a particular ethnic community, the church today is grappling with diversity head-on and finding ways to integrate different languages and ethnicities into one parish-based worshipping community.

While trends in Catholic sacramental practice are disturbing, placing these in historical context provides some perspective. It may be of some consolation to realize that the "fallen away" Catholics that we despair of today are proportionately similar in size to those who never attended Mass back in the 1950s – when three-quarters of Catholics were telling pollsters that they had attended services within the last seven days. We would like to believe that "once a Catholic, always a Catholic," but the reality is that the boundaries that make one a Catholic are somewhat fluid and flexible, and always have been. Look around the next time you are at Mass – one in eight people sitting in that church have come back to the faith after some period of absence. Another one in ten are people who were raised in another faith (or no faith) and have come to the Catholic faith as adults. The declining trends in sacramental practice are certainly cautionary, but they do not necessarily signal despair. There is still plenty of reason for hope.

Finally, the trends in pastoral leadership also signal hope for a church on the move. Despite a shortage of ordained clergy and religious sisters and brothers, and a mismatch between population and resources in many places, the church continues to adapt and explore new models of parish configurations and new models of pastoral leadership. Merged and clustered parishes, international priests, permanent deacons, and lay ecclesial ministers are all creative ways to meet the pastoral needs of the people where they are.

The clergy sexual abuse crisis is a cloud over the church across the United States at the beginning of the twenty-first century. Its effects on the church so far appear to be transitory and perhaps short term. There has been some drop-off in diocesan collections and loss of credibility among bishops, but otherwise little else has changed. It is too early to tell, at this point, just what the longer-term effects will be. Much will depend on how well the hierarchy handles its credibility deficit and whether trust can be restored effectively among the laity.

Predicting the future of US Catholicism is an art, not a science. The trends explored in this chapter describe a church that shows signs of flexibility, of adaptation to change that can give one a great deal of hope for the future. The church must bend with the winds of change, it must learn new lessons from the mistakes of the past, and it must read the signs of the times if it is to remain relevant. These are the very things that give one hope.

FURTHER READING

D'Antonio, William V., Michele Dillon, and Mary L. Gautier. *American Catholics in Transition*. Lanham, MD: Rowman and Littlefield, 2013.

Fichter, Joseph H., SJ. *Social Relations in the Urban Parish*. Chicago, IL: University of Chicago Press, 1954.

Froehle, Bryan T. and Mary L. Gautier. *Catholicism USA: A Portrait of the Catholic Church in the United States*. Maryknoll, NY: Orbis Books, 2000.

Gray, Mark M., Mary L. Gautier, and Melissa A. Cidade. *The Changing Face of U.S. Catholic Parishes*. Washington, DC: Center for Applied Research in the Apostolate, 2011.

Gray, Mark M. and Paul M. Perl. *Sacraments Today: Belief and Practice among U.S. Catholics*. Washington, DC: Center for Applied Research in the Apostolate, 2008.

Zech, Charles E., Mary L. Gautier, Mark M. Gray, Jonathon L. Wiggins, and Thomas P. Gaunt, SJ. *Catholic Parishes of the Twenty-first Century*. New York: Oxford University Press, 2017.

Index